MW00647377

All God's Creatures

DEVOTIONS *for* ANIMAL LOVERS

2025

A Gift from Guideposts

Thank you for your purchase! We appreciate your support and want to express our gratitude with a special gift just for you.

Dive into ***Spirit Lifters***, a complimentary booklet that will fortify your faith and offer solace during challenging moments. It contains 31 carefully selected verses from scripture that will soothe your soul and uplift your spirit.

Please use the QR code or go to **guideposts.org/spiritlifters** to download.

All God's Creatures 2025

Published by Guideposts
100 Reserve Road, Suite E200
Danbury, CT 06810
Guideposts.org

Copyright © 2024 by Guideposts. All rights reserved.

This book, or parts thereof, may not be reproduced, stored in a retrieval system, or transmitted in any form or by any means, electronic, mechanical, photocopying, recording or otherwise, without the written permission of the publisher.

Cover and interior design by Mullerhaus
Cover photos by iStock
Monthly page photos by iStock
Typeset by Aptara, Inc.

ISBN 978-1-961126-48-0 (hardcover)
ISBN 978-1-961251-08-3 (softcover)
ISBN 978-1-961126-49-7 (epub)

Printed and bound in the United States of America
1 0 9 8 7 6 5 4 3 2 1

Introduction

I am an old man now, but on that day I was a young man, wearing my New York Yankees baseball cap, leaning against the fence, arms resting on the top rail, staring at the bull that was staring back at me with menacing, squinty eyes. He was enormous—chocolate brown, with a long, flat back; a huge, muscular neck; and short, spiky horns. I learned later that he was 4 years old and weighed just shy of 1 ton.

I was the interim student minister, newly married, sent from the seminary to serve this small country church over the summer. I resolved to visit every one of my new parishioners during the course of my assignment—a goal I actually accomplished—and that's how I met James and his prize bull, Sampson.

James was a taciturn, rawboned rancher with a permanent gray stubble on his chin, a downy silver dust. A toothpick dangled from the corner of his mouth, and it wiggled slowly up and down as he gnawed on it.

Pointing to Sampson, I asked, "Is he dangerous?"

James thought a moment, took off his hat, scratched his head, put his hat back on, and said, "Nah, not really. You could probably walk around out there in his pasture and he'd pay you no mind. But you'll want to stay out of his querencia."

I asked the same question you are asking. "What is a querencia?"

It is pronounced kay-ren-seeuh, and it is a bullfighting term, I came to find out. It describes a small area inside the bullring, maybe 10 feet by 10 feet, where the bull believes he is entirely safe and secure. Each bull has his own idea of where his querencia is, and if you happen to be standing in Sampson's querencia at the moment he feels frightened or pained, he will bolt in your direction, and in seconds his horns and your groin will occupy the same space. And that is not good.

I asked James where Sampson's querencia was. He thought a moment, shrugged. "Don't know."

We all have a querencia. Several of them, probably. You walk into a crowded room and find yourself among a lot of strangers, people talking. You feel insecure, awkward, maybe a little bit frightened. But then you spy someone you know, an old friend with whom you feel entirely comfortable, and you rush to her side. Now, suddenly, you feel safe, secure. You have found your querencia. A querencia can be almost anything, anywhere—a certain person, a garden bench, a church sanctuary, a rowboat on a pond, your kitchen. It's your retreat, your safe space, the place you go to when you feel frightened, puzzled, pained.

It is my hope, and the hope of Guideposts, that this devotional book becomes a querencia for you. Between these covers you will find stories that will warm your heart, inspire you, challenge you, make you laugh out loud, and occasionally bring a tear to your eye. Gifted writers with an obvious respect and love for animals will draw you closer to God's Word, and to God's world. They will help you to see things that you never noticed before and remind you of things you must never forget—that there is a God, that you are loved, and that in the end all will be well. May this book be for you a safe place, a place of refreshment and renewal, where you can spend a few minutes every day thinking about who you are, and whose you are.

Standing there at the fence, it suddenly occurred to me that James was wearing a red shirt. It was faded and dusty, but definitely red. I asked, "Isn't it dangerous to wear a red shirt when you are standing close to a bull? I mean, bulls charge at the sight of red, don't they?"

James slid the toothpick from one side of this mouth to the other. "Nah, not really," he said. "That's a myth. All cattle, bulls included, are color blind to red."

I felt a sense of relief, and then James added, "It's New York Yankees caps that makes 'em charge."

And for the first time, he cracked a smile.

—Louis Lotz

January

JANUARY 1

Hope Unfurling

Then God said, "I give you every seed-bearing plant on the face of the whole earth and every tree that has fruit with seed in it. They will be yours for food."

—GENESIS 1:29 (NIV)

WALKING ALONG THE creek by my home, movement flashed in my peripheral vision. I turned to find a bird amid the branches of a Russian olive tree. It was January, and most birds were enjoying the tropics. I didn't expect to find many new-to-me species this time of year. Yet I had never seen this bird. And it wasn't his colors or markings that caught my attention, as he was a rather unassuming bird. Rather, it was his antics.

I stood and watched the gray bird perform an acrobatic feat among the branches. He stood on one branch before swooping down, plucking an olive from the stem mid-flight, then landing on another branch before eating it. He repeated this several times. With help from a bird identification app, I found his name: a Townsend's solitaire.

His behavior inspired a personal research project I continued throughout the winter. Each time I saw birds in our olive trees, I noted how they ate the fruit. These birds were braving a harsh Colorado winter, and I wanted to closely observe how they foraged. I discovered that the Townsend's solitaire, along with the European starlings and American robins, gulped the fruit whole. Smaller birds, such as house and Cassin's finches, squeezed the olive to get the seed inside before spitting the fruit to the ground. Evening grosbeaks seemed to dislike the olives and chose them as a last resort, chewing them to a pulp before finally swallowing them.

Several months later, in early June, many of these bird species had left for the summer. Walking along the creek, I noticed delicate yellow flowers erupting from the olive tree branches. On fruiting trees, flowers always precede the fruit. I gently touched the yellow flowers and was filled with hope. Each blossom represented future fruit for my birds upon their return. I thought of God, at the beginning of time, designing entire ecosystems to support these amazing creatures and how He plans even more carefully for my provision. In perfect time, His hope unfolds like a flower at the height of its bloom, promising fruit to come. —Eryn Lynum

But I am like a green olive tree in the house of God.
I trust in the steadfast love of God forever and ever.
—Psalm 52:8 (ESV)

JANUARY 2

Challenges of Life

So do not fear, for I am with you; do not be dismayed, for I am your God. I will strengthen you and help you; I will uphold you with my righteous hand.

—Isaiah 41:10 (NIV)

WE ALL KNOW life is challenging. No question about that. But would we want it any other way? According to my pets, maybe not.

My husband and I always spend a month or two in Florida during the winter, and this year we would bring our dog along but leave our cat at home with a friend. Would Rocky, our cat, miss us, or would he be happy for the peace and quiet? When both pets were together, much of the day was spent in what I term controlled chaos. Lucy, our dog, would chase Rocky endlessly. Rocky did have his hiding places, and when he'd had enough of Lucy, he would retreat to one of them. I wasn't sure whether Rocky enjoyed the sport or whether he tolerated each day's chase. It was no use telling Lucy to stop; she just couldn't.

Messages from my friend on the home front conveyed that Rocky was fine but seemed a little bored. Once we returned home, Lucy and Rocky took off right where they left off, chasing, jumping, fighting. I wondered whether Rocky missed those quiet days. The silent answer to my question happened in front of the fireplace that night. As Lucy finally lay spent in front of the fireplace in nap mode, Rocky tenderly licked her head. He'd missed Lucy. He'd missed the challenge of being chased and outsmarting danger.

And so it is for us humans. It's in the challenges of life that we grow. God promises never to give us more than we can handle. He allows us to stumble and pick ourselves up to gain wisdom. Just like Rocky, who faces a new chase each day, we encounter new challenges, but God also gives us the skill and means to conquer them with His help. —Linda Bartlett

Heavenly Father, help me to remember that the difficulties of life strengthen me. I know You will guide me through them. Thank You for peace and joy along the way. Amen.

JANUARY 3

A Cleansing Flight

One thing I do: Forgetting what is behind and straining toward what is ahead, I press on toward the goal to win the prize for which God has called me heavenward in Christ Jesus.

—PHILIPPIANS 3:13–14 (NIV)

WHAT STRANGE WEATHER. It is January, but the sun is shining and the temperature is in the high 40s. Winter in Michigan usually means pewter-gray skies and frigid temperatures, but today icicles are weeping in the winter sunshine, and melting snow is trickling down the drainpipe.

I bundle up and go outside, tramping through the snow to check on my beehives. As I approach them, I see tiny brown spots on the snow, hundreds of them. Warm weather triggers in honeybees an urge to get outside for what's known as a cleansing flight. The bees have been hunkered down for weeks and have had to keep the hive clean and sanitary. When an opportunity arises for a bathroom break, they take advantage of it. In one quick trip they eliminate all the gunk and impurities they have been storing up.

I have stored up some things I'd like be rid of. Painful memories, hurtful thoughts, self-pity because life did not accommodate my every wish—a lot of emotional and spiritual gunk. Watching the bees return to the hive from their cleansing flights, I silently resolve to copy Philippians 3:13–14 onto a sticky note and tape it to my desktop, where I'll see it every day: "One thing I do: Forgetting what is behind and straining toward what is ahead, I press on toward the goal to win the prize for which God has called me heavenward in Christ Jesus."

Nothing hinders my spiritual growth quite like being mired in the past. I'm not always successful in my resolve to forget what lies behind and strain forward to what lies ahead, to what God has in store for me. But I am not discouraged. I'll keep trying. The bull's-eye is always the last part of the target to wear out. —Louis Lotz

Teach me, O God, that the past is a place to learn from, not a place to live in. Amen.

JANUARY 4

Pancake

In the beginning was the one who is called the Word.
The Word was with God and was truly God.

—JOHN 1:1 (CEV)

MY FRIEND CAROL'S cockapoo was so small that she was easily held in one hand. Because her coloring was identical to their morning griddle cakes, the family agreed that her name should be Pancake.

Pancake liked to try to mimic human words, and even if she was not always successful, it was still easy to know what was on her mind. "I could read her like a book," was an appropriate description of this tiny canine.

One day Carol's husband brought Pancake to the groomer, dropped her off, and left to run some errands. This was not typically Pancake's favorite adventure, but it was far worse when she was left alone with the stylist. Even though she came home with the cutest haircut and lovely bows in her hair, she wanted it known that she was unhappy. She wouldn't move from the top of the entryway stairs until Carol returned home from work. Carol entered the hallway to hear the insistent scolding that only an angry cockapoo could deliver. Once Pancake had voiced her displeasure (whether it was for being left alone or just having to endure the haircut), she left her sentry post and pranced into the family room to recline in peace.

If Carol happened to stay up too far past her bedtime, cooking and baking, Pancake would come into the kitchen huffing and puffing as if to say, "Go to bed!" Carol would respond, "Pancake, you can go to bed without me." Only when Carol headed toward her bedroom would this loving watchdog nestle into her own bed.

Words, attitudes, and actions speak loudly. I love it that God speaks to me through His written Word and through His Son, Jesus. I also love it that He is willing to show me who He is and what He thinks. I want to be so close to Him that I can read Him like a book. —Liz Kimmel

Thank You, Lord, that You don't make me guess at what You are saying to me. Help me to be as open and transparent with You as You are with me.

JANUARY 5

Hummingbird Help

Let everything that has breath praise the Lord.

—Psalm 150:6 (NIV)

THAT WINTER DAY when I saw the hummingbird, the morning seemed grayer than usual. Getting out of bed felt like a chore, and there was a feeling of malaise I couldn't shake. There are highs and lows to life, but that day everything seemed tedious, worn, and old—including me. I got up anyway and began my day as if I felt normal, hoping my mind would follow.

While I was at the kitchen sink washing dishes and thinking about my current circumstances, I glanced out the window and noticed that a hummingbird had appeared. After several minutes, he continued to hover, watching me while I continued to wash dishes and think. The bird was beautiful and happy, and he seemed to be full of energy and color, the very things I wanted in my life.

I remember saying to the hummingbird, "Well, this gray morning sure isn't a problem for you." And that's when I realized that this sweet bird was a message for me. His fluttering wings, his bobbing head—it was all like a dance, a way to praise the One who made him and to be the beautiful thing amid the gray.

Maybe I was going about this day all wrong.

The hummingbird continued to move, darting to the left and right, but returned to face me every few seconds, as if to say, "See, this is how you do it! Just keep praising and keep on going." I finished the dishes with a smile on my lips and praise in my heart. If the birds of the air could praise God during this gray day, then so could I.

That hummingbird changed my entire outlook. When I focused on what was most important—looking for the good, expecting the best, and praising God through it all—everything fell into place, and that gray day turned bright and beautiful. —Heather Spiva

Heavenly Father, thank You for reminding me to take my eyes off my circumstances and to focus on praising You instead. Amen.

JANUARY 6

Unexpected Gifts

If you, then, though you are evil, know how to give good gifts to your children, how much more will your Father in heaven give good gifts to those who ask him!

—MATTHEW 7:11 (NIV)

MY YOUNG ADULT son, Jordan, was out of town and I'd promised to feed his cat, Rocket. On my way, I grabbed our mail and immediately felt my heart drop. The mail contained the medical bill for my husband's recent surgery. We'd been dreading its arrival. I decided not to open the envelope until I got home, but I couldn't stop worrying about it. *God, we're going to need Your help with this,* I prayed.

I let myself into Jordan's house. Rocket was waiting by the door and immediately started rubbing against my legs. "Are you hungry, Buddy?" I asked him. I went to grab the cat food and nearly tripped over Rocket, who was determined to stay close to me. I filled his dish, then sat down at the breakfast bar. Instead of eating, Rocket jumped onto the counter and rubbed his face against mine, purring loudly. I couldn't help laughing. "You want attention more than you want food," I said. I gave in and petted him. He angled his body so I'd scratch his favorite spot. He purred even louder.

I'd come over to feed the cat, but he didn't care about food. He just wanted my attention. It was like I'd given him a gift just by visiting him. But he gave me a gift too—his love took away my anxiety over that bill for a bit.

After playing with Rocket, I headed back home, still anxious about the bill. I handed it to my husband, Eric, and he could see the worry on my face. "No matter how much this is, God is going to help us take care of it," he said. He took a deep breath and opened the envelope. His eyes scanned the page and he smiled. "Insurance covered a lot more than I thought they would," he said. "God was helping us. This bill actually feels like a gift."

Two unexpected gifts in one day. Through them both, I saw God's provision and faithfulness. —Diane Stark

Walk of Faith: *Make a list of the gifts God has given you today and then thank Him.*

JANUARY 7

Lacking Nothing

I have all that I need.

—PSALM 23:1 (NLT)

"COME ON, SCUPPERS. Find your spot." I was jumping up and down in place trying to stay warm as I waited for our dog to relieve himself. It was a bitterly cold day with wind and frigid air seeping into any crack in my clothing and lingering in my bones. I wore multiple layers, from my thermal underwear and glove liners to the hat-and-hood combination of my heaviest and longest coat. Even with all those layers I still hurried the dog along as we walked beside the river.

I looked out upon the water and saw a half-dozen Canada geese gliding along, stopping every now and then to dip their heads and long necks in deep to find something to eat. The bitter cold didn't seem to bother them at all. If I had only seen their movements and not felt the air temperature, I would've thought that it was the height of summer.

I was once again awed by how God prepares His creation for whatever they might encounter. He made the geese with dense insulating feathers and a waterproof outer plumage to protect them from the cold and to equip them for life on the water.

I was reminded of how God had prepared my husband and me for a recent move to another state—our ability to work from home naturally evolving from COVID restrictions, the technology enabling us to keep in touch with our dearest friends, and the blessing of finding a home during a difficult housing market.

Some days I forget how well prepared God made us for this move. All I focused on were the difficulties, things like establishing friends, finding a church home, and working with contractors. Yet when I looked closely, I saw that God had everything covered.

When I remember that God provides all that I need, I, too, can glide on icy waters and not be bothered by my circumstances. —Virginia Ruth

Creator of all things, thank You for providing all that we need.
If only we would pay attention. Amen.

JANUARY 8

The Care of a Cocker Spaniel

Love does no harm to a neighbor. Therefore love is the fulfillment of the law.

—ROMANS 13:10 (NIV)

MY SENIOR COCKER spaniel, Schroeder, is one of my life's greatest gifts. We adopted him from an animal shelter 13 years ago, and he has been a faithful, kind, and sensitive friend to me through hardship, joy, and life's transitions. Though we don't know his exact age, we suspect he was around 1 or 2 years old when we adopted him.

Though he has aged remarkably well, he does require extra care in these senior years. He takes a daily joint supplement for hip pain and a medication to manage Cushing's disease, a condition in which the adrenal glands overproduce hormones. Though he enjoys many more naps these days than he did in his squirrel-chasing youth, he loves his routine and particularly his daily walks—and he will bark at me if I forget to take him!

We began the frequent walks for his heart health, but an unexpected thing happened. Initially I thought a walk a day would help me care for *him*, but I *myself* receive a blessing too. The fresh air, flowers, and birdsong improve my mood, bring me joy, and spark my creativity. Every day, I look forward to slipping on my comfortable shoes, cueing my audiobook, and grabbing Schroeder's leash.

I've heard it said that God's Kingdom works "upside down" from our own expectations of how things will turn out—that when we humble ourselves to care for others, we better allow God's love to work in and through us because Jesus Himself is the ultimate picture of humility. We may *think* we are the ones offering a service. But the beautiful thing about God's sacrificial love is that when we share it with others, we fulfill His law and discover a deeper sense of purpose ourselves.

If you are in a caregiving role today, whether you're nurturing a child, caring for an adult, or tending to your senior pet, I pray that God reminds you of your value and that you find a deeper blessing in the work you are doing. —Ashley Clark

Father, sometimes caregiving is a lot of work, and my heart grows weary. Lift my burden today as I fix my eyes on You, and show me the blessing You have for me right where I am today. Remind me I am not here by accident and I am not forgotten, and may Your love sustain me.

JANUARY 9

The Winter Refuge

He who dwells in the shelter of the Most High will abide in the shadow of the Almighty.

—PSALM 91:1 (ESV)

A COLD WIND BIT my cheeks as I opened the front door to bring in the package delivered earlier in the day. Suddenly, something flew out from the Christmas wreath hanging on the outside of the door.

I ducked, narrowly missing the flying object that vanished into the twilight. After catching my breath, I wondered if a bat or a bird had been in my wreath.

The next day my cat sat inside the front door, staring up through the vertical windows that were mostly covered by the evergreen wreath. I looked to see what had captured his attention.

A small finch fluttered its wings as it chose a spot to land in the wreath. I smiled as I caught glimpses of the darling bird nestling into the evergreen branches. Apparently, my Christmas wreath was going to be its winter home.

As winter continued, turning bitterly cold, I left the wreath up longer than normal so the little finch had a place to shelter from the elements. Every evening, the finch returned to the wreath and hunkered down for the night.

If I opened my front door after five p.m., I had to duck or shake the wreath before venturing out to avoid a collision with the bird. But no matter how many times the finch was spooked and darted away, it would always return as soon as possible to the safe shelter.

As I observed the finch, I realized it was setting an example for me. Too often I am lured away from the Lord by busyness or temptations. At other times, hardship and trials make me stop reading the Bible and spending time in prayer. But to survive and thrive in this life, I need to imitate the finch. I must return daily to dwell in the shelter of my God, where I will find refuge and strength. —Jerusha Agen

For he will hide me in his shelter in the day of trouble; he will conceal me under the cover of his tent; he will lift me high upon a rock.

—Psalm 27:5 (ESV)

A Shepherd's Fun

Let the fields be jubilant, and everything in them;
let all the trees of the forest sing for joy.

—PSALM 96:12 (NIV)

IT WAS BILLED as the snowstorm of the century, so like good Minnesotans we heeded the warning and stayed home. We've dealt with snow before, and we know better than to tempt nature. But after 3 days of being cooped up with everything cancelled, I had a severe case of cabin fever.

Once the plows had done their duty on the fourth day after the storm, I headed out to run errands I had put off. I stopped at the library, the grocery store, and the post office, but I was still antsy, so I decided to make the 25-mile trip to the next small town and do some gift shopping. After all it was only February in Minnesota and we could have more snow tomorrow. We could be stuck at home again. I had to make use of my freedom.

Once on the road, I was behind a small red car with a large German shepherd on board. How did I know? Because he had his head sticking out the window, inhaling as many scents as he could. Only a canine could find it fun to have his head outdoors in 10-degree weather! Apparently, I was not the only one with cabin fever looking for a little excitement. Once on the highway the shepherd pulled his head back in, but as soon as the car slowed down or stopped for any reason his head popped right back out. That shepherd knew how to make the most of his day.

I want to take a page from the shepherd's book and relish the moment. Conditions may not be perfect and the weather may still be cold, but the sun still rises, my body still works well enough, and God still reigns. Life is good. —Linda Bartlett

Happiness often sneaks in through a door you didn't know you left open.
—John Barrymore

JANUARY 11

A Leap of Faith

Now faith is confidence in what we hope for and assurance about what we do not see.

—HEBREWS 11:1 (NIV)

RECENTLY, OUR FRIEND Bob shared a story about squirrels that he and his wife, Jenny, had witnessed. His story really spoke to me about faith.

One day while in their yard, Bob and Jenny noticed four juvenile squirrels playing in a tree. One of them ventured out to the end of a thin branch and launched 4 feet through the air to the end of a branch on another tree. That limb was also thin, and the squirrel swayed as it precariously clung to the branch. But it was able to hang on. Soon after, two more squirrels carefully made the leap. But the fourth one appeared fearful.

It tried several other branches to see if a better—more certain—route could be found. All the while, the other three squirrels were having a grand time in the other tree. Finally, after about 5 minutes, the scared squirrel went back to the original limb, backed up a few feet, and ran to make that leap. Success! Bob and Jenny cheered as it landed safely and joined the others to play.

This story reminds me of how I can sometimes feel God leading me to do something—take on a new project, reach out to invite or help someone, sign up for a class, or join a group study at church—yet fret over the decision. Am I taking on too much? Will it be a good fit? Will I be rejected? Will I fail? Like that doubting squirrel, I waffle and try to find an easier, more familiar, "safer" path.

But I want to have enough faith that when God leads, I'll fearlessly take that leap. I want to be more like the first three squirrels. With God giving me faith, I know I can. —Missy Tippens

He replied, "Because you have so little faith. Truly I tell you, if you have faith as small as a mustard seed, you can say to this mountain, 'Move from here to there,' and it will move. Nothing will be impossible for you."
—Matthew 17:20 (NIV)

The Little Alligator

And lead us not into temptation, but deliver us from the evil one.

—MATTHEW 6:13 (NIV)

THIS WEEK, MY son and I attended a reptile presentation at our local library. Eager to get a good view of the animals, my son hurried to the front of the room where a crowd of children sat in a circle waiting to see turtles, snakes, and other lizards. Each new animal's appearance was met with a round of oohs and ahhs, but of particular surprise was the small alligator the facilitator presented. Much to the delight of the children—particularly my son—the man held on to the baby alligator and stepped into the circle of kids. My son scampered backward, laughing even as he got out of the way.

The presenter explained that when the alligators reach a larger size, he returns them to the sanctuary from which they initially came. If he were to wait too long, the alligators would become a danger to him and the crowds to whom he presents.

While the event was thrilling for all the children who attended, this encounter also provided a solemn warning that everything we allow into our lives, both good and harmful, will grow eventually. Many days I feel as though I have control over the "baby alligators" in my mind and heart, and watching over them may even seem like a playful game. But eventually, those wild things will grow into something untamed, much like the bad habits in my life will also. I am grateful that God provides another option against the dangers of sin: boundaries. I have the ability to guard my heart against the sin that may otherwise consume, discourage, and disillusion me by remaining in God's Word and using wisdom in my choices. Today I choose to release the dangerous habits I have adopted and to replace them with good habits instead. —Ashley Clark

Lord, please show me today where I've created a habitat for things that are not of You. Show me the actions I need to take to set boundaries in my life before the dangers grow even more destructive. Mend the places where my sins have harmed me. And thank You for Your grace, which sets me free from the sins that so easily entangle me.

JANUARY 13

Cowgirl the Comfort Squirrel

I look for your deliverance, Lord.

—Genesis 49:18 (NIV)

MY HEART WAS heavy with many difficult circumstances. I was so lost in thought while running an errand at the grocery store that I almost walked past them.

At the entrance of aisle two was an endcap display featuring peanuts. And there they sat with their open bag of nuts.

The elderly man in his motorized cart was a celebrity in our small town. Called Cowboy, he acted in the 1972 film *Deliverance*. With his long gray beard and familiar leather hat, not to mention his two small pets, he was hard to miss.

He smiled at me. "Howdy!"

"Well, hello there." I knelt beside him. "How are you and the gang today?"

Beaming like a proud parent, Cowboy stroked the squirrel who'd moved to sit on his shoulder. "Well, I'm a-doin' fair to middlin', I reckon. Just been battlin' some aches and pains."

"I'm sorry to hear that." I patted his arm. "How 'bout Cowgirl? Little Man?"

Cowboy fed his squirrel a peanut. "Cowgirl's sweet as ever." Shifting to pet the small dog, he continued. "Little Man? I'm 'fraid he's a mite on the crotchety side."

Little Man cowered, nearly hidden behind Cowboy's beard.

"Hey, wanna hold Cowgirl?"

Hold a squirrel…in a grocery store? But before I could answer, Cowgirl leapt from his shoulder to mine, then sat up nice and tall.

"She's so friendly! Nicest squirrel I ever had." Cowboy clucked, and Cowgirl returned to her owner. "She brings me comfort, no matter what ails me."

We talked for a few more minutes. Before I stood, I told Cowboy I'd be praying for him.

Cowboy knew his Deliverer personally. Talking to him reminded me that I, too, know the One who brings comfort in all of life's troubles. For some, God uses comfort animals—yes, even squirrels.

Jesus. He was Cowboy's Comforter. And He's mine too. —Maureen Miller

Thank You, Jesus, for the gift of Your comfort and for all the many ways it's delivered. I know Cowboy is happiest now, home with You.

JANUARY 14

Created to Do Good Works

For we are God's handiwork, created in Christ Jesus to do good works, which God prepared in advance for us to do.

—EPHESIANS 2:10 (NIV)

BELLE, BELLY, OR Boo Boo—it doesn't matter what we call her. At the sound of our voice, my boss's golden retriever puppy comes loping down the hall and into one of our dental treatment rooms. Belle's favorite patients are children who wrestle on the floor with her or toss her tooth-shaped toy, but she loves nervous little old ladies too. Somehow, she knows just who needs a nuzzle or a lick.

Belle is one of many animals making a significant contribution to our world. Service dogs assist the visually impaired or physically handicapped. Dolphins help the navy protect our waterways. Capuchin monkeys help paralyzed individuals perform daily tasks. And Belle the office dog helps scared children and little old ladies brave the dental office.

As I watch Belle work her magic, I realize the concept of animal helpers isn't a twenty-first century phenomena. God has used animals to assist humans for millennia. Balaam's talking donkey delivered a warning to an evil messenger. Jonah's great fish provided a timely rescue and redirection for the reluctant prophet. Noah's dove confirmed it was safe to exit the ark, and Elijah's ravens fed the prophet during a famine.

These obedient animals, faithfully carrying out the tasks God has assigned them, serve as powerful examples to me. Sadly, I don't always obey as quickly or serve as willingly as they do. Sometimes I lose sight of the fact that God created me—as He created them—to do good works. These amazing animals remind me to embrace the tasks God has assigned to me and, like Belle, bring smiles to everyone I encounter along the way. —Lori Hatcher

Father, thank You for filling our world with animals who assist us, bless us, and make us smile. Help me be as obedient to You as they are. Use me to accomplish the good works You created me to do, for others' good and Your glory. In Jesus's name I pray, Amen.

JANUARY 15

Right-Side Up, with Help

Carry each other's burdens, and in this way you will fulfill the law of Christ.

—GALATIANS 6:2 (NIV)

I PET-SIT FOR AN unnamed eastern box turtle in a household that also includes a Quaker parrot and four guinea pigs. The turtle is fairly low-maintenance—I just change her water, moisten some turtle pellets, and chop up fresh vegetables—but sometimes she escapes her enclosure and goes on a walkabout across the hardwood floor. In that case, I search for her in any space where her shell could fit, then return her to her habitat so she can eat and drink. Occasionally I find her upside-down, frozen on her dome-shaped shell.

In the wild, this position leaves a turtle vulnerable to predators, makes it impossible to eat and drink, and even causes breathing difficulty. A little research let me know that the turtle *is* capable of righting herself. It's just not easy. She would stretch her head to one side, then repeatedly use all four feet to push off the ground or any nearby objects, rocking on her shell until one last push turns her over with an ungentle plop. On this turtle's slick, polished floor, I figure she would have an extra challenge due to lack of traction, so I help her out by turning her over, even though she doesn't technically need my assistance.

Many times I technically don't need help either, but assistance sure would make a task easier and, perhaps, the result better. Yet I resist and try to do the work all by myself. It takes longer and is more difficult, plus I've lost the opportunity to bond with a helper. As Paul implored us to carry each other's burdens, not to always be the carrier, I need to allow myself to be the one unburdened at times. Accepting aid is not a weakness but a blessing. Instead of staying bogged down, I can continue on my way, right-side up like my turtle friend. —Kim Sheard

Help us to help each other, Lord,
Each other's cross to bear;
Let each his friendly aid afford,
And feel his brother's care.
—Charles Wesley

JANUARY 16

No Worries

Therefore do not worry about tomorrow, for tomorrow will worry about itself. Each day has enough trouble of its own.

—MATTHEW 6:34 (NIV)

I LOOKED OVER MY to-do list, sighing at the number of tasks. I preheated the oven and gathered the ingredients I needed to make cookies for our church's bake sale. Then the power went out. "No, not today," I moaned. The power outage triggered every smoke alarm in our house to start beeping. Immediately, my two dogs, Piper and Peyton, startled awake and ran under the table, cowering in fear at the high-pitched sound. I raced from one smoke alarm to the next, trying to turn them off, but they kept restarting. The sound was jarring to my ears, and I knew it must be terrifying for the dogs.

"Come on, girls," I said. "Let's go find a quiet place for you while I figure out what to do." I coaxed the dogs out from under the table, and we headed upstairs. We went into the guest bathroom, and I closed the door. I could barely hear the alarms. I sat on the floor to comfort the dogs. As I rubbed Peyton's belly, I remembered my to-do list. "God, make the power come back on," I prayed. "I have so much to accomplish today." My worrying was kicking into overdrive when I heard a squeak. I turned and saw Piper with her favorite toy in her mouth. I couldn't help laughing. Even in the chaos, Piper stopped to grab a toy. I realized that I needed to follow her example. Worrying wasn't helping anything.

I left the dogs in the bathroom and returned minutes later, carrying a toy for Peyton, a pillow, and a book I'd been wanting to read. The three of us snuggled together on the bathroom floor, enjoying our books and toys. Although it wasn't the day I'd planned, God reminded me that worrying was never the solution. —Diane Stark

Walk of Faith: *In what areas do you need to set aside worry and trust God?*

JANUARY 17

Mesmerizing Manta Rays

Great is our LORD and mighty in power; his understanding has no limit.

—PSALM 147:5 (NIV)

DURING A VACATION on Big Island, Hawaii, my son and I signed up for a nighttime snorkel tour to swim with manta rays. On the day of our adventure, just as the sun was setting, we changed into our wet suits, tested our snorkeling gear, and boarded a small boat with ten other tourists. A few miles away from the harbor, the tour operator turned off the boat motor and set up a large flotation device on the dark waters. He projected a bright light to attract plankton. One by one we entered the water, held on to the flotation device, and submerged our faces, extending our legs behind us.

Ryan floated next to me. My eyes scanned the seemingly quiet and colorful underwater world. Tiny fish darted about, as if upset at our intrusion. While I was still surveying the ocean floor, three manta rays appeared, like superheroes wearing giant capes. With a wingspan almost 10 feet wide, reef manta rays are the second-largest species of rays in the world. Intimidated by their size, I froze as the marine giants swam near me. But after a few minutes of watching them twirl and glide effortlessly and gracefully, my fear turned into awe and admiration. Ryan and I exchanged excited looks through our masks as we watched the gentle giants open their mouths wide to eat the plankton only inches away from us.

The encounter reminded me that that my God, the Creator of manta rays and other bigger creatures, is a great and powerful God. Yet He delights in drawing near to me, a mere human. I feel privileged and loved to be in a personal relationship with God and to be surrounded by His awesome presence every day. —Mabel Ninan

Dear Father, thank You for always being with me. May the excitement and awe of being in a relationship with You never wear away. May I never lose the joy and wonder of experiencing Your intimate presence in my life. Amen.

Impossible Only Until It's Done

Now to Him who is able to do exceedingly abundantly above all we ask or think, according to the power that works in us, to Him be glory in the church by Christ Jesus to all generations, forever and ever. Amen.

—EPHESIANS 3:20–21 (NKJV)

DID YOU KNOW you can potty train a bird? I didn't until my 42-year-old parrot potty-trained himself.

I sat on the couch one evening with my open book propped on the pillow in my lap. My parrot, Lorito, rested on my arm. I rubbed his neck as I read, only pausing to turn the page.

After a while, Lorito said his name and lifted his left foot, indicating he wanted to be picked up. I set my book down, carried him to his cage, and placed him on his perch. He turned to face the front and promptly pooped. Was that a coincidence?

This happened several nights in a row. Sometimes I didn't get him to his cage fast enough or the urge came on quickly and Lorito couldn't make it to his cage before he had to go. Thankfully our tile floor makes cleanup a breeze.

I had never considered potty training my parrot a possibility. I just figured cleaning up poop came with having a bird, but what a joy that I no longer have to do that.

As I considered how Lorito potty-trained himself, I felt God's nudge to believe that He can do great things. To trust that He is bigger than my circumstances. To have confidence in Him for the impossible. That His "voice thunders in marvelous ways; he does great things beyond our understanding" (Job 37:5, NIV). —Crystal Storms

Never tell a young person that anything cannot be done.
God may have been waiting centuries for someone ignorant
enough of the impossible to do that very thing.
—G. M. Trevelyan

JANUARY 19

A Flock of Faith

A friend loves at all times, and kinsfolk are born to share adversity.

—PROVERBS 17:17 (NRSVUE)

I HAVE ALWAYS LOVED the color pink. I even had a pink bedroom when I was a child. So it makes perfect sense that I've also always loved flamingos, especially once I saw them in person.

I learned recently that when in a large flock, flamingos tend to form smaller social groups—usually just two to four birds. And those same groups remain mates or friends for years (the study I read took place over five years).

I, too, have a group I've been friends with for years. My writer friends from across Georgia and Florida have a yearly retreat where we spend several days together at a condo near the beach, eating, sharing, praying, studying, and—of course—writing.

I was tickled when I read this research article, because our group of four named ourselves The Flamingos from the beginning! And each year when we gather in our "flock," we give one another small, fun flamingo-themed gifts.

Now that I know about flamingo social groups, I'm struck by how appropriate our name is. That first year I got invited along, the three other women had already been planning their retreat. When I asked for prayer for a difficult situation on another email loop, one of the flamingo women saw my request and felt moved to invite me on their beach trip. I know this was God at work, because it was exactly what I needed in that moment. It was encouragement when I was at my lowest.

Although the flamingos in my flock aren't pink, I love them, too, especially when we gather in person each year to thank God for our friendship. —Missy Tippens

God, thank You for caring for us through others who listen to Your nudging and obediently reach out to offer love and support. Thank You for the people You place in our lives whom we can depend on. Amen.

JANUARY 20

Supportive Service Dog

I lift up my eyes to the mountains—where does my help come from? My help comes from the LORD, the Maker of heaven and earth.

—PSALM 121:1–2 (NIV)

MY WRITING MENTOR and prayer partner, Xochitl, and I arranged to have lunch with our families one afternoon. When my husband, my son, and I met Xochitl and her husband, Alan, in a Thai restaurant, I noticed that Callie, Xochitl's service dog, did not excitedly approach or sniff us. Callie was hard at work and not distracted, staying close to Xochitl. She had been professionally trained to assist Xochitl, who suffers from chronic pain due to a spinal injury.

Our families exchanged hellos and hugs before sitting down at a table. My friend placed a blanket on the floor below the table so her pooch could settle down. Callie remained calm but alert, undeterred by the delicious smells of fried rice, fish, and chicken. When we finished eating and got ready to leave, Xochitl said, "Brace." The dog stood in front of Xochitl with her side pushed against Xochitl's knees. Holding on to Callie's harness and pulling upward, Xochitl stood up strong. Our families chatted as we walked to a nearby park. I observed, amazed, as Callie, upon Xochitl's command, picked up something from the floor that Xochitl had dropped.

Watching Callie support Xochitl brought to my mind the countless ways in which God has been my Helper. Recently, during my book launch, He provided the right opportunities and brought people into my life at the right time to help promote my book. When I became weary or disappointed, He strengthened me through His Word. He stretched my time and energy so I could multitask efficiently. Just as Xochitl can count on Callie's assistance, I too can depend on God to support and guide me not only in my writing but also in my marriage, my parenting, and other areas of my life. —Mabel Ninan

---

So do not fear, for I am with you; do not be dismayed,
for I am your God. I will strengthen you and help you;
I will uphold you with my righteous right hand.
—Isaiah 41:10 (NIV)

JANUARY 21

This Too Shall Pass

For our light affliction, which is but for a moment, is working for us a far more exceeding and eternal weight of glory.

—2 CORINTHIANS 4:17 (NKJV)

TWELVE FOLLOWED BY twelve zeros—twelve trillion. That's how many Rocky Mountain locusts are estimated to have devoured crops and other vegetation across the Great Plains of the United States in 1874 (just one of many locust plagues that occurred from the late 1700s in Maine and Vermont through the end of the nineteenth century in Plains states). Skies were darkened by the hopping insects, and people reported seeing so many during the day that it looked like snow or vapor blocking out the sun. A report in 1875 estimated that the cloud of locusts covered 198,000 square miles—an area larger than California. People lost their livelihoods, and some lost their lives because their food supplies were destroyed and cut off by the hordes of insects.

States placed bounties on the flying insects, which looked like large grasshoppers, but no human effort could make a dent in the number of the voracious creatures. People reported that the locust swarms piled up more than a foot deep and "ate crops, trees, leaves, grass, wool off sheep, harnesses on horses, paint from wagons, and pitchfork handles" (Wikipedia).

The last major swarms of Rocky Mountain locusts occurred between 1873 and 1877, causing $200 million in crop damage across Colorado, Kansas, Minnesota, Missouri, Nebraska, and other states. And then, 30 years later, for reasons scientists can only speculate about, Rocky Mountain locusts were gone. Extinct. The last known sighting took place in 1902.

I'm humbled by these stories of the courage and tenacity our forebears demonstrated in the face of such challenges. My difficulties pale in comparison. When I think about things that irritate or upset me, I am struck by how trivial they often are. Even when challenges seem truly difficult, I remember the Rocky Mountain locusts and think, *This too shall pass.*
—Jon Woodhams

Dear God, I pray that I will emerge from my difficulties as a better, stronger person. Help me remember that while my troubles are but for a moment, Your love is forever. It will never pass away. Amen.

JANUARY 22

Wild and Free

And he said: "Truly I tell you, unless you change and become like little children, you will never enter the kingdom of heaven."

—MATTHEW 18:3 (NIV)

MY MIDLIFE CRISIS resulted in a horse, a beautiful bay Arabian gelding named Moscato. He has such a lovely gait, whether walking, trotting, or cantering, but I especially love to watch him run. He is the epitome of the Arabian breed, holding his stunning short-muzzled head and thick dark tail high as he gallops across the field. It's a breathtaking sight.

He's 6 years old now, and it's about time for him to visit a trainer and learn to be ridden. Many of my friends have wondered why I haven't had him broken to ride before now. After all, I've waited my entire life for a horse, from the time I first knew what a horse was.

The truth is, I wanted him to have a childhood. I could have pushed him to be tamed and ridden. Many trainers start training horses when they are 2 or 3 years old. But Moscato lives in a herd of horses he's fond of, and he had lots of land on which to run and play. I believe this time in community with his own kind will be to his advantage as he ages, just as a human child benefits from friends and playtime

As I leaned against the fence watching Moscato frolic in the field with his friends, I considered when I'd first been introduced to Christ. When I heard of God's love for me, I immediately started learning everything I possibly could about my faith. Which wasn't a bad thing, as I was hungry to learn the Word of God and to change my life to please the Lord. But I sometimes wonder if I pushed myself too hard. I never took the opportunity to simply enjoy what it meant to be a new Christian and embrace the wonderful feelings of simply being connected to my Creator and the Christian community I'd just discovered. —Deb Kastner

Play is the work of childhood.
—Jean Piaget

JANUARY 23

Slow as Snails

My dear brothers and sisters, take note of this: Everyone should be…slow to speak and slow to become angry.

—JAMES 1:19 (NIV)

I PURCHASED THE FINAL addition to my snail family the other day." That's what my friend Chloe texted, sending me a plethora of photos and several videos.

It's true. She's been adopting, adding to her Mystery Snail brood, for a couple of months, naming each and learning about their aquatic lifestyle.

Her slow-moving children, more in number than the blended family in the *Brady Bunch*, are Mango, Francis, Yolk, Shelby, PS2, Mac, and Roast. Well-cared for, they can live approximately 1 year and grow to be the size of a golf ball. Furthermore, they enjoy a diet of blanched veggies, such as cucumber, carrots, and zucchini. By consuming calcium-rich eggshells, their own conical shells are strengthened.

"Some even like to be held," she texted, adding "Mango *loves* being held!"

And I have to admit, not only did I wonder how she knew snails like to be held, but I also wondered why she found such pleasure in these tiny creatures. In fact, as I watched the videos she shared, I found myself growing a bit impatient.

Can't you hurry up? I thought as an orange gastropod, its antennae swaying in a hypnotic manner, eased its way through artificial sea grass. *Why are you so slow?* And I shook my head to keep from drifting off.

But they're snails. And my attitude? Case in point. Indeed, the very lesson God called these tiny creatures to teach might be patience. To be slow to speak. Slow to become irritated.

While a mollusk might not be what I'd consider the perfect pet, it may be just what I need. In fact, perhaps I'll ponder this—and probably for quite some time. After all, my decision-making is known to be slow…as…a…snail. And to most who know me, that's no mystery! —Maureen Miller

Maker of earth and sea and sky,
Creation's sovereign Lord and King,
Who hung the starry worlds on high,
And formed alike the sparrow's wing;
Bless the dumb creatures of Thy care,
And listen to their voiceless prayer.
—Anonymous

JANUARY 24

The King of the Jungle

And let us consider how we may spur one another on toward love and good deeds, not giving up meeting together, as some are in the habit of doing, but encouraging one another—and all the more as you see the Day approaching.

—HEBREWS 10:24–25 (NIV)

THE CATTY SHACK Ranch Wildlife Sanctuary in Jacksonville, Florida, provides a permanent home to endangered big cats. Among their exotic rescues are lions, tigers, cougars, bobcats, and servals, as well as non-feline residents. Each animal has its history displayed for visitors to read and learn more about its situation. Walking through the sanctuary brings visitors up close to the magnificent cats, and staff are always ready to share information.

I particularly loved the lions and tigers. But a thought struck me as I viewed these creatures. Why is the lion considered the king of the jungle when the tiger is larger and stronger? I learned that the reason is lions are sociable cats, whereas tigers are not. Unlike the rest of its race, the lion lives in groups. Survival depends on getting along, working, and cooperating with one another. But tigers, being solitary animals, generally do not work in teams. To be successful, they must constantly fight and hunt alone.

This powerful example demonstrates how much stronger Christians are and how much more we can accomplish when we live and work as a united group. God created humans to dwell in communities. Surrounding ourselves with fellow believers encourages and strengthens us and gives us boldness to live out our faith. God never called Christians to be loners. Yet, with the advent of modern technology, many Christians are doing just that. Sitting at home watching a live-streamed, prerecorded, or televised church service is a blessing to those who are physically unable to attend church in person. For me, though, nothing can take the place of communal worship. I need the instruction, fellowship, and exhortation of other Christians. Simply being in the presence of God's people lifts my spirits and helps me realize I am not fighting life's battles alone. After all, Christians are lions, not tigers. —Ellen Fannon

United we stand. Divided we fall.
—Winston Churchill

JANUARY 25

The Flight of the Eagle

Do you not know? Have you not heard? The LORD is the everlasting God, the Creator of the ends of the earth. He will not grow tired or weary, and his understanding no one can fathom. He gives strength to the weary and increases the power of the weak. Even youths grow tired and weary, and young men stumble and fall; but those who hope in the LORD will renew their strength. They will soar on wings like eagles; they will run and not grow weary, they will walk and not be faint.

—ISAIAH 40:28–31 (NIV)

AS I WAS walking my dog this evening, I noticed a very large bird not too far overhead. In what seemed like seconds, that same bird was soaring high above me, practically a dot against the landscape. The bird's flight reminded me of God's promise—that those who trust in the Lord will soar on wings like eagles.

What a thought—to hold on to the wing of an eagle. To soar so far above our own horizon that our feet come up off familiar ground. And to gain a different vantage point entirely. When I join my spiritual wings to the Lord's, He freely allows me the opportunity to do all these things. Not only do I rise above challenging circumstances, but I also view them differently. How often I forget that God's kingdom, His way of viewing and acting in the world, is not bound by the same rules and challenges that bind me.

The carefree flight of that large bird challenged me, encouraging me to consider the Lord's invitation to mount on His wings. I know I can get a different view—a bird's-eye view—of my struggles today if I only allow my faith to carry me to His waiting wings. —Ashley Clark

Father, I choose to set my eyes on You today. You are my hope. When heavy circumstances weight me to the ground or things seem out of control, I am tempted to despair. Give me Your perspective and Your wings to rise above instead.

JANUARY 26

The Cat Lady's New Best Friend

In the same way, let your light shine before others, that they may see your good deeds and glorify your Father in heaven.

—MATTHEW 5:16 (NIV)

MY FRIEND AT work rescues cats. At one point she had twelve elderly cats living with her, each with different dietary needs. Their morning routine took almost 2 hours. She loves cats with inspiring devotion. Recently, she told me that I wasn't going to believe what she had done.

"Rescued another cat?" I asked.

Driving home in a rainstorm, she saw a golden ball of wet fluff running in circles at the intersection of two big streets. Thinking it was a cat who had been hit by a car, she stopped and chased it. When she finally caught it, she realized it was a dog, with a tiny snout and enormous foxy ears. It shivered in her arms, burrowing close to her heart. She took it home and introduced it to all the cats, who were indifferent to it, and to her husband, who bellowed, "No more animals!"

She took the little dog to the vet to see if anyone was looking for her. They found no leads, but they did discover that she had heartworms. My friend began to chart the best course of care for this little pup, who she called Missy.

The two of them are inseparable now. Missy accompanies my friend to work riding in a pink carrier and wearing a pink rhinestone collar, which looks very nice with my friend's pink glasses. With their luxurious golden hair and sweet features, they look as if they were created to be best friends. My friend's husband is now Missy's biggest fan, and all our coworkers take turns playing with her in the halls.

I thought about how bad things looked for Missy before my friend's enveloping love healed her and bonded them. When I allow myself to be enveloped by God's love, the same thing happens. Not only do I heal, but love also bonds me to God and makes me more radiant to those around me. Even without a rhinestone collar. —Lucy Chambers

A faithful friend is the medicine of life.
—Ecclesiasticus

JANUARY 27

Haven in the Ruins

And there will be a tabernacle for shade in the daytime from the heat, for a place of refuge, and for a shelter from storm and rain.

—ISAIAH 4:6 (NKJV)

THE RED ABBEY is named for its red sandstone. It is one of the oldest surviving structures in Cork City, Ireland, and dates back to the thirteenth century. As amazing as those facts were when I saw the abbey during my first trip to Ireland, something else comes to mind whenever I think of that landmark. I remember the coo of a pigeon coming from an archway, hearing someone say, "I see a bird up there," snapping a photo not knowing what would show up in it, and zooming in to discover I'd captured a perfectly clear picture of a pigeon peeking out of a hole in the sandstone.

The centuries-old structure was destroyed by a fire in the late 1700s (by then it was a sugar refinery), and the 300 pieces of lead shot found during an excavation indicate that it endured many battles. With this history, it fascinated me to know that the Red Abbey was providing a nesting place for that pigeon and possibly even her babies. Sure, the pigeons most likely came to the abbey knowing Cork is a bustling city full of locals and tourists who would throw them goodies. But that pigeon looked especially content up there in her hole in the archway. I have no idea what caused the miniature cave in the sandstone. The Siege of Cork (I read that the abbey tower was a main vantage point during the battle)? The sugar refinery fire in 1799? Time? Whatever happened, a member of God's creation found a haven in the ruins.

That fat-and-happy pigeon reminded me that since the beginning, God has faithfully provided havens of shelter and sustenance for His children. He has opened nests of safety when my life was chaotic and taken part of my life that had fallen into ruin and transformed it into something others could benefit from. And He will continue to. —Jeanette Hanscome

Walk of Faith: *Reflect on a difficult time when God provided you with a safe haven and thank Him.*

JANUARY 28

Two Dogs on a Summit

A friend loves at all times.

—PROVERBS 17:17 (NKJV)

SMITH ROCK IS one of the Seven Wonders of Oregon, its cliffs overlooking the Crooked River. From the walking bridge, where hikers and climbers start out, its elevation reaches 600 feet. The sheer cliffs are ideal for rock-climbing enthusiasts. The crags, spires, and gorges are breathtaking for any observer, but watching rock climbers scale the heights always takes my breath away.

On a short hike at Smith Rock, at the parking lot level, my husband, Tom, and I noticed two small figures on top of the summit. I couldn't imagine how hikers could get up that high, with rock climbers just below them using ropes and spikes to ascend. Then, to my surprise, we watched two tiny forms frolicking and realized they were the hikers' dogs alongside them!

"How on earth did they get up there—with their dogs?" I asked Tom.

"They have to take Misery Ridge Trail, where dogs are allowed on leashes," Tom explained. "The climb is long and steep with switchbacks. It winds around the back side going up and the front side coming down, like a loop. When hikers reach the summit, which is a few blocks square, they can walk there and enjoy the view—3,360 feet above sea level."

I later pondered how a dog is called man's best friend. It's no wonder—dogs are loyal and caring as they walk alongside us on sunny, joyful paths of life, as well as when we trek paths of hardship, even misery. They sense when we are hurting and when to celebrate with us on the summits of life, where the "view" and new perspective is worth the climb.

I discovered a premise at Smith Rock that day. Sometimes, on our own personal "misery trail," we need a companion—someone to walk alongside us to encourage us, a friend who is a prayer partner or a family member who shows they care. Sometimes, that companion is a four-footed furry friend—as they are gifts from God too. —Kathleen R. Ruckman

Dear Lord, thank You for the gift of Your Holy Spirit, who always walks alongside us—and for friends on earth, too, who walk by our side.

JANUARY 29

Bumblefoot

I cry out to the LORD with my voice....I pour out my complaint before Him; I declare before Him my trouble.

—PSALM 142:1–2 (NKJV)

I ANGRILY SWEPT UP a pile of hay. I was not in the mood for cleaning the guinea pig cage that morning. I was too upset about something a friend had said to me. It seemed she wasn't willing to go out of her way for me, the way I'd gone out of my way for her hundreds of times. I was so upset I wouldn't take her calls or text her like I usually did. I just fumed silently.

My miniature broom whisked vigorously. As Petunia and Marigold scrambled into their hideout, I thought I saw something red on the bottom of Marigold's foot. Recently I'd told my granddaughter about *rumblestrutting*—a funny word for guinea pigs' display of dominance. Now I was worried about what amounted to another funny word, *bumblefoot*, or a painful infection of the foot. I reached for Marigold, and she tucked her little foot underneath her body instead of letting me see it so I could help her.

Hiding pain is an instinct for prey animals, but what about me? Did I sometimes do this too? Maybe not with physical pain, but what about emotional pain? I'd never expressed what was bothering me to my dear friend. Maybe there was a good reason for what had happened. Maybe she didn't even know she'd hurt me. God wants us to foster strong friendships, ones built on trust and sharing. In the same way, He wants us to come to Him with our hurts.

I lifted Marigold, cradled her, and examined her foot. It was just mildly red, but not too bad. I made a mental note to keep an eye on it. And I made another mental note: text my friend to share my hurt honestly and to give her the grace necessary to keep our friendship on strong footing.
—Peggy Frezon

Almighty Father, thank You for being bigger than all my hurts.

No Pee-yew!

Give all your worries and cares to God, for he cares about you.

—1 PETER 5:7 (NLT)

"GRANDMA, I DON'T LIKE the black and white thing outside."

My husband and I followed our grandson outside to save him from what I assumed was a bug. Then I heard his older brother. "Help…help."

We hurried to the yard and saw "the black and white thing"—a skunk! We watched as it circled our grandson where he stood, and before we could reach him, the skunk stood up on its hind legs and bit him! Our grandson screamed. We yelled for him to run, which he did, but not before the skunk bit him again. It chased him onto the porch, ignoring the stick my husband swung at it. We ran into the house without anyone else getting bit or the skunk spraying.

As we checked our grandson's leg, I worried about how we'd get to the car to take him to meet his parents at the ER without getting sprayed. After doing so, the next hours dragged while we awaited word on our grandson's fate (eleven shots as a precaution in case the skunk had rabies), help from the game commission in capturing the skunk, or the return of the skunk. I prayed for no complications for our grandson, for his parents not to blame us (they didn't), and for Jesus to fix this somehow so that my grands wouldn't be afraid to come back to our house.

And did He ever answer! Our oldest grandson not only wasn't fearful to return but he also couldn't wait. Despite the trip to the ER and all the shots, he thought the whole episode was a cool story to share. The next visit we enjoyed several days of good times, albeit inside! And the skunk? We never saw it again. —Cathy Mayfield

Thank You, Jesus, for caring about all our needs—physical and emotional.

JANUARY 31

The Least of These

The King will reply, "Truly I tell you, whatever you did for one of the least of these brothers and sisters of mine, you did for me."

—MATTHEW 25:40 (NIV)

I WOKE TO A wreckage scene in my front garden. It was winter, so there weren't many plants to damage. However, I was determined to faithfully feed our resident birds and provide them with much-needed sustenance so they could make it to spring. Yet many mornings, the feeders in the front yard were flipped over, and the seed was scattered throughout the snow. Then, one morning, I caught the culprit. As I stared out the window with the sun rising on a quiet morning, a young bull elk sifted through the snow in our yard to get at the grass beneath. The bulk of his size knocked at our sapling trees and, no doubt, was the cause of my overturned feeders. He was alone and had only one antler. The other antler looked to have been broken off. Because of his age and size, I thought his missing antler was likely the result of a lost battle with a larger male elk.

All my frustration over strewed seeds melted into compassion as I watched this young elk simply trying to survive winter—just like the birds I was feeding. He nibbled at buried grass and shriveled berries from branches. At once, the phrase "the least of these" came to mind from Matthew 25. Jesus encouraged His followers to serve those they encountered and told them their offerings might contribute to a bigger cause they could not see. Jesus was encouraging them to serve with no questions asked and without conditions. I wonder how often I've missed God's bigger opportunities to serve because I'm absorbed with my smaller agenda. Am I so fixated on feeding the birds that I turn a blind eye to other needs, like the solo-antlered elk? I want to heed Jesus's call and learn to look up and all around with a heart sensitive to the needs around me—and to generously give my time, talent, and treasure, no questions asked. —Eryn Lynum

Therefore, as God's chosen people, holy and dearly loved, clothe yourselves with compassion, kindness, humility, gentleness and patience.
—Colossians 3:12 (NIV)

February

FEBRUARY 1

Letting Go

Forget the former things; do not dwell on the past. See, I am doing a new thing! Now it springs up; do you not perceive it?

—ISAIAH 43:18–19 (NIV)

I FLIPPED THROUGH OLD photo albums, feeling nostalgic about when my kids were little. *Where does the time go?* I wondered, wishing I could rewind time. I longed to be needed again, like I was when they were younger. *God, help me not to miss the past so much,* I prayed.

That night, I attended an Indiana Pacers basketball game with my husband, Eric. The halftime show was a man and his three dogs who could catch Frisbees in amazing ways. He threw Frisbees while jumping on a trampoline, and two of the dogs caught them. He threw Frisbees while riding a little motorcycle, and two of the dogs caught them.

The third dog—a black Lab—caught the first Frisbee the man threw to him. When the man threw the Lab a second Frisbee, the dog chased it, but he couldn't catch it because he still had the first Frisbee in his mouth. He chased Frisbee after Frisbee, but he never caught another one because he wouldn't drop the first one.

I loved the show, even the poor Lab who couldn't let go. He was missing out on new things because he couldn't let go of a previous thing. He reminded me of myself. Was I missing out on the fun of having big kids because I was looking backward? I hated to think I was.

I needed to find a way to cherish the past but to let go of it enough to enjoy the present. I realized that my kids still needed me, but in different ways. Parenting big kids was different, but it was still a rewarding experience.

Just like that poor Lab, I'd been holding on to something that was keeping me from fully living in the present, but with God's help, I'd learn to let it go. —Diane Stark

Let go of the past but keep the lessons it taught you.
—Chiara Gizzi

FEBRUARY 2

Harbingers of Hope

I wait for the LORD, my soul waits, and in his word I hope.

—PSALM 130:5 (ESV)

I WAS WALKING OUR dog around the neighborhood on our daily afternoon stroll. Although the calendar said it was winter, the day had developed into a beautiful springlike day—a blue, cloudless sky with the sun warming up the ground and the birds hopping and flitting between the earth and the trees.

We had recently moved, were remodeling the home, and had not even unpacked any boxes. We were living in limbo land: Some issues had come up with the remodeling and nothing was moving forward. It seemed as if our life was much like the frozen ground and the dormancy of the outdoor life—we were hindered from any growth due to the delay in the remodeling project.

As I walked along I noticed that the birdsong had increased and become different. I heard sparrows, robins, and wrens twittering, all joining in a loud cacophony of sound. The harbingers of spring. I stopped in my tracks to listen. Just as they had returned and their sounds reminded me that spring would come again, a feeling of peace came over me, and I sensed that all would be well with our new home.

I may be in the winter of discontent, yet the presence of those birds gave me hope for the warmer weather and hope that our home project would be completed. When I thought honestly about the remodeling, I realized the work *had* been moving along; in my discontented state I hadn't recognized it.

The chorus of those birds reminded me that when we are at our wits' end, whether with winter weather or our current situation, a day like that day will appear and give us a glimpse of what will come. God in His infinite wisdom knows just what we need, when we need it. —Virginia Ruth

"Hope" is the thing with feathers—
That perches in the soul—
And sings the tune without the words—
And never stops—at all.
—Emily Dickinson

FEBRUARY 3

Loving Missy

But God demonstrates His own love toward us, in that while we were still sinners, Christ died for us.

—ROMANS 5:8 (NKJV)

MY CALICO IS weird." So says my father-in-law when he relates his cat's latest neurotic behavior. He's right. Unusual cat from the get-go.

Missy was a rescue kitten. Dad was attracted to her beautiful marbled colors of tan, cream, and blue-gray. He brought her home with high expectations for a sweet, personable pet.

Now, many years later, Missy remains standoffish. Friendly she is not. A lap cat—forget it. Her human engagement is wary, carefully watching for any peripheral, sudden human movements. There are times when she surprises us by allowing a passing petting. Remarkably, she allows Dad to brush her every morning before she disappears for the day.

A vet told us that calico personalities are variable. You may be blessed with a laid-back cat that enjoys being around you. On the other hand, you may find yourself with a cat who terrorizes humans and other animals in the household. In Dad's case, he has an aloof cat who displays neurotic behavior.

Yet, Dad has accepted and loved Missy unconditionally regardless of her obvious relational indifference and difficult personality. It wasn't until recently, in what turned out to be the last weeks of Missy's life, that she became calmer and actually sought out Dad's lap for the first time.

The story of Dad and Missy is like God's love for us. God loves us as we are, neuroses and all. Even in the midst of our relational indifference, He sacrificed His Son to die for us. God chose to love you and me, regardless of whether we meet His needs or expectations today or ever.

And when we do finally seek a relationship with God—crawling into His lap, so to speak—God never pushes us away. And, like Missy, we finally realize that love is not scary or dangerous. It's comforting, especially when we're dying. —Darlene Kerr

God loves us not because we're lovable but because He is love.

—C. S. Lewis

FEBRUARY 4

An Avian Celebration

This is a day you are to commemorate; for the generations to come you shall celebrate it as a festival to the Lord*—a lasting ordinance.*

—Exodus 12:14 (NIV)

A RARE HARD FREEZE gripped south Louisiana for 3 days, and the flock of sparrows and wrens that usually frequents our backyard was nowhere to be seen. The birdbath was frozen solid, and our feeders were unvisited. Then the temperature suddenly zoomed into the 60s and the dam broke. Half a dozen birds were in the birdbath at the same time, and they were impatiently fighting over the perches on the feeders. The birds' jubilant return was truly an avian celebration and a reminder of our ability to celebrate the Lord's goodness many times in various ways.

Of course, we have many standard celebrations, with religious and family holidays such as Christmas, Easter, birthdays, baptisms, and many more. But there is no need to restrict our celebrations to specific days. Rather, just like the birds, we can celebrate any time the Lord showers us with abundance. As the Mad Hatter *in Alice's Adventures in Wonderland* says, there are 364 "unbirthdays," and each of those deserves to be celebrated. My wife and I enjoy finding something to celebrate each and every day, and every year we produce a calendar for ourselves listing at least one possible celebration for each day of the year. For example, in the first 2 weeks of March, we might celebrate the birthdays of Oreos and Monopoly, Romeo and Juliet's wedding day, the premier of *My Fair Lady*, and one of our former priest's favorites, National Get Over It Day.

Life is full of freezes, struggles, and disappointments, but the Lord always provides reasons to celebrate. Like the birds, every day I want to celebrate the Lord and this wonderful life He has given me. —Harold Nichols

The more you praise and celebrate your life,
the more there is in life to celebrate.
—Oprah Winfrey

FEBRUARY 5

A Place for Snakes

Just as Moses lifted up the snake in the wilderness, so the Son of Man must be lifted up.

—JOHN 3:14 (NIV)

SNAKES HAVE ALWAYS terrified me. I don't want one for a pet, and I don't accept a pet-sitting job for one. I don't even love going into the snake house at the zoo, and those reptiles are behind glass!

But I have felt a conviction about snakes and my hatred, yes, hatred (translation, fear) of the reptile ropes. Lately there have been guests with snakes on my TV show—environmental folks talking about the reptiles' important role in the ecosystem—and so many social media posts about good snakes and all they do. I can no longer ignore the idea that God had more in store for snakes than apples, Eve, and the fall of humankind.

Most recently, in a visit with my zookeeper friend, Jim, and a herpetologist who brought an 8-foot boa constrictor for me to meet, I confronted my own fear and began to learn about this important creature. I risked a ginger touch or two and was pleasantly surprised at the supple movements and intricate patterns of its beautiful skin.

I am struck by the plan God has for every living creature to keep our earth in balance. Just as there is a place for me, there is a place for a snake. Every living thing has a divine plan to complete in the days we are given, and all are to serve the highest plan of creation. On days I feel insignificant and unimportant, God reminds me that if He can use a snake for His needs, He can also use me, even when I'm fearful or uncomfortable. —Devon O'Day

God, use what I fear and what I avoid to draw me into Your divine plan for my life.

FEBRUARY 6

Night Workers

The earth is the L*ORD's, and everything in it, the world, and all who live in it.*

—PSALM 24:1 (NIV)

THE RAINY SEASON arrived and turned our Pacific Northwest backyard into a muddy mess. Earlier, we'd had some trees removed, leaving the area looking like a barren moonscape. I couldn't wait for spring, when I could replant grass and flowers. But in the dead of winter, the mud sprouted mounds that I thought must be raccoon or opossum tracks.

Since our bunny lives out back in an enclosure, I worried that predators were stalking her at night. I pointed out the mounded tracks to my son, an avid angler, and asked, "Do you think it's raccoons?"

He chuckled. "No, Mom. Not raccoons. Those mounds are where the earthworms come up at night."

My mouth hung open. He added, "That's why they're called night crawlers." I stared harder, imagining these worms pushing through the mud to breathe. Growing up, my sons had dangled plenty of the reddish-pink segmented worms in my face, but until that moment I hadn't thought of how hard it must be to excavate the heavy earth.

Technically, a night crawler is different from an earthworm, but they're both annelids, a name that comes from the Latin word for "little rings," and the rings play different roles in worm health. These creatures aren't slimy like slugs or snails. And unlike snails, both night crawlers and earthworms till and enrich the soil. In my yard, I counted dozens of holes and thanked the worms for caring for the earth.

I can't help thinking of these lowly beings as heroes, soldiering on unseen—at least until some robin nabs one for breakfast. I'm thankful for the many people God places in my life to both enrich and stir things up a bit. I asked my angler son to spare our resident worms from a fishhook, knowing they are doing their part to keep God's earth fertile and full of blessings. —Linda S. Clare

Walk of Faith: *Find unrecognized heroes in your life and thank them for their dedication.*

FEBRUARY 7

Advance Notice

Therefore keep watch, because you do not know on what day your Lord will come.

—MATTHEW 24:42 (NIV)

GROWING UP IN India, I was used to stray monkeys. We saw them on the streets, in treetops, and sometimes in our houses. They were harmless, mostly. A large family of monkeys would regularly pay a visit to our neighborhood looking for food. Finding strength in numbers, they would raid the patios, balconies, and outdoor spaces of our gated community for anything edible. The primates were adept at opening fridges and food containers and getting into food packaging. They smashed eggs and stole produce.

Our neighbors came up with a solution to this ongoing problem. When someone saw the monkeys approaching, he or she hollered to warn us. Immediately, we left whatever we were doing and sprang into action, securing any appliances kept outside, whisking away food containers and other items indoors, and locking ourselves inside to keep out of their way. Our family home was particularly vulnerable to these unannounced visits because our dining area was situated in an outdoor courtyard. The advance notice gave us enough time, even if it was just a few minutes, to prepare for the invasion and protect our food and property. Every night after dinner, my family moved fruits and vegetables from the dining table to the kitchen inside in preparation for the inevitable monkey visits.

I chuckle whenever these childhood memories resurface, knowing that the monkeys were probably forced to look for food in our homes as a last resort. But they also remind me that Jesus is coming back, and though I don't know when He will return, He expects me to be ready. The Bible gives us advance notice of the Lord's second coming. I'm also called to wait joyfully and expectantly for that glorious day, even as I faithfully steward my time here on earth in preparation for Jesus's return. —Mabel Ninan

For the Son of Man is going to come in his Father's glory with his angels, and then he will reward each person according to what they have done.
—Matthew 16:27 (NIV)

FEBRUARY 8

Clearing a Path in the Snow

You make known to me the path of life; you will fill me with joy in your presence, with eternal pleasures at your right hand.

—PSALM 16:11 (NIV)

THE INDIANA SKYLINE was clear of trees as my family traveled past fields and country lanes that February day. As I drove, I noticed birds gathering high in the sky on my left. They were not in the classic Canada geese V formation but in loose circles and jumbled lines. Against the setting sun, it was as if a pen had created modern art out of tiny moving pieces—a swirling tornado of movement. As I focused past that first group, I saw what looked like tens of thousands of geese flying for miles beyond, a stunning sight. With the windows down, the honking was as loud as if they were next to us on the road.

A few groups of geese began to descend closer to the ground, close enough that we could see their white fluffy feathers and big black wing tips, giving us a better chance to identify them. We discovered that these birds were migrating snow geese participating in a twice-a-year phenomenon, flying their way from Florida back to Canada.

The patterns of squiggly lines didn't make any sense from the ground. But the Creator of all things has a reason for this mishmash of wings as the geese watch from their view high above. As the geese fly, the patterns on the ground lead them north and back again, the view as familiar as their own flying buddies. From the ground, I couldn't tell which direction they would travel next or where they would land for the evening. A mystery of nature.

Interruptions and tragedy, surprises and sadness—my days have patterns known only by my loving Father. The mishmash of a thousand moments seemingly strung together without meaning. What is my purpose? God tells me my life does have one and promises that in the end, when I arrive home after years of traveling, I will find answers in open arms, alongside my flying buddies. —Twila Bennett

In all my prayers for all of you, I always pray with joy because of your partnership in the gospel from the first day until now, being confident of this, that he who began a good work in you will carry it on to completion until the day of Christ Jesus.

—Philippians 1:4–6 (NIV)

FEBRUARY 9

Gaining Traction

In God, whose word I praise, in God I trust; I shall not be afraid. What can flesh do to me?

—PSALM 56:4 (ESV)

I HELD MY BREATH as my Bernese mountain dog rounded the corner from the carpeted room to our tiled foyer and followed me toward the kitchen. Ossian walked easily across the floor as if he hadn't a care in the world.

Then everything changed.

Ossian suddenly tensed his whole body and clenched his feet so that he was walking on his nails instead of the pads of his paws. He started to slip as he painstakingly tried to move forward.

I hurried to help, putting my hands on his sides to make sure he didn't fall. "You're OK, buddy. You won't slip if you relax. Trust me."

But he couldn't. Seconds before, he'd had perfect traction on the tiles. It seemed he hadn't even thought of the possibility that they could be slippery. Then the risk, the idea of possible danger must have entered his mind. Whatever the reason, he instantly reacted with fear even though nothing around him had changed.

And that fearful response created a danger that hadn't been there before.

That wasn't the first time Ossian had tricked himself into believing a surface was slippery when it wasn't. When I told a friend of my dog's silly habit of manufacturing trouble where there wasn't any, she said, "I wonder if God feels that way about us sometimes."

Her point hit me hard. So often I focus on the risks, dangers, or worst-case outcomes of any given situation. When I focus on fear, I try to take control, micromanage, and become increasingly anxious and stressed as a result. When I let fear control me, I create trouble for myself and others.

The antidote to my debilitating fear is the same as the solution for Ossian. I need to relax and trust that God has me in His hands. He won't let me fall. —Jerusha Agen

Lord, help me to trust You so much that fear cannot shake my confidence in Your sovereignty and goodness.

FEBRUARY 10

Ants Marching

Though one may be overpowered, two can defend themselves.
A cord of three strands is not quickly broken.

—ECCLESIASTES 4:12 (NIV)

IN MANY PLACES on earth, there are barely any roads, let alone highway rest areas. Such was the case in Liberia when we visited friends there just after the country's long civil conflict. Traveling to a remote village, my friend halted his SUV in the rutted trail so we could take a nature break.

"Watch your step here," Jerry said, pointing to what appeared to be a thin black stripe across the road. Looking closer, I saw that the line was moving. Looking closer still, I realized it was a colony of ants, marching.

"Soldier ants," he said. "Nasty things if they get hold of you. They travel in a pack and attack in a swarm."

I took a step back. "Maybe we should get back in the truck," I said.

"No," Jerry insisted. "They're headed somewhere. One of their scouts probably found a carcass. Now they're on the march. Just stay out of their way and they'll leave you alone."

I watched the tiny troopers for a minute or so. Sure enough, they were focused. Hundreds, maybe thousands, passed by in formation. Each one was tiny, but I had no doubt they could do real damage in such numbers.

Often, I feel a bit puny as a believer. Who am I to take on the challenge of world evangelism? What can I do to bring about change in the world? Not much, actually.

That's true for each of us, just as it's true for those ants. Alone, we're tiny, powerless, insignificant. But we're not alone. We are united with others in our congregation, in our denomination, and in the whole Body of Christ. Me? I'm not much of a soldier. But the church militant, that's a force to be reckoned with. —Lawrence W. Wilson

Walk of Faith: *Refuse to live in isolation. Join with other believers in doing something—anything—for the cause of Christ.*

FEBRUARY 11

The Best Nester

In my Father's house are many mansions: if it were not so, I would have told you. I go to prepare a place for you.

—JOHN 14:2 (KJV)

DRESSED IN THEIR finest tuxedoes, the African black-footed penguins waddle-ran toward their caretaker and gathered around her as she started a keeper's chat. A row of small hutches lined the back of the enclosure, and the keeper pointed out four mated couples in the group. She explained that some penguin species mate for life and both male and female penguins share responsibility for raising their young.

"Each couple claims a hutch as its own," she said, "and they often collect nesting material to prepare for laying their eggs. Henry here is our best nester."

She went on to tell us about Henry's penchant for collecting unusual items to line his sweetheart's nest. Anything left in the enclosure was fair game. He had dragged bowls, toys, and even a broom to his hutch. Henry apparently had grand ideas for his family's home.

As splendid as Henry might make his home, it won't compare to the one Jesus is preparing for me in heaven. He described it as a mansion, something I picture as roomy and magnificent and full of light. I won't live in just any mansion, either, but in God's house with my Lord and Savior. What's more, He *wants* me there with Him. Jesus said He provided the way and will come back to take me to my new home. I can't wait!

No doubt Jesus will furnish my mansion just right, and it will have everything I need. While I wouldn't mind bowls and toys, I would just as soon He leave out the brooms. —Tracy Crump

Our permanent home is not here on earth. Our permanent home is Heaven.
—Billy Graham

FEBRUARY 12

Abandoned but Not Forsaken

Because of the LORD's great love we are not consumed, for his compassions never fail. They are new every morning; great is your faithfulness.

—LAMENTATIONS 3:22–23 (NIV)

MY RANCHER HUSBAND, Craig, brought me a living Valentine's week present. No, it wasn't a puppy or a kitten. It was the largest newborn angus calf he'd ever seen in nearly 40 years of ranching.

He was feeding his cattle in a brutal snowstorm early that evening when he noticed a heifer trying to give birth. So he moved the mama-to-be outside the corral to an area next to the haystacks, which provided some protection from the storm. Suddenly she stumbled and fell, so Craig was able to pull on the two calf legs sticking out and bring that large bull calf into the world. But that first-time mom ran away like the dickens, so Craig brought the large calf home—rubbing him down and then settling him in the bathtub. Two days later Craig took him back to the ranch, but the mom wouldn't take her calf, so Craig continued bottle-feeding before he could eventually get a dairy cow to take on an extra. It's not unusual, he said, that first-time mama cows walk away from their calves. What was unusual about that calf—which I named Hungry—was that he immediately took to the bottle, taking everything he could get, sucking it nonstop.

Like that abandoned calf, we might also feel a bit forsaken. Perhaps a relationship dissolves. Or a long-time friendship gradually dissipates. We might even think that God has ignored our cries for help if our prayers go unanswered. But instead, He is faithful to love us, provide for our needs, and direct our steps when we are confused. Like a good rancher, He does not forget us and will hold us to Himself when others seemingly walk away. —Janet Holm McHenry

Great is Thy faithfulness, O God my Father,
there is no shadow of turning with Thee;
Thou changest not, Thy compassions they fail not;
as Thou has been Thou forever wilt be.
—Thomas O. Chisholm

FEBRUARY 13

The Catnap

The righteous care for the needs of their animals.

—PROVERBS 12:10 (NIV)

SOON AFTER I drove home in my brand-new CRV, I parked it in the carport, then stopped to admire it for a while. It was exactly the vehicle I wanted. My beautiful, pearlescent-white chariot. Luxurious enough for comfort but also fully utilitarian. All-wheel drive with plenty of room to store my handmade twelve-string guitar and case safely. Almost dancing into the house, I seemed to be walking on air.

Behind me, I heard a troubling thump. Stopping mid-step, I caught my breath. Had something fallen on my new car? I rushed back and spotted Niner, a large, tortoiseshell cat, spread out on the still shiny, white hood. What chutzpah! My temper flared and I flailed my arms, warning him off. He gave me a side-eye look, apparently not interested in removing himself from the hot, white warmth of the Honda's hood. The February chill hardened my heart. Was I to expect his paw prints littering the purity I'd just purchased? Niner needed to nest next door, not on the hood of my new baby.

Apparently, he disagreed. Even though I persuaded Niner to vacate his shiny throne more than once, he always sneaked back. I might find him cozied up against the vents, asleep. Or discover evidence of a visit—paw prints. Afraid to get tough with him and end up with scratches in the paint job, I began to pray about the situation. And God gave me some insight.

He loved that little cat. And cared about his welfare. God made humans and land animals on the same day. Didn't that give them a special connection? They have much value in the kingdom and are good gifts from the Father.

My eyes began to open. I had been thinking of Niner as a pest sleeping atop my new car, but God asked me to be generous with an inanimate object. An expensive object, yes. But one that offered care and comfort to an animal lovingly created by God. And needing a warm place to rest.
—Cathy Elliott

Treat all creatures kindly, then, so far as you can,
for the great Creator's sake.
—Charles Spurgeon

FEBRUARY 14

Love Languages

Trust in the LORD *with all your heart and lean not on your own understanding.*

—PROVERBS 3:5 (NIV)

IN THE FAR southwestern tip of Ireland, I had the opportunity to watch a shepherd working his flock with two beautiful border collies, Cooper and Declan. The dogs were brothers, as alike yet as different as any siblings. Cooper was black and white; Declan, rusty red and white. I was fascinated to discover that Cooper only understood English and Declan only Irish.

Before they could work together to care for the sheep, the shepherd had to train them separately so they knew all the commands in their individual languages. The shepherd, a weathered young man with a lovely brogue, explained that if the dogs were to work on the same task, they would get competitive and perhaps unwittingly drive the sheep over the cliffs into the deep emerald sea below. But when each dog heard the shepherd's voice speaking directly to him, he would only execute those commands. Then that dog would follow the command to sit while his brother accomplished a different job.

Though they were only a year and a half old, Cooper and Declan worked like cogs in a fine machine, each moving on command to follow the shepherd's instructions. The sheep responded to the dogs' movements and flocked together to return safely to their pasture. I thought of all the sheep analogies in the Bible—none so flattering to the sheep, but all revealing the tender care the Shepherd provides. It had never occurred to me that not only does the Shepherd know how to tend all of the creatures in His care, but He also knows how to speak to us individually so we can hear His voice without being distracted by instructions or paths that are meant for others.

Focusing on God's voice, rather than all the noise around me, I can better accomplish the good work that He intends me to do. —Lucy Chambers

The King of love my Shepherd is,
Whose goodness faileth never;
I nothing lack if I am his
And he is mine for ever.
—H. W. Baker

FEBRUARY 15

Diminishing Obstacles

You have hedged me behind and before, and laid Your hand upon me.

—PSALM 139:5 (NKJV)

I WALKED MY YORKIE north along the Fred Marquis Pinellas Trail in Florida. The trees shaded the path and protected us from the morning sun. Minnie and I entered Wall Springs Park and circled the butterfly garden, pausing to notice the fresh blooms. I walked along the sidewalk to the wooden boardwalk that went over the spring.

I lingered to view the waters. A school of mullet made circles and figure eights as they traveled. A crab lay at the bottom of the muddy waters. Beige grass surrounded a dark-colored turtle.

It took a minute before I noticed the turtle's small head peeking above the water. As I stood there, the tide changed, and the grass seemed to close in on him. I feared he would become trapped. The grass nearly obscured his algae-covered shell before I saw him swim under it. I watched and waited.

After a few minutes he popped up in a different spot a few feet away, still surrounded by grass. He seemed to welcome the barrier.

I realized that what I viewed as his prison was really a shelter that allowed him to remain hidden. The grass protected him from intruders and concealed him from unsuspecting prey.

Sometimes I view my limitations as prison walls, obstacles to moving forward and hindrances to progress. But watching the turtle reminded me that my limitations are merely proof of my humanity. They cause me to turn to God as my strength and guide, leading me straight to the shelter of His arms and His presence. —Crystal Storms

The name of the LORD is a strong tower; the righteous run to it and are safe.

—Proverbs 18:10 (NKJV)

FEBRUARY 16

Learning to Love

Dear children, let us not love with words or speech but with actions and in truth.

—1 John 3:18 (NIV)

THE LITTLE BOY toddles around the large black dog, who is lying in the driveway with the hubbub of family around him. The boy squats down next to the dog, reaching out a small hand, and the dog's tail wags lazily as the boy pets the dog—though to the undiscerning eye, it might look more like the boy was hitting the dog with the palm of his hand. Still the dog stays motionless, except for his wagging tail, patiently allowing the kind of rough love that only a toddler can provide.

I am, or was, that little boy, and the scene was captured on 8-millimeter film by my camera-loving dad. The images on the screen flicker a bit, but the relationship between boy and dog is unwavering as the scene clicks by at 16 frames per second.

I barely remember Jet, my family's dog of unknown heritage. He was a loving and beloved farm dog and pet for my first few years. And then he was gone, much too soon. Seeing my interaction with him more than 50 years after we were filmed made my heart swell.

Much like my toddler self, I don't always know how to show love. I've lived much of my life trying not to be a bad person more than I have trying to be a good person. Don't rock the boat, don't offend, don't say how I really feel in case someone might not like it (or me). Back away if there's conflict or differences. But I'm learning that loving others isn't about what I don't do, and it isn't about not being true to myself. It's about what I *do* that matters, and I can't share my heart if I'm hiding half of it from everyone.

I'm still learning to love, as I will be for the rest of my life. I just hope and pray that others will be as patient with me as Jet was so long ago and accept the love I offer in whatever form it takes. —Jon Woodhams

Dear God, help me learn to love as You love, to love my neighbor as myself. Amen.

FEBRUARY 17

Praying for People and Pups

Do not be anxious about anything, but in everything by prayer and supplication with thanksgiving let your requests be made known to God.

—PHILIPPIANS 4:6 (ESV)

POOR HALSEY. LIKE many French bulldogs, my grandpup suffered from a spine disorder. Surgery to remove three degenerating discs left him with a long recovery. He endured months of crate rest (no zoomies), weeks of being carried up and down stairs (challenging for owners *and* pup), and neighborhood walks in the indignity of a doggie stroller. Finally, he received the all clear—permission to walk outdoors.

When I visited, we explored the neighborhoods in Old Town Alexandria, Virginia. Every morning, Halsey trotted out with a glorious doggie grin on his smushed-in face. Ears tuned to every sound and eyes alert for squirrels, he was in his happy place.

On the day I returned home, I made him a promise. "The next time I see you, you'll be at my house, and you can run around in my backyard." The only place Halsey loves more than the back streets of Alexandria is my backyard.

Sadly, a flare up just before he visited put him back on crate rest. No zoomies in my backyard. No long walks through the neighborhood. He wasn't even allowed to walk around indoors for fear he'd rupture another fragile disc.

One day, he and I sat outside on the screened porch. He stretched out in a sunny spot, closed his eyes, and fell asleep. As I petted his silky fur, a prayer rose in my heart: *Lord, this poor pup has been through so much. Strengthen and heal his back. Restore his mobility. Give him a long and happy life.*

As I lifted my prayer to *Jehovah Rapha*, Hebrew for "God who heals," a peace settled over my soul. I've often asked God to bring about human healing, but that day the Holy Spirit reminded me it was OK to pray for my furry friend too. I could bring my requests to God in confidence, knowing He saw, He cared, and He would do what was best. —Lori Hatcher

Father, I know it's not always Your will to heal, but oftentimes it is.
Help me remember to bring all my needs to You in prayer,
on behalf of my human and my furry friends.

FEBRUARY 18

Persistent Woodpecker

But as for you, be strong and do not give up, for your work will be rewarded.

—2 CHRONICLES 15:7 (NIV)

A RED-BELLIED WOODPECKER HAS been visiting our bird feeder. It's the first one I've ever seen, and I think he's beautiful. The slight blush on his belly, for which he was named, is hard to see, but the bright red cap on his head really stands out. I can even identify him perched amid the leafless branches of our lilac bush, where many other birds don't show up as well.

But it isn't only his appearance that attracts my attention. It's also his behavior. First of all, most of the birds—including blue jays, red-winged blackbirds, mourning doves, evening grosbeaks, chickadees, and goldfinches—appear in flocks. Even the cardinals, downy woodpeckers, hairy woodpeckers, and nuthatches appear in pairs. But the red-bellied woodpecker always comes alone.

Unlike other woodpeckers, he didn't know how to grip our suet feeder and eat at the same time. The poor bird tried clinging to the feeder pole and stretching to the hanging suet rack. But his weight made the suet feeder swing, and he couldn't get a nibble. He also tried hanging upside down on the block of suet, but his head fell too far below the feeder for him to eat. If only I could go outside and show him what to do. But obviously, I couldn't. Days passed, but the persistent bird didn't quit.

As for me, I'm a freelance writer, and I was struggling to write a magazine piece for kids. Frustrated at my inability to get the words right, I wandered into the kitchen for a cup of tea. That's when I looked out the window and saw the red-bellied woodpecker again. To my delight, he was eating! He had learned to hold onto the suet feeder with his feet, stay upright, and peck at the food.

I returned to my computer feeling inspired. If that woodpecker could stick to his work until he succeeded, so could I. And I did. —Aline Alexander Newman

Believe in yourself! Have faith in your abilities! Without a humble but reasonable confidence in your own powers you cannot be successful or happy.
—Norman Vincent Peale

FEBRUARY 19

Missy and the Mailman

But the Lord is faithful, and he will strengthen you and protect you from the evil one.

—2 THESSALONIANS 3:3 (NIV)

MY MOTHER-IN-LAW, Corinne Landry, lived in a neighborhood where mail was delivered to a mailbox attached to the house right by the front door. She had a wonderful Chihuahua named Missy who decided that the mailman was evil and took it upon herself to protect the house and its occupants.

Missy had a routine. Her nose told her when the mailman entered the neighborhood, and she would begin racing around the house from room to room growling at this menace she couldn't see. Her activity intensified as the mailman drew nearer and continued even after he delivered the mail. It was after he actually left the neighborhood that she collapsed for a well-earned rest.

One day when Mrs. Landry was retrieving the mail, Missy slipped out. Her nose led her straight to the unsuspecting mailman, and by the time Mrs. Landry got outside to rescue him, Missy had cornered the poor man against a neighbor's front door. His eyes were as big as saucers as he tried to ward off this raging menace. We have joked that Missy may have been solely responsible for the change in mail delivery, with boxes now on posts at the street.

Missy's fierceness keeping the house safe and the evil intruder out brings to mind God's fierceness in protecting me. He has promised to protect and shield me from whatever the evil one throws at me. And like Missy, He will frequently warn me of dangers before my limited vision becomes aware of them. I simply need to remember that He is always one step ahead of me. —Harold Nichols

Even though I walk through the darkest valley, I will fear no evil,
for you are with me; your rod and your staff, they comfort me.
—Psalm 23:4 (NIV)

A Special Arrival

So you also must be ready, because the Son of Man will come at an hour when you do not expect him.

—MATTHEW 24:44 (NIV)

MY SON SPOTTED the long-haired cat on his morning walk. Several days later, he pointed out the cat to my husband, David, and me. The orange, black, and cream-colored tortoiseshell cat warily kept her distance. When she moved away from us, we saw she was pregnant. Very pregnant, it seemed.

After checking with neighbors, we realized she was ownerless. We've never been a cat family because we're all allergic—my husband, son-in-law, and grandson terribly so. But this sweet mama-to-be captured our heart with her beauty and helpless plight. We fed her, first in the front yard and then on the front porch after luring her there for mealtimes.

David removed the front of a cardboard box, leaving a lip to keep kittens contained, and I lined it with soft towels. We thought erroneously that she was due any day. I was surprised how excited I was for the birth of kittens. I told everyone about "our" mama cat and sent pictures of our new furry friend to family and friends.

When David and I left for a work trip combined with a fortieth anniversary getaway to Italy just 5 days after we adopted Mama Feline, she still hadn't delivered. I said a prayer, hoping she'd wait another 2 weeks until we returned home. Even though I was anxious about not being around for this exciting event, we put our son in charge of feeding and taking care of her and whatever kittens might arrive. "We'll figure out what to do with them after that," I said.

Lucky for me, Mama Cat didn't deliver until 4 days after we returned. My anxiety—and excitement—reminded me of Jesus's second coming. God promised us that Jesus will return, though none of us know the day or hour. I certainly hope my enthusiasm for Jesus's arrival is as evident to others as that of my new kitty friends! —Julie Lavender

Perfect submission, all is at rest,
I in my Savior am happy and blest,
Watching and waiting, looking above,
Filled with His goodness, lost in His love.
—Frances J. Crosby

FEBRUARY 21

Remembering Donna the Hippo

Surely the righteous will never be shaken; they will be remembered forever.

—PSALM 112:6 (NIV)

A FEW MONTHS AGO my husband and I visited Mesker Park Zoo in Evansville, Indiana, so we could view the bronze sculpture designed as a memorial to a beloved hippopotamus. We had been there several years ago during the final birthday party for Donna who, at the time, was the oldest living Nile hippo in captivity. School children made cards for her, and we took photos of memorable moments. I remember that Donna's arthritis prevented her from walking normally, but, in her wading pool, she was buoyant. Donna didn't mind sharing her hippo-shaped birthday cake with us and a few thousand others. She chomped down on her own floating Popsicle cake made with frozen fruit.

When we located the bronze tribute, I thought the placement in the playground was perfect. Donna and one of her eight offspring were sculpted as if they both were submerged in the soft blue flooring. A staff member explained to us, "We placed the memorial down low so small children can climb around on her back." I hoped that meant mature women like me also, because I posed on board for my photo op.

As I reflected on the events from both visits, I experienced a mixture of excitement and grief. That's the way my life memories are too. I am joyful during my family's celebrations, but I experience pain from the absence of my parents, my grandparents, and the animals I loved. I wondered what God advises about remembering those who are no longer with us. I learned there are 231 verses in the New International Version of the Bible that contain the word *remember*. God sets the example—reminiscing about loved ones and being honest about our loss, but not continuously focusing on the past. So I remember those I loved and move forward in perpetuating their memories. —Glenda Ferguson

Because of the LORD's great love we are not consumed,
for his compassions never fail.
—Lamentations 3:22 (NIV)

FEBRUARY 22

Goldfish Switcheroo

Therefore each of you must put off falsehood and speak truthfully to your neighbor, for we are all members of one body.

—EPHESIANS 4:25 (NIV)

MY NEIGHBOR IS a gruff sort, scaring away trick-or-treaters with a nickel and the warning "Don't do drugs." But she also has a soft spot. For turtles. Her backyard is a turtle refuge. Apparently some turtles outlive their charm as pets—sometimes by decades—and are abandoned. Lucky ones live out their days next door, in man-made ponds under chicken wire that keeps out raccoons.

When my family planned to be away for several weeks, this neighbor was the obvious candidate to care for our goldfish. How hard could it be to add one bowl of two fish to the habitat? Our fish seemed to have fared very well under her care. When we returned the fish were twice the size they had been when we left them! But their behavior had changed too. Formerly they would come to the water's surface whenever we entered the room, and we had fed them by hand. They were simple little fish rescued from the feeder tank at a pet store, but they were our little fish, and we loved them.

Months passed before I asked the neighbor, "What did you feed our fish that they grew so large?" She confessed that the goldfish had died, and she had replaced them with the hearty-looking goldfish. By this time the kids had come to love the new fish, which they believed to be the over-fed old fish. No reason to explain the switch to them. But my neighbor clearly felt terrible. I wondered how long she had harbored her secret and the guilty feeling she now expressed to me. I offered forgiveness, and the clandestine goldfish switcheroo became a joke between us.

I no longer think of her as my gruff neighbor. I think of her as a friend. When I travel, I ask her to water my plants. But I leave the goldfish with someone else. —Susie Colby

Honesty is often very hard. The truth is often painful. But the freedom it can bring is worth the trying.

—Fred Rogers

FEBRUARY 23

The Heart of a Lion

Finally, all of you should be of one mind. Sympathize with each other. Love each other as brothers and sisters. Be tenderhearted, and keep a humble attitude.

—1 PETER 3:8 (NLT)

MY CAT FRIEND, Stella, was visiting for a few months. After being alone for the day, she loved to cuddle together and nap while I watched TV. One evening, *The Lion King* live-action movie was on, and to continue my cat theme situation, I watched it.

Simba appeared on screen, and not-sleepy-anymore Stella sat up with a start as his young roar filled the room. She jumped from my lap and climbed onto the television stand with caution, nose to the screen. She sat in front of that large lion cub and looked up at it with big eyes. When Simba moved, she watched him closely, pouncing toward each side as he ran off-screen and out of sight. From her perch, she was engrossed in every lion, watched other characters, and looked distraught at loud noises. Then came the scene where Mufasa lay dying.

I watched as Stella's small cat paw reached up to pat Mufasa as he lay suffering. She was somber and quiet, instinctively connecting with this very real, yet fake, lion. Stella sincerely saw Mufasa's pain. I was overwhelmed by her show of compassion and emotion.

Her reaction continues to make me reflect on how much compassion I show when others have pain. Of course I want friends to reach out to me when I'm in pain—it makes me feel good, and their tenderness brings me to tears. But do I really focus on someone else's terrible news or horrible situation? Am I willing to draw near, listen, and put a hand on their shoulder without putting myself first?

I am trying. To me, this is something we can learn from all God's creatures. The memory of that cat's care can help me to pause and reach out with love. —Twila Bennett

Walk of Faith: *The next time your friend is hurting, stop. Really listen. Put your arm around them or put your hand on their shoulder. Showing deep compassion can take one simple gesture.*

FEBRUARY 24

Tangled Up

My eyes are ever toward the L*ORD, for he will pluck my feet out of the net.*

—PSALM 25:15 (ESV)

LIKE MANY DOGS, Snowy enjoys chasing squirrels. He is fiercely protective of our backyard, especially during the summer when our plum and pear trees bear fruit, attracting birds, squirrels, and other small animals for a quick snack. One evening when my husband, Simon, was working from home, he heard unusually loud and squeaky noises and rushed to the backyard to investigate. To his shock, he found a squirrel stuck in our son's mini soccer net, dangling from its hind legs.

Surprisingly, our pooch did not show interest in harming the squirrel but stayed near the net, sniffing curiously. He may have been frightened by the rodent's frantic movements. Simon chased Snowy back inside the house and approached the net to figure out how he could help the creature in crisis. But the squirrel became more terrified, squealing, kicking the net, and showing his teeth. Simon backed off. He waited a few minutes so the squirrel could calm down before tiptoeing slowly behind it. With a pair of scissors, my husband carefully cut the portion of the net around the animal's hind leg. He shook the net a little. Within seconds, the creature untangled itself and scampered onto the backyard fence before disappearing out of sight.

I can be like that squirrel sometimes. I resist God's help during tough times. When I find myself in a difficult situation, I don't always run to God first. I exhaust all other options, wanting to be independent. I fight the thought of giving up control and depending on God. Often, this leaves me frustrated and feeling even more tangled up. It's only when I surrender my problems to Him and put my trust in Him that I can relax and let God be God—the Savior, the Miracle Worker. —Mabel Ninan

Walk of Faith: *If you're struggling to deal with a sticky situation on your own, write a prayer of surrender to God today and ask for His help. Also write down a Bible verse that reminds you that God saves and rescues His children.*

FEBRUARY 25

Equipped and Empowered

[God will] equip you with everything good for doing his will, and may he work in us what is pleasing to him, through Jesus Christ, to whom be glory for ever and ever.

—HEBREWS 13:21 (NIV)

TOY WAS MY great-grandmother's African gray parrot. Although I'd never met Toy in person, I'd heard countless stories about him and seen pictures of him on his perch. He felt like one of the family.

Many parrots can repeat words, but Toy was extremely smart and had a strong personality. If you asked him, "What does the little dog say?" Toy would respond with a soft, "Yip, yip, yip!." When asked, "What does the big dog say?" Toy would give out a loud "Woof, woof!"

My great grandmother ran a boarding house, and Toy loved to play tricks on the boarders. Sometimes Toy would imitate sirens and yell, "Fire!" in order to watch the boarders flee from their rooms. Then he would laugh at his practical joke. If he was in his cage on the front porch and one of the men was sitting with him, Toy would whistle at the young ladies walking by, much to the young man's embarrassment.

Toy exceeded the perceptions many people had of a pet parrot, and demonstrated far more intelligence than they expected. As a teenager, hearing stories about Toy, I was inspired to never be held back by limitations others had for me. I wasn't naturally athletic, but I tried out for sports in high school and made the team. My brothers had not attended college, but I wanted to, and I not only got accepted but also earned several scholarships. I thought of Toy whenever I was facing a challenge, and it helped me believe in myself.

More important, I grew to know that God believed I could do great things. He equipped and empowered me to follow His call. Still does. If there is something God puts on my heart to achieve, I know He will give me what I need to see it through. After all, He put such a bold spirit in a lively parrot. —Peggy Frezon

Father God, thank You for giving me all that I need.

FEBRUARY 26

Patterns of Faithfulness

This is what the Lord says:"Stand at the crossroads and look; ask for the ancient paths, ask where the good way is, and walk in it, and you will find rest for your souls."

—JEREMIAH 6:16 (NIV)

YESTERDAY, WHEN I delivered my goldendoodle, Honey, to Martha, the groomer, Honey did what she always does. Even though Honey tends to act anxious about being left at the groomer, after we entered the small grooming studio and Martha took hold of the leash, Honey pulled to the back where there are kennels for the dogs to wait their turn. Honey always goes to the exact same kennel, and Martha always remarks on that. Honey likes to show me and Martha that she understands what is expected of her; she knows the ways and the routines of her day at the groomer. Also a creature of habit, Honey feels safest and best when she can follow patterns that she knows are right and good. Patterns comfort her. Later, when I picked Honey up midday, Martha commented that everything went very well, and I think this has to do with Martha helping Honey know the patterns and Honey following them well.

When I watch Honey keep the patterns of her life—and there are many—I think of the patterns that exist in my walk of faith. I think of reading my Bible at the dining table while drinking my second cup of coffee after breakfast. I think of praying with my family at the same table. I think of regularly attending worship with my larger family of believers, and the ways, even, that we follow patterns in our worship service that help us know and love and understand our relationship with God better. Many of these patterns are ancient practices taught to me over a lifetime by parents, pastors, and other spiritual mentors. They guide me day by day, and week by week, closer to God.

When I make a deliberate choice to read scripture, pray, and attend worship, I know that I choose a good way. And when I walk these straight and steady paths, I am at peace. I find restfulness in the patterns. They are both restorative and instructive to my daily life journey and my future. —Katy W. Sundararajan

Be faithful in small things because it is in them that your strength lies.
—Mother Teresa

Upside-Down World

You turn things upside down, as if the potter were thought to be like the clay! Shall what is formed say to the one who formed it, "You did not make me"? Can the pot say to the potter, "You know nothing"?

—ISAIAH 29:16 (NIV)

WHILE VISITING A small zoo, I became fascinated with the two-toed sloths. Though known for being slow, one of the sloths moved steadily along ropes strung from one side of his long cage to the other. He certainly wouldn't win any races, but he moved faster than I had imagined. His long, curved claws helped him maintain his grip as he gently swung upside down on his journey.

A zookeeper later pointed out that the sloths' fur grows backward from the way most animal fur does, allowing rain to flow off as they hang from tree branches. Their internal organs are also arranged to accommodate this upside-down life.

As the keeper talked, she fed the sloths bits of cucumber and zucchini, some of their favorite treats. In the wild, they eat relatively little food because it can take up to a month to digest just one leaf. The only time they drop to the ground is to defecate—*once a week*. Since moving on the ground exposes sloths to predators and puts undue stress on their lungs, the more they remain in the trees, the better.

Though I enjoyed hearing about the sloths, I prefer to stay right side up with my feet planted firmly on the ground. Without Jesus, though, my world would turn upside down. As my Lord and Savior, He not only keeps me right side up but also helps me stay grounded in God's Word. He is the only one who can keep me on the right path in this topsy-turvy world. —Tracy Crump

Jesus, keep me ever mindful that You are first in my life.

FEBRUARY 28

The Paws of God

"'If you can'?" said Jesus. "Everything is possible for one who believes."

—MARK 9:23 (NIV)

OUR BLACK LAB, Ruby, goes to a wonderful school where she serves as a coach to younger dogs. The trainers are remarkable in how well they understand what dogs need and how to communicate with them. Recently, they called and asked if Ruby could come in on a day she was not scheduled to coach. A shy Lab boy was scared to venture into the Fit Paws area where the dogs learn how to climb on different surfaces and go around obstacles. This fear was keeping him from enjoying his time at school. The trainers thought Ruby could help him.

When we picked her up that afternoon, everyone was ecstatic. Ruby was wagging her tail, the shy boy was licking her, and his person was relieved that school was not scary anymore. The trainers explained what had happened: They introduced the two dogs outside, and they became friends. The boy liked Ruby and enjoyed playing with her. When they opened the doors to the Fit Paws room—one of Ruby's favorite places—she bounded in and started working the course. He saw how delighted she was to be there, and he trusted her and followed. Once his new friend showed him the way, he was able to enjoy all of the aspects of the school, and they had a great day.

Ruby's ability to help her new friend reminds me that all of us—humans and Labs, other animals and other organisms—are put here to work together, according to God's beautiful design. When I am feeling like the shy dog, I need to trust God and the community He has provided me. When I do, the world opens up, offering increased joy. And just as Ruby lent a paw to help her friend overcome his challenges, I can be the hands of God for others. —Lucy Chambers

Trust the past to God's mercy, the present to God's love
and the future to God's providence.
—Augustine of Hippo

March

MARCH 1

Not an Itsy-Bitsy Spider

Have mercy upon me, O God…blot out my transgressions.

—PSALM 51:1 (NKJV)

MOM! COME QUICK! Hurry! Mom!"

The shouts came from the bathroom, where our oldest daughter was taking a shower. Holly hadn't turned on the water yet, so she couldn't have slipped in the tub. Nor could she have cut herself on a dull razor. I hurried to see what prompted such hollering. I nudged the door open to see her wrapped in a towel, standing in the tub. No blood—that was good. Then I noticed her pointing inside the tub.

"I need a container."

Oh no, not another one. Holly held the title of Spider Rescuer in our home. I also hated killing anything, though the third time a large, hairy wolf spider crawled across the floor in the kitchen in as many days, I wished she would re-home them farther away. This spider had decided to bathe with her, so I bravely went for a container big enough to capture a typical wolf spider; however, the one eyeing us from the floor of the tub could've filled the bottom of a soup bowl.

As I walked outside with the monster spider, I must admit the temptation to toss it into the trash can crossed my mind. Still, I supposed I could be merciful to this creature caught in a situation he didn't really intend to make. Just like Jesus—hanging on a cross for the sins I wouldn't intend to commit but couldn't help doing. His mercy covers much more than I did in releasing the spider outdoors. Bye, spider, but please, don't come back! —Cathy Mayfield

Apart from the mercy of God, there is no other source of hope for mankind.
—Pope John Paul II

MARCH 2

Sweet, Humble Juncos

Humble yourselves in the sight of the Lord, and He will lift you up.

—JAMES 4:10 (NKJV)

A FLOCK OF TINY birds foraged on the ground of my courtyard. The dark-eyed juncos were new to me when we moved to the foothills of Oregon's Cascade Mountains. Part of the sparrow family, these birds are sweet to behold. Their delicate, high-chirping notes, like a quiet serenade, match the appearance of humble little songbirds.

Because they are ground birds, the gray-and-brown juncos blend in with the earth and are easy to overlook. I watched them hop around at the base of my shrubs, eating the seeds on the ground rather than take flight to find food. When larger, more aggressive birds hung from our bird feeder until it swayed, knocking seeds to the ground, the juncos had a feast.

The behavior of the juncos intrigued me, and I decided to read more about these petite and beautiful birds. I learned they are the original snowbirds, taking on that name because they are basically winter birds that inhabit higher elevations; they are also considered mountain birds. In parts of Oregon, we are blessed to have them year-round.

While watching the juncos, I discovered something about life. We are all individuals, some taking flight to high places, gracing the tops of symbolic trees and skies. Others prefer the lowlands, content to stay grounded, acknowledging the value of what others leave behind. I thought of Ruth in the Old Testament, who gleaned in the barley field, gathering the leftover grain dropped by workers during harvest. These little birds, too, don't waste a thing.

The humble dark-eyed juncos have touched my heart. I am inspired to not waste what is around me, to be more frugal, and to be content to take the low road where I am often unnoticed. It is there where I find God's provision and grace, because I depend on Him. —Kathleen R. Ruckman

Dear Lord, may I walk humbly before You, singing songs of praise and finding treasures others overlook or leave behind.

MARCH 3

The One Lost Puppy

Suppose one of you has a hundred sheep and loses one of them. Doesn't he leave the ninety-nine in the open country and go after the lost sheep until he finds it?

—LUKE 15:4 (NIV)

DANTE, A POMERANIAN-CHIHUAHUA cross, was a 2-pound snowball. If I fully opened the dishwasher door, he could walk under it without bumping his head. His small stature held a huge puppy heart and an adventurous spirit. He'd race around the house, chasing his ball, then leap into my arms, instantly falling asleep. My husband and I were smitten.

Our townhouse community curled around a hilly courtyard. One afternoon, Dante learned to push the screen door open. Within seconds, he had bolted. We didn't even see it happen. We noticed the open door and our stomachs knotted. We raced outside and over the lawns. We called his name. We scanned every dark corner for a glimpse of white. We prayed he'd stay on the grass and not wander into the road. As the seconds ticked by, we started to panic. He was so small! It would be so easy for him to get lost or hurt or stolen or…

Suddenly, a little ball of white raced over the hills! Dante's ears blew back as he ran toward us, his sweet face bursting into a smile. He jumped into my husband's arms. I broke into a rush of tears. We covered him in kisses, lifting fast and grateful prayers.

As we held Dante, I thought about God as the Good Shepherd. I've read of the shepherd leaving the whole flock to chase one lost sheep, but it always feels so extravagant. How can one small lamb matter that much? But as I held our little lost Dante, I had the tiniest glimpse into God's heart. For the briefest moment, I understood how distraught God must be when one of us is lost and how excited He must be to finally cradle us again. —Allison Lynn

Loving God, sometimes we allow the distractions of our lives to draw us away from the comfort and security of Your flock. But You have promised we can never outrun Your love. Thank You for chasing us down when we wander and always welcoming us home! Amen.

MARCH 4

A Peacock's Glory

To them God willed to make known what are the riches of the glory of this mystery among the Gentiles: which is Christ in you, the hope of glory.

—COLOSSIANS 1:27 (NKJV)

MY HUSBAND, TIM, and I went on a getaway for our twenty-seventh anniversary. We stayed at the Putnam Lodge in Cross City, Florida. Lush gardens surrounded the historic site. Peacocks, chickens, and cats roamed freely.

The front desk clerk gave us a tour of the beautiful building as she showed us to our room. She revealed the lodge's history and called our attention to the pecky cypress–adorned walls. We admired the wood stenciling throughout the building. The sitting room with its coffee-table books invited me to linger.

Our host pointed out the signs by the exits on the garden side that remind guests to latch the doors to prevent peacocks from entering. I asked about the signs, and she confided that one of the peacocks had entered the lodge through an unlatched door in the middle of the night. Once in, he did not want to leave. His loud hooting calls woke up guests, and it took several people to corral him and take him outdoors.

The next morning, I walked through the gardens and followed a peacock, hoping to see the fullness of his beautiful plumage. He disappeared into the woods without fanning his train.

I felt God prompt my heart to believe that a peacock reflects His glory in the beauty of his feathers. But that is not the same for me as a follower of Jesus. Beauty fades, skin sags, and clothes wear out. Accomplishments get forgotten and trophies get dusty. Possessions rust and break down. Christ is in me, and that is the way I reflect His glory. —Crystal Storms

Father, guard me from the dangers of pride. Give me a humble heart that exalts the name of Jesus and brings glory to Your Name alone. Amen.

MARCH 5

When Life Doesn't Seem Fair

In their hearts humans plan their course, but the LORD establishes their steps.

—PROVERBS 16:9 (NIV)

IS HE HOUSETRAINED?"

"I don't know."

Josh's frown deepened, "What name did you pick?"

"Mister Magoo."

That got a chuckle.

Josh left for work, unconvinced that this adoption was a good idea.

I, however, was thrilled. I'd been praying daily about the young pug that came into the shelter where I work. Josh and I usually adopt senior dogs, but the energy of this 1-year-old captured my heart. Today, God willing, he'd join our pack.

I barely got his harness on before he bolted from the kennel and chugged down the hall. The sounds of panting pug and the stench of stray dog filled my car. Introductions with our three older dogs were short. Soon they realized they couldn't keep up with Magoo's frantic exploration of the backyard and retired inside.

Magoo raced after them, jumped on and off the couch, dashed out to the yard and back inside to repeat the course. This went on for hours. During one intermission, he flipped the toy basket and strewed a couple dozen stuffed plushies and tug toys throughout the house. His pant-snorting echoed off the walls well past midnight.

I'd prayed hard about this precious pug becoming part of our family, but his abundant energy was too much for us. I brought him back the next day and cried all the way home.

Was I overtired or relieved? A little of both, but I was also disappointed that my prayers were unanswered. Yet the more I thought about it, I realized this wasn't about me—it was about Magoo and what was best for him.

When I pray for God to do His will and open my heart to whatever He's designed, I can't be disappointed at His choices. I may be sad that it didn't work out the way I wanted, but I can also be joyful to have been part of His plan.

Though my heart was broken, everything worked out as God intended it to. Magoo was adopted within a half hour of his return to the shelter. And for that I'm thankful. —Jean Alfieri

Dear Lord, please help me to embrace the many blessings in my life, including Your answers to my prayers.

MARCH 6

The Hamster Wheel

Be still, and know that I am God.

—PSALM 46:10 (NIV)

I WANDERED DOWN THE aisle of the pet shop on my way to buy some small-animal food, and my attention was immediately diverted by a furry little rodent in a glass cage moving vigorously on his exercise wheel. I had never seen a hamster move so fast before, and that wheel just spun around and around and around.

How I could relate to that! I find myself spinning around and around on my hamster wheel of worry all the time. I worry about my health, the health of my husband, my kids, my grandkids, my pets. I worry about finances. Safe travels. Making good decisions. I worry about a lot of things I can't change. Sometimes I worry about things that never even happen. But I keep on worrying.

When I worry, I'm like a hamster on a wheel. I just keep spinning and spinning, obsessed with the same concerns but getting nowhere. It is not until I get off the wheel and trust God that I can begin to let go of the worry. Trusting God isn't always easy—it takes faith. Faith that someone else is in control. But our God is worthy of being in control. Scripture tells us that we can cast our anxieties on Him, because He loves us (1 Peter 5:7). God is bigger than all our worries.

I don't know how long that hamster continued spinning on that wheel. And I don't know if hamsters worry—at least not in the same way we do. But I do imagine that when the little guy finally got off that wheel, he probably lay down in a corner, heaved a big hamster sigh, and felt a little better relaxing and being still. I know, because that's the way I feel when I finally trust in faith and get off the wheel of worry. —Peggy Frezon

Worry is carrying tomorrow's load with today's strength—carrying two days at once.

—Corrie ten Boom

MARCH 7

Baby Love

He tends his flock like a shepherd: He gathers the lambs in his arms and carries them close to his heart; he gently leads those that have young.

—ISAIAH 40:11 (NIV)

BABY THE RABBIT was a mother at last. After a visit from another family member who brought a male rabbit, Baby birthed four black male bunnies, each one her little replica—black satin colored and soft as velvet.

Baby's babies had come in the quiet of night. The next morning, Becky awoke to Baby's scratches on the door, alerting her mistress, wanting her to follow. Becky did follow, and the bunny showed her where the new little family nestled. Four perfectly black babies, irresistibly silky.

Becky was thrilled. Always sweet, loving, and very well-trained, Baby played nicely with Becky's dogs and gave kisses on request. Why not more bunnies just like her? She was a perfect pet, except for one thing: Baby absolutely would not feed her babies unless Becky held her at the same time. So Becky helped raise them, holding Baby while the bunny nursed her littles. Cozy in Becky's lap, being snuggled and cuddled, lovingly energized to do her duty.

When Becky told me about Baby, I was moved. The story was precious and reminded me of a verse in Isaiah about God's tender care "...he gently leads those that have young." I was amazed that Becky had to hold her beloved bunny to entice her to feed her own babies. What magical trust was this? It felt like natural love usurping nature.

Once the babies were old enough, Becky found homes for all of Baby's beautiful offspring. But she was careful to keep Baby from breeding again, since the rabbit would expect Becky to stop her day job and become the bunny's babysitter full time. Again.

God's loving care is for all His creation—for those of us who call Him Lord and Shepherd and for all who recognize Him as Master. Without words. —Cathy Elliott

He's got the whole world in His hands.
—Black American Spiritual

Comforting Presence

Scorn has broken my heart and has left me helpless; I looked for sympathy, but there was none, for comforters, but I found none.

—PSALM 69:20 (NIV)

IT WAS A horrible day at work, and when I got home that night, I just wanted to cry. But being a mom meant I had to hold things together. Unfortunately, the kids also had had bad days. Both of my kids are in middle school, so I understand the trouble of their social world. Math homework plus bullies in the hallway meant two sad kids at the dinner table. It was definitely not a night for me to complain about my job.

Finally, it was time for bed. As I got under the covers, I felt the weight of my little dog, Fizz, as he curled against my side. He was such a comfort! All day I had felt alone, but the simple presence of my puppy was enough to take away my sadness.

Our dogs are such good companions for us. They don't need to know the details of all the things that have gone wrong with our day. They are just happy to be by our side. I am so thankful for all my dogs (I have three), but especially for Fizz on my hard days. He is my little cuddler.

Sleeping at the foot of the bed, lying under the kitchen table, and jumping up to greet me when I come home, my dogs remind me of the abiding love of God. When there is no comfort to be found among people, God—and my pets—provide the comfort and sympathy I need. —Heather Jepsen

Thank You, God, for Your presence in my life,
especially on my hardest days. Amen.

MARCH 9

A Transformation Process

Therefore, if anyone is in Christ, the new creation has come: The old has gone, the new is here!

—2 CORINTHIANS 5:17 (NIV)

THE DOOR FROM the garage to our mudroom flew open as I watched Dane run into the house with excitement. My son had just received the delivery of a special birthday gift from his cousin. With great enthusiasm, he tore open the package to find a butterfly kit. It came complete with two cups, each inhabited by five caterpillars.

Over the next several days we let those cups sit on our family's kitchen table. They were a source of real-life entertainment. I watched as my children would lean their elbows onto the table to try to get as close as they could to visit the caterpillars. They whispered to them, tried to name them, and would often tell the caterpillars about their day.

Once the caterpillars turned into chrysalises, it was time to move them from the cups to a pop-up netted enclosure. A few days later, beautiful painted lady butterflies emerged. My children were amazed to see these wonderful creatures in their home for a few more days. Eventually, we let Dane release them into the outdoors.

This special kit taught us about how God can take the same exact creature and make it into something that looks like a completely new one. In the same way, God does the same with us human creatures through His resurrection power. It might feel uncomfortable at times, but change is what transforms me into His beautiful child. In doing so, He has helped me to reconcile my past so that I can be reborn in order to live out His purposes and plans. This kit was an inspiration to spread my wings and fly in all areas of life for God's glory. —Stacey Thureen

Walk of Faith: *Take a few minutes to reflect and thank God for the transforming work He has done in your life. How has He changed you for your good and His glory?*

MARCH 10

A Place to Heal

This inheritance is kept in heaven for you, who through faith are shielded by God's power until the coming of the salvation that is ready to be revealed in the last time.

—1 PETER 1:4–5 (NIV)

WHAT I NOTICED first was the lizard's tail as he crossed the porch to hide under a planter. Or I should say, the lack of a tail. We'd recently had a severe freeze, which was quite abnormal for our part of Texas. It could be that the lizard lost his tail in the freeze. Or maybe he'd been in a fight. Perhaps a predator caught him and he chose to sacrifice his tail to save his life. I didn't know.

Each day I watched for him. I knew lizards could regrow their tails. I also knew it took an awful lot of effort and energy to do so. Losing his tail cost him much. The lizard kept close to the shelter of the porch. He didn't dart around. He moved slowly. He was hurt. Whenever he moved, he stuck to areas with places he could hide if necessary. This lizard needed a safe place to heal. My porch provided that place.

After several weeks, I saw a small dark bump where the lizard's tail should be. His tail was growing back! Although the lizard ventured past the planter, he still stayed on the porch. A couple of weeks later, there was definitely a tail. Not very long, but it was there.

The lizard was healing. He was improving. In time, he would be whole. It wasn't long before the lizard had a completely regenerated tail. Fully restored and healthy, he left the porch to return to his normal life.

Just like that lizard, I also need time to heal from a loss. It also takes a lot of energy. Just as the lizard sought a place of safety to heal, so must I. When storms, adversaries, or loss hit, the safest place for me is in the shelter of God's wings. —Sandy Kirby Quandt

He giveth more grace when the burdens grow greater,
He sendeth more strength when the labors increase;
To added affliction He addeth His mercy,
To multiplied trials, His multiplied peace.
—Annie Johnson Flint

MARCH 11

Mike's New Name

The nations will see your vindication, and all kings your glory; you will be called by a new name that the mouth of the LORD will bestow.

—ISAIAH 62:2 (NIV)

YOU BETTER GRAB that dog! He's a pit bull! And I will sue!" shouted a very angry woman who came to my door to sell me something.

I quietly stepped outside my door and closed it behind me. I explained to the woman that she had come to the dog's house and was unfamiliar to him. I had not invited her. And that this dog had come from a really scary background and sometimes his past made him react with fear. That fear to some looked like aggression. She huffed and puffed and walked away mumbling something about all aggressive breeds needing to be put down.

When I walked back in, Mike wagged his tail and covered me with kisses, so glad that he'd scared off the mean woman who to him undoubtedly meant me harm. He was proud of himself for doing his job.

Like that woman, many of us judge others on appearances and reactions. I have watched well-meaning Christians come across as rude, angry, and judgmental toward people they deem dangerous without knowing a thing about them. How many people have become outcasts because they were born into a certain group of people or have made poor decisions based on desperation?

I am so glad that God judges on the heart He created within us all. He doesn't throw away even the most sinful beings that come to him. He greets every one of us with kisses and hugs and great joy because He sees us as His creation. His love gives us all a new name. Mike's new name is Mike the Farm Dog. Because love gave him a new name too! —Devon O'Day

God, thank You for my new name: Beloved.

MARCH 12

Surprise Inspection

"It is easier for a camel to go through the eye of a needle than for a rich person to enter the kingdom of God." And they were exceedingly astonished, and said to him, "Then who can be saved?"

—MARK 10:25–26 (ESV)

THE STATE OF Pennsylvania motor vehicle laws require annual car inspections. I want our cars to pass and not have to deal with major repairs that can be costly, so I try to stay on top of things to avoid any unwanted surprises. One of my daughters scheduled her older car's inspection with some concern about the outcome.

On inspection day, she drove to the shop, parked, and grabbed the necessary paperwork. Although she was preoccupied with the owners' toddler playing in the waiting area, familiar sounds came out of the mechanic's bay through the open door. Then everyone heard a loud scream. Thinking there'd been an accident, the mechanic's wife raced into the bay to see what was wrong. Then she screamed! My daughter wondered what could possibly be so bad with her car.

All the commotion was the result of the mechanic removing the tire and finding a snake coiled up around the brake housing. Apparently, the milk snake had crawled onto the car at our house and hitched a 12-mile ride with my daughter. The snake was harmless but created a memorable surprise inspection.

Seeing and hearing the unexpected shocks me at times. I think my daughter's mechanic would agree. Surprises can be either good or bad. The passage in Mark shows that Jesus surprised His disciples when He explained how hard it was for a rich man to enter heaven. It wasn't what they expected to hear. I am guessing they thought if they simply stuck with Jesus, they would gain some earthly rewards.

Fundamentally, I am glad to know that nothing surprises God. He is omniscient and all-knowing and can use the surprising things in my life to carry out His plan and purpose for me. —Ben Cooper

Nothing is a surprise to God:
nothing is a setback to His plans;
nothing can thwart His purposes;
and nothing is beyond His control.
—Joni Eareckson Tada

MARCH 13

Just Float for a While

But seek first his kingdom and his righteousness, and all these things will be given to you as well.

—MATTHEW 6:33 (NIV)

IT WAS AN especially busy season, and I'd hardly had a moment to rest in weeks. As the mom of five kids, I met so many volunteer opportunities, and I couldn't seem to say no to any of them. Between bake sales, book fairs, and the PTA, I was wearing myself down. Today I was chaperoning a field trip to the Indianapolis Zoo with my son's first-grade class. I was in charge of a dozen 6-year-old boys, including my son, Nathan.

We entered the aquarium, and the boys ran toward the huge tanks. "Don't bang on the glass," I reminded them. They tore around the room, excitedly pointing at the different fish. I followed them as best I could. The boys ran to the seahorse exhibit. "I love how they swim by wiggling their tails," Nathan said.

I watched as the seahorses swam around the tank for a bit and then wrapped their tails around a plant so they could float for a while. It might sound silly, but I actually felt envious of them. When a seahorse got tired, it could just hang onto a plant and rest. I wished I could do that, but I had too many people counting on me.

After several more hours of chasing the boys around the zoo, we boarded the bus to go back to school. I was exhausted, but I still had dinner to prepare. When Nathan and I finally arrived home, he took my hand and led me to the couch. "It's time for you to stop swimming and float for a while, just like a seahorse," he said.

I realized that God didn't mean for me to wear myself out every day. *Help me find ways to rest,* I prayed. My phone buzzed. It was a text from my husband, offering to bring home pizza for dinner. Thank You, God. I put on some worship music and lay down, finally able to rest in Him for a bit. —Diane Stark

Lord, help me to find rest in You instead of carrying my burdens all alone. Amen.

MARCH 14

The Cat's Best Gift

Therefore I tell you, do not worry about your life, what you will eat or drink; or about your body, what you will wear. Is not life more than food, and the body more than clothes? Look at the birds of the air; they do not sow or reap or store away in barns, and yet your heavenly Father feeds them. Are you not much more valuable than they?

—MATTHEW 6:25–26 (NIV)

A KINDHEARTED WOMAN WHO used to work at my dog's vet now runs a rescue organization for dogs and cats. Several weeks ago, she posted a plea on social media. An 18-year-old cat who calls the rescue his home is very attached to a particular bunny toy that he has had for many years. Unfortunately, over time the toy wore out. The woman at the rescue asked if anyone had this years-old toy shoved away in an old toy bin, but nothing came of her request.

Last week, as I watched my senior dog playing with his favorite toy, my heart ached for this cat. Time and age take a toll on all creation, and to still find joy in a toy or special treat is truly a gift for a pet as it ages. With a heavy heart and feeling a bit silly, I petitioned God to *please* provide that same bunny toy for this aging feline. I'll be honest—I did not expect God to do it. My prayer seemed so insignificant in the grand scheme of life.

Imagine my surprise when I signed on to that social media platform this evening and saw a picture of the cat with the bunny toy. Turns out, a family who keeps up with the rescue and knew about the bunny search has a dog themselves. Last week, with no provocation, the dog went to his toy bin and pulled out an old toy he hadn't played with in *years*. He carried it into the living room to show his pet parents. You'll never guess what toy he found.

The exact. Same. Bunny.

The family promptly donated it to the rescue for this elderly cat to enjoy.

Friend, God cares about the details of your life. If He can provide a stuffed bunny for an 18-year-old cat from a mustard seed of a prayer, just imagine how much more He loves you. —Ashley Clark

Father, when the circumstances of life distract me from You, I begin to doubt Your presence in my life. Remind me just how deep and sweet Your love is for me today, and help me, in return, to share Your love with others.

MARCH 15

Sing Your Praise to the Lord

I will bless the LORD at all times; His praise shall continually be in my mouth.

—PSALM 34:1 (NKJV)

THE EARLY MORNING silence was broken by a melodious chirp. It was a birdsong I hadn't heard before. It was late winter, so I assumed the song came from a migratory bird. As I listened, I searched for the bird. Since its song was strong, I expected to find a large bird. However, when I spotted the tiny bird, I couldn't help but smile.

It appeared to be a type of wren with brown-and-cream markings. Nothing flashy or remarkable about it. Nothing to draw attention to it, except for its song. In fact, it blended right into its surroundings. What caused me to finally spot it was its bounce. With each tweet, the bird hopped off the branch, then bounced back down. Over and over.

I don't know what I enjoyed the most. The bird's song or its hop. The hop wasn't accidental. It was intentional. Tweet. Hop. Tweet. Hop. It seemed as if the bird was pleased with itself with each tweet and hop. It sang for several minutes without stopping.

Although I was privileged to hear it sing, I couldn't help wonder if that bird's concert was meant for its Creator. It was so joyful. So full of praise. So pure.

When I think about the tiny bird who sang for an audience of one, I think about our world that says I must be bigger and better. A world that says I must have a platform with thousands of followers. The tiny bird showed me that no matter how small I might appear in the world's eyes, God hears my offerings of praise. I don't need a large platform. I don't need thousands of followers. All I need is a heart full of praise for the One who gives the song. —Sandy Kirby Quandt

Let us ever remember that God recognizes every expression of praise and of His people's love. He knows so well what His love and grace are to us that He must expect us to praise Him.
—G. V. Wigram

MARCH 16

Flunked

Many are the plans in a person's heart, but it is the LORD's purpose that prevails.

—PROVERBS 19:21 (NIV)

BUT WE HAD a plan," I said to my husband, while patting our golden retriever Petey. The dog wiggled and waggled with excitement.

Our plan was to have two golden retrievers and train them to be therapy dogs. One for my husband to handle and one for me. We already had one certified therapy dog—Ernest, also a golden. He'd had no problem passing the test. Calm, sweet, and lovable Ernest.

Then we got Petey. Enthusiastic, fun, and boisterous. He loved everyone, but in a different way from Ernest. Petey couldn't greet someone without barking, grabbing a toy, and jumping. We took him through therapy-dog training classes. On the day of the test, Petey held it together for about 6 minutes. Then he burst up, bouncing, lunging, and barking with all his inappropriate energy. He flunked right then and there.

It had been several years since that disastrous test, and we'd worked hard with Petey. "Maybe he can do it this time," I said on the day of another test. But before the words were even out of my mouth, Petey was spinning all across the room, panting joyfully. I thought about how Ernest sat still when we patted him, putting his head gently in our lap and sighing with contentment. I shook my head slowly. "I don't think Petey wants to be a therapy dog."

God has gifted us all with talents that can be used for His glory. We might sing, or write, or help others. It's different for all of us. We shouldn't try to change to fit into some other mold. Petey may not be cut out for therapy-dog work, but he does use his canine gifts. He makes us smile and laugh. His silly personality brings joy and lightness to our days. His boisterous energy is delightful. Psalm 138 reminds us that the Lord will fulfill His promises for us so we're not to forsake the work of our hands. Or paws! —Peggy Frezon

Be who God meant you to be and you will set the world on fire.
—St. Catherine of Siena

MARCH 17

The Not-So-Ugly Duckling

Then Peter began to speak: "I now realize how true it is that God does not show favoritism but accepts from every nation the one who fears him and does what is right."

—ACTS 10:34–35 (NIV)

THERE'S A PARK on the banks of the bayou that I pass frequently when riding my bike. One day, I noticed two big ducks gliding around the reeds at the water's edge. They were mottled black and white; their heads, bumpy and red. *Too bad these ducks don't have iridescent green heads or little crests to make them beautiful,* I thought.

The next time I passed the park, the big ducks had a large flock of ducklings in tow. Fluffy and funny, yellow and brown, and endearingly wobbly, they teetered around in the grass, with their mother hovering nearby. *So cute,* I thought. *Too bad they are going to grow up to be ugly ducks.*

On my third visit, the ducklings were much bigger. They swam strongly behind their mother, and she seemed proud. The way they were growing and learning moved me. I remembered my judgment of them as ugly, and I couldn't reconcile that thought with the nurturing mother and her flock. They were uniquely beautiful, and I was sorry I had been dismissive of them. Although they would never grow to be mallards or swans or pintails—any of the birds that my limited imagination had deemed as worthy—they had a role to fill in God's kingdom. I later discovered they were Muscovy ducks, which clear algae, eat mosquitoes, and do good work for the environment. They were fully engaged in doing what God had created them to do, not wasting their time comparing or ranking as I was.

As I continued on my journey, I vowed to hold the ducks in my heart as a reminder to spend less time judging and more time loving the world God has created. —Lucy Chambers

Our job is to love others without stopping to inquire whether or not they are worthy. That is not our business and, in fact, it is nobody's business. What we are asked to do is to love, and this love itself will render both ourselves and our neighbors worthy.

—Thomas Merton

MARCH 18

A Whole Herd!

Thou art worthy, O Lord, to receive glory and honour and power: for thou hast created all things, and for thy pleasure they are and were created.

—REVELATION 4:11 (KJV)

GRANDMA! COME QUICK!"

Hearing this cry from one of our young grandsons could mean blood or a broken toy. I hurried to the backyard where the boys had been playing. Both appeared nearby, seemingly intact, no red smears.

"Hurry! They're going this way! A whole herd of deer!"

I ran with the boys toward their vegetable garden. We'd seen a few deer now and then across the road in the woods. Not quite a whole herd, but to imagination-filled boys, I suppose it could have seemed that way.

"Wait! They're going around the other way! Quick, Grandma, come on!"

Instead of following the deer around the house to the front yard, the boys went back in the back door and out through the front door, making this mini safari expedition even more atypical. I followed and saw what definitely deserved to be called a herd of deer, at least eight of them, crossing the road and dashing through the woods. After the deer disappeared over the hill, the boys went back to their play, but their excitement stayed with me.

Seeing wildlife always brings joy to my heart, but the boys usually remain stoic about deer sightings. I humbly realized their excitement was for me. They knew how much I'd love to see the deer herd and expended their energy to make sure I did. I felt loved and cherished.

I bet their enthusiasm resembled what God felt when He created deer, elephants, lions, puppies, kittens, and all His wondrous creatures. He made them with love, for His enjoyment and mine. I can imagine His pleasure while watching how excited I get each time I see His creations. —Cathy Mayfield

From raccoons to rabbits, bats to bugs, ducks to doves,
God delights in creating to display His love.

—C. M.

MARCH 19

Chicken Whisperer

As a shepherd seeks out his flock when he is among his sheep that have been scattered, so will I seek out my sheep, and I will rescue them from all places where they have been scattered on a day of clouds and thick darkness.

—EZEKIEL 34:12 (ESV)

ONE DAY WHILE walking home from school, my 11-year-old grandson Bodhi spotted two light tan hens wandering next to a busy road. The air still smelled like wet grass from rain, and the clouds hung low and gray. He'd been walking fast in case the sky opened up again, but now he stopped and kneeled down. Both chickens flapped their wings, but Bodhi assured them that he meant no harm.

He spoke in a low, gentle voice. "You must be lost." Instead of running away, the hens edged closer, until Bodhi could stroke their feathers. He picked up a hen. "I'll keep you safe." Juggling his backpack and one of the chickens, the boy straightened up and walked the rest of the way home, where he secured the chicken inside their dog run.

Bodhi's mom hugged him, thanking him for rescuing a stray hen. But the boy wriggled out of her embrace. He called over his shoulder, "I have to get the other one." He ran out before she could say more.

A few minutes later, he came home, cradling another buff-colored hen. Bodhi reunited the pair and then set about hanging up "Lost Hen" flyers in his area. After weeks of searching, no owner came forward, but by that time my grandson had named them Rebecca and Honey Boo-boo. He faithfully cares for his feathered friends, along with two mastiff dogs and a cat.

We call Bodhi a chicken whisperer, but his faithful love for animals reminds me of the ways that God cares for us. Bodhi went out of his way to keep both hens safe, much like the shepherd in the parable of the lost sheep. No matter how far off the road we wander, our loving Creator will never leave us stranded. Like my grandson, the chicken whisperer, God is *always* ready to rescue us. —Linda S. Clare

Walk of Faith: *Practice being a "whisperer" with a lost or scared animal or human, demonstrating God's compassion.*

MARCH 20

A Safe Nest

In peace I will lie down and sleep, for you alone, LORD, make me dwell in safety.

—PSALM 4:8 (NIV)

THE PAIR OF house sparrows had worked diligently on their nest in the eaves of my back patio, but it wasn't a good location. Gusting wind and prowling neighborhood cats wouldn't allow the nest to be completely secure. After several failed attempts to construct a nest sturdy enough to withstand both wind and cats, the birds moved on to find a better location, leaving behind a messy tangle of sticks and grass.

I felt sorry for the sparrows who were unable to make their nest work in the eaves, but a couple of months later I saw them again, this time busily hopping on the top of my fence, frantically feeding a trio of noisy baby sparrows perched there. Obviously, they'd found a safe place to raise their brood! Seeing God's provision for these birds made me grateful for my own secure home.

Like the house sparrows, I do the best I can to shield myself and my family from harm, but some things are out of my control. We sometimes have earthquakes where I live, and wildfires have burned through my area more than once. But I trust that God will lovingly and faithfully watch over me and my family no matter where we live or what perils we face on this earth.

The world can be an unpredictable and dangerous place for birds and humans alike, and while it's not always easy to find a safe place to build a nest, I know that no matter where I make my earthly home, I'm already in my safest place—in the palm of God's hand. Nothing can remove me from there! —Marianne Campbell

Children of the heav'nly Father
Safely in His bosom gather.
Nestling bird nor star in heaven.
Such a refuge e'er was given.
—Karolina Sandell-Berg

MARCH 21

The Squirrel Sign

You will seek me and find me when you seek me with all your heart.

—JEREMIAH 29:13 (NIV)

ABOUT A YEAR ago, when my husband announced a family bike trip in Ireland as a special surprise, I was dismayed. I didn't even own a bike. I had sworn off riding because of the traffic. But I really wanted to go to Ireland, so I found a bicycle and started training. It was hard. It took a long time. My seat hurt.

While I wasn't enjoying the actual riding, being on the trails was wonderful. When I saw a heron fishing, a rabbit darting across a meadow, or a fish leaping from the water, I felt a little more connected to the world, a little more peaceful. Maybe I *was* a person who rode bikes on trips.

Winter came with rain and cold and other excuses for not getting on the trails, and I lost that vision. My family counted the days, and all I could count was the miles I hadn't ridden. Maybe I should just ride in the support van.

The first day the weather permitted me to get back on the bike, I asked God for a sign. I imagined the familiar animals stopping their foraging and fishing to cheer me on. But my return to the trail was not this children's book fantasy—no animals were even visible. Wanting a sign, I took their absence as an omen.

I had just worded my resignation from riding when I saw him walk out of the brush. I stopped my bike a respectful distance away. With the sun shining on his glossy fur and the wind ruffling his thick tail, he looked straight into my eyes. Here in this land of gray squirrels was a magnificent black squirrel, a sign if I ever saw one.

I got the message: Get out of your comfort zone. Don't let pride keep you from exploring this wonderful planet. Trust God and you will be delighted by the surprises that will appear on your path. Get back on that bike and ride. And so I did. —Lucy Chambers

Ask and it shall be given unto you,
Seek and ye shall find;
Knock and the door shall be opened unto you.
Allelu, Allelujah!
—David Huff and Karen Lafferty

MARCH 22

The Patience of an Egret

Through patience a ruler can be persuaded, and a gentle tongue can break a bone.

—PROVERBS 25:15 (NIV)

A SNOWY EGRET HAS recently taken up residence in our neighborhood. I first saw it in a neighbor's front garden, and it was standing so still that I asked my wife, "Is that a statue, or is it real?" It was indeed real, and it soon migrated to the neighborhood's back pond, where it can be found almost every day as it waits patiently for a meal to swim past.

The hallmark of this egret is supreme patience. It can seemingly stand in the same spot for an hour or more without moving. It is far more patient than most fishermen who try their luck in the pond. After a few minutes of futile casting, they often become vexed and move elsewhere or give up altogether.

The egret is also far more patient than I am in my daily spiritual walk. I find it difficult to sit still for long periods of time and wait for the Lord to speak to me without my spirit feeling the need to check notifications on my phone or get up and do some work or it becomes distracted by some vagrant thought.

Our world is certainly filled with trials and temptations. But God uses those difficulties in daily life to increase our faith. James emphasizes this connection in chapter 1 verses 2–3 (NLT): "Dear brothers and sisters, when troubles of any kind come your way, consider it an opportunity for great joy. For you know that when your faith is tested, your endurance has a chance to grow." Patience, endurance, perseverance—these are some of the most wonderful blessings we can receive from God.

I need to try harder to emulate the snowy egret and approach every day with patience and stillness. Only then can I hear God's gentle whisper as He walks beside me. —Harold Nichols

Dear Lord, Help me to remember this egret every day as I encounter the trials and temptations of this world. Let the patience of the egret inspire me to listen for Your voice as I make choices in my daily walk.

MARCH 23

Special Delivery

For he will deliver the needy who cry out, the afflicted who have no one to help.

—PSALM 72:12 (NIV)

OUR POOR LITTLE kitty had been in labor all day, but no kittens had yet arrived. Cuddly, the soon-to-be mommy cat, had settled in the bathtub, perhaps seeking a cool place in her travail. My mom tried to help the panting cat, but what to do? Finally, a tail emerged, and a small white bottom appeared; the kitten was presenting breech. Desperate, Mom grabbed her phone book, scanned the emergency numbers scrawled inside, and began dialing.

The receptionist seemed perplexed by Mom's description of our plight but put the doctor on the line. He patiently walked my mom through the kitten's delivery, then suggested Cuddly might not have strength to birth the rest of the litter. "Keep an eye on her. She might need medical assistance."

While Cuddly washed her tiny orange kitten, licking it into life, a gray kitten slipped out, but exhaustion seemed to be getting the best of Cuddly as she lay her head back in the tub. Mom and I scooped cat and kittens into a basket and headed for the vet.

"Cuddly needs help," we told the receptionist who seemed befuddled by our abrupt arrival. "She's having trouble with the rest of the litter," we explained. The receptionist reached for the phone. "I'll call in the doctor."

"But he was just here...." Mom started.

The receptionist eyed us curiously as she dialed.

The vet arrived and delivered two more kittens by cesarean section. Cuddly and her brood came home the next day into our loving care. We'd made up a comfy bed and hoped Cuddly would prefer it to the bathtub.

The phone rang. "How is your cat? Did the kittens arrive safely?" It was my mom's obstetrician calling to follow up. In her panic, my mom had called not our vet but her own doctor. It was he who had coached us through the difficult delivery.

I suspect that my mom was equal parts embarrassed and grateful. You never know where help will come from when you call for it! —Susie Colby

As for me, I call to God, and the LORD saves me.
—Psalm 55:16 (NIV)

MARCH 24

The Healing Power of an Oreo

Blessed be the God and Father of our Lord Jesus Christ, the Father of mercies and God of all comfort.

—2 CORINTHIANS 1:3 (NKJV)

LIVING ALONE AFTER the passing of her longtime spouse, my sister had one of the best attitudes of anyone I'd known facing similar circumstances. Susan soldiered on with life, attending church, showing up for family gatherings with a smile, and even recovering from serious heart surgery. Her only complaint, "It gets kind of quiet in the afternoons with just me."

Enter Oreo, a miniature dachshund with dappled gray-and-white fur. As I knocked on the door and entered Susan's house, a wriggling mass of puppy padded its way to greet me.

"Watch out for Oreo," my sister hollered out to me.

"He's hard to miss," I said.

Indeed, he was quite the sight as he flipped and flopped all over the floor with excitement. I bent over and picked up the 3-pound puppy. His whole frame quivered as he tried to climb my shirt to affix puppy kisses to my beard.

A new playpen stood prominently in the family room amid colorful toys and a small blanket tossed among them.

"Looks like you have a new baby," I said.

"He's a bouncing bundle of joy, that's for sure."

The smile on my sister's face shone with contentment and new hope for the future. Of course, nothing could replace her dear husband of 40 years. However, it seemed Oreo was making a major dent in the quietness that had engulfed her home. The squirming mass full of life overcame the darkness of solitude that tried to obscure the mercy of our Savior.

I learned something about God's comfort that day. While my humanity may long for the familiarity of comfort that has been lost, the Father might have a new kind of joy in mind for me. My job includes the willingness to reach out and accept His gift—even if it's a different kind of joy for a new season of life. —David L. Winters

I really try to enjoy life and have joy with what I do.
—Tim Tebow

MARCH 25

Big Snow, Little Snow

This is the day the Lord has made; let us rejoice and be glad in it.

—PSALM 118:24 (ESV)

MY SISTER'S DAUGHTER, Lisa, lives in the wilds of Colorado on the western slopes of the Rocky Mountains. Their winters are snowy, which provides endless delight for their silver Lab, Hoyt. Their home is within easy walking distance of a dog park. One of Hoyt's favorite things to do at the park is to get a running head start for the hill and then travel down the snowy slide on his belly as fast as he can possibly go.

His limitless energy is exhausting to watch. After several times up and down and back again on the hill, Hoyt will stop mid-slide and begin wiggling his body around on the slope as if he is trying to create snow angels. His tail never stops moving. He often runs back to his human walking partner with a huge doggy smile on his face as if to say, "Did you see that? Wanna see me do it again?" And off he goes.

But snow, even on a mountain, doesn't last forever. After arriving at the park one spring day, Hoyt discovered that his snowy slide was no longer a hill. Instead it was a narrow strip of packed-down iciness. Not to be deterred, Hoyt bounded toward the smaller slippery stretch with as much vigor as he'd had on the whole hill just a month prior. He checked out its taste before flopping down and rolling exuberantly from tummy to back, back to tummy, squirming his way over the entire section before starting all over again.

I want to exhibit joy like Hoyt had no matter what situation confronts me, even if my snowy hill disappears and I have only a small strip of ice left. Whether from big delights or little surprises, my spirits can be lifted to equal heights because my joy is not dependent on my outward circumstances. My joy comes from Jesus. —Liz Kimmel

Lord, teach my heart to find joy in the small things in life. Help me not to be disappointed if my expectations are not met, no matter what is happening around me, no matter the time or season.

MARCH 26

Malcolm, the Cat that Came with the Farm

If the home is deserving, let your peace rest on it;
if it is not, let your peace return to you.

—MATTHEW 10:13 (NIV)

I HAD JUST MOVED into the farm and was sitting in a lawn chair amid boxes, feeling overwhelmed and tired. The sound of an insistent little cry drew my attention, and I began looking for its source.

Soon a tiny gray-and-white kitten appeared, and its sounds went from a plaintive cry to a scream. I opened a can of kitten food. He licked the plate until every bite was gone. When I went inside, he followed me. He had a collar, so I knew he must belong to someone, but he slept with me that night and disappeared into the morning. I didn't see him for a week or so, but he showed up eventually. He grew too big for his collar, so I removed it. He never stayed for long periods of time but turned up regularly for meals and love. I took him to the vet, thinking that if he was going to be a regular stop-by visitor, he needed a clean bill of health. I gave him the name Malcolm and told the vet that he wasn't mine but came with the farm. That's when I learned that a community cat like Malcolm returns to the place where he finds peace, even if he doesn't stay for long.

A good friendship is like that. Like Malcolm, I want to return to the people who nourish my soul and give me peace. Time may pass between our visits, but the love is always there waiting. —Devon O'Day

God, reveal the good people and places that You have placed in my path so I might return to bless and be blessed.

MARCH 27

Broken Twigs

...having been built on the foundation of the apostles and prophets, Jesus Christ Himself being the chief cornerstone, in whom the whole building, being fitted together, grows into a holy temple in the Lord...

—EPHESIANS 2:20–21 (NKJV)

EVERY YEAR AFTER our harsh winters, I clean up the twigs, branches, and pine cones scattered by the seasonal strong winds. This past winter was exceptionally windy, causing several trees to blow over. Providing more evidence of the unusually high winds were several bird nests on the ground. While gathering them up, I examined and admired the materials and diversity used in their construction.

Robins use broken twigs and mud to attach their nests to tree branches or structures. Some birds weave baskets that hang from trees, making them look more like a basketball net. Swallows build on the floor beams of my barn. Still other birds, like the killdeer, create a nest on the ground near rocks so their speckled eggs will blend in. Each species has its own signature nest design and will use common debris for the foundation. Amazingly, they perfectly construct these without having hands.

Discarded twigs, dead blades of grass, and random pieces of string appear as debris to passersby. But in the avian architecture, they become integral building blocks that result in a home to hatch the next generation and shelter them from storms.

Inspecting these fallen nests makes me think about how God builds His church. He gathers up broken people who might be seen as debris and creates something for a higher purpose. I am like a broken twig selected out of many to become part of His church. God uses me to raise up another faithful generation of believers to fortify His structure—the church—to withstand the storms that come. He selected me and placed me in just the right spot, one He reserved just for me. Amazingly, He does this without using hands. —Ben Cooper

Dear Lord, thanks for selecting me and making me acceptable nesting material for building Your church. You have taken what was dead and broken to be fitted together as an essential building block. Use me in Your Kingdom. In Jesus's name, amen.

MARCH 28

Finding Sanctuary

All the believers were together and had everything in common.

—ACTS 2:44 (NIV)

THE DONKEY SANCTUARY in Liscarroll, Ireland, has become a home for thousands of injured and neglected donkeys since the Barrett family started it in 1987. Thanks to the Barretts, there are apparently more donkeys in the small village of Liscarroll than there are people. During a long-awaited visit to The Donkey Sanctuary, I reveled in the peace and beauty of the place. I'd learned while preparing for the trip that because donkeys are herd animals, they thrive in community, much like people.

While walking one of the shady paths with my friends, I noticed a donkey grazing under the shelter of an oak tree. He stood out to me among the clusters and pairs of donkeys. I took a picture of him and found myself looking at it often during the rest of the trip, and even after I got home. The donkey looked content there in the shade, eating grass, alone but not lonely. I didn't know the story behind how he came to the sanctuary, but I'd heard enough about some of the others to understand that being safe, healthy, and well-fed made a big difference in his life.

Seeing him reflected how I felt when I realized I'd finally found a healthy, nurturing Christian community. The safety of my spiritual family gave me a place to heal past wounds, grow in my relationship with God, and become the person He'd created me to be. We supported one another, honestly admitted struggles, and celebrated God's work in one another's lives. Like that donkey grazing under the tree, I'd found a sanctuary.

My photo of that one donkey in Liscarroll continues to remind me of our human need for safe community. When we find it in the family of God, we can see His love at work, let Him tend our wounds, and be part of a sanctuary for others. —Jeanette Hanscome

I'm so glad I'm a part of the family of God.
—Bill and Gloria Gaither

MARCH 29

A Golden Love

Love bears all things, believes all things, hopes all things, endures all things.

—1 CORINTHIANS 13:7 (ESV)

I WATCHED AS MY mom, a veterinarian, prepared to take a blood sample from our golden retriever. Since Thor's cancer diagnosis, we had to draw his blood regularly to monitor his condition. As she attached the needle to the syringe, Thor stood up, walked to the top of our basement staircase, and lay down.

My mom and I stared at each other in astonishment. She always drew the blood with Thor lying at the top of the stairs so she could walk down a few steps below him, giving her an easy angle to take the sample from his leg. But normally, we had to guide Thor into position and ask him to lie down.

Tears filled my eyes as I went to my sweet boy and praised him. While many dogs balk at needles or refuse to hold still for pokes and exams, Thor was voluntarily submitting to what we needed to do. Due to his remarkable cooperation, I realized I didn't have to hold onto Thor while my mom took the sample.

After that first time, he would voluntarily get into position when we needed to collect another sample. Thor became such an expert that I no longer had to help at all—he and my mom could do it alone. It was one of the most powerful demonstrations of love I've ever seen.

Thor sensed we weren't trying to hurt him or frighten him. I believe he understood we were acting out of love. Because he loved us and knew we loved him, he could submit to even painful circumstances.

I'll never forget Thor's example of how love produces trust and endurance. I can endure difficulties with joy when I think of Thor. God allows difficulties in my life and leads me through dark valleys, but He does so out of His great love for me. —Jerusha Agen

One of the greatest truths of the Bible is that...God loves us—and because He loves us, He wants to give us what is best for us.

—Billy Graham

MARCH 30

The Woods Are Alive with Thrush

The birds of the sky nest by the waters; they sing among the branches.

—PSALM 104:12 (NIV)

IT FELT NOTHING like the Colorado we had grown familiar with as we walked through wet, dripping woods. After years of drought and wildfires, this spring greeted us with weeks of rainfall. The landscape erupted with color and fragrance. My husband and I had taken our kids hiking after a storm to see the forest's response to all the rain. High-water creeks wound between trees and puddles, hosting tiny ecosystems abounding with life. Spotted coralroot orchids poked up from the wet soil; not yet budding their elegant orchid blossoms, they looked like purple asparagus across the forest floor. Above us, hermit thrushes sang their unique, echoing chorus. They sang in jubilation through a forest canopy dripping with life. It seemed as though they, too, were celebrating the rain and all the flowers, berries, and insects it brought to the forest.

A few days following our hike, my mom texted me from her home in the Ozark mountains.

"The woods are alive with thrush," she wrote. I thought back to our hike and the wood thrushes' choruses. Their mechanical yet stunning notes seemed to echo across raindrops and wet dew. My mom was right; the woods were alive with thrush. Their melodies were a refrain from Psalm 104:13 (NIV), where we read of God as "He waters the mountains from his upper chambers; the land is satisfied by the fruit of his work." The forest was bursting with bounty, and the thrush couldn't help but sing for God's provisions. Their refrain is contagious. Walking through the wet woods, I want to carry on the notes of the thrush and worship the One who satisfies the earth with the fruit of His works. —Eryn Lynum

Walk of Faith: *Take a walk through a wooded area and notice every natural sound you hear. Listen to creation singing praise to the Creator, and join their chorus through song or prayer.*

MARCH 31

Teasing an Orc

For our struggle is not against flesh and blood, but against the rulers, against the authorities, against the powers of this dark world and against the spiritual forces of evil in the heavenly realms.

—EPHESIANS 6:12 (NIV)

FOR THE LAST few springs, we've enjoyed watching a family of owls in a neighbor's backyard. When it's time for their babies to leave the nest, their survival depends on quickly becoming adept hunters. A recent incident underscored their challenging learning curve.

One of the young owls made a serious mistake by sitting on a fence post in plain sight in daylight. Spotting a squirrel on a nearby tree trunk, he made his dinner reservation. Alas, the squirrel evaded each of the owl's swoop maneuvers by speedily moving to the other side of the tree trunk and flattening itself against the bark, remaining frozen in place. The owl would dive; the squirrel moved around the tree. The owl tried again; the squirrel moved to another side. Again and again, same tactic, same result. After numerous failed attempts to ensnare and devour, the owl finally gave up.

When I relayed the squirrel versus owl altercation to my neighbor, she observed that squirrels can be teasers. Recently, she had witnessed a squirrel nonchalantly sitting on a fence just barely out of a dog's lunging reach. "I don't know," I responded, "would you tease an orc?" In J. R. R. Tolkien's fantasy world, orcs are a race of evil, monstrous, and vicious creatures. I wouldn't seek a playful encounter with an orc. Likewise, I suspect a squirrel wouldn't tease an owl.

Owls are predators in the natural world, while orcs belong in fantasy books. For humans, our all-too-real adversary is found in the spiritual realm. Satan and his followers are determined to ensnare and devour us, separating us from God. But, like the squirrel plastered to a tree, our security, our salvation, and our confidence reside in hanging on to Him.
—Darlene Kerr

But the Lord is faithful, and he will strengthen you and protect you from the evil one.
—2 Thessalonians 3:3 (NIV)

April

APRIL 1

Beetle Buddies

Perfume and incense bring joy to the heart, and the pleasantness of a friend springs from their heartfelt advice.

—PROVERBS 27:9 (NIV)

MY GRANDSON COLLIN loves bugs. At age three, he can tell you the difference between an insect and a spider, where to find the fattest slugs, and how to build a good bug habitat. He wakes up in the morning thinking about bugs and goes to sleep at night dreaming about them.

One spring day, I took him and his siblings on a walk in the woods. Sharp-eyed Collin soon spotted a shiny beetle on a piece of pine bark. He carried the bug on its bark-boat all over the forest. When it was time to leave, he batted his long-lashed eyes at me and asked, "Gigi, can I bring him home?"

Since the beetle hadn't budged from the bark, I assumed it couldn't fly. Sure enough, it sat there contentedly all the way home. All afternoon and into the evening, Collin carried his bug everywhere he went—the backyard, the garage, and the playground. Never was a bug so loved.

As night approached, the beetle stirred. Before Collin could cup a hand over it, it rose in a graceful arc that carried it over the house and into the woods.

I've never had a beetle friend, but Collin's bug buddy reminded me of human friends who have come and gone from my life. Some I've known for years, others for months. Some I've met in chance encounters and never seen again, but all have brought me joy. Friendship—two-legged, four-legged, or six-legged—is a precious gift from God. —Lori Hatcher

I cannot even imagine where I would be today were it not for that handful of friends who have given me a heart full of joy. Let's face it, friends make life a lot more fun.

—Charles Swindoll

APRIL 2

The Sound of the Oriole

And we know that in all things God works for the good of those who love him, who have been called according to his purpose.

—ROMANS 8:28 (NIV)

IT WAS A picture-perfect spring day: sunny, cloudless blue sky, with a gentle breeze and a just-right temperature. I was walking our dog outside our home and noticed a distinctive hee-haw sound. The Baltimore orioles were back! One orange beauty would call out and then another would sound; it was music to my ears. The return of the birds was a reminder of the return to warmer weather and the promise of summertime.

I had difficulty seeing them at first. I followed the sound but couldn't locate the birds. I stood before one tree and then moved to the next, straining my eyes upward. They were making their presence known through their calls, but I wanted to see their beautiful color. Only after I remained still and focused could I spy a flash of orange as a bird flitted from one branch to another. The glimpse of feathers confirmed that the sound was coming from an oriole.

Sometimes I have trouble "seeing" God, too, most recently when I would pray for a troubled family member but wouldn't see progress toward an answer. I would ask God, *Why don't You answer? Are You listening?* I thought God was there, but my lack of "God sightings" gave me doubts. Only when I would be still could I glimpse His presence through an encouraging phone call from a dear friend or through an applicable Bible verse. Those glimpses confirmed that God was working on the situation even if I didn't see or feel Him all the time.

Just like the sound of the orioles reminded me of their presence, God's voice reminds me of His. Even when I can't see Him, I can be assured that He is working all things together for my good. —Virginia Ruth

Creator God who sees and knows all things, thank You for the reminder that although we may not see You, You are always there. Amen.

APRIL 3

Someone's at the Door

Here I am! I stand at the door and knock. If anyone hears my voice and opens the door, I will come in and eat with that person, and they with me.

—REVELATION 3:20 (NIV)

A DOOR, OGDEN NASH said, is what a dog is perpetually on the wrong side of. My dog is on the wrong side of the door just now. It is a lovely spring day, and I just let him out 10 minutes ago, but he is already at the door, barking and whimpering, wanting to come in. The thing is, when I let him in, 10 minutes later he'll want to go out. Let him in and he wants to go out. Let him out and he wants to come in. I would be within my rights to say, "You're the one who wanted to go out, so quit bothering me." But of course I don't say that. I let him in.

He walks triumphantly to his bed, turns two circles—a genetic predisposition inherited from some primeval lupine ancestors—and lies down. I rub my hands over his fur, across his flanks, under his ears, down his legs. I scratch his neck where the collar presses his fur flat. I rub his warm tummy. I tell him he is a good boy, and he looks up with melting brown eyes, agreeing with me. Ten minutes from now he'll want to go out again, but for now he is content, and so am I.

If only I could open the door of my life that readily to people who want to come in, people who want only a hug, a shoulder to cry on, a kind word, an assurance that, their sins and failings notwithstanding, they are still good, still loved. Instead, way too often I find myself acting like the biblical Elder Brother: "You wanted this life, you made your choices, so don't come crying now to me." Wouldn't the world be better if we opened the door when people repented their choices and came knocking? Wouldn't I be better? —Louis Lotz

Merciful God, who in Jesus Christ stands at the door of my heart and knocks, give me the grace always to open the door to You and to receive others the way You receive me—with grace and forgiveness. Amen.

Let It Rain

For I will pour water on the thirsty land, and streams on the dry ground; I will pour my Spirit upon your offspring, and my blessing on your descendants.

—ISAIAH 44:3 (ESV)

THIS YEAR I have rediscovered the fact that May flowers are definitely preceded by April showers. It's been a rainy spring. While driving to church one Sunday through the pounding rain, I noted the absence of people strolling along the city sidewalks. I didn't even see any umbrellas. The rain was so intense that most people just stayed inside (unless it was to dash to their car, as we had done). It also occurred to me that there were no birds mingling on the power lines above the streets, nor were there any squirrels and rabbits scampering from tree to tree in search of nuts or seeds to eat.

As we got farther out into the country, it was clear that horses and cows were not as intimidated by the idea of getting wet. So many of them were standing patiently in their fields, munching on clover or grass or hay. One field held a covered shed for the horses, but it remained empty as the horses chose to stand in the middle of the field. They were seemingly content, totally unconcerned that their hair was damp and their feet were muddy.

Sometimes the blessings God bestows on me don't come in a neat, dry package. At times, they cause me some kind of inconvenience, and sometimes they require me to step out of my comfort zone. But my sovereign Lord knows what I need, when I need it, and how I need it, whether during sunny days or storms of life. With Him, I can be content in every kind of weather. —Liz Kimmel

Thank You, Father, for both the sun and the rain that You send into my life. Help me to recognize that both are from Your hand and have a purpose that overflows with ultimate blessing. Thank You, Spirit of God, for pouring Yourself onto, into, and through Your people.

APRIL 5

Two Doves Singing Down the Sun

You will keep in perfect peace those whose minds are steadfast, because they trust in you.

—Isaiah 26:3 (NIV)

FOR MANY YEARS, I remained in a toxic relationship, afraid to pull the rip cord and leave, for a variety of reasons. I was afraid of my reputation being marred. I was afraid of my security and finances being on rocky footing. I was afraid of...everything. But I carried a stone in my pocket every day that simply said "peace." That was my prayer. If I was afraid of taking the step, I prayed God would hear the prayer I could not pray and give me peace.

And He did. Every afternoon as the sun would set on the most beautiful of valleys behind the house, I would hear the song of two doves. They would gently coo and woo, calming my heart with their sounds. I knew those doves could only be a gift from God. He'd heard my prayer and brought me peace in my storm. I added courage to my peace prayer, and eventually I was able to walk away from the secret pain that was destroying me. God heard that prayer too.

Those doves that met me every day did not squabble or fight. They didn't fly away from each other in disgust. They joined in perfect choruses. When I could not find peace in my own life, God made certain peace found me.

After I'd moved into a new place to begin my life again, I was met with the familiar song of two doves. Peace had followed me! God speaks to my heart in many tongues, and this sweet dove peace song is one of my favorites yet. —Devon O'Day

Dear God, sing over me with Your peace and give me the heart to hear.

APRIL 6

The First Voice to Call Out

And you, my child, will be called a prophet of the Most High; for you will go on before the Lord to prepare the way for him.

—LUKE 1:76 (NIV)

MY FAMILY RECENTLY returned home from spring break in sunny Florida, but here in Michigan the early mornings are still dark and chilly as we rise for school. I brush my teeth and shuffle back to my room to make the bed, dreading the work of coaxing my children from slumber in a few minutes. Then I hear a lone bird calling from the still sparsely leafed tree out front. If I took time to peer out my window into the developing morning light, I might see the bird singing. If I opened a special app on my phone to record the birdsong, I also might determine what kind of bird it is. But I do not. I just listen while I smooth the sheets, plump the pillows. This almost automatic process continues for several days, interrupted only by letting the children sleep in on the weekend.

Early the next week, according to routine, I trudge back to my room with minty breath and hear the bird calling again, but now there is more singing. One bird sings, and two more reply, a trio singing the day awake while I go to rouse my children. I listen to this for another week or two, and the trio becomes a small choir. Soon there are too many voices singing to really even count.

Despite how the choir becomes a cacophony, I still think of that singular bird calling out the week after spring break. I think about how sometimes it takes just one bold individual offering a message of hope before two or three more join in, and then a whole crowd starts singing in hopeful unison. John the Baptist prepared the way for our Savior—one voice crying out in the wilderness—until Jesus Himself arrived and fully set the story of salvation in motion. Even now, I know that my singular voice has a message of hope to offer an aching world. And if I am bold, like that bird, I will gather others so that together we are a small chorus of hope for all to hear. —Katy W. Sundararajan

Praise to the Lord, the Almighty, the King of creation!
O my soul, praise him, for he is your health and salvation!
Come, all who hear; now to his temple draw near,
join me in glad adoration.
—Catherine Winkworth

APRIL 7

Paddy Beaver

Commit to the LORD *whatever you do, and he will establish your plans.*

—PROVERBS 16:3 (NIV)

WHEN I WAS a child, I was a voracious reader. My mother says I got my first library card when I was 5 years old. Among my first books were those by conservationist Thornton Burgess. Burgess created a magical realm, the Green Forest, and filled it with animal friends—Prickly Porky the porcupine, Lightfoot the deer, Reddy Fox, and my favorite, Paddy the beaver. I think I was drawn to Paddy because, like me, he was shy, ungainly, awkward-looking.

I enjoy hiking in the woods and wetlands along Michigan's Pigeon River. There is a footbridge that spans the river, and if you stand there long enough and still enough, you will see beaver. I am standing on that bridge just now, leaning on the railing, watching Paddy beaver, a poplar twig in his mouth, swimming along the surface of the shallow pond he has created. In the center of the pond is his dome-shaped lodge, with underwater entrances not accessible to predators, and at the far end of the pond is his dam.

A beaver dam is not built with one big log. It's built a stick at a time, each twig, reed, and sapling caulked into its proper place with mud. I've learned the hard way, which is pretty much how I learn everything, that if I try to undertake a large, complex project, I tend to get overwhelmed and discouraged. But if I break big projects and big problems into small pieces, I can much more easily deal with them.

I'm still shy and ungainly, but I have a beaver-like worth ethic, and I've learned to deal with life's big projects and big problems one stick at a time. Did I mention that today, April 7, is International Beaver Day? Let's get to work! —Louis Lotz

Walk of Faith: *What large, complex problem has got you depressed and demoralized? Ask God to show you how to break that large problem into small, manageable pieces.*

APRIL 8

Unexpected

And the Philistine said, "I defy the armies of Israel this day; give me a man, that we may fight together." When Saul and all Israel heard these words of the Philistine, they were dismayed and greatly afraid.

—1 SAMUEL 17:10–11(NKJV)

WHEN VACATIONING IN Honduras, I was super-excited to have the opportunity to visit with sloths, but the iguana farm that came along with the excursion? Not so much. To be honest, I was more than a little nervous about walking through a village of loose iguanas that were anywhere from 6-inch babies to 6-foot adults. But since I knew this would be a once-in-a-lifetime experience, I psyched myself into being prepared to hold a baby iguana. *Surely I could do that without panicking too much,* I thought as I waited anxiously for my turn to hold one of the cute little guys in my palm.

At that moment, one of the group leaders who worked for the farm came over and, without asking, deposited a 3-foot-long adult iguana on my shoulder and then walked away. Imagine my surprise that not only was my new iguana acquaintance a friendly fellow, but I also didn't even experience a freak-out moment. The iguana farm was one of my favorite experiences, and I have some great photo memories.

I don't know how many times I've looked at something coming up in my life and believed it was too much for me to handle, as if I were David up against a giant. I've regularly psyched myself out, crying out to God, practically begging Him to go easy on me because I simply couldn't do whatever it is He's planned for me. Often I think He must gently and nonchalantly slip His will onto my shoulders before I've had a chance to realize it's there, so I don't have time to grumble or worry about it. And by trusting God, I know He wouldn't send me out to fight an army if I wasn't ready.

I eventually realized that getting to hold that huge iguana was a gift that no one else in my group got to experience. The best gift, though, is the one I get from God every day—His constant presence. —Deb Kastner

Dear Lord, help me to recognize how much more I can do through You.

APRIL 9

Dogs Will Be Dogs

If it is possible, as far as it depends on you, live at peace with everyone.

—ROMANS 12:18 (NIV)

I'D RIDDEN MY bike past the house often enough to know that the mixed-breed dog kept there was no sweetheart. Yes, I'm sure he was a loyal and loving pet to the family. To me, he displayed no such affection. More than once he'd lunged for my ankle as I pedaled furiously to get away. One day I stopped to plead with the owner.

"I hate to be a pain," I began, addressing the elderly woman who lived there, "but would you mind keeping your dog in the yard? It's really dangerous for cyclists when he runs into the road."

By this time, the pup was sitting meekly at her feet. He didn't seem to have a care in the world. His master appeared less comfortable. She looked at me, then her multicolored companion, unsure of what to say. Her son stepped out of a pickup truck to join the conversation.

"Well, you're the only one that's complained about it," he said. "Bicycles go by here all the time, sometimes in big groups. Nobody thought it was a problem before."

I sighed. No use arguing. Shaking my head, I turned around and rode off.

That night, I lay awake, fuming. *It's a public road. I have a right to travel without being attacked,* I thought. *Even in the countryside, you can't let your dog roam off your property. I ought to call the law on them.* First thing tomorrow, I would contact the sheriff and file a report. *That'll fix 'em.*

Over breakfast, the Holy Spirit asked for my attention. *She lives alone, that lady. Her son may visit, but the dog is her real companion. And he loves her. That's why he chased you. He thought you were a threat. You don't really want to separate them, do you?*

Of course I didn't. Before my coffee cup was empty, I realized that it was I, not the devoted mutt, who was causing anxiety. How could I have let such a small annoyance disturb my peace—and theirs? —Lawrence W. Wilson

Lord Jesus, help me get over myself.

APRIL 10

Spinning My Wheels

Run in such a way as to get the prize.

—1 CORINTHIANS 9:24 (NIV)

WHEN I WAS in veterinary school, I had a pet mouse. (Yes, a *pet* mouse.) I rescued the little rodent from becoming snake food, although I'm sure he didn't grasp the fate he escaped. I named him Squeak, which I realize is not a terribly original name for a mouse, but it wasn't for the reason one might think. His name came from the fact that he ran on his squeaky little exercise wheel all night long. Pocket pets have a proclivity to literally run in circles and get nowhere, but since this is often their only source of exercise and they have to run off energy, many of these creatures become addicted to their wheels.

The irony is not lost on me that I often run in circles or spin my wheels going nowhere. How often do I get busy with unproductive activities that don't matter or bring glory to God? How often do I try to do things the same way, again and again—especially in my own power—expecting different results? Sometimes I even get busy with church work while neglecting prayer, Bible reading, or quiet time with God. There are some activities that, although good in and of themselves, are not necessarily what God has called me to do. Many times I use the excuse that I am doing good works—things I *want* to do—and am too busy to do better works, perhaps the harder or more sacrificial things God would prefer I spend my time on.

I don't want to waste my life spinning my wheels, running in circles, and getting nowhere. Unlike Squeak, I don't want to become addicted to my activity wheel, burning off energy that would be better spent doing God's will. The only way I can know His will is to step off my wheel long enough to spend time in His presence, allowing the Holy Spirit to "squeak" to my heart. —Ellen Fannon

Therefore I do not run like someone running aimlessly.

—1 Corinthians 9:26 (NIV)

APRIL 11

Diligent Doves

And let us not grow weary of doing good, for in due season we will reap, if we do not give up.

—GALATIANS 6:9 (ESV)

I SMILED WHEN I saw the mourning dove sitting on the mystery nest. I had wondered what kind of bird was building a new home on our drainpipe that spring. The previous year, robins had built a nest there and raised four broods.

I was delighted to discover that mourning doves were responsible for the new nest. While I've always loved those birds, I had never seen their babies before. Now all I had to do was wait. And wait. I watched the doves take turns sitting on the nest day and night for weeks. They were incredibly dedicated to the task. I never saw the nest left unattended.

Growing impatient to see the chicks, I found information on mourning doves and learned that 14 days was the normal duration between eggs being laid and hatching. By then, it had already been 2 weeks.

I waited longer. And so did the doves.

While robin and sparrow eggs hatched, and fledglings hopped around my yard, the mourning doves remained—sitting on the nest, waiting for their eggs to hatch.

I wondered if the expectant parents were discouraged. If they were, they didn't show it. They faithfully persevered in the work God designed them to do.

Yet at the same time, I was struggling to persevere in work God had called me to do. Discouragement pressed in when the work was hard and the expected results didn't happen. But the diligent doves inspired me to remain obedient to God no matter the results.

When little mourning dove heads appeared in the nest at last, the doves and I had a demonstration of God's promise—obedience will always lead to success in His way and His timing. I simply need to do what God designed me to do and never give up. —Jerusha Agen

Walk of Faith: *What are you working on that hasn't yielded the results you hoped for? Ask God for perseverance and trust His promise that your work will yield fruit in due time.*

APRIL 12

All Play and No Rest

The Lord replied, "My Presence will go with you, and I will give you rest."

—Exodus 33:14 (NIV)

OUR TWO RESCUE dogs are estimated to be more than 2 years old, and they're both still very playful. They play hard all day and typically settle on the couch around 7 p.m. But sometimes, Honcho has another burst of energy later, right when Simone is happily snoozing beside me.

I know he's about to disrupt the peace when he gets in the play pose and starts making little huffing sounds, as if he wants to wake her up, all the while knowing he's not supposed to. Frustrated, he'll launch from his spot on the couch to hers. No response. More huffs and whines follow, and then he'll nip at her heel.

I have taken many photos of him in that play position, chin on the couch, eyes bright and expectant, rear end up in the air, tail wagging like crazy. Finally, he'll nip at her heel again, leading to a quiet warning snarl in return. He hops away, avoiding her, and starts vocalizing excitedly because he knows she's awake now. Eventually, she launches herself at him, and the play begins all over again. We know it'll be a while before they settle in for the night and give us a bit of peace (and the ability to hear the TV!).

Sometimes I'm a little like Honcho fighting the need to rest. I "reward" myself by staying up late to watch TV or read or play games on my phone. Thus, I don't get enough sleep. I am trying to do better, to listen to the nudging of the Spirit telling me I need to take better care of my body. My body is a tool that glorifies God, and getting adequate rest is pleasing to Him. I'm going to take my cues from Simone and learn how to rest. —Missy Tippens

Come to me, all you who are weary and burdened, and I will give you rest.

—Matthew 11:28 (NIV)

APRIL 13

Rescuers Be Blessed

Blessed are those who have regard for the weak;
the LORD delivers them in times of trouble.

—PSALM 41:1 (NIV)

A CAT CARRIER BY a pond? What in the world...?

"I think it's a rescue in progress," my friend whispers.

We creep closer as a goose, presumably just released from the repurposed plastic cage, plops into the water and tiny goslings follow.

"How old are they?" I ask the ladies standing by, who I now notice are wearing matching Wildlife Rescue Association T-shirts.

"They hatched last night. The silly goose had laid her eggs in a planter box in that condo's rooftop garden," the woman answers, gesturing skyward.

Honk, honk, honk, honk.

"She's calling for her mate, letting him know where she is," one woman explains.

"He'll find them," the other woman adds reassuringly.

A sense of relief settles inside me at the thought of this family's reunification, no matter that I'd been ignorant of their plight until just moments ago. The relief is short-lived. In the evening I learn that while we were witnessing the successful goose rescue, our city council was approving a measure to cull geese throughout the city. I understand the city's dilemma. Geese create real health and safety problems in public places. But I am grateful to live among people like these goose rescuers who empathize with the wild animals with which we share our home, people who regard the plight of others as an opportunity to lend a hand. —Susie Colby

The LORD protects and preserves them—they are counted among the blessed in the land—he does not give them over to the desire of their foes.
—Psalm 41:2 (NIV)

APRIL 14

Boxy the Elder Bugs

In my Father's house are many mansions: if it were not so, I would have told you. I go to prepare a place for you.

—JOHN 14:2 (KJV)

WHEN MY IN-LAWS came over to help us demolish our basement last April, I knew there was no turning back on an enormous home-remodeling project. Along with all the disruptions came a big change to part of our basement that had become living quarters to several boxelder bugs.

As God designed them to be, boxelder bugs like warm areas and are attracted to environments that get a lot of sunlight. With the remodeling came the time to clean up and seal a large area of the basement—that included three windows, where many of the bugs liked to squeeze their way into our home and camp out.

Not only did these small bugs make their home in our basement, they also liked to journey their way upstairs to our kitchen and dining area. Our children were initially shocked at having these harmless black-and-orange creatures sit so close to us at mealtime. Eventually, they politely welcomed them to join us by naming all of them Boxy the Elder bugs.

After several months of remodeling our basement, we noticed fewer boxelder bugs upstairs in the kitchen and dining area and in the basement by the windows. They made our family life interesting at times, and there is a part of me that misses them. Not having them around has reminded me that while we are remodeling a home, God is preparing a new place for me to live in heaven. Although I wonder where the boxelder bugs' new home is, I don't have to wonder about mine. I will be in my forever home, basking in the Son's radiant glory and perhaps sharing a meal with Him too. —Stacey Thureen

Heavenly Father, during my time on earth, please help me to respect Your creatures. And thank You for preparing a place for us, and all Your creatures, with You in heaven. Amen.

APRIL 15

Finding My Voice

Then Moses answered, "But behold, they will not believe me or listen to my voice."

—EXODUS 4:1 (ESV)

HAVING FREE-RANGE CHICKENS can be both beneficial and aggravating. My wife tends to the flock, while I handle coop maintenance. A few hens became broody, and my wife thought it would be great to raise our own replacements. Having hatchlings is a "chick magnet," especially during their first week, when visitors come. Then later, the prognostication begins. Will they be hens or roosters?

We tend to get plenty of roosters when we only need one for the flock. As these young roosters develop, they reach the stage where they try to find their crowing voice. It can be entertaining listening to their pathetic attempts. They remind me of a teenage boy when his voice changes. Here's what usually happens: The dominate rooster crows, and in turn each of the others sound off their attempts. It can get noisy at times and marks when my wife begins to find new homes for them.

I remember well the first time I was asked to speak in front of the entire student body at my high school. I was just a freshman and probably sounded a lot like those young roosters trying to crow for the first time. But as I was offered more opportunities, I became more comfortable in my voice.

Moses didn't think he could speak for the Israelites to Pharaoh. When he asked God who should he say gave him his authority, God said to tell him, "I AM has sent me to you" (Exodus 3:14, ESV). It is hard for me to grasp the full meaning of having the all-knowing, all-powerful God of the universe giving Moses the authority to speak. Yet, God had his back. And when God grants me the opportunity to speak on His behalf, I have that same backing. I find my voice when I let it get lost in His Word. —Ben Cooper

I sought to hear the voice of God,
—And climbed the topmost steeple.
But God declared: "Go down again,
—I dwell among the people."
—Louis I. Newman

APRIL 16

A Delightful Dance

Take me with you, and we'll run away; be my king and take me to your room.

—Song of Songs 1:4 (GNT)

MY HUSBAND AND I were driving one day, heading out of the city but still technically in the metro area. The road under us became an overpass that lifted us up into the sky and brought us very close to a most amazing sight. Flying right over our car was a beautiful pair of bald eagles. They spiraled around each other in what reminded us of the double helix pattern of a DNA strand. Time stood still as they spun together in the air within easy view of our windshield. They stayed above us for some time, following the track of the highway on which we were traveling. Their movements were intricate, beautiful, and full of life, and the sighting was a lovely gift from God.

The proximity of our interaction with these majestic creatures was another astounding aspect of this experience. I had never seen an eagle this near to me. Usually they are so high up in the air that my husband has to identify them for me. And even then, though I appreciate the sighting, I'm unable to really *see* them.

I shared this experience with a friend who had lived in that area for many years. She was familiar with those particular eagles and told me we were passing close to their regular nesting area. Bald eagles mate for life and typically renest on the same sites, often in the same trees.

I can't say with certainty that these birds loved each other. I assume they are mates, and as such, their behavior will be faithful and supportive for the remainder of their lives. What I can say with certainty is that God chose me for life. He loved me before I even knew Him, and His deep desire is that our relationship be mutually enjoyed, everlasting, and intimate, just like that of the eagles. —Liz Kimmel

Thank You, loving Father, that there has never been a time when Your love for me was not present. Create in me a desire to know You intimately and to want more than anything to spend my days in a beautiful, delightful dance with the King of the Universe.

APRIL 17

Be Like Mikey

Consider it pure joy, my brothers and sisters, whenever you face trials of many kinds, because you know that the testing of your faith produces perseverance. Let perseverance finish its work so that you may be mature and complete, not lacking anything.

—JAMES 1:2–4 (NIV)

THE TIME WAS coming for the baby lambs to be born. Each morning, we trekked out to the barn, hoping they had arrived. Finally, two beautiful lambs appeared. One stood tall in the straw. The other stayed on the ground. On further inspection, we discovered the little one had three broken legs. We rushed the little ram to the vet, who put all three legs in casts and added a metal frame on the broken leg in the back. We christened him Mikey and took him home.

Despite his painful beginning, Mikey proved to be an indomitable force. He delighted us with his friendly personality and playful spirit as he tried to chase us around his pen. The only trouble was the metal frame on his back leg was longer than his other legs, so he would end up spinning in circles. To keep up our play, we ran in circles with him as we laughed at our undefeatable lamb.

Sometimes things don't go my way, and I end up spinning in circles on a "broken leg." When I face difficult life situations, however, I can look at Mikey and realize I have a chance to persevere and develop character. These chances for growth come in all shapes and sizes. Sometimes they're smaller disappointments, like when I wasn't cast in a play for a role I desperately wanted. Other times they're life-altering moments, like when my mom told us of her cancer diagnosis. Whatever comes my way, I'm thankful that God always steps in and gives me the strength to be like Mikey. In those moments, when I focus on the Father and enjoy His presence, I find the hope He gives me as He walks with me through the situation. —Kristen G. Johnson

Each life is made up of mistakes and learning, waiting and growing, practicing patience and being persistent.
—Billy Graham

APRIL 18

One-Legged Balance

The LORD detests dishonest scales, but accurate weights find favor with him.

—PROVERBS 11:1 (NIV)

AS SOON AS my son and I entered the Oakland Zoo, our eyes were drawn to the large exhibit right in front of the main entrance. There they were. More than twenty flamingos, standing tall, looking classy and elegant, dressed in perfectly layered orange-pink and white feathers. "My favorite bird!" I exclaimed. Ryan joined me in admiring the birds as they walked with ease on sticklike feet. Some socialized, communicating with one another through noisy calls, while others lowered their hook-shaped heads to feed from the pond. A few of them rested, undisturbed by the noise and movement around them. With their heads tucked inside their fluffy bodies, these flamingos napped on one leg.

For a long time, scientists theorized that flamingos slept on one leg to conserve heat. But recent research suggests that these birds adopt a one-legged stance while resting probably because it's the most stable position to assume. When one leg is pulled directly beneath the flamingo, it activates the locking mechanism of the standing leg in such a way that the creature's center of gravity falls just over its leg. Maybe the bird can sleep on one leg because it is most balanced in that position.

The flamingos' odd napping position made me consider the relationship between balance and rest. I had been struggling to rest. An endless stream of thoughts and to-do lists ran through my mind because I had been juggling various roles as mom, author, podcaster, Bible teacher, and seminary student. I was always busy and stressed out, spending less time in prayer and Bible study. That day, God invited me to revisit my habits and daily routine and depend on Him to reset my priorities and reschedule my calendar. Only He can help me find balance and give me rest. —Mabel Ninan

The key is not to prioritize what's on your schedule
but to schedule your priorities.
—Stephen Covey

APRIL 19

Open Doors

Ask and it will be given to you; seek and you will find; knock and the door will be opened to you.

—MATTHEW 7:7 (NIV)

I HANDED A CUP of coffee to my teenage daughter, Julia, and carried my own cup to the table. She was home from college for the weekend, and we were talking about the summer internship she'd been offered. "It's halfway across the country, Mom," Julia said. "I won't know anyone, and I'm scared to be that far from home all by myself." I didn't know what to say. I reminded her that she'd worked so hard for this opportunity and said we should pray about it. We joined hands and asked God to show her what she should do.

A few hours later, I was working in my home office. I heard our two dogs, Piper and Peyton, coming up the stairs. My office door was cracked open, but Piper pushed the door wide, raced in, and scooped up her favorite toy. Peyton ran in a second behind her and lay down at my feet.

Julia poked her head in. "The dogs just did the weirdest thing," she said. "Peyton reached your door first, but instead of going in, she sat down and waited for Piper to nudge the door open."

I nodded. "It happens all the time. Peyton acts like she's afraid to push open the door." I reached down to pet her. "But the poor girl always misses out on the best toy because Piper gets to it first."

Julia thought for a minute. "I don't want to be afraid to go through doors that have been opened for me," she said. "I think God used Peyton to show me that I need to take the internship."

I nodded. "I think you're right, Jules. We know that since God opened that door, you won't be there alone. God will be with you this summer."

She bent down to hug each dog. "Thanks for the reminder about trusting God, even when I'm nervous to try something new." —Diane Stark

Walk of Faith: *What doors has God opened that you need to walk through?*

APRIL 20

Making a Home

Even the sparrow has found a home, and the swallow a nest for herself, where she may have her young—a place near your altar, LORD Almighty, my King and my God.

—PSALM 84:3 (NIV)

IT IS SPRING and all the animals are busy making their new homes. The leaves are just starting to bud, so I can still see deep into the trees and notice what is happening in the animal world. Today I see a squirrel building a nest in the tree outside my window.

This weekend my daughter told me she had seen a squirrel running around grabbing sticks and then throwing them into a pile between two tree branches. I'd missed him that day, but today as I sit at my computer to write, I can see him out the window. He is gathering leaves from the bushes below and carrying big mouthfuls up to his pile high in the tree. It is just the cutest thing.

Whenever I see an animal building a nest, it reminds me of Psalm 84:3, one of my favorite lines in Psalms. I love this idea of the sparrow and swallow building nests near the altar of God. Birds sometimes fly into my church, and I am certain there were nests high in the rafters of the Lord's temple. What a wonderful image of drawing close to the presence of God.

My kids are getting older, so I am not building a nest anymore. I remember that energy, though, wanting to paint and organize while I was at the end of my pregnancy. Now I spend my energy going to dance recitals and football games.

Why did the squirrel choose to build in my backyard? Maybe so it is in proximity to my bird feeders, but still I wonder about God's hand in this. Perhaps He is drawing me closer to His altar today, reminding me that He is guiding me to build my life the way I do. His presence is the foundation of my home and my life. —Heather Jepsen

Walk of Faith: *Take a walk outside and observe the birds and critters building their nests. Think of some ways He is drawing you closer to His altar, then thank Him for giving you space in His presence.*

APRIL 21

Do Not Fear

When I am afraid, I put my trust in you.

—PSALM 56:3 (NIV)

WHEN MY SON and his family helped us with a building project in our backyard, our granddaughter Nellie happened upon a five-lined skink. She squealed and backed away from the colorful lizard.

My husband captured it and held it out. "Do you want to hold it? It won't hurt you."

"No!" she said.

Stan didn't try to force her but set the skink on his shoulder while he showed her the neon blue lines that ran down its tail. Nellie came closer and closer, and before we knew it, she held out her hand. She stood holding the skink for a long time and giggled as it climbed up her arm and down her back.

"He's adorable," she said, running her finger along its tail.

So how does a skink go from terrifying to adorable? I guess just as many of my fears go from a looming catastrophe to something that never happens. But even when my worst nightmares do come true, I know God will strengthen me for the battle. He is patient with me, as my husband was with Nellie, and draws me closer to Himself while I work through my fear.

He certainly did that when He called me to speak in front of groups, something that struck terror in my heart. But I started with small groups and worked my way up. Little by little, knowing that God was by my side, I lost my fear of public speaking.

Just as Nellie found she could trust her granddaddy when he said the skink wouldn't hurt her, I have watched God prove Himself faithful over and over. —Tracy Crump

If the Lord be with us, we have no cause of fear. His eye is upon us, His arm over us, His ear open to our prayer—His grace sufficient, His promise unchangeable.

—John Newton

APRIL 22

Crazy Little Thing Called Love

There are three things that are too amazing for me, four that I do not understand: the way of an eagle in the sky, the way of a snake on a rock, the way of a ship on the high seas, and the way of a man with a young woman.

—PROVERBS 30:18–19 (NIV)

SPRINGTIME IN THE animal kingdom is quite mysterious. I'm convinced male mockingbirds have a death wish as they attempt to attract a mate. Several times a day one will demonstrate its bravery by swooshing across the road in front of my car, narrowly escaping a collision.

On Edisto Island in South Carolina, spring ushers in mating season for horseshoe crabs. The warm water draws the crabs out of the surf and onto the beach to gather at the water's edge. I watched one love-struck pair circle each other five or six times in what looked like the crustacean version of "Ring around the Rosie."

I also witnessed a beautiful courtship display at the local park, Swan Lake Iris Gardens. Like graceful ballet dancers, two trumpeter swans moved to music only they could hear. They raised their heads until they were eye to eye, then lowered their beaks demurely, still gazing at each other. Did they know their graceful necks formed a perfect heart shape?

God designed His creation, from mocking birds to horseshoe crabs, to swans to humans, to delight in courtship rituals. Think of the beautiful—and sometimes crazy—things you've seen people do as they pursue love. Perhaps you've done a few yourself. My husband drove 600 miles round trip almost every weekend to visit me when we were dating. During our 4-month-long engagement, I wouldn't go to sleep at night until I'd written him a mushy letter sealed with a kiss and spritzed with my perfume.

In the words of Agur son of Jakeh, "There are three things that are too amazing for me, four that I do not understand."

Courtship—in the animal world and in the human world—is just another example of the complexity and beauty God has built into each one of His creations.

Don't you just love it? —Lori Hatcher

To love at all is to be vulnerable.
—C. S. Lewis

APRIL 23

Laurel

Give thanks to the Lord, for he is good; his love endures forever.

—1 Chronicles 16:34 (NIV)

THE WEATHER MAY be cool and the sky a soup of gray drizzle, but there is romance in the air. In Michigan, turkey breeding begins in April, triggered by increasing sunshine and a subsequent hormonal response in the birds. The National Security Agency has a term—*loveint*—that refers to intelligence gained by spying on lovers. That's what I'm doing right now, binoculars in hand, spying.

For weeks I've been watching a wild flock, especially the two prominent males, whom I've dubbed Laurel and Hardy. Laurel is easy to recognize because he's lost one of his rear-end fan feathers. The two toms are doing the ritual mating dance—strutting, gobbling, fanning their feathers as if to say, "Look at me, girls!" Hardy approaches a hen, but she gives him the cold turkey shoulder, sashays over to Laurel, and crouches before him, the sign that she has chosen him to be her mate. But moments later the fickle hen jumps up and walks back to Hardy, making her final selection. Poor Laurel. "'Tis better to have loved and lost," the saying goes, "than never to have loved at all." Still, rejection hurts.

Why does rejection hurt so much? All the other kids in class get invited to the birthday party, but you are excluded. You are ostracized by your family. You are let go by the company. Worst of all, the one you love doesn't love you back. Rejection hurts, but I take comfort in the fact that the One who loves me the most will never, ever cease loving me. —Louis Lotz

Because of the Lord's great love we are not consumed, for his compassions never fail. They are new every morning: great is your faithfulness.

—Lamentations 3:22–23 (NIV)

APRIL 24

On Guard

The Lord *will watch over your coming and going both now and forevermore.*

—Psalm 121:8 (NIV)

OUR FAMILY LOVES the meerkat exhibit at Riverbanks Zoo in Columbia, South Carolina. One spring day, we gazed through the glass that separated us from the colony and watched their antics.

In one corner, a plump male with toast-colored fur dug furiously in the soft sand. Dirt flew as the tunnel grew deeper and deeper. Soon, all we could see was his furry rump and long tail. In the center of the exhibit, Mama Meerkat squatted beside a food dish, nibbling at something she'd plucked from the pile. Scampering around her was a tiny replica of herself. Its shiny black eyes, pointy nose, and tiny paws prompted 7-year-old Caroline to exclaim, "It's so *cute*!" At the back of the habitat, three meerkats tunneled busily while two others slept in a sun puddle.

"Look, Gigi!" My 9-year-old granddaughter Lauren pointed. "There's the sentry." Sure enough, perched on the highest point in the habitat stood the colony's sentinel. "His job is to guard the rest of the meerkats," Lauren informed me, scrolling through her encyclopedic memory of random animal facts. "Meerkats can't watch for predators while they're digging, so one meerkat always stands guard."

Tasked with the job of keeping his friends and family safe, this sentry was on point. He stood erect, nose to the sky, scanning for danger. Like a lifeguard during summer swim, he appeared to be counting noses as he glanced from one side of the exhibit to the other. When a shadow passed overhead, he barked a warning that sent every kat racing for shelter. With this sharp-eyed watchman on duty, the meerkats were free to work, eat, and sleep without fear.

Watching this sentinel of the animal world reminded me that I have a sentinel too. One even more vigilant than sharp-eyed meerkats. Psalm 121:8 (NIV) describes His faithfulness: "The Lord will watch over your coming and going both now and forevermore." With God watching over me, I can work, play, and even sleep without fear. Nothing will touch me that He hasn't allowed for my ultimate good and His glory. —Lori Hatcher

In peace I will lie down and sleep, for you alone, Lord, *make me dwell in safety.*

—Psalm 4:8 (NIV)

APRIL 25

Finding Fluffy

For I am sure that neither death nor life, nor angels nor rulers, nor things present nor things to come, nor powers, nor height nor depth, nor anything else in all creation, will be able to separate us from the love of God in Christ Jesus our Lord.

—Romans 8:38–39 (ESV)

FLUFFY WAS MISSING. She had strayed from her home 6 months ago, but her desperate owner was not giving up hope.

In a neighboring state, the local "cat lady" had been trying to reach a small ginger cat living under a dumpster. After several days of the encouragement of tantalizing morsels, the cat came to her, and she was able to take it to a vet to be examined. The veterinarian called her and said, "You won't believe this, but this cat was microchipped, and I've been able to get in touch with the owner. She lives in the next state." Fluffy had wandered a good 200 miles from home. A joyful reunion took place between Fluffy and her owner.

I heard this cat story on the radio during a time when I was feeling distant from God. No specific situation had caused it. The busyness of life and work was distracting me from staying close to God. I skipped my daily Bible reading and prayer time and soon found myself in a place of alienation. Dear Christian friends who noticed this gently encouraged me to return to my spiritual "home" and my daily spiritual practices.

Fluffy's reunion reminded me that I am microchipped—that is, sealed—with the blood of Christ and I am God's child. He doesn't give up on me when I stray and faithfully waits for me to come back to our relationship. Sometimes it takes the kindness and grace of those around me to bring me back to God. —Virginia Ruth

Loving God, You are the patient parent waiting for me to come home. Thank You for the people in my life who return me to You. Amen.

APRIL 26

A Lucky Duck

Keep me safe, my God, for in you I take refuge.

—PSALM 16:1 (NIV)

ONE OF MY favorite family stories is how my father acquired Billy, his childhood pet duck. Billy belonged to the neighbors up the road, who planned on serving him for Sunday dinner. When my father learned of Billy's fate, he ran home crying. My grandfather went to the neighbors and bought Billy for the price of 50 cents. I don't know what the going cost of a duck was in the early 1900s, so I can't say whether my grandfather got a bargain or paid a fortune for Billy. My father kept Billy for many years until the duck died of old age. I doubt Billy ever realized how close he came to disaster and what a lucky duck he was.

Likewise, God has rescued me from many dangerous situations, such as the time when I was 3 years old and thought sticking car keys in an electrical socket was a good idea. Or the time I accepted a ride with a stranger when my car broke down in the middle of nowhere. Or the many times I met with clients alone at my veterinary clinic for after-hours emergencies. I can think of several other examples in my life in which circumstances might have turned out differently had it not been for God's protection. But how many disasters escaped my notice because God's divine intervention protected me? When I got delayed by red lights, an unexpected phone call, or someone with an urgent need, did God keep me from an accident or being in the wrong place at the wrong time?

Just like Billy, so blissfully unaware of his near death, I doubt I will ever know the number of times God has sent His angels to watch over and shield me from harm. But I do know I am grateful for His continual watch, care, and protection. —Ellen Fannon

Safety is not the absence of danger, but the presence of God.
—Jeanette Windle

APRIL 27

One Day at Tractor Supply

"For my thoughts are not your thoughts, neither are your ways my ways," declares the L*ORD.*

—ISAIAH 55:8 (NIV)

I SAW THE SIGN at the entrance of Tractor Supply: "Do you want to add some peeps to your family?"

"Mike, it's Chick Days!" I dragged my husband to the back of the store, where the baby chicks were housed in huge metal bins covered by heat lamps. I peered over the edges at the soft yellow, chirping balls of fluff. One little baby was so cute, I wanted to jump into the bin with it. Yes, I wanted to add some peeps to my family—baby chicks are adorable! The grandkids would love them. And think of the eggs! Each year I suggested getting some. Each year Mike gave me the same discouraging look in return.

If I'd acted in accordance with my thoughts that day, we'd have walked out the sliding doors with a carrier of peeping chicks. But would it have been the right thing to do? Later, upon reflection, I considered that there were some good reasons *not* to get baby chicks. Our three golden retrievers might bark at or try to chase the chickens. We'd need to build a coop and allow for feed and other expenses in our budget. And many more reasons I didn't think of when I was blinded by downy feathers.

I recalled other times when my desires were probably not aligned with God's plans for me. Recently, I was hoping for a certain outcome to a complicated problem and became frustrated when it didn't work out. But my reaction was based on my own imperfect view. Only God has a perfect view, and only His ways are right, even when I can't see why because they are too vast for my limited understanding. When I remember that, I'm able to shake off my disappointment.

God's ways are higher than my ways; His thoughts are higher than my thoughts. Even when it comes to bringing home baby chicks. —Peggy Frezon

My wise God, help me to trust Your thoughts and accept Your ways, which are right and good and perfect forever.

APRIL 28

Safety from Life's Lions

Lord, how long will You look on? Rescue me from their destructions, my precious life from the lions.

—Psalm 35:17 (NKJV)

NOTHING AT THE zoo inspires as much fear and respect in me as the lions. Of all the big cats and other prey animals, the lion is the one I can readily imagine encountering in the wild. What defense could I mount in the face of a starving lion? He could run faster than me, scale available trees, and tackle me faster than I could resist. The wild cat's strength would be overwhelming.

Fortunately, I don't run into a lot of actual lions in Ohio, outside of a zoo or wildlife sanctuary. Staring through the glass at the specially created lion habitat in the Columbus Zoo, I am reminded of an important biblical truth: some foes in this life are greater than my ability to prevail against them—at least within my own strength.

Often in Psalms, lions are used to represent insurmountable foes. The writer calls out to God for help in facing the awesome power, cunning, and weapons of the king of the jungle. In Psalm 57:4, the lion's teeth are compared to spears and arrows, while the tongue is imagined to be a sharp sword. Like many big cats, lions can actually cause a wound just by repeatedly licking prey with their sandpaper-like tongue.

Staring at the lions through the glass wall evoked some of the same emotions David must have felt as he wrote his psalms. Each of our lives contains its fair share of battles, whether at work, at the grocery, in relationships with those we love, and even within our own minds. Words and actions of close friends and family can hurt us, even send us to our knees in prayer.

Thank God that we have an intercessor in Jesus. No matter how serious or trivial the situation, our Savior cares and wants to bind up our wounds. His ability to change our attitudes, circumstances, and future goes far beyond any self-help strategies or truisms. With Jesus by my side, I can prevail against any foe. —David L. Winters

Lord, save us from the "lions" around us. Hear our humble cries for help and grant us the victory that only You can win.

APRIL 29

Jealous for My Attention

For I am afraid that when I come I may not find you as I want you to be.... I fear that there may be discord, jealousy, fits of rage, selfish ambition, slander, gossip, arrogance and disorder.

—2 CORINTHIANS 12:20 (NIV)

SCOUT LIVED NEXT door. She was a friendly brown-and-white beagle mix. Her owners had a tomato planter attached to their fence—a planter that Scout climbed onto every time my husband or I pulled into our driveway. From her perch, Scout would peer over the fence at us. She stood on hind legs, wagged her tail, and waited for us to come scratch her chin.

My husband and I were in a season without a dog for the first time in over 20 years. We missed our dogs greatly, and Scout filled that void. We loved Scout. We looked forward to her greeting us when we came home. If we were in the backyard and she was out, we'd talk to her. Whenever we poked our fingertips between the wooden-fence slats, she licked them.

Things changed the day we brought a brand-new puppy home. Scout still met us when we pulled into our driveway, but her behavior in the backyard was different. She was no longer the friendly tail-wagging sweet dog she'd always been. Whenever our puppy, Daisy, went to the fence, Scout barked menacingly at her.

It saddened me that Scout's jealousy turned her sweet disposition into unfriendliness around Daisy. Even though we still talked to Scout, still scratched her chin, and poked our fingers through the fence, that wasn't enough for her. Scout seemed to want us all to herself.

There are times when I've behaved like her. I've allowed jealousy to alter my behavior. I've allowed jealousy of another's abilities, opportunities, and friendships to change my disposition from pleasant to disagreeable. Jealousy didn't look good on Scout, and it doesn't look good on me either. —Sandy Kirby Quandt

Father, in those moments when I am tempted to become jealous of another, please remind me of Scout and keep me from following her example. Amen.

APRIL 30

Kiki Come Home

Then he calls his friends and neighbors together and says, "Rejoice with me; I have found my lost sheep."

—LUKE 15:6 (NIV)

OUR CAT, KIKI, had been missing for a few days. Kiki has always been a wild thing, spending most of her time outside and wandering beyond the bounds of our backyard. One day she did not come home for dinner, which wasn't completely unusual. But when she missed breakfast the next morning, I started to worry.

Three days passed with no sign of Kiki. Mealtime calls went unanswered, and I began to fear the worst. I told my kids that Kiki may be gone for good. Together we took long walks in the neighborhood calling her name, but nothing.

My son, Henry, was growing increasingly troubled. He has a sensitive heart and is often worrying. As the days passed with no sign of Kiki, he was growing more and more downcast.

The Sunday morning after Kiki went missing I was leading the church in prayer time. As I collected prayer requests from the congregation, I was surprised to see Henry's hand in the air. "I want to pray for our lost cat, Kiki" he said. Luckily my church is super supportive of animals and no one batted an eye to think that someone would ask for prayers for a pet. Together we lifted our concerns for Kiki along with the other prayers of the day.

Later that same afternoon my daughter was headed outside to water the flowers when who should appear on the porch, but Kiki! My daughter squealed with delight, scooped up the kitty, and ran inside. "It's because we prayed," she said.

We don't always get such a direct answer to our prayers in life, so I am hopeful my kids will remember the day Kiki came home. God heard our prayers and answered them. And together we rejoiced that what once was lost was now found. —Heather Jepsen

Amazing grace, how sweet the sound, that saved a wretch like me.
I once was lost, but now am found, was blind, but now I see.
—John Newton

May

MAY 1

The Ordinary

When they saw the courage of Peter and John and realized that they were unschooled, ordinary men, they were astonished and they took note that these men had been with Jesus.

—ACTS 4:13 (NIV)

I FELT A SURGE of joy when I saw an American robin fly past me with a twig in its beak. It was a mini taste of the joy Noah must have felt when the dove returned to the ark with an olive leaf. Noah endured the flood and its aftereffects for more than a year, and I had finally gotten past the 88 days of winter.

The robin's nest building put an image to the clear, lilting song I'd been hearing over the last 2 weeks. Some people describe a robin's delightful string of clear whistles as saying: Cheerily, cheer up, cheer up, cheerily, cheer up.

An engaging song. One of the early broadcasters of spring. Hooray for robins! Yet robins are often underappreciated and dismissed. I've heard it thoughtlessly slip out of people's mouths (mine included), "Oh, it's just a robin." Perhaps the attitude is not surprising since nearly one out of 30 birds in North America is a robin.

Likewise, how many individuals are overlooked within the teeming mass of humanity? There are now more than 8 billion people on the earth. Most live quiet lives in humble circumstances. Not fabulously wealthy. Not so beautiful, brilliant, or talented. Lives lived outside the limelight.

Thankfully, God has a much larger view. In the Bible, we read of ordinary people whose lives were weaved into the extraordinary plan of God. Consider the poor immigrant Ruth, Rahab the prostitute, and an unnamed boy with five loaves and two fishes.

Isn't it exciting to know that God's extraordinary can and does intersect with the ordinary? The same God who created robins to proclaim spring likewise created us to proclaim the good news of Jesus Christ in the setting and circumstances in which He's placed us. Like Peter and John, I have the imprint of Jesus on my life. Suddenly, my ordinary no longer feels, well, quite so ordinary. —Darlene Kerr

The only way to live a truly remarkable life is not to get everyone to notice you, but to leave noticeable marks of His love everywhere you go.

—Ann Voskamp

MAY 2

Safety of Home

But the Lord your God will keep your life safe like a treasure hidden in a bag.

—1 Samuel 25:29 (NIRV)

WHAT A CRAZY, busy morning. Although I was thankful to work from home, many tasks lay between me and a busy day at my workstation. First and foremost, the dogs needed hugging and then feeding. Snowy, a purebred golden retriever, and Teddi, a goldendoodle, eyed me intently as I made my way to the couch before giving them their expected vigorous morning hugs and a brief petting session.

They smacked their lips as I got up and headed toward their empty food bowls. Knowing what to expect, Teddi let out an excited whine punctuated by a short bark. Soon, they munched away as I went to my office to turn on the computer. By the time I logged on, both dogs appeared next to my chair, reminding me to let them out in the backyard.

With a 6-foot-high privacy fence, I felt confident opening the back door and watching them trot out to the green lawn where they could do their business in peace. I returned to my desk and got busy on an email.

After several minutes, it felt like time to let them back in, but when I opened the back door and called out, no dogs appeared. I scanned my modest-size backyard—the pooches were not there. Then my eyes landed on the gate, which stood wide open. The previous evening, I must have forgotten to close and lock it. Before panic set in, I prayed and then called out one more time. Teddi peeked her head in and walked through the open gate first, followed by Snowy.

Even though the dogs could have run away into the neighborhood, both valued the safety of their backyard more than the adventure that lay beyond. I choked up a little, thinking about God. Though I might wander from Him through the open gate of free will, He always welcomes me back with grace and love. I have all I need with His love. —David L. Winters

Thought for the day: God provides all that we need.

MAY 3

The Right Place for a Blue Heron

Whom have I in heaven but You? And there is none upon earth that I desire besides You.

—PSALM 73:25 (NKJV)

THE BLUE HERON and I startled each other as I hiked over boulders toward the waterfall at Sugarloaf Ridge State Park. Usually, I see these large, shy waterbirds in wetlands or near the Russian River, not hidden away in a rocky landscape.

"Boy, are you lost," I said with a chuckle as I watched it fly up and away. But then I went over to where it had been standing in the shallow water. There was something moving beneath the surface. A crayfish! That blue heron hadn't been lost at all. I'd interrupted his lunch. And I didn't even realize we had crayfish in this creek! It got me to thinking.

The blue heron knew exactly where it wanted to be and why, and it knew right where to find the good food it craved. That's how I feel each Sunday morning when I go to church to worship. I've often jokingly said, "At least once a week I know I'm in the right place at the right time!" but it is the literal truth.

Like the blue heron seeking tasty crayfish at the foot of a hidden waterfall, I show up at church seeking my beautiful Savior. I look forward to being fed by His Word and worshipping His magnificence with fellow believers. Certainly, God is everywhere and always with me, but I do find special uplift in gathering with my spiritual family, uplift that is different from when I privately pray daily to my Father in heaven.

Just as the heron can find nourishment in different terrains, I appreciate that God provides me with different means to connect with Him, directly or through my brothers and sisters in Christ. Each week, as He feeds me and His followers, I know I'm in the right place. —Marianne Campbell

And if I go and prepare a place for you, I will come back and take you to be with me that you also may be where I am.

—John 14:3 (NIV)

MAY 4

A Hopping Harvest

So let's not get tired of doing what is good. At just the right time we will reap a harvest of blessing if we don't give up.

—GALATIANS 6:9 (NLT)

OUR PROPERTY HAS a ditch with a small seasonal stream that pools next to the house. A few months ago, after a particularly rainy couple of weeks, we noticed hundreds of tadpoles swimming in the pooled area. Our grandson, Benaiah, loves to look for frogs and toads when he comes for a visit.

So when the hot southern Georgia spring days began to evaporate our little tadpole-filled pool, my husband and I took turns adding water to it with a garden hose. (I've watered a lot of God's creations in my lifetime, but I can't say I've ever watered tadpoles!) We kept up our vigil faithfully, checking daily to see if enough water remained for our future hatchlings.

One day after returning from a grocery run, I came in fuming. "I try my best to be nice to cashiers," I grumbled to David as I put away my goods, "because I know it's such a challenging job dealing with the demands of customers. I know if I'm not careful, I can be a real grouch by the time I get ready to check out. But I'm so tired of encountering rude clerks nearly every time I shop."

"Darling, just the other day you told me about a wonderful conversation with a cashier. Why don't we go for a walk to cheer yourself up?"

Wandering around the backyard plants, I spotted movement in the grass. I bent over for a closer look and saw a tiny toad. Then another and another. "Babe, we did it! Toads are everywhere!" Maybe not hundreds, but certainly a nice couple of dozen hopping amphibians to show Benaiah. I guess our efforts were worth it.

I think I'll keep up my efforts to be kind to cashiers too. I know it will be worth it. —Julie Lavender

Therefore, whenever we have the opportunity, we should do good to everyone—especially to those in the family of faith.

—Galatians 6:10 (NLT)

MAY 5

Make a Joyful...Hee-Haw

This is the day the Lord has made. We will rejoice and be glad in it.

—Psalm 118:24 (NLT)

WHAT'S THAT?" MY granddaughter's face crinkled.

"Oh, that's just our neighbors' donkeys, Cyrus and Billy Ray."

Their hee-haw came again, echoing through the valley, and Lila giggled. "They're silly!" Cupping her hand over her ear, she asked, "But what are they saying?"

I paused. What *were* they saying? "Perhaps they're praising God for the beautiful day. Or maybe they're thanking Him for the fresh hay Farmer Duckett forked over their fence."

Lila was quiet. Finally, "Can we take them a treat? Maybe they'll thank us too."

After slicing several apples, we strolled down the country road. Seeing us, the pair approached, then brayed again. Once more, Lila couldn't contain her laughter.

I smiled. *Thank You, Father.* My silent praise came from a place of gratitude, despite my earlier grumbling. My heart was aching over what I considered unanswered prayers.

Two days later, strong gusts of wind sent rain in torrents, striking our windows with force. Suddenly we heard them.

Placing her puzzle piece down, Lila walked to the window, then peered out over the pond to our neighbors' pasture. Joining her, we saw two drenched donkeys standing in the downpour.

With her face pressed against the glass, "It's raining. Why would they say thank you?"

I considered my answer. "God tells us we're to praise Him in all circumstances—on sunny days and on rainy days too. Know why?"

My granddaughter thought a moment before speaking. "Because there's something good in every day."

"That's right, dear. We can find something to praise God for, no matter what."

And right on cue, as if they knew both the joy and the aching of my heart, Billy Ray and Cyrus sang out again—*hee-haw. Hee-haw.*

And I heard God's whisper. *This teachable moment wasn't just for Lila. It's for you too.* —Maureen Miller

Again I will say, rejoice!
—Philippians 4:4 (NKJV)

MAY 6

Seasons of Change

He made the moon to mark the seasons, and the sun knows when to go down.

—PSALM 104:19 (NIV)

THE SPRINGTIME SEASON brings stray and feral cats to the rescue ranch. I feed not only them but also any other wildlife that comes at night for food. Some nights there might be twenty creatures that I do not know or even recognize showing up to be fed. This year, though, the usual feral cat population, the opossums, and deer are few and far between. And it is in these seasons of fewer animal responsibilities that I have learned that life is about to change.

This change equates to a void in my life. I get attached to strays, fosters, and my own pets. And when a beloved pet passes away or I find a home for a foster, I feel an ache in that void. In the past, I would take more pets right away. Often, a call about a dog or cat needing a home would come, or an animal who needed me would just show up. But in the past year, I have felt the void, and I have felt the need to allow the void to be just that—a void. One I didn't fill with another rescue dog or horse or cat. I felt God's push to allow the empty space.

In that empty space, life began to challenge me. An elderly parent needed me. My job became more demanding. I had opportunities to experience things that my old normal would not have accommodated. God has freed me up to live differently.

As uncomfortable as change can be, it opens the door for something God has been planning for us. And what God has planned always has a gift in it. —Devon O'Day

God, even though I am not comfortable in this place, I am willing to walk in the path You are creating. Help me see the gift in each step.

Hidden Things

They search the sources of the rivers and bring hidden things to light.

—JOB 28:11 (NIV)

IT WAS EARLY morning, and we were standing by a quiet pond at a Texas bed-and-breakfast when the owner approached with a question. "Have you seen any fish?"

"Not a single one," I replied.

He put a finger to his lips to signal silence, and then began humming the *Jaws* theme: *dodo dodo, dodo dodo, dodo dodo*. Instantly the pond was in turmoil, with hundreds of catfish coming to the surface as the owner fed them their breakfast. And then just as quickly as it started, it was over. When the last morsel of food had been consumed, total quiet descended once again.

As I contemplated this sensational display, I thought, *Aren't I a lot like that pond?*

Deep inside, I'm filled with memories, emotions, thoughts, triggers that can rise suddenly to the surface. Sometimes those thoughts are negative, but sometimes they are positive: dreams, hopes, and treasures. And unlike those fish, those memories and emotions don't always go away quickly. Instead they stay in my mind, affecting my mood and my interactions with my colleagues, my neighbors, and my loved ones. As Charlotte Bronte said, "The human heart has hidden treasures,/In secret kept, in silence sealed;/The thoughts, the hopes, the dreams, the pleasures,/ Whose charms were broken if revealed."

My challenge is to let my life be ruled by the positive rather than the negative hidden things, so that my daily interactions reflect my love of God and spread that love to others. —Harold Nichols

Dear Lord, when my emotions, thoughts, and dreams surface like those fish, please help me to be ruled by thoughts of Your love, and help me reflect that love to everyone I meet. Amen.

MAY 8

Joy Comes with Wings

Weeping may endure for a night, but joy comes in the morning.
—PSALM 30:5 (NKJV)

HAS JOY RETURNED?" I've been pondering that question since receiving an email from someone whose husband is deathly ill. She wonders how I endure bereavement.

Joy never left, but it's different now. I laugh with friends, and I laugh more deeply still with my grown children, but the deepest joy was that which I shared with my husband. Now I inhabit that deepest place alone.

For almost a year, I spent hours each day at my kitchen table, plowing through death chores—taking my husband's name off accounts, filing government forms, checking the "widowed" box over and over. Occasionally I would look up and see a hummingbird visit the salvia I'd planted in boxes outside my kitchen window. While I was on hold with yet another agency, a jewel-colored friend hovered at my window. While I typed away, a tiny bird dipped its beak into each bloom.

Hummingbirds visit a thousand flowers each day. These hummingbirds chose my window box as part of their flying feast. Their arduous work of survival encouraged me in mine. For all their labor—hummingbird hearts beat twenty times per second—the hummingbirds never looked stressed as they eyed me through the pane of glass. They seemed curious, even joyful. Is that possible? To be under so much stress and yet remain curious about the world and joyful in response?

In Psalm 30:5 and 11 (NKJV), the Psalmist claims, "joy comes in the morning" and further declares, "You have turned for me my mourning into dancing; you have put off my sackcloth and clothed me with gladness."

Each day, joy returns like the hummingbirds, my beautiful small companions. I am not yet dancing; neither am I clothed with joy. But I am grateful for the tiny jewellike birds who offer reason to be glad and grateful every day. —Susie Colby

Finally, brethren, whatever things are true, whatever things are noble, whatever things are just, whatever things are pure, whatever things are lovely, whatever things are of good report, if there is any virtue and if there is anything praiseworthy—meditate on these things.
—Philippians 4:8 (NKJV)

MAY 9

Rosebush Redemption

I will repay you for the years the locusts have eaten—the great locust and the young locust, the other locusts and the locust swarm—my great army that I sent among you.

—JOEL 2:25 (NIV)

LIKE ANY GARDENER, I love springtime. In addition to the early blooming perennial flowers, bushes, and trees, annuals in front of and around the sides of my house require a lot of time and effort. Soon, everything seems alive with new growth and color.

Roses are one of my favorites, though I don't have a lot of history with them. Recently, I purchased a new home and inherited the prior owner's rosebushes. Blooms burst forth with vivid yellows, pinks, and reds. The roses begin blooming in June and last through the summer, but not without some trouble and work along the way.

Imagine my indignation when seemingly overnight almost all the green leaves on several of the rosebushes developed holes; some were almost entirely eaten away. On closer inspection, I discovered tiny bugs and worms. These little terrorists intended to ruin not just my rosebushes but my entire garden!

I sprang into action, rushing to the gardening department of a large hardware chain. "Help me. My roses are being attacked," I said dramatically to the first store employee I encountered.

A bit surprised at my outburst and obvious angst, a patient young man invited me to follow him to the gardening department. Once there, he pointed to a wall of cures to heal my hurting roses. The choices were nearly overwhelming, but I chose one with natural ingredients that wouldn't harm bees, my dogs, or other animals.

Once I resolved that crisis, I thought about God's promise to us in the book of Joel. He knows that tribulations in life will exact a toll. Random problems and even our own bad choices can lead to hurt, loss, and regret—the garden of our life damaged by our enemies. Yet we only have to rely on His promise in Joel 2:27 (NKJV) to be healed: "I am the LORD your God and there is no other. My people shall never be put to shame."
—David L. Winters

I try to avoid looking forward or backward, and try to keep looking upward.
—Charlotte Brontë

MAY 10

The Very Large Toad

The Lord is my shepherd, I lack nothing. He makes me lie down in green pastures, he leads me beside quiet waters, he refreshes my soul.

—Psalm 23:1–3 (NIV)

ALONGSIDE MY HOME is a protected walkway where I grow several potted plants. It's a quaint spot that's well-protected from weather and predators. Imagine my surprise when one day I was walking along the path and noticed that a toad had burrowed into the soil of one of those pots. What a perfect habitat it had found for itself. While we have many toads around our property, I quickly realized this was no ordinary amphibian—in fact, it may have been the largest one I'd ever seen!

No doubt this guy had grown to such a robust size because its chosen habitat provides both safety and plenty of food. Seeing the toad brought a smile to my face, but beyond this small joy, it also taught me an important spiritual lesson.

I have a choice where I make my own habitat in life. If I choose scant protection from predators and life's storms, I will not be safe. If I choose poor nourishment, I will not be spiritually fed. But when I choose to abide near the Lord—just as the toad lives next to my house—then I will know abundance. Simply put, being near the Lord allows me to burrow under the soil of His spiritual covering, just as the toad does in its pot. My spiritual striving will always lead to weariness and insecurity, but when I rest in His presence, I will find my needs met. The choice is mine to make today—in my heart and mind and soul. —Ashley Clark

I need thy presence every passing hour.
What but thy grace can foil the tempter's power?
Who like thyself my guide and strength can be?
Through cloud and sunshine, O abide with me.
—Henry Francis Lyte

MAY 11

Choose to Protect

Like birds hovering overhead, the LORD Almighty will shield Jerusalem; he will shield it and deliver it, he will "pass over" it and will rescue it.

—ISAIAH 31:5 (NIV)

WHY WON'T THE crows leave that poor bald eagle alone? Overhead a murder of crows mercilessly badgers an eagle as it soars on the thermals. I sympathize with the poor eagle, who swoops to evade their pestering.

Just as I'm pondering the bullying crows above, a car flies through the intersection in front of my house. The driver, laughing and talking on his cell phone, doesn't even slow or glance both ways as he sails past the Stop sign. Furious, I follow the car, waving my arms and yelling. My heart rate rises. I feel desperate as I contemplate options. My neighborhood is full of children who cross the intersection en route to and from school, the park, and the tree house in my yard. How dare this driver endanger them!

Suddenly I understand why the crows are in such a state. It's nesting season. Very likely the eagle had threatened a nest. Mama or Papa Crow summoned allies to ward off the predator. I switch sides from Team Eagle to Team Crow, feeling sorry I had judged the crows so harshly. I think about my arm-waving, yelling self and wonder if I could have taken some more effective action. I had wanted to punish that careless driver for putting kids at risk, but maybe he himself had been a kid playing in the neighborhood not long ago.

I thank the crows for enlightening me and then order a neon-green plastic Slow, Children at Play sign for the corner of my front yard. My anger subsides as I choose to protect the neighborhood kids rather than fume pointlessly. Maybe I need to recruit some allies! —Susie Colby

When adults speak up for the vulnerable and the weak, working and demanding that safety and respect prevail, God's little lambs are protected and nourished. They know they are not abandoned; they are loved. And the world becomes a little more like heaven as a result.

—Wess Stafford

MAY 12

Squirrel Love

Can a mother forget the baby at her breast and have no compassion on the child she has borne?

—ISAIAH 49:15 (NIV)

I'VE SEEN A lot of strange things in a car's engine," David said, "but this was the strangest." My husband works for a car dealership that sells and services cars. "When the mechanic lifted the hood, a ball of gray fur flew out, hit the ground, and scampered off into the woods behind the garage."

"A squirrel?" I guessed. He nodded.

Apparently, the fuzzy rodent had ridden to the dealership under the hood on the interstate for more than 10 miles.

"But that's not all," David continued. "We realized there was only one reason the squirrel didn't jump out as soon as we started the car."

"Babies?"

"Babies. The mechanic looked around the engine, and sure enough, there was a nest—with a tiny squirrel curled up inside. We knew it wouldn't survive without its mother, so we gathered up the nest and set it at the edge of the woods. Sure enough, within a few minutes we saw Mama Squirrel crawl inside, grab her baby, and race off into the woods."

I understand that Mama's commitment to her baby. She was an example of how mothers through the ages—human and animal—have bravely protected and defended their young. A mother's love is fierce and forever. Nothing—not a roaring engine, a 10-mile interstate, or a greasy mechanic—could separate her from her baby.

Perhaps this is why God our Father used the example of a mother to describe His commitment to His children. "Can a mother forget the baby at her breast and have no compassion on the child she has borne?" He asked in Isaiah 49:15. When the Israelites feared God had forgotten them, He responded through the prophet Isaiah, "I will not forget you! See, I have engraved you on the palms of my hands" (Isaiah 49:15–16, NIV).

When circumstances cause me to wonder if God has forgotten me, I picture the nail-scarred hands of Jesus and know He hasn't. As David's traveling squirrel reminded me, Jesus has engraved me on His heart (and His hands) forever. —Lori Hatcher

Walk of Faith: *Read Isaiah 49 and bask in God's declaration of love for His children—including you.*

MAY 13

The Big Flock

For just as each of us has one body with many members, and these members do not all have the same function, so in Christ we, though many, form one body, and each member belongs to all the others.

—ROMANS 12:4–5 (NIV)

MY NEW FLOCK of chicks huddled together in the corner of a cardboard box under a heat lamp. I'd just brought them home from my local feed store and put them there for safety. Crowded together, they looked like a small ball of fluff with many shiny eyes and tiny beaks sticking out. In a few short weeks, though, their down had turned to feathers and soon they were hardy enough to be moved outside.

Once outside, my free-range flock continued to move as a single unit. They did everything together—foraging, dust bathing, and exploring the yard. If one started clucking, the others were sure to join in. In the evening, they crowded together near the back patio door where they could see my family in the house. The chickens were a flock, and my husband and I laughingly referred to ourselves and the chickens together as The Big Flock.

My chickens wouldn't thrive if they were separated from their flock. They're simply not wired to be alone. And, it turns out, neither am I. I need a big flock. And the best flock for me is other Christians. I need them with me to gather and worship our great God together. I need them around me to celebrate the good times and to comfort me in the bad times. I rely on their wisdom, teaching, and guidance. And I grow through them and with them as we share our Christian faith. Of course, there's a time for me to be alone with God, but His desire is for me to be part of a flock of believers.

Like my backyard flock, I benefit from the close connection to others who share my love of Jesus Christ. I love my flock, both chickens and believers. —Marianne Campbell

Our relationship with each other is the criterion the world uses to judge whether our message is truthful—Christian community is the final apologetic.
—Francis Schaeffer

Two Birds

Then God said, "Let the waters abound with an abundance of living creatures, and let birds fly above the earth across the face of the firmament of the heavens."

—GENESIS 1:20 (NKJV)

TWO SEAGULLS. TWO events. Two very different emotions.

Several years ago I was attending a writer's conference in San Antonio. Texas. As beautiful as it was, I was having a difficult time adjusting. I'm a major introvert who finds it hard to speak to people or join in group conversations. My hotel roommate and I didn't know each other, but she had friends there and was usually out with them. To be honest, I was feeling deeply lonely and left out. I decided to go to a banquet but couldn't find an open seat, so I changed back into jeans and went out to eat by myself. I was sitting on the deck at a restaurant not exactly enjoying my solitary meal when a seagull decided to join me, perching on the table and eyeing my food. Great. Now I had a bird for my only dinner companion. I could not have felt worse.

Some time after that, my husband and I took a cruise. We docked in a Caribbean port, and I grabbed something cold and sweet to drink and sat out on my balcony to watch the waves. I was just as much alone as I'd been in San Antonio, but this time I was relaxed and, to borrow one of my grandson's favorite words, *chill*. Suddenly a seagull joined me, perching on the railing and surveying me with curiosity, cocking his head to the side and focusing one eye on me. His expression made me laugh out loud.

I had a happy conversation with that second seagull, regaling him with all the fun I was having. But later, as I relayed the story to my husband, I remembered that first seagull and how dissimilar I'd felt back then. What was the difference? Was it the circumstances? My attitude? Maybe both?

Since that time, I think of seagulls as a turning point in my relationship with God. Now whenever I see one of those birds (not often, as I live in landlocked Colorado), I am reminded of two very different experiences that had the same takeaway—that every circumstance is part of God's plan. And then I take a moment to thank God for both my circumstances and the seagulls. —Deb Kastner

Never be afraid to trust an unknown future to a known God.

—Corrie ten Boom

MAY 15

Good Goat, Baaaaaaad Goat

If our hearts condemn us, we know that God is greater than our hearts, and he knows everything.

—1 JOHN 3:20 (NIV)

I WAS AWAKENED BY one of those calls from a neighbor you just hate to get: "Your goats are out. Just thought you'd like to know."

I rushed to pull on rubber boots over my pajama-covered legs and ran outside to get the babies back in. There in the front yard were the two little girls, Tink and Lizzie, just munching away on the green grass as if they were supposed to be there. I live on a busy highway, so this was terrifying to me because I knew the danger these two were unaware they were in.

"Goats! What are you doing out here?!" I yelled, hoping to admonish them, not scare them so they'd run into the busy early morning traffic.

Stopping mid-chew, the two little runaways froze and looked at me, then each other. Thankfully they ran back through the hole in the fence they must have been working on for awhile. They'd been caught in the act and knew they were in the wrong place, doing the wrong thing.

Can you remember ever being caught doing something you weren't supposed to be doing? I don't know why we try so hard to convince God of what He already knows. All He ever wants is for us to be on a path to the higher purpose He created us for. Heading back to the place where we went wrong is a beautiful place to start over. And the wonderful thing about God is that He always welcomes us home to His grace that is waiting. —Devon O'Day

God, sometimes I end up in a place that You did not prepare for me. Please help me find my way back to You.

MAY 16

Press toward the Call

In him we were also chosen, having been predestined according to the plan of him who works out everything in conformity with the purpose of his will.

—EPHESIANS 1:11 (NIV)

MY MOM AND I arrived at the stables in Idaho Springs, Colorado, and signed in. The leader asked me about my riding experience and gave me Bullet, a beautiful chestnut quarter horse, to ride.

I stepped into the stirrup and hoisted my other leg over his back. Years had passed since I'd sat atop a horse. Once positioned in the saddle, I felt the muscle memory return. I rubbed Bullet's neck and ran my hands along his coarse mane. I turned to look at my mom. She sat atop Cookie, a solid black beauty whose coat gleamed in the sun.

The trail ride began at 2 p.m. The riders lined up single file. Instructions were given. Nothing faster than a canter. Absolutely no galloping. Everything about the ride was done by the book.

But Bullet didn't read the book.

The guide led us along the dirt road to the backcountry trails. Bullet navigated the rocky path with ease. We paused to gaze at the vista of trees down the mountain.

The horses sped up on the way back and trotted along the dirt road. The stable came into view when we rounded the corner. Someone had left the gate open. Ready to return to the barn at the end of the day, Bullet accelerated from a canter to a full gallop.

The guide called out, "Pull the reins. Don't let him run." I enjoyed the speed, the freedom of moving forward. I feigned innocence and let Bullet race home. Those few minutes of joy outweighed the small reprimand I received when I dismounted.

Just as Bullet raced for the stables, I need to race toward my calling, disconnecting from the things of this world to better connect with God and His Word. Then without hindrance I can press toward the call He has given me. —Crystal Storms

Walk of Faith: *What distracts you from seeking God? Ask Him to help you release it so you can pursue Him in greater measure.*

MAY 17

Beyond the Blue

You have searched me, L*ORD*, *and you know me.*

—PSALM 139:1 (NIV)

IT IS MAY, and spring has come bounding in like a Labrador puppy. The air is damp and warm, my black raspberries are in full bloom, the rhubarb stalks are already as thick as a broom handle, and there, perched on the telephone wire, is the first indigo bunting of the year. Often described as "a scrap of sky with wings," the brilliant blue bunting is one of those migratory birds that unlike me, can afford to spend the winter in the tropics. But come May, they return to western Michigan, where I dutifully mark their first appearance on my little chart. Some buntings stay only for a quick meal of insects and then push on into Canada. Hopefully, this fellow will remain here, and I will enjoy him all summer.

Indigo buntings are easy to spot because of their bright sapphire coloring. The thing is, buntings aren't really blue. They lack blue pigment. Their jewellike cerulean color comes from a microscopic oddity in their feathers that refracts and reflects blue light. Buntings appear to be blue, but they're not.

I try to appear fine and flashy to the world. Now and then I get away with it, and people see in me virtues that I don't really possess. But there is One who knows I am not as high-minded as I pretend to be. God knows the truth about me—not the self-serving story I sometimes try so hard to project to others and even to myself—but the real story, the unvarnished truth. An unnerving thought. And yet comforting at the same time. God sees the truth behind my sleek fluffy feathers. And yet He loves me, utterly and completely. Now there's a reassuring thought for a lovely May day. Come on, let's you and me go pick some rhubarb. —Louis Lotz

Search me, God, and know my heart; test me and know my anxious thoughts.
See if there is any offensive way in me, and lead me in the way everlasting.
—Psalm 139:23–24 (NIV)

MAY 18

Safe with My Father

I lift up my eyes to the mountains—where does my help come from? My help comes from the LORD, the Maker of heaven and earth.

—PSALM 121:1–2 (NIV)

MY HUSBAND; OUR Lab-pit mix, Bear; and I were winding up our 3,259-mile trip through the Southwest in our RV camper. After we checked into the campground in Carlsbad, New Mexico, the owner explained what the tall metal structures near a grove of fruit trees were—hail cannons. They fired loud booms every few seconds whenever storms approached and continued firing until the storms passed. Their intent was to interrupt the formation of hailstones in the atmosphere in order to keep hail from damaging the fruit trees.

Thunderstorms made Bear nervous. He didn't like them at all. I really hoped we had no need for a hail cannon demonstration while we were there. Bear displayed his weather sensitivity earlier in the day when he hid under the dash at my feet. Although there was no evidence of a storm that we could see, our dog knew. Turns out, we were in the path of a tornado.

As we ate dinner that evening, it began to rain. Hail cannons boomed right along with the thunder. If thunder didn't already upset Bear, it surely would by morning. Three severe storms passed through during the night, each filled with wind, rain, thunder, lightning, and hail.

Although Bear is not allowed on our bed, that is exactly where he went during the storms. He knew we were there. He knew he would be safe snuggled next to us. Bear understood we would protect him. Most importantly, our dog knew we wouldn't turn him away in his time of distress.

In my times of storms, I need to be more like Bear. I need to go immediately to my heavenly Father, who will protect me and keep me safe. I know He'll never turn me away. —Sandy Kirby Quandt

The raging storms may round us beat,
A shelter in the time of storm;
We'll never leave our safe retreat,
A shelter in the time of storm.
—Vernon J. Charlesworth

MAY 19

What Matters Most

For where your treasure is, there your heart will be also.

—LUKE 12:34 (NIV)

PEOPLE RESPOND WITH unvarnished skepticism when I tell them that Windsor, my sweet and feisty schnoodle, loves salad. Green salad. Specifically romaine lettuce. And more specifically, the crunchy hearts of romaine.

There is little in this world that excites Windsor more than a handful of the greens in his bowl. In fact, he will leave behind a hamburger, a piece of steak, or some shredded turkey if there's salad to be had. He will literally pick off the individual pieces of lettuce from his food if he's feeling especially finicky. Windsor will hover around the kitchen if he hears the telltale crackle of the salad bag, watching in case a sneak preview drops to the floor. If it's just a leaf, he might ignore it, but if it's any sort of crunchy bit, he's all over it.

People's disbelief is understandable. Windsor is not like other dogs in many ways, and his infatuation with romaine is just one of them. I have no idea where this passion for this lettuce came from. I don't even remember how I discovered that he liked it so much.

Windsor's romaine obsession makes me think about what *I* value most. A recent reunion with my siblings took me back to the small town where I grew up. Being in the rural setting of my childhood, I couldn't help thinking that the time I spend on social media, as well as the vocational and artistic pursuits that consume my time and energy at home, felt trivial and removed from how I was raised. I felt a twinge of regret that I had moved away from home early on and never returned, that I had missed out on precious time with my mom and my siblings. It made me examine where my heart is. I can't change the past, but I can be more mindful going forward about what matters most. —Jon Woodhams

Stay centered on what matters by keeping what matters at the center.
—Richie Norton

His Eye Is on the Sparrow

I will take you as my own people, and I will be your God. Then you will know that I am the LORD your God.

—EXODUS 6:7 (NIV)

I HAD A MORNING of waiting ahead of me in a town that was distant from home. First coffee and some email before heading back to my car. As I watched the sun hit the buildings in front of me, I noticed sparrows flying in and out of a puddle, splashing and fluttering about. I started humming the old hymn, "His Eye Is on the Sparrow," delighting in their joy.

I decided to take a walk around the small downtown and noticed a young woman ahead of me with a cane and a puzzled look on her face. When I asked if I could help, the woman explained that she was trying to walk to her bank on the other side of the busy road and that she was blind. She had gotten turned around after coming down from her apartment above the coffee shop. She was trying to feel the sun on her face to know which direction to go.

I let that sink in for a moment.

She needed an arm and a friend. And there I was. We linked arms while she explained that after losing her sight a few years prior, she went to school to learn how to live independently in a seeing world. Her spirit was happy and silly. Her impressive confidence astounded me as she told me stories of maneuvering through town and how her parents worry about her.

It was an unexpected divine connection. I am never in that town, but God knew that on that morning, I needed to be right there.

God had His eye on the sparrows that needed a drink that hot day and provided the water. He also had His eye on the one who needed a helping hand and the only one who could give it. —Twila Bennett

I sing because I'm happy,
I sing because I'm free,
For His eye is on the sparrow,
And I know He watches me.
—Civilla D. Martin

MAY 21

The Eagle Has Landed

Be completely humble and gentle; be patient, bearing with one another in love.

—EPHESIANS 4:2 (NIV)

AS MY HUSBAND and I walked in the park, we heard the cawing from two displeased crows overhead. I suppose the crows were just as surprised as we were about encountering an adult bald eagle invading their airspace. Spotting the once endangered bird is not that rare an occurrence in our southern Indiana area anymore. But one this far from its preferred lake habitat was unusual. As we watched, the protective pair circled and pursued the trespasser halfway across the park. Maybe the two were paying it forward for the many times smaller birds had been aggressive with them.

One returned to its crow's nest. The other insistent partner shadowed the intruder. The eagle soared and gracefully landed on a sycamore tree next to the creek that flows along the park trail. But the boisterous crow circled around, flapping its wings and cawing out. Foolishly, the crow chose a perch only a few feet from the eagle's sharp beak and the curved yellow talons that were curled around the limb.

My husband remarked, "That crow better watch out. Any minute that eagle could have enough and strike."

Luckily, the majestic bird of prey was more focused on keeping an eagle eye on us rather than any threat from the compact clamorous crow.

Just like that noisy bird, I tried a similar method in solving a minor disagreement with a friend. I circled around the discord, flapped my mouth, and complained about it to others. That really did not produce any lasting effect. I learned I have three options: First, walk off, procrastinate, and let the spat keep us further apart; second, "crow" about it to whoever may listen and suffer the consequences; or third, take a deep breath and pray about it.

Eventually my friend and I, with God's help, confronted the problem and resolved the conflict. Just like the crow, I learned all that squawking about a frivolous matter is for the birds. —Glenda Ferguson

Dear Father, my Mediator, forgive me when I permit trivial matters to derail my loving relationships with others, and let Your gracious mercy intercede and restore unity.

MAY 22

Leader of the Pack

Lead me to the rock that is higher than I. For You have been a shelter for me.

—PSALM 61:2–3 (NKJV)

WHEN I WAS young, I had a small terrier-mix rescue named Pepper, a vivacious ball of black fur. Even though technically she was the family dog, in my 6-year-old mind, I thought Pepper was exclusively mine. After all, she slept on my bed every night. I was in charge of feeding her and cleaning up after her, although in hindsight, I doubt that actually happened. Somehow I expect my mom did a lot more feeding and cleaning up than I ever did.

Because in my mind, at least, she was *my* dog, I didn't understand why Pepper faithfully followed my mom around all day—to the kitchen, the laundry room, the living room, her bedroom. Wherever Mom went, so followed Pepper. It didn't seem fair. Why did Pepper look to my mother for guidance when she was my dog?

Of course, now that I'm not only the mother of three but also a grandmother of three, with two dogs and two cats, I understand what it means to be the leader of the pack. Though dogs are no longer considered pack animals in a strictly survival sense, there's still a social aspect. They enjoy spending time with their leader. That would be me. Our dogs always follow me wherever I go, and usually the cats do as well, though they'd never admit to wanting to be in any way social. I'm the one who feeds them, cares for them, and keeps them safe. They both love to play with my grandchildren, but they never take their eyes off me.

As the Good Shepherd, Jesus is the leader of my pack. I'm so grateful to be able to point the way for my children and grandchildren to discover the One who feeds us, takes care of us, and keeps us safe. —Deb Kastner

Lord Jesus, thank You for leading my pack and taking care of all our needs.

MAY 23

Grateful Pigeons

Rejoice always, pray continually, give thanks in all circumstances; for this is God's will for you in Christ Jesus.

—1 THESSALONIANS 5:16–18 (NIV)

MY DOG PETEY barks at pigeons. This is curious, because he isn't bothered by any of the other birds at the feeder. He quietly watches the finches, sparrows, and blue jays. But whenever he sees a pigeon, he jumps at the window and tries to scare it off.

Me? I give thanks for pigeons!

The other day I was enjoying the fresh breeze on the porch when Petey started barking. Sure enough, four plump pigeons sauntered by. "Thank You, God, for these beautiful birds," I said. Yes, beautiful. I love their bright orange feet and the pretty iridescent band of green around their necks. I also love their slow and steady walk, their heads bobbing as if in time to music. And the pleasant cooing sound they make—a gentle, trilly sort of song.

Most of all, I love the way they hang around at the base of the bird feeder, pecking at the seeds. I've never seen them compete for a perch above or try to fight off an interloper. They are happy with what falls to the ground. With every little peck, peck, I feel a special message, just for me—"Don't compete with others. Be thankful for what you have!" I may not always remember to be grateful for the little things, for that which seems like crumbs on the ground. Or for the times that are lean and I desire more. But I can be grateful that I am provided for by a good and loving God. He has bestowed His blessings upon me.

As I continued to relax on the porch rocker, I heard that funny, sweet cooing noise again. I turned to see a particular friendly avian fellow under the feeder. Was he cooing his thank-you? I like to think he was.
—Peggy Frezon

Thank You, God, for all my many blessings, for the way You provide for my needs and never leave me. And for this humble bird, the pigeon, who reminds me to be grateful for even the little things.

The Hummingbird and the SWAT Officer

But the Lord *said to Samuel, "…The* Lord *doesn't see things the way you see them. People judge by outward appearance, but the* Lord *looks at the heart."*

—1 Samuel 16:7 (NLT)

I recently read about a Georgia man named Mark Cardenaz who, a few years ago, found an injured hummingbird near his front porch—some of the feathers on one of its tiny wings had broken off, and it couldn't fly. Cardenaz scooped the hummingbird up and took it into his home for the next 8 weeks—the time needed for it to molt its feathers and grow new ones—feeding it sugar and Pedialyte. Cardenaz gave him the hummingbird-appropriate name of Buzz, and in those few short weeks, Buzz became a member of the family.

By his own admission, Cardenaz is not someone you might look at and assume he'd be willing to nurse such a small creature back to health. But the tough, tattooed, and bearded ex-SWAT officer has a tender spot for animals. As Buzz regained his strength—and his feathers—he began to take short flights around the yard, eventually coming back to Cardenaz when he tired.

As winter approached, Buzz was ready to migrate south, and as Cardenaz watched him depart, he wondered if he'd ever see his feathered friend again. To his delight and surprise, Buzz returned to Cardenaz the following spring—and landed in his hand! And he returned for the next four years. Skeptics might question how Cardenaz could know it was the same bird, but Cardenaz dismisses their disbelief: "Random hummingbirds don't land in your hand."

The story made me think of Paul's reminder to honor one another and to show hospitality and love in Hebrews 13:2 (ESV): "Do not neglect to show hospitality to strangers, for thereby some have entertained angels unawares." "Angels unawares"—unassuming people we meet who just might be angels. Like Buzz, I've experienced the kindness of strangers. They surely seemed heaven-sent when they aided or cared for me, and I wouldn't be surprised if some of them were angels. Since God sometimes uses the most unlikely people to help, I want to avoid making assumptions about others based on their outward appearance—and see their hearts instead. —Jon Woodhams

Surprises are everywhere in life. And they usually come from misjudging people for being less than they appear.
—Brownell Landrum

Dining with Deacon

Create in me a clean heart, O God; and renew a right spirit within me.

—PSALM 51:10 (KJV)

DO YOU REMEMBER how Deacon would walk along the edge of the wall when we were eating in the dining room?" We were having a family dinner, and my in-laws were recounting their memories of their beloved dog Deacon. Because their previous dog had a habit of jumping and hitting your arm while you were eating, when they acquired Deacon, they decided to proactively prevent any bad habits like that. They had disciplined him to not enter the dining room while the family was eating.

"Over the years, he interpreted our rule that as long as he didn't walk on the center of the dining room carpet, he was not in the room," my father-in-law explained. "He would enter the room and slink along the edge of the carpet, rubbing against the baseboard. He would come in through the kitchen and hug the wall until he traveled through to the other side door."

As we laughed at the antics of Deacon, it caused me to think about how I have interpreted some of God's rules. How many times have I skirted along the edge, thinking that I would be OK if I didn't actually enter into an active sin. *God would not notice. Surely He wouldn't mind those little white lies that didn't hurt anyone? Wasn't it OK if I silently grumbled and complained while I helped another person? That person wouldn't know my thoughts or heart? After all, I did help out.*

But of course God noticed! When I try to sneak past what God desires for me, I am only deceiving myself. Like Deacon, I need to be reminded of God's rules: to love Him with my whole heart, mind, and soul and to love my neighbor as myself. —Virginia Ruth

Holy Spirit, create in me a clean heart—one in which my thoughts and actions are fully God's. Amen.

MAY 26

Standing Attentive at the Bush

"Do not come any closer," God said. "Take off your sandals, for the place where you are standing is holy ground."

—EXODUS 3:5 (NIV)

MOM, I FOUND these weird bugs on the bush in the yard. They are blue, black, and orange, like caterpillars but with six legs."

As detailed as my 10-year-old son's description was, I had difficulty picturing what he was explaining. I followed him out to the front yard to investigate the strange creatures. True to his description, strange bug-like creatures crawled all over the leaves of our bush. We also discovered tiny hatched eggs clinging to the leaves, along with small, stationary orange pods. Pulling out my magnifying glass and holding it over one of the creatures, we could also see other nearly microscopic green creatures. With some research, we discovered that we were observing ladybug larvae snacking on aphids, tiny sap-sucking insects. We watched our bush over the following week, witnessing the entire life cycle of ladybugs, including seeing the adult insects newly hatched from their pupa state.

In the preceding weeks, I'd been lamenting that my fascination with nature felt like work. As a naturalist and nature teacher, hikes and explorations often involve lesson planning and presenting. I love my work, but I'd been yearning for the joy of pure discovery—to revel in the wonders of creation and tap into the childlike awe of finding something new. My son gave me that opportunity by welcoming me into his wonderful discovery. Although my bush was filled with beetles and larvae—not fire—I felt a bit like Moses, as if God had used something as unexpected as a bush to get my attention. Observing the intricate systems and details of a ladybug's life cycle, I remembered the God of Abraham, Isaac, and Jacob, the great I Am who created the vast universe and the tiny creatures that fill it with wonder. —Eryn Lynum

In all things of nature there is something of the marvelous.
—Aristotle

MAY 27

The Rebel

I have strayed like a lost sheep. Seek your servant,
for I have not forgotten your commands.

—PSALM 119:176 (NIV)

WHILE ATTENDING A writing seminar in Burtigny, Switzerland, I went out for a morning walk to enjoy the crisp air and the jingle of cowbells. The seminar took place at the Youth with a Mission (YWAM) base in a small farming village, so cows were part of the landscape.

On my way to a walking path, I saw a black-and-white cow standing all by herself. I strolled over for a closer look. A small section of the fence had fallen, but she was oblivious to it, perfectly happy to be away from the herd.

I said hello to the pretty Swiss cow and took a picture of her, hoping she wouldn't escape by way of the broken fence. Then, out of nowhere, one of the young YWAM workers ran over. She clapped her hands and in French gently shooed the cow back to the pasture. The cow lumbered back to where she belonged. I imagined her grumbling, *Aw, man. I was having so much fun.* But she was safer in the pasture than hanging out alone by a fallen fence.

I often joke that God has always kept me on a short leash. Though it would be tempting to brag that I've never been the type to rebel, as I look back on my life, I see a pattern of occasionally wanting to go in a direction that wasn't good for me, only to have God gently coax me to where I belonged. Sometimes redirection felt like Him taking me away from something exciting or fun, until I looked back on the whole picture and saw His kindness in it. Like that Swiss cow, I am just as prone to wander as anyone, but I have a loving Father watching out for me, ready to hold me back from wandering too far off His course. —Jeanette Hanscome

Prone to wander, Lord, I feel it,
Prone to leave the God I love;
Here's my heart; O take and seal it;
Seal it for Thy courts above.
—Robert Robinson

MAY 28

Completing the Ambience

So all of us who have had that veil removed can see and reflect the glory of the Lord. And the Lord—who is the Spirit—makes us more and more like him as we are changed into his glorious image.

—2 CORINTHIANS 3:18 (NLT)

OUR HEADLIGHTS STRAINED to cut through the fog as we drove the country roads near home. Peering out the passenger side window, I noticed large black blobs in the field.

"Phooey! Rotten fog! I can't see the cows' ears or their eyes! It's like when we're spotting deer, and the light's too dim to see theirs." I humphed.

My husband turned his head a moment, raised an eyebrow, and laughed. "You're silly!"

"You don't understand. Their ears are the perfect shape! They complete their…their…their ambience!"

At that, my long-suffering husband roared in laughter. Honestly confused, I asked him the reason for his mirth. I mean, anyone knows cow eyes and doe eyes bring gentleness and calm to the spirit of the onlooker.

"You and your choice of words," came his reply.

Oh…my words…again. I'd gotten used to Kevin and our daughters shaking their heads over my word choices. Seeing several deer in a meadow brought out "creation's scenes of serenity." A pair of squawking crows? Why, a "cacophonous cantata," of course. And a plethora of birds…a "winged kaleidoscope."

As we continued down the road, my eyes strayed back to the hazy cows. I turned to Kevin and asked, "Well, what completes *your* ambience?"

Ah, a question I should ask myself too. Indeed, a doe's eyes may fulfill the delicate peace their visage hints at, something I feel the Creator made them to do. But what about me? What ambience does Jesus want me to exude? And what can I do to complete it? —Cathy Mayfield

Father, if my ambience is to exude acceptance, grant me smiles of encouragement. If love, grant me arms to hug. If joy, let my laughter ring out. And if someone needs to laugh, whisper a "choice of words" to produce a belly full!

MAY 29

Hummer Dancing

But as it is written, Eye hath not seen, nor ear heard, neither have entered into the heart of man, the things which God hath prepared for them that love him.

—1 CORINTHIANS 2:9 (KJV)

I LOVE HUMMINGBIRDS. FOR me, these tiny birds are proof that God works wonders. Hummingbirds seem supernatural, with their iridescent feathers and ability to hover and fly backward in search of nectar. Where I live in the Pacific Northwest, hummers tend to be rufous or red-throated Anna's, which stay year-round. I planted red flowers and feeders to attract them and any of their hummingbird friends.

One of my sons has acute senses, including hearing, due to his autism. This means that he hears everything before anyone else. Hummingbirds' high-pitched wingbeats alert him before he sees them. He always yells for me to come, but I seem to show up after they've flown away.

One afternoon in late spring, my son hollered, "Mom! Quick! Hummers!" I tossed down the book I was reading and ran to the patio door. But as I stood next to my son, I saw and heard nothing. I started to head back inside, but my son grabbed my arm. "Be patient," he said. "There's an Anna's female, see? Right up there in the branches. See her small reddish throat patch?" I squinted but saw little except the neighbor's cherry tree. My son added, "The males will be back."

We stood for several moments, shading our eyes from the setting sun, listening. Suddenly, my son's face lit up. "Here they come," he announced. Sure enough, two beautiful Anna's males flew into view seconds later. The male birds, with their more pronounced red throat, or gorget, showed off for the drabber female.

My son said, "They dance for one another. And for God." While autism spectrum often leads to challenging social interactions, my son was relaxed with hummingbirds and their secret language. We linked arms, thanked God, and watched the hummers dance. —Linda S. Clare

Lord, help me to watch for chances to dance in praise to You.

Persevering when the Waves Knock You Down

Blessed is the one who perseveres under trial because, having stood the test, that person will receive the crown of life that the Lord has promised to those who love him.

—JAMES 1:12 (NIV)

DAVID AND I saw the large walking whelk as we strolled along Driftwood Beach on Jekyll Island in Georgia. Anxious to get a close-up video to show our 4-year-old grandson, Benaiah, I approached the edge of the water. "Too close," I said to David when I saw the hermit crab's legs disappear, and the whelk shell, the discarded home of a sea snail, come to a halt in the sand.

My biologist husband gingerly picked it up, turning it slowly so I could show Benaiah the hermit crab peaking from the opening. David replaced the shell, and we stepped back to keep watching.

Soon, the shell appeared to be walking on its own again, but the next wave rolled it over. We saw legs floundering about until another wave tumbled the shell upright, and again, our new friend kept moving forward.

As I watched the hermit crab persevere, I couldn't help but think about my mom's newest challenge with macular degeneration. Just a couple of days before my husband and I escaped to Jekyll Island for an overnight getaway, the doctor informed my mom and me that her eye disease had progressed enough that she could no longer drive.

Discouraged but taking it in stride, Mom accepted the change, anxious to discuss a new routine as I delivered her safely to the home where she lives alone, just 7 minutes from my house.

When the waves of this world knock me down, I certainly hope I can persevere like that hermit crab and my 83-year-old mom. I know I'll need God's help to do so. —Julie Lavender

Walk of Faith: *Who do you know who needs encouragement to persevere through a difficult situation? Make time this week to share words of encouragement through a phone call, text, email, or card. What can you also do physically that will help your friend during their time of need?*

Broken Beauty

Therefore we do not lose heart. Though outwardly we are wasting away, yet inwardly we are being renewed day by day.

—2 CORINTHIANS 4:16 (NIV)

THE BRIGHTLY COLORED anise swallowtail butterfly landed on a pale pink wild radish bloom several feet from me. It was a gorgeous spring day, and I'd decided to take a walk on the creek trail nearby in town. Now I was being treated to the sight of this striking yellow-and-black butterfly fluttering its pretty wings. Lifting my camera, I zoomed in to get a close-up shot of the butterfly. When I got home, I downloaded my pictures and looked them over on my desktop computer. The one I took of the anise swallowtail was beautiful. It was perfectly in focus, which allowed me to see that one of the wings was missing a large part of its distinctive tail.

The anise swallowtail had to have been in some kind of altercation to have lost a big chunk of its wing. Although it may have been impaired, it was still able to fly and navigate from flower to flower. The butterfly was beautiful in spite of its damage.

I think this is how God sees me. He sees all my imperfections, my brokenness, and my missing parts, and He loves me anyway. Like the butterfly, I, too, have had my share of altercations that took a chunk out of me—physically, mentally, and spiritually. Sometimes, in my human frailty, the damage has been self-inflicted through stubbornness or misplaced pride. Yet God doesn't cast me away as deficient and of no use to Him. Instead, He gives me what I need to carry on despite the damage. And even in my brokenness I can glorify God and His great and unconditional love. —Marianne Campbell

God loves human beings. God loves the world. Not an ideal human, but human beings as they are; not an ideal world, but the real world.

—Dietrich Bonhoeffer

June

JUNE 1

The Powerful Lion

Then one of the elders said to me, "Do not weep! See, the Lion of the tribe of Judah, the Root of David, has triumphed. He is able to open the scroll and its seven seals."

—REVELATION 5:5 (NIV)

MY YOUNG SON has always liked to feign terror when he sees a picture of a lion to get everyone laughing. But beyond the joke is a simple and universal truth: lions *are* terrifying. I was recently on a safari-style ride at a theme park when I had the opportunity to see two lions sauntering in the area. I'll be honest—even from the safety of the ride, I stiffened. The power of these magnificent creatures inspires respect.

While we commonly and rightfully associate the "Lion of Judah" with Jesus Christ, I recently learned that the symbol of a lion had been associated with the tribe of Judah long before Jesus walked the earth. In fact, Jacob refers to his son Judah as a lion cub all the way back in Genesis 49:9. Imagine what life must have been like, then, as an Israelite when Jerusalem was destroyed. Jerusalem was the capital of Judah at the time and likely a beacon for success and power. The lion, by all accounts, must have appeared fallen and even hopeless. Yet God was not done with His people. He was about to send a different type of lion—the Lion of Judah—to protect and redeem them.

Sometimes I forget God's power in my life. I fear Him out of worry rather than fearing Him out of reverence. But the same God who sustained Judah and brought about the redemption of the Israelites is the God who sustains and redeems me. I do not have to convince Him to be powerful or kind or good. He is already all of those things, and He ever lives to intercede for me. —Ashley Clark

Wrong will be right, when Aslan comes in sight,
At the sound of his roar, sorrows will be no more,
When he bares his teeth, winter meets its death,
And when he shakes his mane, we shall have spring again.
—C. S. Lewis

JUNE 2

Wonderfully Made

*I praise you because I am fearfully and wonderfully made;
your works are wonderful, I know that full well.*

—PSALM 139:14 (NIV)

AS THE WEATHER got warmer, my family welcomed a very pregnant robin outside our home. At first, my husband, Kyle, didn't like the idea of letting her nest where our family liked to walk past, play, or pass the time away.

When Kyle first attempted to move her nest, the robin came right back to the same spot above our front porch and rebuilt another. After he made a second and then third attempt to move her home, I shared with him that when a woman is in labor, she just wants to be comfortable. So I encouraged Kyle to support the robin by letting her stay put, and he did.

What happened over the next several weeks was a wonderful depiction of the awesomeness of Creator God. My husband took pictures of the nest, and the whole process of becoming a mama bird, to remember our visitor. We all read and learned about the specifics behind a robin laying her eggs and the things she—and the dad—go through until the chicks leave the nest. I soon realized that this bird graced us with excitement and curiosity, because I watched our children come home from school and smoosh their faces right up against the front window to watch nature unfold. And then, to our joy those little blue eggs cracked open and new life started.

Although the robins might have initially seemed like an inconvenience to the exterior of our home, I realized I had learned a springtime lesson about praising God for the gift of new life. I watched the mom and dad robin care for those little chicks with grace and love in a way similar to how God cares for His children. —Stacey Thureen

Heavenly Father, thank You for creating me. Remind me today of Your amazing care, loving-kindness, and grace toward myself and all Your children. Thank You that I am fearfully and wonderfully made in Your image. Amen.

JUNE 3

Hummingbird Doppelgänger

If you need wisdom, ask our generous God, and he will give it to you. He will not rebuke you for asking.

—JAMES 1:5 (NLT)

IT FLITTED THROUGH the garden. It hovered over a long-necked flower, extending its substantial tongue deep into the bloom to sip nectar. It was small and colorful.

"Oh, look, a hummingbird" quickly morphed into "Hey, that's not a hummingbird" and then into "Umm, what is it?" Fortunately, a local resident and frequent visitor to the garden spoke up and correctly identified what we had spotted.

This was the first time I had seen a white-lined sphinx moth. These moths often initially fool observers who think they must be a hummingbird. Both wings and body are covered with striking white, pink, and tan stripes. Adding to the confusion is their size. Their large wingspan (2 to 3 inches) is closer in size to those of hummingbirds than other moths. However, there are differences upon closer inspection—a plumper body, a long tongue that rolls up when not in use, and a tail that opens into a fan. And it's less attractive than a hummingbird.

Admittedly, my moment of bewilderment was trifling. So what if this creature remained a mystery to me? It's nothing compared to the confusing times in my life when the stakes are higher if I get it wrong, such as those related to relationships, finances, my future, and medical interventions. I stop to consider how I approach those situations and decisions. Do I waste days, even months, ruminating, worrying, and fretting in disquiet, or do I turn my uncertainty over to the God of all wisdom? Seeking God's perspective and guidance is the best way for me to navigate those troubling times and decisions.

That day in the garden, I was fortunate that someone could solve my confusion. Yet I'm more fortunate to have the Lord to turn to every time confusion comes calling. —Darlene Kerr

For the LORD gives wisdom; from his mouth come knowledge and understanding.
—Proverbs 2:6 (NIV)

JUNE 4

Slug Mama

But as many as received Him, to them He gave the right to become children of God, to those who believe in His name: who were born, not of blood, nor of the will of the flesh, nor of the will of man, but of God.

—JOHN 1:12–13 (NKJV)

MY THREE-YEAR-OLD GRANDSON Matthew and I had already had a busy day. We began by going to story hour at the library, stopped by the park to spin on the merry-go-round, and came home for lunch. After the required mac and cheese, we planted zinnia seeds and relaxed with refreshing apple juice ice pops.

Then Granddaddy called us over to check out his find. "Look, here's a slug."

I plucked off the violet leaf on which the slug rested and placed it in Matthew's hand. He watched as it stretched out, extending its body a full half inch, and surveyed its surroundings with tiny antenna-like tentacles. Matthew touched them and giggled when the slug immediately retracted the feelers. After observing for a few more moments, my grandson placed the leaf on the ground with serious care and said, "He needs to go back to his mama now."

Hmm. I'd never thought of slugs as having mamas.

Matthew's tender heart extends to all creatures. He helps his daddy carry twenty to thirty frogs from their pool to the pond every week. "They have to find their families," Matthew says.

I'm glad I don't have to search for my family. With God as my Father and other believers as my brothers and sisters, I'm surrounded by those who love me. My belief in Jesus's sacrificial death, burial, and resurrection assures me that I will always remain a child of God. As such, I try hard to imitate my Father by showing love as Christ did. That's the tender heart I hope to display. —Tracy Crump

Therefore be imitators of God as dear children. And walk in love, as Christ also has loved us and given Himself for us, an offering and a sacrifice to God for a sweet-smelling aroma.

—Ephesians 5:1–2 (NKJV)

JUNE 5

A Protector and Friend

The Lord will keep you from all harm—he will watch over your life; the Lord will watch over your coming and going both now and forevermore.

—Psalm 121:7–8 (NIV)

LAST SUMMER, MY husband had set a ladder against the side of our home to remove a satellite dish on our roof that we were no longer using. While climbing the rungs and getting closer to the dish and other materials attached to it, he noticed two large round eyes staring at him from inside a box that was part of the dish.

"Come quickly!" he said to me, as he slowly started backing down the rungs. "I think we have a new friend." I was gardening and looked up to see what he was talking about. Sure enough, a very small owl was tucked safely inside a part of the materials we'd intended to take out.

"Looks like we won't be removing this anytime soon," I said. That little owl had taken residence just outside our master bedroom window. Over the next few weeks, we would watch him come out and watch us. Most of the time he retreated into his hideout during the day. In the evening, he would climb out of his box and perch on a wire, awaiting dusk for his nighttime food search.

Just knowing I had this sweet owl outside my window made me feel safe and happy. Even though I couldn't see him, I knew he was there, protecting us from any vermin and happy to be near us like a dear friend. These lovely but simple attributes of the owl reminded me so much of our loving Father. We may not see Him and we may not know what He's doing, but He is our faithful friend, always watching out for us and protecting us. —Heather Spiva

Walk of Faith: *We have a Heavenly Father who is with us every step of our day and night, even if we can't feel or see Him. Choose to believe He is watching you and will keep you from harm. Have faith that He can be trusted.*

JUNE 6

Pack Your Trunks

Therefore, as we have opportunity, let us do good to all people, especially to those who belong to the family of believers.

—GALATIANS 6:10 (NIV)

MY HUSBAND SAID, "Come look at the news about these three elephants." Watching the television news report, from Tennessee, we saw local firemen escorting the three pachyderms out of the back of a semitrailer to the shoulder of the interstate. Thankfully no one had been hurt when the truck cab caught on fire as the trio was traveling from southern Indiana to Florida for the winter. The bystanders commented on how the elephants had behaved so calmly, even though all this took place in the early morning darkness. We watched as the news camera zoomed in on the threesome munching down on hay, their favorite snack.

I yelled, "I know those elephants!"

I recognized the three African elephants as residents from the nearby Elephant Encounter. When I stopped by last month, they were luxuriating in a bath, then children painted bright red polish on their oversize toenails. Each of the elephants has a distinct personality. Lou has a fondness for the ranch's spa routine, Lovie is known as the one-tusk jokester, and Makia rules as the matriarch. Those three grew up together, which created an unflappable bond that is beneficial during times of stress.

Preceding their trip, the elephants' caretakers, who were part of our church family, mentioned their trunks were packed, and all of them were headed for Sarasota. Our pastor led us in prayer for our friends' safety on the road and arrival at their winter residence. That included a ring of protection around the elephants.

When trouble strikes, I strive to be more like the elephants, bonding with those who support me. After a disappointment in my teaching career, I wanted to retreat into solitude. However, God has gifted me with a group of believers who have become a family, and my husband assured me the best course of action was gathering together with our Christian brothers and sisters. Through them, with God's guidance, I gained strength from our prayer circles. —Glenda Ferguson

Walk of Faith: *Think of three people from your church family who will surround you with love if you encounter a stressful situation. Thank God for those Christian brothers and sisters.*

JUNE 7

The Joy of Wildlife

Let the land produce living creatures according to their kinds: the livestock, the creatures that move along the ground, and the wild animals, each according to its kind.

—GENESIS 1:24 (NIV)

WE ARE FORTUNATE to own a three-season waterfront cottage in the Adirondacks, in Upstate New York. One of the best things about it is our nearness to wildlife. Every year, we see a surprisingly wide variety of animals without leaving our little half acre. Black bears, whitetail deer, coyotes, groundhogs, red and gray squirrels, skunks, great blue herons, turkeys, chipmunks, bald eagles, kingfishers, Cooper's hawks, turkey vultures, beavers, loons, snapping turtles, river otters, raccoons, mallards, mergansers, and Canada geese swim or wander by. Most are gone in minutes. But some, like the darling black bear cub who delighted us by lying under a tree for an entire day, stay awhile. Or the statuesque great blue heron who waded along our shore long enough for me to watch him spear a fish.

And these are just the animals I've seen. Others I have heard, like the unknown creature that woke me and my husband in the middle of the night screaming like a banshee. We thought it was a fisher but have since learned that it is more likely to have been a red fox.

"Come and see the works of God," says Psalm 66:5 (NASB), which resonates with me whenever I see or hear one of these wild animals. It's also why I spread the word to the rest of the family, saying, "Come and see." I want everyone to revel in the same wonder and gratitude I feel for the beautiful world God created and filled with such unique and diverse creatures. It always amazes me how each animal is perfectly designed to survive in whatever portion of the environment they occupy and how much their very presence enriches my life.

The Bible also uses the phrase "come and see" many times, as a reminder that we must first come to God before we can fully understand who He is. Just like His creatures, God's constant presence enriches my life. —Aline Alexander Newman

May all the animals of the earth, and the animals of the sky, and the animals of the sea be at peace. May they be free of hunger, may they be free of fear, and may their hearts and minds be calm.

—Daniel Kirk

JUNE 8

Outward Appearances

Do not judge, or you too will be judged.

—MATTHEW 7:1 (NIV)

AS I PLANTED flowers along the back fence, the aggressive barking coming from the other side caused me to jump. Up to that moment, I didn't know our back-fence neighbors had a dog. Staring at me with one eye pressed against a knothole in the fence was a gigantic black mastiff–Great Dane mix. She cast a large shadow. She jumped repeatedly. Her nails scraped against the wood. The force of her weight shook the fence. Speaking softly to her did no good. When her owner arrived to take her inside, I learned that her name is Basker, named after "The Hound of the Baskervilles."

Whenever I was in the yard, Basker barked, peered through the knothole, jumped at the fence, and clawed it. Things got worse once we brought our new puppy home. Each time Daisy went to the fence and whimpered, Basker barked and jumped. It wasn't long before both of them started digging under the fence. My fear for Daisy rose to the point of being afraid to leave her outside alone. Basker's size worried me. I didn't know what would become of our puppy if she got into Basker's yard.

Several months later, something that I wasn't expecting happened. The two dogs began racing up and down the fence line together. They were playing. Basker barked and jumped the whole way. She didn't bark to be aggressive. She barked to get attention. Basker was lonely. All she wanted was someone to play with her.

Basker is a massive dog with a fierce bark that jumps on the fence in a threatening way, but she's not a threat. After I got to know her, I discovered that behind her fierce bark, she's simply a lonely dog looking for a friend.

I think of Basker whenever I encounter Dell, a fierce-barking resident at the nursing home where I help lead a monthly church service. Perhaps, after I get to know Dell better, I'll discover that like Basker, behind her fierce bark she is simply a lonely person looking for a friend.
—Sandy Kirby Quandt

How easy it is to judge rightly after one sees what
evil comes from judging wrongly!
—Elizabeth Gaskell

JUNE 9

A Colorful World

By faith we understand that the universe was formed at God's command, so that what is seen was not made out of what was visible.

—HEBREWS 11:3 (NIV)

I STOOD WITH MY husband and young children beside the Gunnison River. We were hemmed in by the daunting 2,000-foot walls of the Black Canyon. It was hard to believe any large animals would call this narrow canyon, with its impressively steep hillsides and cliffs, home. And so I was surprised at my husband's exclamation, "There's a bear in the river!"

A large bear was wading in the waters on the opposite riverbank. We watched as it masterfully snatched a fish from the water and then ran up the steep hillside back into the woods with lunch clutched in its jaws.

Afterward, my husband commented on how light the bear's coloring was. We knew we have black bears in Colorado, but this bear looked brown. We mentioned this to the ranger behind the desk at the visitor center.

"Oh yes! That's our cinnamon bear. She has two cubs right now," the ranger explained. Now we understood we'd witnessed the mama sow catching lunch for her cubs. I'd never heard of a cinnamon bear. After some research, we discovered that the ranger and we were talking about the same animal, and that a cinnamon bear is a black bear. We also learned that black bears come in many colors, including cinnamon, blonde, silvery gray, and even white. These bears are known as "color phase" black bears. How creative God is. He dreamt up every color and then used those colors to add wonder to our world.

If I had seen the bear that day and settled on simply calling it a bear, I would have missed out on the wonderful discovery of color phase bears. Instead, by remaining curious, I discovered a creative Maker who splashes the world in color. —Eryn Lynum

Walk of Faith: *Go on a walk through a natural area and notice all the colors you see, particularly of creatures. Bring a notebook and record those colors in your own descriptive words.*

JUNE 10

Glorious Birds

For the eyes of the Lord range throughout the earth to strengthen those whose hearts are fully committed to him.

—2 CHRONICLES 16:9 (NIV)

WATCHING PELICANS SWOOP down to search inches from the ocean waves for their next meal mesmerizes me every time I am in Florida. One of my favorite pastimes is observing these birds and the skills they demonstrate. I often sit on our deck with my eyes glued to the water, hoping for a flock of pelicans to glide by. These astute fishermen not only fly effortlessly but can also spot their prey, dive in, pick up their meal, and carry it to a safe place to enjoy. No bait or expensive fishing gear needed. Man should be so clever.

I'd like to think that God also swoops down over the entire earth in the same way. I see Him with piercing eyes checking for that one person ready to meet Him in a more personal moment. And I see Him pluck that human up from the crowd and whisk that person into a personal relationship. I've had moments of deeper understanding when God has been close. Yet I fear I have missed chances He has given me to have more of those moments simply because I don't tune in to Him as often as I could.

Like the pelican after his prey, God is always alert to the opportunity to lift up and save us from our sin. He carries us to safety and fills us with His love. I hope I can become better at waiting and watching for His personal touch so I can experience more uplifting moments. —Linda Bartlett

Patience is learned through waiting.
—E'yen A. Gardner

JUNE 11

Aloha Cats

Where shall I go from your Spirit? Or where shall I flee from your presence?

—PSALM 139:7 (ESV)

CAT-SITTING FOUR KITTIES is a small price to pay for luxurious accommodations in Hawaii. Two of the cats turn out to be kittens who want to play all the time. On our first day of vacation, my daughter and I play with the kitties, then run off to enjoy the beach. On the second day, we play a little longer, then drive up the coast to a renowned outdoor market. After playing with the kittens until noon on the third day, we go in search of a coffee farm tour, where we find a feral cat who has adopted—or has been adopted by—the farm staff. By the fourth day, we decide we've had enough gallivanting, and we stay home with the cats. We play and throw treats, then we lounge around indoors, then outdoors, flanked by the kittens. We all settle down for a group nap in the afternoon before dinnertime. We feed the cats on the lanai, then take our own dinner out there too.

This trip has been in the making for a long time. After some arduous years of school, illness, and grief, we are finally celebrating something—my daughter's graduation. This is her dream trip, one that makes the exotic promise of sunshine, rainbows, sunsets, beaches, and more beaches. But it's the cats we are assigned to feed that capture our hearts. By the time we are preparing to leave, the cats—who have taken up residence in our half-packed suitcase, a protest against our departure—make it hard to say goodbye to Hawaii.

Our long-awaited trip is coming to an end. But at home, our own cat, Tango, awaits our return. She isn't quite as playful as the kittens, but she is just as glad to see us. —Susie Colby

Blessed shall you be when you come in,
and blessed shall you be when you go out.
—Deuteronomy 28:6 (ESV)

JUNE 12

Soft and Cuddly

For with what judgment you judge, you will be judged; and with the measure you use, it will be measured back to you.
—Matthew 7:2 (NKJV)

ON A RECENT visit to Honduras, I had the amazing opportunity to visit with and cuddle an 8-year-old sloth in my arms. Holding him was somewhat similar to holding a 1-year-old human baby, as he put his paws over my shoulders and snuggled his head under my chin. It was an absolutely delightful feeling, having this wild animal trust me so implicitly. I think he would have continued cuddling all day if I'd let him.

I'll admit I had some preconceived ideas about sloths. Watching them on television, I expected them to be ridiculously slow moving and not very responsive. My friend may not have been the fastest animal I encountered, but I didn't find him to be excessively slow either. He was also friendly and reactive. Another misconception I had was about a sloth's fur—that it would feel rough, pointed, and jagged—the way it looked on TV. I guess I was expecting to feel something like a porcupine. In truth, the sloth's fur was wonderfully soft and a joy to pet. I couldn't have been more surprised.

I made a lot of judgments about the sloth based solely on what I'd seen at a distance, and it made me wonder how often I do that with people as well. How many times have I made up my mind about someone before I really got to know them? I'm ashamed to say perhaps far too often.

Jesus knew humans would struggle with judging and He contained a warning in Matthew 7:1 (NIV): "Do not judge, or you too will be judged." Thankfully, Jesus accepts me when I fall and loves me regardless. —Deb Kastner

Lord, help me not to judge people before I get to know them.

Take a Chance on Me

God demonstrates his own love for us in this: While we were still sinners, Christ died for us.

—ROMANS 5:8 (NIV)

SOMEONE SAID THERE were shih tzus at the shelter, so there I was, being shown around the dog area by a staff member. A former neighbor's shih tzu had absolutely adored me (it was mutual), so that seemed like a good place to start.

It didn't take long to realize that no shih tzus graced the shelter. The other dogs either ignored us or lunged or barked at us inside their cages. Except one—a scruffy little dog whom the shelter folks had aptly named Shaggy. He'd been found wandering in a ditch somewhere, and he was dirty and unkempt, his black coat matted. By appearance alone, he had little to recommend him. But he had one major thing going for him: He, alone among all the other dogs, stood at the end of the cage, front paws against the mesh, looking intently at us, as if to say, "Pick me! Pick me!"

"Would you like to take him out to the yard?" the woman asked. She slipped a leash around Shaggy's neck. We reached the grass in the backyard, where Shaggy proceeded to do his business. He'd waited until he was outside—a very promising sign.

Long story short: Shaggy came home with me and became Windsor (it was the year of Queen Elizabeth's diamond jubilee, after all). A trip to the groomer revealed another surprise. Windsor was not a black dog—he was a gorgeous silvery gray. The hopeful clues I'd seen at the shelter about his house training turned out to be true. *Plus,* he doesn't shed. At all.

People who meet Windsor are astonished that he came from a shelter and not a breeder. He's a sort of designer dog—a schnauzer-poodle mix called a schnoodle, and he really has been The. Best. Dog. Ever. All because we took a chance on each other that day. —Jon Woodhams

Dear God, I thank You that You took a chance on me.
Thank You for adopting me into Your family. Amen.

JUNE 14

What Brings Us Joy

He who did not spare His own Son, but delivered Him up for us all, how shall He not with Him also freely give us all things?

—ROMANS 8:32 (NKJV)

I WAS DISAPPOINTED LAST year when the family of swallows that nested outside my window two springs in a row chose the roof overlooking our back patio as their seasonal home. Instead of waking me with joyful chatter, showing off their flying skills, and using my two birdhouses as play structures, this group made a mess on the patio and circled me and my parents whenever we went outside. I decided this little band of hooligans couldn't possibly be *my* swallows. Mom and Dad joined the neighbors in creating a harmless barricade to discourage them from nesting in the same place this year.

I missed my friendly family of swallows. It made me sad to have them nest in a place that made them a nuisance instead of welcome spring guests and to know my days of looking forward to their yearly migration to the spot outside my bedroom window might be over.

Then I returned from a trip to Ireland, jet-lagged and already missing the lush beauty of the countryside. As I rolled my suitcase toward the stairs leading to my room, Mom informed me, "Jeanette, you will not believe this. The swallows are outside your window again. Dad and I have been watching them all week."

I woke up the next morning to their chirps and chatter, sensing that God knew just when to send my little friends back to the place where they would be appreciated. They kept me entertained while I caught up on deadlines and smiling when my family had a stressful week. It seemed like such a little thing to get excited over, but the timing confirmed something God had been teaching me—that He knows and cares about my needs. The One who created the world and sent His Son to save it also loves us enough to send gifts of joy. —Jeanette Hanscome

Heavenly Father, thank You for providing not only for my needs but also for what makes me happy. You are such a kind Father. Amen.

JUNE 15

What's in a Name?

But now, this is what the LORD says—he who created you, Jacob, he who formed you, Israel: "Do not fear, for I have redeemed you; I have summoned you by name; you are mine."

—ISAIAH 43:1 (NIV)

LITTLE DID I know when I named my cat Rocky that in another year we would adopt a dog named Lucy. Of course, that meant that I'd have to rename my cat Ricky so that they could be known as the *I Love Lucy* team. Ricky sounded almost like Rocky, and as owners of two dogs called Cesar and Cleopatra in the past, Ricky and Lucy seemed like the logical names for the new pair.

"Oh, no, you don't," my husband said. "Rocky is Rocky."

"But Rocky doesn't answer to his name anyway," I argued.

It wasn't worth the fight, so I relented. But sometimes, just under my breath and not loud enough for anyone but a cat to hear, I still whisper RickRock, Rickster, or just plain Ricky. Rocky (aka Ricky) doesn't seem to mind or even notice. All he cares about is that his food dish is filled and his litter box cleaned.

On the other hand, people usually like to be called by the right name. That's why I think it's wonderful that God knows us by name (John 10:3) and in fact even knows the number of hairs on our heads. He comes to us personally no matter what anyone calls us.

RickRock comes when I use that name seemingly only if he's in the mood. I sometimes treat God like that—ignoring Him when He calls to me, whether to help in service to Him, to be more diligent in prayer, to read the Bible thoughtfully, or to just take time to listen for Him. While I love RickRock unconditionally, I'm overjoyed when he answers me by coming when he's called. Doesn't that sound a lot like God? Now I just need to be a little better at answering His call. —Linda Bartlett

A rose by any other name would smell as sweet.
—William Shakespeare

JUNE 16

Two Goats, One Good Friendship

Two are better than one.

—ECCLESIASTES 4:9 (NIV)

OUR FARM HAS been home to a number of Nigerian dwarf goats. The original two, Abraham and Amy, arrived with their names. Soon, the couple gave us triplets—daughters we called Rachel and Leah and a son we named...You guessed it!

Isaac, who's affectionately nicknamed Sir Isaac Neutered, is now 10. Except for him, all have returned to their Creator, the most recent being father Abraham.

Isaac mourned. Like other breeds, Nigerian dwarf goats prefer to dwell among their kind and are discontent being alone. Therefore, after Abe passed, we searched to find another goat. Within days, Carnival, who also came with his name, joined Isaac, settling in the grassy, fenced-in paddock shared with several varieties of laying hens.

Unlike Isaac, Carnival is all male, though there's little hope for him to ever sire children since we don't plan on breeding him. His high level of testosterone presents itself in an unpleasant odor. Hence, this newcomer has been nicknamed Smelly Nival, though he doesn't seem to mind.

Neither does Isaac. They're the best of friends—two kids chumming around, taking in the sunshine, and sharing grain poured into a common feeding trough each evening. Now and then, they might raise up to stand on hind legs before butting heads in playful banter, but it's never out of anger or jealousy.

Sometimes the wind blows a barn door closed, and the two are separated. I always know from the frantic bleating I hear all the way inside the house. I hike up to open the stall door, then offer them apple treats to celebrate their reunion.

Isaac and Nival remind me that I, too, was created for relationship. From the beginning, God planned this, fashioning humankind in His image that we might walk with Him as friends. Though sin separates, He's there to rescue—throwing open any door slammed shut to embrace me, reminding me whose I am.

Indeed, God called friendship good, even sending His only Son to demonstrate—to reconcile, reuniting us to Him.

And His name? It's Jesus, and He's my very best friend. —Maureen Miller

Kind Creator, thank You for the gift of friendship in its many unique forms!

JUNE 17

Where Is Your Focus?

I lift up my eyes to the mountains—where does my help come from? My help comes from the LORD, the Maker of heaven and earth.

—PSALM 121:1–2 (NIV)

MY PARROT AND Yorkie don't get along. Lorito, the parrot, bites at Minnie, the Yorkie, if she gets close, and Minnie barks at Lorito if he fluffs his feathers. For my own sake, I'm thankful they tolerate each other. In an attempt at fairness, I give Lorito his breakfast first in the morning, and I give Minnie her dinner first in the evening. I don't know if Minnie loves her dinner or loves that she's first, but she often finishes her last bite before Lorito even gets served.

One morning I sat in my quiet-time chair with Lorito on my shoulder. Minnie lay in her bed, and I called her to come. Minnie lifted her head and glared at who was sitting on my shoulder. I tried again. Her eyes remained glued to Lorito, and she refused to turn toward me. The third time I called for Minne, she finally broke her gaze from him to look at me. I called for her to come. She stood up, stretched, and walked toward me. I picked her up and set her on my lap.

As I snuggled Minnie close and gave her a back rub, I considered how difficult it was for her to turn away from Lorito and look at me. It reminded me that I often do the same. I can be so focused on my problems and plans that I don't turn to God. Thankfully, in His kindness and grace, He continues to extend the invitation to come to Him. —Crystal Storms

Jesus, help me to keep You as my focus and to magnify You and not my problems. You are my help and comfort. In You I trust. Amen.

JUNE 18

A Fish Story

The heart of the discerning acquires knowledge,
for the ears of the wise seek it out.

—PROVERBS 18:15 (NIV)

BROWN BULLHEAD FISH thrive in the cool Adirondack lakes near our seasonal cottage on the Fulton Chain of Lakes in upstate New York. Having gone there since childhood, I've seen many of the distinctive, medium-size dark brown fish, with their broad, flat heads. Bullheads scared me as a kid because of the long, sharp-looking dark whiskers around their mouth. Not until I grew up and began fileting them did I realize those sharp-looking whiskers, or barbels, are actually soft feelers that help compensate for the fish's poor eyesight. It's the barbs on their fins that you need to avoid—they really are sharp.

Then came one day last June. Two large bullheads were circling around in the shallow water at the foot of our dock. Not only were they mere inches from shore, but they stayed all day. *What on earth is going on?* I wondered.

Late that afternoon I saw it—a black mass, like an inky cloud, in the water between them. Itty-bitty baby bullheads! Probably thousands of them. I had never heard of fish pairing up and raising their young together. So I did some research and was fascinated by what I learned.

Bullheads build nests in shallow water underneath logs or other objects. This pair probably built one under our dock, unknown to me until the eggs hatched. But guess what? Bullheads, sometimes dubbed trash fish because they're bottom feeders, make excellent parents.

It turns out that Mom and Dad stay together building the nest, incubating the eggs, and guarding the babies until they're ready to leave the nest. Then the parents herd their clouds of offspring around until the babies swim off. The whole process can take a month. During that time, if a baby strays from the group, a protective parent will find it and bring it back in its mouth.

Seeing and learning about bullheads made me think about how ignorant I am of God and how much more there is to discover. Reading the Bible answers some of my questions, but there is so much I don't know and will never understand. For that I must rely on faith. —Aline Alexander Newman

The only journey is the journey within.
—Rainer Maria Rilke

JUNE 19

Groundhog Legend

All the ends of the earth will remember and turn to the LORD, and all the families of the nations will bow down before him.

—PSALM 22:27 (NIV)

AS I PULLED into the long driveway at my sister's house, I noticed an unusual creature slowly moving up the walk toward her front door. The round beast looked something like a beaver, but I soon learned it was a groundhog. As my friend Gary and I exited the car and followed it up the walk, the groundhog turned to acknowledge us. The furry mammal stood on its hind legs, measuring his height against our own.

With an unhurried wave of his front paw, he seemed to dismiss us, then lumbered off toward the side of the house. Gary followed in hot pursuit.

"We're here for lunch," I said, entering the front door.

"I'm back here," my sister replied. "I'm starting to get hungry, so you're right on time. Where's your buddy?"

"He chased the groundhog into the backyard. He wants to get a picture."

"Oh, that's Chuck. He's lived out back in the bushes for several years. Doesn't bother anything really. Chuck's a local legend. All of the neighbors see him walking back and forth from the woods at the end of our street."

I smiled and looked out the back window. My friend rapidly snapped photos, even trying to get a selfie with the famous Chuck. This made me think of earthly fame. It amazes me sometimes to see half-crazed fans crawling over one another to get a photo of their favorite sports star or music icon. They seem desperate to memorialize the occasion and pay homage to a personal hero. In my younger years, I might have been one of them.

Truly, only One is my hero, worthy of my adoration. God deserves awe for everything He is, from glorious sunsets to the very animals that capture our imagination. He loves us so much that He sacrificed His own Son for our eternal life. He's the only legend worth celebrating.
—David L. Winters

Lord, I worship You and give You the highest praise. You truly are the greatest.

JUNE 20

Watching for Birdies

When we heard of it, our hearts melted in fear and everyone's courage failed because of you, for the LORD your God is God in heaven above and on the earth below.

—JOSHUA 2:11 (NIV)

TIM AND I both enjoy watching for birdies, but in different ways. Since Tim is a golfer, a birdie means one stroke under par for a hole. For me, birdies are an abundance of my fine feathered friends visiting our yard. I especially enjoyed watching the pair of swallows that built a nest in the eaves of our garage. From ground level, I strained my neck to observe the graceful birds snatching insects midair. The aerialists performed with the greatest of ease, never bumping into one another.

Recently Tim invited me to watch the ladies' golf tournament at the Pete Dye Course, located on the highest elevation in our southern Indiana county. We walked up the steep hill and perched on the rock wall so we could observe the golfers on the green below.

I was somewhat interested in observing the ladies' golf skills. What really drew my attention, though, was a trio of swallows directly in my field of vision, swooping high above the golfers. The fliers' maneuvering would make a stunt pilot envious. From my vantage point, I couldn't help but marvel at God's winged ones against the backdrop of the brilliant blue sky.

My early perceptions of God was that He scrutinized me from above. I had the sense God looked down on me, so I always prayed up to Him. I thought since He resided in heaven, He didn't interact with me. Now I know that my God is "God in heaven above and on the earth below." He does not critically observe my life but rather guides me in the correct way I should go.

As we finished watching the golfers, Tim said, "That was an amazing birdie!" I thought so too—I had never seen swallows dive from this angle. Maybe the next time we visit the golf course, both of us will have an eagle sighting. —Glenda Ferguson

The only time my prayers are never answered is on the golf course.
—Billy Graham

JUNE 21

The Naked Stranger

Are not two sparrows sold for a penny? And not one of them will fall to the ground apart from your Father. But even the hairs of your head are all numbered. Fear not, therefore; you are of more value than many sparrows.

—MATTHEW 10:29–31 (ESV)

MY HEART SANK as I looked to the ground and spotted a nest lying on the wet grass. In a cup made of twigs and feathers lay a strange orange creature. He appeared to be only hours old, completely naked with his eyes tightly closed. The tiny bird wriggled energetically, trying to make himself at home.

I assumed the rain knocked down the fragile nest, so I scanned the area for the mother. She was nowhere to be found.

I felt powerless and wondered how I could save this innocent life. A young bird requires intense care—care I could not provide. I was on vacation away from home and my return flight would depart in a few hours.

I picked up the nest and gently rolled it, so the bird could lie comfortably in the center. I put the nest between two sturdy branches, guessing this was the safest place, the one Mama Bird would have chosen.

I pleaded with God to bring the mother back and commended the precious creature to His mercy and love. As I walked away with tears in my eyes, I said a prayer and trusted God to take over this situation.

World events and personal adversity often make us feel powerless. We hear about war and famine in distant lands and think there's nothing we can do. Sometimes we try to help. Other times, we shrug our shoulders and walk away, feeling guilty.

But we are not powerless. We are one with God and His unlimited might. Our job is to say yes to the actions the Lord calls us to do, including saving a newborn bird. —Sonia Frontera

Walk of Faith: *In times of trouble, offer up a prayer to God, listen for His wisdom, and then release your worries, knowing that He always acts for the highest good.*

JUNE 22

Take the Plunge

The fear of man lays a snare, but whoever trusts in the Lord is safe.

—PROVERBS 29:25 (ESV)

FIVE PEACOCKS, FOUR males and one female, were confused by a small gulley at the zoo. It wasn't a gigantic obstacle. The sides were only about 5 feet high and gently sloped. At the bottom ran a tiny stream of water, only about 1 inch deep and 3 inches wide. But the peacocks were clearly afraid of making the crossing. First one male would take a few steps down the side, only to retreat to the safety of the top. Then another male would make the attempt, only to retreat as well. Finally the female got tired of all the tomfoolery and hesitation. She took the plunge, racing down one side of the gully and up the other, and the males quickly followed.

It was funny to watch, but as I thought about the situation, I realized how like me it was. How often have I been hesitant to take the plunge and follow the quiet voice in my head urging me to try something new, whether taking a class, visiting a new place, volunteering at a place where I am needed, or asking a friend, relative, or neighbor if I can pray for them? It's easier to stay inside my comfort zone, even when I know the Lord is leading me elsewhere. Shakespeare put it this way in *Julius Caesar,* "There is a tide in the affairs of men,/Which, taken at the flood, leads on to fortune;/Omitted, all the voyage of their life/Is bound in shallows and in miseries."

I need to trust that the Lord is with me, follow that peacock, and take the plunge more often in my daily life. —Harold Nichols

You miss 100 percent of the shots you don't take.
—Wayne Gretzky

JUNE 23

June Morning

I will give you a new heart and put a new spirit in you.

—EZEKIEL 36:26 (NIV)

IT IS A warm, damp morning in June, and strawberries do not weed themselves, so out to the garden I go, weed bucket and trowel in hand. I had built raised beds in my garden, which make it easier to weed and water the berries, and now the deer don't have to bend over so far to eat. I am sitting on the edge of a bed, uprooting weeds, lifting berries off the sandy soil and propping them up on pillows of straw, when I spy an intruder. It is a gastropod mollusk—a snail. He is munching on a strawberry. Studying the little fellow, I find myself thinking: *He's just earning a living, doing what comes naturally. He has the right to exist. He probably serves some important ecological purpose, although I can't imagine what it is.*

I used to think that snails shed their calcium carbonate shells as they grew, the way snakes shed their skin. But no, snails keep the same shell for their entire lives. But the shell gets harder and harder as they age. I am afraid, sometimes, that something similar is happening to me. That is, the older I get, the harder I become—intolerant, inflexible, unsympathetic. I am too quick to find fault, too slow to forgive. I am reluctant to give others the benefit of the doubt. I never used to be this way. When did I become so hard? Lord, soften me. Help me not to be so hard on others and even on myself.

Snails do not elicit in me the "yech" response that they arouse in others, but I'd rather this fellow dine somewhere other than in my strawberry patch. I put him in the bucket, along with the weeds. Later, I'll toss him in the compost pile. He can eat there to his heart's content. —Louis Lotz

Soften my heart, O God. Rebuke me when I am intolerant and closed. Give me a new heart that accepts Your grace and forgiveness and extends it to others. Amen.

Never Easy, Always Good

Be on your guard; stand firm in the faith; be courageous; be strong.

—1 CORINTHIANS 16:13 (NIV)

WHEN MY BROTHER suggested a motorcycle tour of the fabled Route 66, I went right out and bought a bike, the first I'd owned since high-school days.

While you never forget how to ride a bicycle, I'd forgotten most of what I knew about piloting a motorcycle. Shifting, leaning, and navigating road hazards were all skills I had to relearn. Fortunately, I had several months to practice before our end-of-summer tour.

On a trial run through rural Ohio, I found myself relaxing on the bike. It was a fine day, and the wooded landscape and gentle curves of a county road made for a fun time.

Then, a deer.

She darted across my path, leaving me just enough time to grab the brake lever with one hand and mash the pedal with my right foot. The bike skidded to a stop, narrowly missing the deer's waving white tail as she dashed into the woods.

That evening, I returned home and considered my situation. I'd been a little zoned out, enjoying the sunshine. That was my fault. But riding is inherently dangerous. Potholes, gravel, rain, other drivers—even animals—threaten your safety. It's impossible to reduce the risk to zero. Was it worth risking my brittle bones on a long summer ride? I realized that two things are true about motorcycling. You must be alert at *all* times. And you must be willing to accept some uncertainty.

Following Jesus is the same. No one can make it perfectly easy for you. Opposition and temptation can appear at any time. You must be vigilant. And you must be prepared to accept the difficulties that come with this trying but rewarding life.

I took that ride with my brother. We had the time of our lives. I'm so glad I pushed through the fear to do something worthwhile. —Lawrence W. Wilson

Lord Jesus, You call me to travel an exciting and difficult path. I'm often tempted to turn back. Give me the courage to get back in the saddle every day.

JUNE 25

Uniquely Called

Before they call I will answer; while they are still speaking I will hear.

—Isaiah 65:24 (NIV)

MY DAUGHTER, AVERY, became fond of horses after talking about them with a neighborhood friend. That girl took horseback riding lessons, and the details of those interactions caused Avery to play with her horse dolls even more. She also became curious about meeting them in real life.

So for her birthday, my husband and I let Avery have a horse party. She invited a half dozen of her closest friends to join her on a trail and arena ride. With all the details in place, waivers signed, and a horse-shaped cake from the grocery store, the girls were ready to have fun. Everyone met at the stable, where they were fitted with a helmet and then greeted the horse they would be with for the allotted time. Each horse had a unique personality. It was fun to witness the girls ride a horse that directly suited their own qualities and characteristics. For example, one horse was very silly in its mannerisms, which completely suited Avery's friend who was an only child with a lively personality.

What struck me about the horses was that while they each had their own way of handling themselves, they knew to listen for the main instructor's voice. Each horse responded to the sound of the person calling for them and could pick it out from all the other noises around them. Witnessing the instructor interacting with the horses reminded me of how God has made me unique and calls out to me. Sometimes I'm caught up in all the noise around me, yet when my Father calls, I can pick out His voice from all the others. I know God's voice, just as He knows mine. —Stacey Thureen

Walk of Faith: *What has God uniquely called you to do? Ask Him for the strength to take the next step in your journey with Him.*

JUNE 26

I Otter Know Better

Moreover, when God gives someone wealth and possessions, and the ability to enjoy them, to accept their lot and be happy in their toil—this is a gift of God.

—ECCLESIASTES 5:19 (NIV)

MY GRANDSON, NICK, and his mom, Heidi, often visit the beach near their family's Monterey, California, home. They typically have an extra hour before picking up Nick's sister, Sissy, from school, so they go watch the otters play. It's a favorite pastime of my daughter and Nick's. Armed with his mom's turquoise binoculars, he watches the otters and giggles at their antics. "I like that otter—he's so funny!" But Nick is so soft-hearted that his voice is edged with emotion, as if he is seeing a new baby and saying, "Aww, look how cute he is!"

Because of their thick whiskers, sea otters are referred to as "old men of the sea." It's said that no one can resist a smile from an otter, and their impish antics spark more smiles from onlookers. Beyond entertaining humans, they have important work to do: God created sea otters to keep the kelp beds in order so they don't take over the sea. He gave them the water to sleep, hide, play, and feed in. The Provider's plan is perfect.

Nick tells me that the otters' hair is so thick, it helps keep them warm. He explains how they sleep at night, all bundled up in what's called a raft, floating in the kelp, and how their babies lie atop their tummies. Again and again I'm inspired by Nick's anecdotes about the magnificent old men of the sea.

When I hear the stories from Nick, I'm impressed anew at God's flawless plan carried out by His animal kingdom. He created these hardworking, whiskered creatures not only to do His work but also to do it while bringing joy to others. They, like Nick, are teaching me about doing our Master's work with gladness of heart. —Cathy Elliott

They seldom reflect on the days of their life, because God keeps them occupied with gladness of heart.

—Ecclesiastes 5:20 (NIV)

JUNE 27

Perfectly Still

Six days you shall labor, but on the seventh day you shall rest; even during the plowing season and harvest you must rest.

—EXODUS 34:21 (NIV)

I PLANTED A FLAT field with pollinator flowers, laid out in 5-foot-wide strips with alternating strips left in the grass. Even though I plant this garden for my bees, I enjoy seeing the other insects that visit the variety of flowers it produces. While walking the strips, a rust-colored object caught my eye. It was a newborn fawn laying perfectly still and hiding in one of the densely flowered strips.

I knew my daughter was stopping by soon, so I waited until she came, then asked her to take a short walk with me and to bring her cell phone. She gasped when she discovered the fawn. It lay perfectly still as if frozen in place, only 3 feet away from us. Without disturbing it, my daughter took some great photos, and we both quietly walked away.

Although it looked abandoned and alone, the fawn was doing exactly what instinct and its mother taught it to do—be still. Fawns will spend most of their first days alone, even if they have a twin. The doe will hide them separately until they are strong enough to outrun danger. But in almost every case, the mother is close by and may even be watching over her young.

As we walked away from that fawn, I realized there have been times in my life when it appeared I had been abandoned and left all alone. The reality, though, is that God will never abandon me. Many times in Scripture, He reminds me that He will never leave me. Like the doe that stays close by, God is with me always, keeping a watchful eye on me and listening when I call out. My responsibility is to be perfectly still. —Ben Cooper

In times when I feel abandoned and alone,
reassure me that You are still on Your throne.
The only thing I need to follow Your will
is to quietly remain perfectly still.
—B. C.

JUNE 28

The Sound of the Crickets

If I speak in the tongues of men or of angels, but do not have love, I am only a resounding gong or a clanging cymbal. If I have the gift of prophecy and can fathom all mysteries and all knowledge, and if I have a faith that can move mountains, but do not have love, I am nothing.

—1 CORINTHIANS 13:1–2 (NIV)

ONE OF THE things I love about warm evenings is the sound of crickets. I like to sit on the patio as my dog smells the yard before bedtime and listen to the sound of crickets chirping. Sometimes it seems as though they're welcoming the evening, the dip in temperatures a sweet reprieve. Other times, their song blends into the evening—the sound so normal that it's easy to forget the crickets' presence.

The other day, as I was sitting outside and listening, it struck me that I rarely live without some kind of background noise. Sometimes I pay attention to the noise, as I do with the crickets, and other times I do not. Whether the television or the air conditioner, the songs of birds or the buzz of bees, a chorus of music sings.

The same can be said of my faith walk. Rarely do I walk in silence—in fact, something is almost always singing in my ear. The question becomes whether that sound is melodic or dissonant. Harmonic or discordant.

I have a responsibility to guard that sound and pay attention to the metaphorical song playing around me. Is it life-giving? Healthy? Lovely and pure? Or is it harmful to my mind and heart? Have I let discouragement and doubt, grudges and anger, all play notes I choose to ignore? I pray God's Holy Spirit produces a chorus of sweet melody in and through me, that I never become a "clanging cymbal" to the ears of those around me. —Ashley Clark

Father, make a sweet sound resound through my life. Show me any discordant influences I have allowed in my heart and mind that have thrown me off-key, and tune my heart by Your love to sing even as creation praises Your name.

JUNE 29

Riding the Storm

God is our refuge and strength, an ever-present help in trouble.

—PSALM 46:1 (NIV)

IT WAS A blustery day on the water. As I walked along the shoreline by the cove near our house, I noticed the outline of a solitary bird silhouetted against the gray sky. It was a red-tailed hawk drifting with the wind. I stood fascinated by his movements and the ease in which he allowed the gale-strength winds to move him along. The gusts would carry him off-course, then he would turn back and head where it seemed he intended. Each time this happened, he would fly a little bit farther. It was a back-and-forth movement, but eventually he appeared to get to where he needed to go.

His flight pattern reminded me of an emotional storm I had journeyed in years past—a broken engagement that left me alone in a foreign city. At the time, I thought that I was on the steady, predictable path of marriage and family. I'd met a man who swept me off my feet and with whom I planned a future. Sadly, the relationship did not work out, and I found myself alone. I was blown completely off course and onto a path that I hadn't intended or desired. Yet God in His mercy provided the means to move me forward even as I wove through the back-and-forth of life. I learned to be reliant on Him and His work in my life. I joined a church, met other singles, and eventually met my current husband there. We have been blessed with 32 years of marriage, two wonderful sons, and a daughter-in-law.

I learned that sometimes we have to go along even in a storm or in a direction that is not planned in order to end up where we need to be.
—Virginia Ruth

God of our troubled times, thank You for being our help and guide even when we are off course. Amen.

Putting in the Work

He who began a good work in you will carry it on to completion until the day of Christ Jesus.

—PHILIPPIANS 1:6 (NIV)

MY 8-YEAR-OLD SON, Nathan, sat down at the table beside me and sighed. "I hate cleaning my room. I've been working for hours, and it's not any cleaner than when I started."

I hid a smirk. "That's because you play with every toy before you put it away."

He ate a snack and then headed back upstairs. Moments later, he called, "Mom, come look at this!" I found him standing on the stairs, pointing at the ledge outside, right above our front door. There was a small pile of leaves on the ledge that I hadn't noticed before. Nathan gasped as a robin flew up, another leaf in her beak. "She's building a nest!"

Nathan was fascinated as he watched the mama bird leave and return with leaves and twigs, again and again. But after a while, he grew discouraged. "She's working so hard, but her nest doesn't look like it's getting bigger. Where will she put her babies?"

"Sometimes when we're working on something, it doesn't feel as if we're making progress, but we are," I said. "It might be slow, but if we keep putting in the work, we'll get there."

"I'm going to ask God to help the mama bird not give up," he said.

"You know you can ask Him to help you too."

Nathan headed back to his room, and I watched the mama bird for a while. Her hard work with not much to show for it reminded me of my own parenting struggles. My goal was to help my children become more like Jesus. It was a lofty goal, one I'd set for myself as well. But the progress was slow. I'm selfish by nature, and acting like Jesus is hard.

Days later, Nathan and I spotted four blue eggs in the nest we thought would never be finished. Just as the mama robin completed her important work, God would help me with mine. —Diane Stark

Lord, help me to trust You to finish the good work You've started in me. Amen.

July

Hole in the Trough

You earn wages, only to put them in a purse with holes in it.

—HAGGAI 1:6 (NIV)

WE LIVE ON an animal rescue farm. In summer, I fill the water troughs at night. When the day cools down, the water stays cool for quite some time before the summer sun warms it up. The horses love to drink in the morning, when the water is refreshing and clear.

For awhile I had been coming home to a completely empty trough and just attributed it to very hot days and very thirsty animals. It was always dark when I filled the tank, so I totally missed the tiny hole in its side that drained the water without my knowing.

One day, God spoke to me about this discovery. I felt Him telling me that some parts of my life had become like my water tank. I was overwhelmed, overworked, and overextended, yet I continued to fill my "tanks." I showed up late for appointments or forgot them altogether. I never got enough sleep. My eating was limited to what was open when I wasn't working. I just couldn't get ahead because there was a hole "in my trough," and no amount of replenishing my trough—me—could help.

The only way to fill the holes in our lives is with Living Water. When our lives are too full and unmanageable, we must be willing to examine them in the light so we can find the holes and ask God to repair them. Only He can fill what cannot be filled by anything or anyone else. Only then will we thirst no more. —Devon O'Day

Dear God, please find the holes in my life that deplete me and fill me completely me with Your living water.

JULY 2

Hiccups in Flight

But when you ask, you must believe and not doubt, because the one who doubts is like a wave of the sea, blown and tossed by the wind.

—JAMES 1:6 (NIV)

EVERY YEAR, MY kids and I would participate in the Great Backyard Bird Count sponsored by the National Audubon Society. While homeschooling, we found counting birds provided fun and education. For each count, we would choose one aspect of the birds to study, researching that trait for each species we saw.

One year, we studied flight patterns. Until then, I'd never noticed how various birds fly. Some fly straight, the basic beeline pattern. Some soar on the air currents in circular motions. Some dive, some wobble. But the ones we liked the best were the woodpeckers' hiccupping flight patterns.

From the tiny downy to the large pileated woodpecker, they all flew in an up-and-down fashion as they crossed the yard from the feeder to the trees. Seeing the little ones do so brought chuckles, but watching the 19-inch-long pileated woodpecker hiccup its way across our front yard turned those chuckles into full-blown laughter. Imagine watching a bird with a wingspan of almost 30 inches, its body undulating as though it was hiccupping while in flight.

Watching those woodpeckers reminds me of my chaotic lifestyle. I often feel as though I'm hiccupping through life—up one day while writing devotions, down the next when worrying about family needs, up for a birthday party, down with a stomach virus. Believing God's promises one minute, doubting His sweet love the next. Oh, that I would fly on a straight and narrow path, not letting hiccups overtake my faith. —Cathy Mayfield

Walk of Faith: *Either in your backyard or on a video, watch the flight patterns of birds and see which match your lifestyle—hiccupping with doubts like the woodpecker or circling endlessly like some birds of prey. Ask Jesus to help make today's flight be straight and true.*

JULY 3

Snail Races

And let us run with perseverance the race marked out for us.
—HEBREWS 12:1 (NIV)

GARDENERS STAY VIGILANT to keep slugs and snails from devouring tender plants. In response to slime trails, we sprinkle bait, spread diatomaceous earth, or resort to squishing to discourage these hungry mollusks. I've always hated to dispatch any of God's creatures, but a girl named Lucy showed me a better way.

While dealing with a rare medical condition, 8-year-old Lucy discovered snails. She kept one as a pet, naming it Beige Swirl, and even corresponded with snail aficionados. She learned that in Norfolk in the United Kingdom, folks hold a World Snail Racing Championship.

Lucy begged to go, but international travel wasn't possible for her. Then she discovered that pet snails are popular with autistic children and organized a snail-racing championship in our town.

Nearly 200 people attended. With numbers affixed to their shells, forty-six snail competitors lined up around a small circle in the middle of concentric circles. The humans timed how long it took any contestant to reach the outer circle. Believe it or not, some snails are faster than others, and one snail took the prize. Lucy's Snail Races is now an annual event. Her hobby distracts her from worrying so much about her medical challenges.

Because of Lucy, my garden now makes way for snails. I do admit to spreading snail repellent around my tender veggies, but instead of squishing snails, I relocate them. I feel better about being a good steward of the earth and letting the snails live to slime another day.

Lucy still keeps a pet snail named Cinnamon Swirl and dreams of traveling someday to the United Kingdom championships. I admit that banana slugs—the largest of them all—still make me shiver, but snails are rather cute. No matter how slimy the trail, Lucy and her snails inspire me to appreciate and be grateful for all God's creatures. —Linda S. Clare

Your speed doesn't matter—forward is forward.
—Wesley Snipes

Grateful for Freedom

For you have been called to live in freedom, my brothers and sisters. But don't use your freedom to satisfy your sinful nature. Instead, use your freedom to serve one another in love.

—GALATIANS 5:13 (NLT)

GREEN BEANS, SIMMERED for an hour in chicken broth and a tad of bacon grease. Two Crock-Pots of homemade macaroni and cheese, bubbling with butter, eggs, milk, pasta, and melted cheddar, Parmesan, and Romano cheese. A frosted, sugary sheet cake from the bakery section of a favorite grocery store because it was my daughter's favorite over a homemade one. Chips, dips, and chocolate.

The delicious smells permeated the inside of the van but didn't brighten my mood. It had taken such effort to get everything ready for the family celebration that would bring together three dozen adults and nine kids under the age of 7. Besides, the weatherman predicted it would be the hottest Fourth of July we'd experienced in years, with the heat index climbing above 100 degrees.

With less than 5 minutes to go of our half-hour drive to my brother's in the next county, a doe ran across the road. My husband slammed on the brakes, and I covered my eyes when a spotted fawn followed her steps.

Crock-Pots tumbled, green beans sloshed, and the cake slid. But fortunately, no animals or humans were harmed in the process. On the rest of the drive, however, I couldn't help but think about the freedoms I enjoy not just on holidays but every day. Although we might not be free to roam in the wild as those deer are, I can thank the people who lost their lives to afford me the freedoms I have today. Most important, I thank God for His Son, who came to earth to give me the greatest freedom of all—eternal life with Him as my Savior. Thank You, God, for freedom. —Julie Lavender

He left His Father's throne above,
So free, so infinite His grace;
Emptied Himself of all but love,
And bled for Adam's helpless race.
—Charles Wesley

JULY 5

Swaddled in Love

Love is patient, love is kind....It always protects.

—1 CORINTHIANS 13:4, 7 (NIV)

I'M NOT SURE exactly when the swaddling began, but it may have been on the Fourth of July. Fireworks popped and crackled in the night sky. Even with our doors and windows closed, we heard the bangs and booms. Our toy poodle, Stanley, ran for cover.

Since dogs have ultrasensitive hearing and he was so young, Stanley ran and hid behind the sofa. I scooped him up, snuggled him in my arms, and told him everything would be OK. Then I took a second step to comfort him by wrapping him in a soft velour blanket. Just under 4 pounds, Stanley was easy to swaddle and hold. I put him in his bed, and he stayed there until morning, when I unwrapped him.

This became a nightly tradition, and I remember the sounds Stanley made—like those of contentment and security—when I swaddled him and put him to bed. His face peeked out of the blanket as he laid his head into the softness of a small doggie pillow.

This tiny dog reminded me of an angel in his disposition and sweetness. Like people, dogs have personalities, too, and some people don't like to be fussed over, just as some dogs might resist over-fussing. But Stanley loved it, and I sensed that God was pleased I would tuck this gentle little dog in at night. When his dark eyes met mine, I think he was saying, "Thank you for your care for me."

Dogs protect us, and even Stanley's shrill little bark would alert my family if a stranger came near. But Stanley taught me that I should be a protector of *all* that God has given me, too, caring for His creatures great and small, in faithfulness and kindness.

Stanley went back to his Creator after 19 years. But my memories of this special gift from God remain—of one swaddled in a blanket and knowing he was loved. —Kathleen R. Ruckman

God requires that we assist the animals when they need our help.
Each being (human or creature) has the same right of protection.
—St. Francis of Assisi

JULY 6

The Light and Wings of a Firefly

You are the light of the world. A town built on a hill cannot be hidden. Neither do people light a lamp and put it under a bowl. Instead they put it on its stand, and it gives light to everyone in the house. In the same way, let your light shine before others, that they may see your good deeds and glorify your Father in heaven.

—MATTHEW 5:14–16 (NIV)

FIREFLIES. LIGHTNING BUGS. Glow worms. Depending on the area of the world where you live, you may call these little creatures something different, but their gentle glow is universally beloved. When the spring flowers have fallen from their buds and the temperatures have warmed, my favorite thing about the arrival of summertime is the return of the fireflies. I'll sit on my back patio with my dog each evening and wait in expectation for the fairy-dust glow across the trees.

I was out late last night with my dog when something on the ground caught my eye. A flicker—once, twice, thrice. When I stepped closer, I realized a firefly was resting on the grass beside me. I've since learned that female fireflies do this as they watch the males fly above. She must have noticed me and sensed danger, because she then quietly flew away.

I don't think I've ever seen a firefly so close-up before, and initially I was stunned by the experience. But then I considered what a perfect metaphor this encounter was for the life of the believer: Christ has given us both light and wings. I am to flicker His love in the dark world, and I am also given a responsibility to remove myself from dangerous places that hinder His light from shining. By setting boundaries with my time, my mindset, and my relationships, I allow His light in me to shine freely—and that is a beautiful thing. —Ashley Clark

This little light of mine, I'm gonna let it shine!
Let it shine, let it shine, let it shine!
—Harry Dixon Loes

JULY 7

Bear-Size Fears

The angel of the Lord *encamps around those who fear him, and he delivers them.*

—Psalm 34:7 (NIV)

When I was a kid, my family went backpacking in Canada's Banff National Park. We saw massive bear prints all along the way, and I remember putting my little hand up against the giant indentations while marveling at how big those bears must be. The second day into our trip, we made it to our destination and set up camp by a lovely creek that was on a bit of a slope. We ate our rehydrated dinner and headed for bed.

In the middle of the night, my mom woke me. "There's a bear!"

My senses blared. A bear was out there. Outside our tent. What could he be looking for? All the food swung high in a tree. Our backpacks were in the tents with us. So that only left…us! I shivered, and my ears strained as they listened for bear noises above the flow of the creek. Finally, exhausted, I fell back asleep, praying the bear didn't decide to come in for a snack.

The next morning, I mentioned the bear, but my mom looked at me, confused. "Mom, during the night you screamed, 'There's a bear out there!'"

She calmly replied, "No, I didn't. I said 'Get up here,' because you had slid down the slope."

Isn't it funny how sometimes we imagine the worst, causing our anxiety to build as we "awfulize" situations—or even make them up. As someone who struggles with anxiety, I've been guilty of overthinking, worrying endlessly, and wondering about all the what-ifs when I allow my fears to overwhelm me. My imagination runs wild in the same way it did so many years ago when I thought a bear was prowling around outside our tents. Turns out, I simply need to adjust my position so that I'm right in front of the Father, who knows all the details and who reminds me that whatever the situation, it's in His hands. —Kristen G. Johnson

Meet your fears with faith.
—Max Lucado

JULY 8

The Deer and the Hydrangea

When you send your Spirit, they are created,
and you renew the face of the ground.

—PSALM 104:30 (NIV)

SHE STARED AT me boldly as she chewed on my prized hydrangea's leaves. Three feet from my home stood the lonesome doe that roamed the backside hill.

For years, our garden had been ravaged by the herd of deer that invaded the yard. My husband painstakingly fenced the property hoping for glorious blooms. We scratched our heads wondering how the intruder outsmarted us again.

The doe remained indifferent as I chased her away, finally taking off after I performed an animated pantomime. I rushed to assess the damage. I felt infuriated to find a leafless shrub sporting a handful of flowers that survived the attack.

Weeks later, I looked out the window. The branches the deer had feasted on were bursting with life. Tender green leaves sprouted on the previously bare stems.

In spite of the "enemy" wreaking havoc in my garden, God's life and love continued to flow through His creation, restoring beauty and wholeness where devastation seemed to rule.

Isn't that just like our lives? Challenging or adverse events such as illness, loss of employment, or the death of a loved one can make us feel hopeless, depleted, and defeated. But God is constantly renewing us, His life and love supporting us and making us stronger.

I'm sure another deer will find my hydrangeas. But I trust that God will continue to show me how He renews life in the midst of adversity—and hungry deer. No situation is hopeless to God. —Sonia Frontera

Walk of Faith: *When life seems hopeless, instead of giving in to despair, turn within and identify the ways God is using your problems to help you learn and grow. Trust that His action plan is always at work in spite of negative appearances, knowing that something valuable will emerge out of the situation.*

JULY 9

A Foreign Language

Day unto day utters speech, and night unto night reveals knowledge.
There is no speech nor language where their voice is not heard.

—PSALM 19:2–3 (NKJV)

I NEVER KNEW BLACKBIRDS could be so beautiful until our family moved to a subdivision with two lakes inhabited by the red-winged variety. Accustomed to rather dull grackles and starlings, I was impressed by the flash of scarlet and gold bands across ebony black wings as these blackbirds took flight.

Though they don't travel in large flocks like other blackbird species, the red-wings do seem to congregate in family groups around the lake. And these robin-size birds demonstrate an amazing ability to perch on the smallest tuft of water plant that seems too flimsy to bear their weight.

While I admire the red-winged blackbirds, my husband has a different view. On his bike ride every morning, Stan pedals down the levee where a lone red-wing sits atop a light pole and scolds my husband with a harsh *chak-chak-chak*. We've both been similarly admonished on our evening walks. I've even seen a couple of these brave birds chase off a great blue heron, many times their size. Though we don't speak red-wing, their meaning is clear: Stay out of my territory!

I really don't mind. Their speech is all part of God's creation, declaring the glory of His handiwork. In their song, I hear God's voice, sometimes correcting but more often comforting or uplifting me or instilling in me wisdom to equip me for another day. All I have to do is listen for it.

However, unlike the blackbirds, God doesn't tell me to stay away. Instead, He wants me near, for I'm part of His creation too—a part He loves and cherishes. —Tracy Crump

Walk of Faith: *Take a few moments to sit outside, close your eyes, and immerse yourself in the sounds around you. Listen for God's voice. Keep your heart open to His instruction, His love, and His peace.*

JULY 10

Infinite Possibilities

For nothing will be impossible with God.

—LUKE 1:37 (ESV)

I PULLED THE SHEET up over me in the stifling, un-air-conditioned 1970s summer heat. The window was open in a futile effort to catch a nonexistent breeze. Despite the swelter, I was covered in goose bumps—not from cold but from a shiver of fear that ran up and down my spine and spread to my extremities. I ventured a timid glance at the window near the foot of my bed, which glowed slightly from the streetlight at the nearby intersection. Wait! Did that shadow just move? Was that a twig snapping? *Was something peering in my window?*

When I was in junior high, a slew of sensational pseudo-documentaries was released—both on TV and in the movies—about unknown creatures. My best friend and I had gone to see an awful low-budget movie at our local theater about a cryptid monster terrorizing a group of Boy Scouts camping in the woods. Afterward, I was both fascinated by and fearful of—or at least creeped out by—this mysterious hominid creature, known in popular culture as Bigfoot or Sasquatch. And now I was sure he was peeking in my bedroom window!

Of course, nothing was at my window that night. (Right?) But Bigfoot had captured my imagination, and although I'm embarrassed to admit it, he still does. If a supposed sighting makes the news, I immediately find the video online—shaky, blurry, distant, dark, inconclusive—of some unknown creature (or someone in a gorilla suit) walking briskly away from the camera.

Silly, I know. But while I won't say I believe, I still like to hold out the possibility that Bigfoot might exist. After all, scientists are finding new species of creatures all the time. Who's to say there isn't one out there that walks on two legs as we do? Who knows what wonders still await discovery? After all, nothing is impossible with a Creator who continually shows us glimpses of the infinite possibilities of His exuberant, lavish creativity. —Jon Woodhams

Dear God, may I never forget that with You, nothing is impossible, for You are able to do immeasurably more than all I ask or imagine. Amen.

JULY 11

Little Swimmers

We who are strong ought to bear with the failings of the weak and not to please ourselves.

—ROMANS 15:1 (NIV)

ON A BEACH vacation, my wife spied a poster from a conservation center advertising the release of baby sea turtles. "Sounds like fun," I said. "I've always wanted to see how they make their way out of the sand and into the surf." We decided to check it out.

Arriving at the site, we found a spot along the roped-off area, right near the shore. We'd have a perfect view of the turtles making their way from the release point to the water, a distance of at least 30 feet. Before long, park employees emerged from the turtle tent, each holding a young turtle.

I nudged my wife. "Let's see how fast they can run."

But they didn't run at all. They didn't even walk. The turtle bearers carried their treasure all the way to the ocean, waded in about knee deep, and gently lowered the turtles into the water. They swam as if they'd been doing it forever, and quickly disappeared into the emerald-green bay.

"Whaaat?" I said. "I thought the whole point was to watch them race to the ocean."

It wasn't, of course. The babies had been hatched in the conservatory precisely because of the danger they'd face on a beach filled with tourists. The point wasn't for the turtles to entertain us. It was for us to see them safely into their forever home—and to learn something in the process.

I remember those turtles every once in a while, usually when I find myself frustrated with other people at church or at work or even in my own family. Most often it's not because they're trying to be rude or troublesome or disappointing. Maybe they've simply had a bad day or received some bad news or been wounded by life. It isn't their job to make my life easier. It also isn't their job to make my life complete. Rather, they are my opportunity to lighten someone else's load. —Lawrence W. Wilson

Lord, place a helpless baby turtle in my path today. And help me not step on it.

JULY 12

Bumblebee Play

A cheerful heart is good medicine, but a crushed spirit dries up the bones.

—PROVERBS 17:22 (NIV)

IN LIFE, PROUST said, we end up doing whatever we do second best. If flower gardening is what my wife, Mary, does second best, I can't imagine what she does even better. She really is quite good.

Just now I am on my morning walk, strolling among her flowers. Enormous white peony blooms, as big as babies' heads, are nodding in the breeze, and beyond them is a rainbow swath of primrose freckled with pink poppies. There is a plastic pinwheel stuck in the ground—one of those whirligig thingamabobs that spin when the wind blows—and sitting on one of the plastic wings, spinning gently in the breeze, is a fat bumblebee. I nudge him onto my finger, but he promptly turns around and walks back to the pinwheel.

Watching him go slowly round and round, I recall reading a magazine article about an experiment with bumblebees. Researchers presented captive bumblebees with two pathways to a food source. One pathway was unobstructed; the other pathway led to the same food source, but it contained a number of small plastic balls. Throughout the experiment, the bumblebees consistently chose the latter pathway, rolling the balls on the way to the food source, then rolling them again on the trip back. Studying this amusing behavior, researchers could think of only one explanation—bumblebees like to play. Maybe that's what that little guy on the pinwheel was doing—playing.

I work, I study, I exercise, but I don't play much. I need to be more playful, more fun-loving. Just now there is a tap at the window. Mary waves at me and blows me a kiss. I catch it out of the air, plant it on my cheek, and swoon with great exaggeration, touching the back of my hand to my brow. She laughs and claps at my performance, and I bow. Now that was fun. —Louis Lotz

Gracious God, let me never become so stressed and so serious that I lose the sheer joy of existence and the happiness of being numbered among Your children. Amen.

JULY 13

Surprise!

This is the day the Lord has made; we will rejoice and be glad in it.

—Psalm 118:24 (NKJV)

ONE SUMMER MY husband and I took a road trip to Utah to visit the Golden Spike National Historical Park, where we planned to watch a reenactment of the 1869 ceremony that completed the construction of the transcontinental railroad. On the way, we had an unexpected surprise: a cornfield filled with hundreds of maroon-colored birds with long curved bills and bright red legs. The sight took our breath away.

A quick consultation with our birder's guide revealed that these were white-faced ibis. But what were the large wading birds—their feathers glinting green and purple in the sunlight—doing out here in a high-country cornfield? We had no idea. Perhaps they'd flown in from the Great Salt Lake. We didn't know for sure. We pulled the car over to the side of the road to enjoy watching the spectacle. It was one of the highlights of our trip, and we praised God for the joy of this unexpected treat.

Upon reflection, I realize that our Lord is the God of the unexpected. The Bible is full of surprises orchestrated by God—many of them difficult to explain. He parted the Red Sea to provide an escape for His people as they fled the Egyptian army. Jesus, the King of kings, was born to a humble Hebrew virgin and laid to rest in a manger. The twelve disciples witnessed many unexpected and surprising things while following Jesus. They had difficulty understanding most of them. I can't explain them, either, but I've learned to accept the unexplainable because I trust Him. And I'm grateful for the pleasing surprises He's blessed me with over the years—like a cornfield filled with bright, long-legged ibis. —Shirley Raye Redmond

Walk of Faith: *Do something unexpected for someone today. Send flowers to a shut-in. Order a large pizza for a neighbor. Call a faraway friend.*

JULY 14

On Finches and Finishing

Now finish the work.

—2 CORINTHIANS 8:11 (NIV)

HEY LOOK," MY husband, David, said, pointing to the corner of our porch. "They're building a nest."

Sure enough, a pair of finches were gathering sticks, pine straw, and grass and carrying it to the top of a post.

"Those finches disappoint me every spring," I said. "I get all excited when I see them building a nest, then they abandon it halfway through."

To be honest, some days I'm a lot like those finches. I get excited about a project, idea, or ministry and dive into the work. Then my enthusiasm wears off, my interest fizzles, and I struggle to see it through. Sometimes I abandon the task altogether. I disappoint others, and I disappoint myself.

The apostle Paul wrote to the Corinthian church about a love offering they'd promised. He commended them for their enthusiasm and willingness. "Last year, you were the first not only to give but also to have the desire to do so" (2 Corinthians 8:10, NIV). Now it was time to send the gift.

Because he was a student of God's Word and human nature, he knew it was much easier to promise than to see a commitment through. Perhaps this was why he encouraged them, "Now finish the work, so that your eager willingness to do it may be matched by your completion of it, according to your means" (2 Corinthians 8:11, NIV).

Paul's words remind me to think and pray before I make a commitment. Do I have the time, energy, and desire to see it through? Once I give my word to the Lord and to others, I want to do everything I can to finish the task. —Lori Hatcher

Father, help me choose my commitments wisely and give me the desire and ability to see them through.

JULY 15

Wishes Come True

Every good and perfect gift is from above, coming down from the Father of the heavenly lights, who does not change like shifting shadows.

—JAMES 1:17 (NIV)

WHEN OUR YOUNGEST, Bethany, visited this summer from Hawaii, she arrived with a full schedule of hiking, kayaking, and sightseeing. She also had a heart's desire—to see an eagle in the wild. While eagle sightings are not rare here in the Sierra Valley, she had never seen one in her growing-up years.

After she, her brother Josh, and I kayaked in the crystal-clear waters of Lake Tahoe, we decided to take a back-roads route home through the Tahoe National Forest. Navigating gravel roads around yet another lake, we stopped at a creek crossing that sliced through a beautiful mountain meadow.

Suddenly Bethany gasped. "There! An eagle!"

Sure enough, a bald eagle sat in the highest branches of a Ponderosa pine.

"And there's another one!" Josh added, as a golden eagle flew into the very same tree.

We took pictures as the two eagles flew from one tree to another along the borders of the meadow and then finally left. Because roads were closed, we never made it through the back-roads route, but we all agreed that our side trip was less about reaching the destination we had in mind and more about God's way to fulfill a heart's desire. Seeing not just one eagle but two different kinds of eagles together—a rarity!—that day was a perfect gift for my daughter. The added blessing was that we three got to share the pleasure of that gift together.

God loves to bless His children. He simply asks us to follow Him. Sometimes that path or journey seems to go nowhere. Sometimes there's a detour, and we're sent around another way. But when we ask the Lord to guide us, He blesses us with His presence and grants our greatest heart's desires—often with more than we ask. —Janet Holm McHenry

Lord, thank You for the sweet blessings You pour over me each and every day. Help me to follow You closely, so that I do not miss seeing them.

JULY 16

Companions on the Journey

For if they fall, one will lift up his companion. But woe to him who is alone when he falls, for he has no one to help him up.

—ECCLESIASTES 4:10 (NKJV)

YESTERDAY THE SUN was setting as my children and I drove home from a small remote beach on the shores of Lake Michigan. Being more used to driving around town, we were enjoying the countryside and the bright green of early summer. Up ahead, two small animals appeared in the middle of the road, and as I slowed, we tried to guess what they were. Squirrels? Opossums? We finally figured out that the odd-looking creatures, lacking in girth and only just beginning to sprout some early-summer fur, were baby raccoons. Coming to a complete and total stop about 10 feet from the babies, we watched with curiosity as they sniffed around at the yellow line for awhile, tripping and tumbling as they went. Next they moseyed along in front of our car, taking their careful time and sticking close together until they slowly made their way down the embankment and into the waiting woods.

I was concerned about them. Where was their mother? Did they even know they had to be careful when crossing the road? To my eyes, it didn't seem they could possibly have enough life experience to be out on their own in the world. Yet there they were, picking their way from one side of a country road to another, steady and unperturbed. Side by side, neither raccoon cast a glance in our direction; they were just two brave little companions getting where they needed to go.

At home later, I thought back to those baby raccoons. It brought to mind my early years of college, living in a new state, with a new crowd of companions. How many times did someone see me then and wonder whether I knew what I was doing? My companions in those days were new girlfriends who could only have been a gift from God. Together we learned to navigate college, early adulthood, and then still more of life, looking out for one another every step of the way. I've learned I can be braver and better able to get where I need to go when I stick with my trusted friends. —Katy W. Sundararajan

Jesus, thank You for friends on the journey who provide an extra measure of wisdom and safety.

JULY 17

The Butterfly Ballet

Where can I go to escape your Spirit? Where can I flee from your presence? If I go up to the heavens, you are there; if I make my bed in the depths, you are there. If I rise on the wings of the dawn, if I settle on the far side of the sea, even there your hand will guide me; your right hand will hold me fast.

—PSALM 139:7–10 (NIV)

IT HAD BEEN a rough time at work. The steady flow of support that normally marked the interactions between my coworkers and me had dried up, and I lost my enthusiasm. When I jumped on my bike to ride the trails that follow our bayou system, that normally refreshing respite felt stagnant too. No fish jumped, no herons perched on the shore, and no cat's-paws sparkled on the water.

I pedaled methodically along, realizing it had been quite some time since God had shown up to delight and amaze me. The lack of nature's beauty along the path amplified this lonely thought, and each rotation of my pedals became a prayer that I might see some sign of life besides rushing cars and zooming bikers. Had this city sucked all the life out of these waterways?

Rounding a corner, I came upon a long stretch of unmown grass, thick with sunflowers. White butterflies darted in and out. Larger yellow butterflies swooped in intersecting arcs. Dragonflies performed angular dives though all the sunflowers and butterflies, and above this dancing corps, a bright pair of goldfinches twirled in a perfect pas de deux.

The skyline, so oppressive just a moment before, appeared behind them like a stage set, showcasing this beautiful ballet so I could fully appreciate it. Once again God reminded me that when I start fretting that He is absent, I am just not focusing on seeing the wonders He has wrought. The delicate orchestration of this scene provided a gorgeous reminder of His omnipresent creativity and love. I decided to take that vision back to work with me on Monday. —Lucy Chambers

Happiness is a butterfly, which when pursued, is always just beyond your grasp, but which, if you will sit down quietly, may alight upon you.
—Anonymous

Escape Route

No temptation has overtaken you except what is common to mankind. And God is faithful; he will not let you be tempted beyond what you can bear. But when you are tempted, he will also provide a way out so that you can endure it.

—1 CORINTHIANS 10:13 (NIV)

OH! LOOK AT that!" I cried.

"What? Ooooh!" said my hiking partner, Carolyn.

A fuzzy brown pocket gopher had popped its head up out of its burrow. No sooner did I pull out my camera than it dived back down its tunnel and out of sight. But my disappointment didn't last long when it popped up again from another hole!

We played this harmless version of Whac-a-Mole for a few minutes, laughing quietly and taking photos of the gopher each time it popped up. We didn't want to scare it. But no matter where it appeared, when it thought we were getting too close, it vanished only to reappear in another spot. The system of tunnels gave it ample opportunities for escape.

I couldn't help but think of the Scripture verse that tells me God "will also provide a way out" of temptation. That's a promise I rely on! As I've gotten older and have been confronted with temptations that could lead me away from God, I've tried to remember that promise. Instead of telling myself, *I have no choice,* and doing what I know isn't right, I look for the way out that He has provided. Some of them have been pretty creative, let me tell you!

Just as that pocket gopher had many emergency exits, I *always* find that God has provided me with an escape, another route I can take to avoid trouble, needless confrontation, and hurt feelings. Sometimes it's not the way *I* want to go, but it's the way *He* wants me to go.

Thank You, Lord, for the example of the pocket gopher. What a blessing—what a promise—to be provided a way out of trouble. —Marianne Campbell

No evil leads my soul astray; I walk with Jesus all the way.
—Hans A. Brorson

JULY 19

Lessons from a Hermit Crab

Wisdom belongs to the aged, and understanding to the old.

—JOB 12:12 (NLT)

CHECK OUT THE one with the stars on it!" My husband and I perused the souvenirs. The kites failed to tempt me, but the hermit crabs were a blast from the past. After we left the souvenir shop, I thought of lessons I'd learned from raising them when I was a kid, lessons my husband and I could use in our empty-nest years.

First, as hermit crabs grow, they need larger shells, which we provided. They'd pull their bodies from their current ones, twist sideways, and stick them into their next shells. Though a move to our next home is on the horizon, wisdom says it won't be larger, as the crabs needed, but still a necessary change.

Another tip pertains to the type of housing. Sure, stars or stripes on the shells may have enticed us, but the crab couldn't care. Home is home. With 5 acres and a creek, both my husband and I despair of moving. But we need to consider our diminishing capabilities. After all, we can still hang my husband's hat in a small, serviceable house with little outside upkeep.

And then, there is the hermit crab's leisurely lifestyle, moseying along his cage, only needing food and shelter. Hmm…a slower pace might be good. Maybe there would be time for our kids to visit us then. Maybe we need to forget the dream of backpacking the Appalachian Trail and stick to state park trails.

As God gives us strength and opportunity, we want to live a life our hermit crab friends would approve of, one with wisdom and contentment in our time left on this earth. —Cathy Mayfield

Father, help me learn from the hermit crab's lessons, gleaning wisdom and contentment as I age.

JULY 20

Always Hungry

But grow in the grace and knowledge of our Lord and Savior Jesus Christ.

—2 PETER 3:18 (ESV)

EVERY YEAR IT seems a robin decides to build a nest somewhere within a few feet of my regular walking routine. This year, one constructed her mud-and-stick nest in the grape arbor. I pass by this area daily on my way to our garden and the mailbox. Each time I do, she vacates the nest using her scolding voice to make sure I know that I'm invading her space.

On one of my more recent passes, there was no flitting about or agitated chirping. All was quiet. Did she abandon her nest because of my frequent intrusions? Curiosity caused me to investigate a little closer. Peering into the nest created a flurry of activity from the three hatchlings that had taken the place of the blue eggs that previously occupied the space. They each raised themselves up to stretch higher with wide-open mouths in competition for better feeding position.

I could only suppose that Mama Robin had shifted from being a protector to being the food gatherer for her demanding brood. Those baby robins reacted the same whether it was me moving in close or their mom with a fresh meal. All they cared about was positioning themselves for their next meal. Their development depended on it. Nothing else mattered.

Just like those robins, I was hungry as a new believer. I got as much spiritual nourishment as I could by participating in Christian youth activities such as Sunday school, Awana (a ministry that teaches kids a biblical foundation), and church camp. As an adult, I still have a growing spiritual appetite. Although I am not competing with my brother or sister in faith, feeding my godly appetite is a necessity if I am to grow daily in the Lord. "For he satisfies the thirsty and fills the hungry with good things" (Psalm 107:9, NIV). —Ben Cooper

Father God, may I never lose my hunger for Your Word. As I grow, let me nourish others around me for Your glory. Allow me to mature and grow in the knowledge of Your dear Son. Amen.

Whimsy on the Forest Floor

Let them praise his name with dancing and make music to him with timbrel and harp.

—PSALM 149:3 (NIV)

MY HUSBAND SLOWED our car to a stop in front of a small creature on the dirt road ahead of us. The strange-looking bird did not hesitate or scurry away. Instead, almost in a trance, it continued its course across the road in a rhythmic fashion.

"It's a woodcock!" my husband exclaimed. I had never seen one, and my husband had not in over a decade. The small shorebird, which curiously prefers forests over sandy beaches, bobbed his entire body back and forth in a silly dance as he made his way into the woods. Although we were 10 feet away, he seemed completely unaware and unconcerned with our proximity. He remained fully absorbed in his unique dance.

Scientists have several theories about why the woodcock performs its intriguing stride. It might be to alert predators that it is aware of their presence and ready to take flight. Another idea is that while the woodcock plods on its front foot in a rocking motion, it gets worms beneath the soil moving around, making them easier to detect and hunt. Whatever the reason for this comical walk, it made me smile. I wonder if God, too, had a smile as He designed the rocking walk of the woodcock. Perhaps He was adding a bit of whimsy to the forest floor.

I believe that when God rested on the seventh day, after creating everything in the natural world, He rested not because He needed sleep but because He wanted to delight in all He had made. On my days of rest, I always think about the root word for *Sabbath* and how it can mean to "stop and delight." Watching the woodcock's dance, I couldn't help but stop and delight in God's design—and humor. —Eryn Lynum

God wishes to see people happy, amidst the simple beauty of nature.
—Anne Frank

JULY 22

Blocking the Way

Now Joseph, a Levite of Cyprian birth...was also called Barnabas by the apostles (which translated means Son of Encouragement).

—ACTS 4:36 (NASB)

I HESITATED WHEN I saw the group blocking the entrance. Three of the four seemed to be minding their own business, but the fourth watched me with a defiant look. I started walking again, slowly, toward the only means of entry available to me, trying not to provoke them or let them sense my concern. The others stopped what they were doing and stared at me, too, but I pressed forward, not wishing to appear intimidated by this tough-looking gang. When I approached the gate, one stepped away to let me pass, but another looked straight at me...and hissed.

These delinquents were Canada geese, and the entrance they seemed to be guarding was the gateway to the park where I often walk. The geese this year are numerous, and it seems as if their numbers have made them bold. That, and the fact that many of the goose pairs have goslings in various stages of development. The four that stood around the gate didn't have goslings nearby, but I was wary of rousing their ire nonetheless. They might look comical, with their long necks and waddling walk, but geese can be fierce when threatened, and I had no desire to fight off their beaks and beating wings.

Trying to get them to move without feeling threatened, I clapped my hands quietly from a distance and spoke to them with quiet authority: "Come on, now, move along. That's right. There you go." Eventually they moved with seeming reluctance away from the gate, and I slipped through and onto the path.

I thought about my encounter afterward and wondered if I'm like those geese sometimes. Do I encourage other people, or do I stand in their way and keep them from reaching their potential? There have been times when I've been thwarted, even crushed, by a discouraging word. And yet there have been other times when someone used a smile, a word, or another encouragement to embolden me to do things I didn't think I could do or to change course even with some reluctance or trepidation. My goose encounter reminded me not to stand in others' way but to encourage them instead. —Jon Woodhams

Dear Lord, help me be a Barnabas. Amen.

Staying on the Right Path

Do not enter the path of the wicked, and do not walk in the way of evil.

—PROVERBS 4:14 (NKJV)

OUR SEVEN-WEEK-OLD KITTENS scrambled under the bottlebrush bush, playing hide-and-seek and tackling one another. The two black kittens with hints of tan, both smaller than the cream-colored one, enjoyed getting the better of the bigger one with stealthy sneak attacks.

When they tired of roughhousing, the smallest black kitten wiggled between lattice slats underneath the front porch stairs. The second black kitten skittered in next. Not to be left out, the lighter-colored one wedged and squeezed under the bottom edge. After a game of chase and bat the spiderwebs, the two dark kittens tumbled out of a different hole in the lattice, running pell-mell one after the other. We watched as the cream-colored kitty tried several exits, all unsuccessfully.

I couldn't help but think about all those times as a teenager when a well-meaning adult asked, "If your friend jumped off a cliff, would you?" I never thought that adage applied to me because I was a scaredy-cat, pardon the pun, choosing not to partake in drinking, smoking, drugs, or other potentially harmful activities.

Something about the kitten's predicament reminded me of a conversation just the day before with a group of women from my church. The discussion had turned to a fellow church member who'd recently been arrested for embezzlement. Without hesitation, I added the rumor-mill information I knew.

That kitten's adventure reminds me to not get trapped in following the ways of others when I know better. I also don't want to be the one to lead others down a wrong path. Rather, I want to be the one who helps others in their time of need, like I did with that kitten. When I couldn't bear to watch its struggle any longer, I moved a piece of lattice so it could escape. —Julie Lavender

All of us knows, not what is expedient, not what is going to make us popular, not what the policy is, or the company policy—but in truth, each of us knows what is the right thing to do. And that's how I am guided.

—Maya Angelou

JULY 24

Safe Like a Baby Bird

Surely God is my help; the Lord is the one who sustains me.

—PSALM 54:4 (NIV)

MY SON AND I were in the backyard inspecting a few birdhouses that he has built over the years through our children's program at church. Looking up beneath a squatty gray house, I was surprised to see that the birds had stuffed the inside so full of twigs that its tiny brown roof had begun to rise off the base. Remarking about this to my son, I reached up and was able to just grasp the bottom of the house, turning it to show him what I was talking about. Well, the very moment I touched the birdhouse, I heard the murmuring, wondering, twittering sound of baby birds—baby birds in the birdhouse! I looked at my boy with wide eyes, and he looked back with his mouth in the shape of an O.

It took but a light touch and a small shift of their small, safe house for the baby birds to begin chattering and mewling for their mama. Whether they were hungry and hopeful, thinking that she had returned with snacks, or whether they were fearful because the movement of the house was unfamiliar, the birdies cried out for their sustainer and protector, Mother Bird. My son and I did nothing more to incite the babies, not wanting to confuse or worry them, certain their mother would return in due time and tend to their needs.

The wee baby birds felt what all babies somehow feel: an innate sense of safety and provision. They were safe in their snug home. And I imagine they had also quickly learned that any slight movement of their house was most often the soft landing of Mother Bird on the perch with something fresh to eat. I'd like to feel just as certain as a baby bird of my safety in this life, and to know just as well that the movement around me is my good Father, near to protect and provide. —Katy W. Sundararajan

Walk of Faith: *Choose something in your life around you that reminds you of God's care and provision, and murmur a prayer of gratitude each time you see it.*

JULY 25

Butterfly Days

You will receive the gift of the Holy Spirit. The promise is for you and your children and for all who are far off—for all whom the Lord our God will call.

—ACTS 2:38–39 (NIV)

IT'S BUTTERFLY SEASON. The air around my home is full of western tiger swallowtails, yellow and black hummingbird-size creatures flitting and diving among blooming flowers and abundant shrubs. Schoolchildren, released for the summer, are flitting around the neighborhood too. I'm sitting on a park bench watching a young girl in a cotton-candy-pink sundress waving a net like a sparkler on the Fourth of July. She's trying to sneak up on a tiger swallowtail, but like its feline namesake, the butterfly is swift and agile. The little girl's pursuit is futile, and I am relieved for the butterfly.

But then comes her dad. I imagine he sees his daughter's plight and longs to be her hero. He takes the net, and with much more height and arm span he poses a greater threat to the butterfly. Western tiger swallowtails are not endangered, so I suppose if this dad were to capture the butterfly, no harm would be done to the species. And with a lifetime of only 6 to 14 days, this particular butterfly would not suffer much diminishment if he were to spend his last days in a repurposed pickle jar.

Yet, I am cheering for the butterfly and for its freedom as it dodges its pursuer, flying high above us into the treetops. Dad drops the net and scoops up his daughter, placing her on his shoulders to better see the swallowtail. The butterfly's days are brief, but so are the days of childhood. Soon it will be the little daughter who evades her father's grasp. But for now, the two enjoy a summer's day together, chasing butterflies, chasing each other.

My own children are now grown, but those butterfly days seem like yesterday. The companionship we forged is the foundation of friendships we enjoy today. Letting go is disappointing in the moment, but the beautiful creatures we love return to us as lovely companions one day. —Susie Colby

May He bring you home rejoicing once again into our doors.
—Northumbrian Morning Prayer

JULY 26

The Patience of a Seagull

But if we hope for what we do not see, we wait for it with patience.

—ROMANS 8:25 (ESV)

ONE MINUTE MY grandkids were happily munching popcorn on the beach. The next minute a wayward piece blew across the sand and caught the eye of a passing seagull. Faster than you can say, "Dinner!" the seagull had snatched it up and swallowed it. My granddaughter threw another piece its way, and the frenzy began. Birds came from everywhere, swarming the kids and deafening us with their raucous cries. From that point on, the rule on the beach was No Feeding the Seagulls.

The next day, we surreptitiously munched our sandwiches, careful not to attract the seagulls' attention. We were successful, except for one red-beaked laughing gull. As I neared the end of my lunch, I noticed him. He stood quietly on one leg, gazing at me. No frantic fluttering. No deafening squawks. Just a patient, attentive gaze.

I turned my face away. When I turned back, he was still there. Same patient gaze. Same quiet disposition.

I thought of the beauty of patience as I watched the seagull and it watched me. Should I eat the last bite of my sandwich or throw it to the gull?

That day on the beach, the seagull waited for what it could see—the last bite of my lunch. Christians wait for what we do not see—our reward for serving God. Do we wait noisily, moaning, groaning, and squawking, or do we wait quietly with patient and confident hope? Romans 8:25 describes the patient hope God delights to reward.

Turning toward the seagull, I tossed the corner of bread into the air. "Well done, little guy," I said with a smile. "Well done." —Lori Hatcher

His master said to him, "Well done, good and faithful servant. You have been faithful over a little; I will set you over much. Enter into the joy of your master."
—Matthew 25:21 (ESV)

JULY 27

What a Catch!

How many are your works, Lord! In wisdom you made them all; the earth is full of your creatures. There is the sea, vast and spacious, teeming with creatures beyond number—living things both large and small.

—Psalm 104:24–25 (NIV)

WE DROVE NORTH into Ontario for hours and hours, passing lakes beyond number and naming. I remember thinking: *This is a long way to go to catch fish. I hope the trip is worth it.* We fished on the big lake for 3 days, getting out early, when steam was still rising from the water, and fishing till nightfall, when the mosquitos chased you ashore. I thought, *Keep count of your fish, because when you get home someone will ask how many fish you caught on your trip to Canada.* I stopped counting at 25. I decided if someone asked me how many fish I'd caught, I would say, "Enough."

On the morning of the third day, I caught the fish of a lifetime. The rod tip shuddered and the reel shrieked as the fish made a long, powerful run. Eventually he tired, and little by little I horsed him toward the boat. He made one last dive, bending my rod into a hoop and sucking the quivering tip into the water. Then he gave up, exhausted, and I steered him into the net. It was a huge sag-belly pike, thicker than a fence post, glassy-eyed and gills heaving. From his lower jaw hung two old, frayed lengths of fishing line, trophies from some long-ago victories. I cut the two old lines, removed my hook, and let him go. He rested there at the side of the boat for a moment, then flicked his tail and disappeared.

That pike grows larger with my every telling of the story, and whenever I think of him, I feel young again. I am grateful to God for many things, not the least of which is His decision, on that fifth day of creation, to fill the waters of the world with fish. And to think I wondered if the trip would be worth it. —Louis Lotz

Many go fishing all their lives without knowing that
it is not fish they are after.
—Henry David Thoreau

JULY 28

Cultivating a Grateful Heart

Let the morning bring me word of your unfailing love, for I have put my trust in you. Show me the way I should go, for to you I entrust my life.

—PSALM 143:8 (NIV)

ONE AFTERNOON MY husband brought home a cardboard box with a small gray-and-brown kitten inside. He'd found the cat stumbling around the college campus. Small and vulnerable, the little guy had only one eye, and his so-called good eye was filmy. I felt sorry for him and resolved to give him a safe and comfortable home. We named him Dead-Eye Dick, after the long-ago cartoon character of a pirate with one eye. It took Dickie a while to learn to navigate the house, but he was a scrappy little fellow and seemed to resent my efforts to assist him.

We'd had him for barely 2 months when he suddenly disappeared. He must have gotten out of the house somehow. We looked high and low but never found him. I worried that a hawk had swooped down and carried Dickie away. Had he been hit by a car? Or perhaps he'd chased a mouse into the nearby cornfield and gotten lost. We never knew what became of Dickie. I felt wretched by his loss.

I sometimes wonder if God feels that way when we stray from Him. Just as Bill and I had been willing to adopt Dickie into our family, the Lord was willing to accept us into His family through His Son Jesus Christ (Ephesians 1:5). His desire is for us to dwell with Him forever in a close, trusting relationship. But too often I'm as scrappy as Dickie—eager to do things on my own. I've taken God's grace and goodness for granted sometimes, failing to express my gratitude for all He's done for me. I confess that my vision is sometimes as poor as Dickie's. I need to work on that. —Shirley Raye Redmond

It is only with gratitude that life becomes rich.
—Dietrich Bonhoeffer

JULY 29

The Swallowtail Release

Finally, brothers and sisters, whatever is true, whatever is noble, whatever is right, whatever is pure, whatever is lovely, whatever is admirable—if anything is excellent or praiseworthy—think about such things.

—PHILIPPIANS 4:8 (NIV)

EVERY YEAR, I say I am not going to interfere with my butterfly garden, and every year, I end up bringing caterpillars into safe habitats on my porch. With ants, birds, and flies all out to get them, these little caterpillars seem to beg for a helping hand. Though my heart aches with each release, watching the transformation firsthand as they go from caterpillars to pupae to butterflies is nothing short of incredible.

My first butterfly of the summer emerged yesterday, much to my son's delight. As I looked at the intricate patterns on its wings, I was struck by the detail of God's creation. We have all heard the familiar metaphor that butterflies' metamorphoses are similar to changes in the human heart—most notably the spiritual rebirth when we come to the Lord. But yesterday, as I looked at my swallowtail, a new thought occurred to me.

Wings are not only beautiful, but they are also purposeful. When I invite God into my heart and He begins a spiritual transformation within, He equips me with agency. I have the ability to first seek out nourishment and then establish a heritage through future generations. My thoughts, words, and actions become flight patterns—and I pray God gives me eyes to see the blooms He has set before me to strengthen me along the way.
—Ashley Clark

I come to the garden alone,
While the dew is still on the roses;
And the voice I hear, falling on my ear,
The Son of God discloses.
And He walks with me, and He talks with me,
And He tells me I am His own,
And the joy we share as we tarry there,
None other has ever known.
—C. Austin Miles

Living on the Edge

Suppose one of you has a hundred sheep and loses one of them. Doesn't he leave the ninety-nine in the open country and go after the lost sheep until he finds it?

—LUKE 15:4 (NIV)

WALKING IS MY preferred form of exercise these days, and for a week in the summer I'm able to do it on the perfect white sand beaches of Florida's Emerald Coast. Generally, I walk near the shoreline, where the wet sand is firm underfoot. I'm seldom alone on these morning strolls. Sandpipers dot the shoreline, digging their pointy beaks into the hard-packed sand.

They amuse me, these happy little birds that seldom fly. I love to watch them follow each receding wave, prospecting for whatever edible thing the water may have carried in. They don't actually like water, though. The moment a fresh wave comes, these tiny creatures scurry back to dry sand and safety.

Over and over they repeat this process, rushing out with one wave and in with the next. They scurry here and there, always staying one tiny step ahead of the incoming surf. Are they brave for facing the waves or timid for shying away? Perhaps they're simply realistic. Whatever there is to be found is out there, near the point of no return. God has given them a near-perfect sense of when to rush in and when to withdraw.

Whatever there is to be found is always out there, where courage and danger meet. That's true for sandpipers hunting food, and I think it's true for Christians carrying out Christ's mission too. Sitting in church, meeting with a small group, studying Scripture at home are all important preparations for the dangerous work of reaching lost people or bearing witness to Truth in godless society. But church is not where the action is. It's out there, within an inch or two of the harsh reality of a broken world. With God by our side, though, we know when to rush in and when to withdraw. —Lawrence W. Wilson

Some want to live within the sound of church or chapel bell;
I want to run a rescue shop, within a yard of hell.
—C. T. Studd

JULY 31

Bats Are Beautiful

Stop judging by mere appearances, but instead judge correctly.
—JOHN 7:24 (NIV)

THE TWILIGHT SKY was filled with fruit bats on the island of Sumatra, Indonesia. With a wingspan of 5 to 6 feet, these are some of the largest bats in the world. As I watched these creatures take over the dusky sky, I couldn't help but feel that I was in the middle of a science-fiction horror movie.

My husband and I were part of a relief effort sent by the International Mission Board to the city of Banda Aceh, on Sumatra, after the devastating tsunami of 2004. Banda Aceh is known as the front porch of Mecca due to its extreme form of Islam. This area suffered more loss than any other in that part of the world, with buildings and vegetation in ruins and over half the population wiped out. Having lived in Indonesia for two years, we were familiar with the culture and language. But the devastation was beyond anything anyone could have prepared us for.

As we set up medical clinics and worked to help people rebuild their lives, I came to the realization that we humans were not the only creatures helping to rebuild the area after the tremendous destruction. I had to acknowledge that God created fruit bats for a specific purpose, although their physical appearance still gave me the creeps. The bats play a role in agriculture, both economically and ecologically. They are pollinators, transferring pollen when they fly between trees to consume nectar or fruits. Pollination is necessary for a variety of plants that grow in Indonesia, including bananas, agaves, and watermelons. Fruit bats are also efficient seed dispersers, moving more seeds than other fruit-eating animals as they help rebuild and maintain plants and forests. In addition to their impact on the environment, which helps maintain the balance of nature, they eat small insects, just like other bat species.

I had to look beyond the bats' appearance to appreciate how God equipped them for His purpose.

And sometimes I have to do this for people as well. —Ellen Fannon

Father, thank You that You have designed all Your creatures for their unique part in maintaining Your world.

August

AUGUST 1

Knees in the Tundra Soil

Hear this, O Job; stop and consider the wondrous works of God.

—JOB 37:14 (ESV)

MY KNEES WERE pressed into the harsh tundra soil. It was the final day of a 3-day Master Naturalist wildflower workshop I was attending in the Rocky Mountains. Eleven participants, including myself, lay across the tundra floor. We were above tree line—so high in elevation that trees do not grow—with magnifying lenses bringing the minute details of tundra botanicals into clearer view. Each of us was fully absorbed in our studies while identifying these hardy plants that grow in the harsh tundra climate.

I lifted my gaze from the dainty sky pilot flowers I was studying and found a beautiful scene. Each participant knelt or lay on the tundra floor. We were scattered about the hillside. At 12,000 feet high, towering summits surrounded us. A herd of elk lay about 100 feet away, sunning themselves and nibbling at the tundra grasses.

"They're just like us!" our teacher exclaimed. She was right. Our group mimicked the elk scattered about the hillside in the prone position. On the road above us, tourists drove by in cars, camper vans, Jeep tours, and buses. But like the elk, we didn't notice. We focused on the flowers, including tiny yellow Draba flowers dotting the landscape. The late naturalist Aldo Leopold once wrote of these tiny blossoms, "He who hopes for spring with upturned eye never sees so small a thing as Draba....He who searches for spring with his knees in the mud finds it, in abundance." With our knees pressed to the soil, I was pretty sure only we and the elk noticed the Draba flowers that day. I determined to do as the elk do and make my way slowly through nature, never missing the intricate details of God's designs. —Eryn Lynum

Your first observations...can be done simply by learning to drift gently through a wood; a naturalist in hurry never learns anything of value.
—Gerald Durrell

AUGUST 2

God Gives Hope

May the God of hope fill you with all joy and peace as you trust in him, so that you may overflow with hope by the power of the Holy Spirit.

—ROMANS 15:13 (NIV)

WE NAMED THE dog Hope because we were literally her last hope. She showed up one day, swimming to the dock in my clients' backyard. I went to their house to examine the dog and found a completely unsocialized animal—afraid of everything and everyone. After sedating her, I vaccinated her and took samples for testing. I advised my clients to contact an animal behavioral specialist.

To my horror, the person who evaluated Hope told my clients to put her to sleep because "she had no soul." I knew nothing about this at the time, and my veterinarian colleague went out to euthanize Hope. But when she arrived, the dog had disappeared. Later that week, Hope reappeared, and the dreaded task fell to me. However, I just couldn't bring myself to put a healthy dog to sleep simply because she was unsocialized. My clients couldn't deal with her special needs, so I brought her to a friend who took her in and worked with her, finally gaining her trust.

Sometimes animals just need a little extra love and encouragement to realize their potential. Sometimes people do too. How many times have I overlooked someone's value to the Kingdom because it seemed they had little to offer? Despite my narrow-mindedness, I know that God has blessed all His children with unique gifts. When I look beyond my preconceived notion of someone's worth, I find amazing qualities in the most unlikely people. I have to guard against my pridefulness and prejudice in judging others' usefulness to God's work. Moreover, I need to be kind, patient, and encouraging in helping them develop and use their gifts.

Just because Hope will never be outgoing and friendly like a golden retriever doesn't diminish the joy and special relationship she has with her owner. Hope does, indeed, have a doggy soul. In the same way, each of God's children has a beautiful soul, created in the image of Him just the way He intended them to be. —Ellen Fannon

Father, help me see the beautiful soul in all Your children.

Hovering Hawk

But hold fast what you have till I come.

—REVELATION 2:25 (NKJV)

WOULD YOU LOOK at that hawk?" I said to my husband as we were walking along the beach. I pointed to the bird hovering over the beach grass on the dune. The hawk was not leaving its location in the sky but rather flapping and dipping with the wind, all in a steady effort to stay located over one patch of grass.

"He must be hunting something," my husband said. Sure enough, after a couple of minutes in his stationary mode in the sky, he swooped down and attacked a small creature in the grass.

His resilience and steadfastness made me think of a recent trial where I was struggling to persevere and remain steady. Sadly, I am easily blown off course when circumstances do not go smoothly. When circumstances get a little tough, I am ready to collapse and give in. I was in a leadership role at church, and we were going through some personnel difficulty. It was tiring and stressful trying to make the right choices, and I was contemplating resigning.

Watching the hawk made me realize that his gaze was continually fixed on the prize. He didn't waver. He wasn't distracted by our walking past, fazed by the wind gusts, or ready to move on to something easier.

I am reminded of Paul's words in Philippians 3 about keeping our eyes on Jesus as we run this race of life. I needed to be steadfast and unwavering in my commitment to serve God and to remember that He would provide me with strength and guidance. Times may be hard, but by focusing on the One who is in control, I can complete what He has called me to do. —Virginia Ruth

Holy Spirit, help us stay focused on Jesus so that we are pressing forward toward the goal of life with You. Amen.

A Mute Swan

And to make it your ambition to lead a quiet life: You should mind your own business and work with your hands, just as we told you.

—1 THESSALONIANS 4:11 (NIV)

I AM SITTING ON my boat on a small Michigan lake, and I am watching a swan. It is a mute swan, a large male with elegant white plumage and an orange bill. Mute swans are not really mute, but they don't make much noise; when they do speak, their voice is softer than those of other swan species. Mutes can be aggressive when threatened, but this fellow glides along silently and peacefully without even giving me a sideways glance, his long neck held in the characteristic S curve. I must not be threatening, or he must not be aggressive.

Watching him sail quietly along, just an oar's length from my boat, I suddenly remember a scene from my childhood. I was a small boy, sitting with my mother in the waiting room at Miss Annette's School of Dance, while my older sister and a dozen other middle-school ballerinas were put through their paces. From the hall next door came rhythmic piano music and a weary female voice, "And one and two and...girls, you are swans, not wildebeests. Swans!...Graceful, graceful, graceful...Yes, that's better... and three and four...."

There are no wildebeests out on the lake today, but there is a mute swan, and he really is graceful, graceful, graceful. He is calm and quiet, and he moves without exertion. In a loud, angry world with people forever shouting at one another, I long to live a quiet, simple life, doing the Lord's work zealously and cheerfully, with a minimum of noise and frenzy, like a swan on the water.

It is getting late, and we part company, the swan and I. The evening clouds are a soft orange, lit by a sun already halfway to China. I give the swan one last look as I row to shore. There he is out there on the water, gliding along, graceful, graceful, graceful. —Louis Lotz

A happy life must be to a great extent a quiet life, for it is only in an atmosphere of quiet that true joy can live.
—Bertrand Russell

AUGUST 5

Big Mama

The Lord is my light and my salvation—whom shall I fear?

—Psalm 27:1 (NIV)

WHAT'S MOVING IN the grass over there?" I was out in the backyard watering my plants on a warm summer day when I noticed a rustling in the grass. I stepped closer, then jumped back with a start. It was the biggest spider I had ever seen!

Curious, I drew closer again. I'd found a wolf spider, and it was a big mama. She was carrying all of her babies on her back and heading toward my blackberry patch.

I felt my adrenaline rush as fear spiked in my body. I don't like spiders; in fact, I'm afraid of them. And this one was huge! But at the same time, I was intrigued to see her and her babies. I knew it was a rare sight, so I didn't really want to run away.

As I peered down, I was in awe of her size and determination. I'm not sure where she was coming from, but she was definitely moving with a purpose. I'm a mama, too, and I know what it's like to hustle with the kids.

I began to wonder if she noticed me as well. Was she afraid too? Had I startled her when I was watering, and now she was frantically trying to get her babies to safety? Imagining the spider's motivation in that moment moved me with compassion. I knew she wasn't going to hurt me. Wolf spiders are big and scary looking, but they don't often bite humans, and they don't have venom. This one was no threat to me.

Having compassion for animals who scare us can be difficult. But then I recall His words in Genesis 1:24, 25 (NIV): "And God said, 'Let the land produce living creatures according to their kinds: the livestock, the creatures that move along the ground, and the wild animals, each according to its kind.'...And God saw that it was good." No matter how many legs His creatures have—two, four, or even eight—my faith reminds me that I don't need to fear nature and the wonders God created. —Heather Jepsen

Loving God, You have created so many wonderful things. Help me not to be afraid of the wonders of Your creation. Amen.

AUGUST 6

A Bee on My Belt Buckle

And which of you by worrying can add one cubit to his stature?

—LUKE 12:25 (NKJV)

GROWING UP, WE lived in Colorado and were only able to vacation to see our grandparents in Oregon every other year or so, as it was a long drive with three small children. I always looked forward to those trips, partially because my grandfather lived on a small ranch and had a hodgepodge of farm animals—chickens (and a mean ole rooster), donkeys, and horses, my favorite. For a kid who lived in suburbia, this was as close to paradise as a person could get. Behind the house was a bubbling crick that you could cross on a plank and Grandpa's shed, which smelled of old leather and horses. In the evenings, Grandpa would pull out his fiddle and play by ear, while Uncle Jack would accompany him on guitar.

I spent many pleasant hours at that ranch, wandering around and exploring and interacting with the animals. One day, however, I was leaning against the fence watching the palominos Suzy and Cindy frolic in the field when a great big bumblebee buzzed right up and landed on my large Western belt buckle. I was terrified of bees, and this one was huge. I did as I was told, freezing like a statue, afraid to so much as breathe.

Finally, the bee flew away, and I made a beeline (pun intended) into the house, screaming the whole way, the screen door slamming behind me. "Bee! Bee! Beeeeeeee!"

My mom and grandma tried to calm me down enough to discover where I'd been stung. Imagine their surprise when they realized I hadn't been stung at all—I was merely frightened. I remember that feeling to this day.

I can sometimes make more out of problems than perhaps they deserve. Making a mountain out of a molehill? Yeah, that's me. It's in times like these that I remember the belt buckle incident and remind myself that worrying doesn't do any good. God's got it covered! —Deb Kastner

As for me, I will call upon God, And the LORD shall save me.

—PSALM 55:16 (NKJV)

AUGUST 7

Birds of Paradise

Then God said, "Let the waters abound with an abundance of living creatures, and let birds fly above the earth across the face of the firmament of the heavens."

—GENESIS 1:20 (NKJV)

IN THE TELLING of the creation story, Genesis mentions the seas being filled with many living creatures and birds flying free across the sky. Often, I've looked at birds as a symbol of life and freedom.

Even now, I sit in my backyard and watch the birds come and go from a small water feature. A series of large and small rocks on an 8-foot-tall hillside allows water to cascade over ledges and collect in a pond at the bottom. Birds of many types descend on the oblong rocks, splash about for a while, and fly away in the opposite direction. There seems to be a landing pattern and flow—they come in from the east and fly out toward the west.

There is something about the abundance of birds in the summertime that fills my heart with gratitude. Despite dire warnings about environmental concerns for the future, right now I sit and listen, watch, and pray as countless birds chirp from nearby trees and flit around. God must love me a lot to create such beauty from the winged creatures He brings to my yard, including cardinals, blackbirds, and bluebirds. Each has a personality, unique physical features, and colors that set it apart.

God's gifts of sight, sound, and smell enhance my interaction with His world. I'm learning with age that it takes moments of rest to fully enjoy all of what He has prepared for us here on earth. As I intentionally quiet my mind, He makes the promise of heaven's new joys even more exciting. As wonderful as nature is in our earthly home, God's Word promises us that even more marvelous joys lie ahead in paradise. I wait with anticipation of creatures even more wondrous than the myriad birds. —David L. Winters

But as it is written:
"Eye has not seen, nor ear heard,
Nor have entered into the heart of man
The things which God has prepared for those who love Him."
—1 Corinthians 2:9 (NKJV)

AUGUST 8

Dog Days

When you were younger you dressed yourself and went where you wanted; but when you are old you will stretch out your hands, and someone else will dress you and lead you where you do not want to go.

—JOHN 21:18 (NIV)

WALKING AROUND THE seaside community where my family vacations, I often see people taking their dogs out for a bit of exercise. One day I encountered an older man walking beagles, an unusual and, in this case, comical sight. There were three of them: a puppy, an adult, and one elderly hound that looked old enough to be Snoopy's brother. They were quite a sight, and quite a handful for their handler.

The pup was all energy and eagerness, sniffing the concrete sidewalk for any hint of a rabbit. He changed direction about every three seconds. The adult dog was alert and a bit wary in this semi-urban environment. He moved more purposefully, sniffing the air, eyes flitting from side to side. And the older beagle, with grayed muzzle and cloudy eyes, lagged behind, laboring to climb curbs and keep pace.

When I was a kid, my grandmother kept a beagle named Judy on her rural farmstead. Judy was highly adept at slipping out the back door to run through the woods and fields. I loved to do the same on those long, play-filled summer days.

I recalled, too, the long days of study in graduate school when my rabbit chasing morphed into the disciplined pursuit of a career. Then came the seemingly endless days of laboring to earn a living while raising small children, then teenagers. Watching the three beagles, one playing, one working, and one struggling, gave me pause.

The carefree days of childhood are now a distant memory. The days of focus and achievement have been going on for some time. How long will it be before I am the old dog, energy waning, strength diminishing, laboring to keep pace with life? —Lawrence W. Wilson

Teach us to number our days, that we may gain a heart of wisdom.
—Psalm 90:12 (NIV)

AUGUST 9

Conquering Giants

And everyone assembled here will know that the Lord *rescues his people, but not with sword and spear. This is the* Lord*'s battle, and he will give you to us!*

—1 Samuel 17:47 (NLT)

TAKING PHOTOS AT Camp Roger typically leads me deep into the woods. One day I was taking a break with friends near our utility terrain vehicle and a giant horsefly landed on the hood. We were stunned by its size, knowing that the bite would have been terrible if it had landed on an arm. Suddenly, with a flutter of wings and surprising swiftness, a bird dropped down from above, snatched that giant right off the hood, and flew to a nearby tree. We yelled in disbelief from our front row seat to the wild kingdom.

Searching the branches above, I saw a tiny gray bird cocking his head at me. This creature didn't look large enough to have a 2-inch fly in its belly. It turns out that eastern wood pewees are pros at catching flies and had indeed conquered that monster with ease.

When David wanted to fight the biblical giant Goliath, his brothers reminded him that as a "peewee" and a boy, he could not and should not fight this battle alone. Using skills that he knew best from his daily job, David took out a slingshot and five stones and proved them wrong. Right in front of his brothers and an entire army. David's cry to the Lord for help was the force that allowed him to take down an incredible foe.

I can recall many times in my life where the task at hand seemed impossible—learning a new job, forgiving someone, and moving through difficult physical recovery. Calling on God brought sustaining power to tackle the impossible every time, pushing those giants down one by one, thanks to His divine strength. —Twila Bennett

The Lord *is for me, so I will have no fear. What can mere people do to me?*

—Psalm 118:6 (NLT)

AUGUST 10

Wonderful Giraffes

I praise you because I am fearfully and wonderfully made;
your works are wonderful, I know that full well.

—PSALM 139:14 (NIV)

WHEN MY FRIEND Linda and I visited a wildlife park in Oregon, she rubbed her temples. "This morning I stood up too fast and nearly fainted. Ever wonder if that happens to giraffes after drinking water?" I stared at the long neck of the giraffe in the park.

"I don't," I admitted.

My friend had spent much of her working life in Africa with the Peace Corps, so I figured she'd be an expert on giraffes and other wild animals. But if she knew the answer to her question, she kept it to herself. During our excursion, we chatted about all kinds of things, but I kept thinking about the tallest mammals in the world.

Our trip featured zebras, lions, tigers, and even black bear cubs. I still get goose bumps remembering the giraffe's peaceful gaze, beautiful patterned coat, and majestic height. Not to mention the blue tongue and long neck.

Like my friend, if I stand up too fast, I often experience brief dizziness. How did God make giraffes able to lean down to drink and then stand erect without feeling dizzy or losing consciousness?

I learned that giraffes possess blood vessels with elastic, muscled walls and strong valves that prevent their blood from pooling in their extremities or head. Their necks don't reach the ground, so they must splay their forelimbs to drink.

The more I learn, the more I'm in awe of the ways God fashioned His creatures. Every living thing is lovingly created to reflect God's mercy and care—from giraffes to people. Giraffes remind me to count myself fearfully and wonderfully made to praise the God who thinks of everything. —Linda S. Clare

So we say with confidence, "The Lord is my helper;
I will not be afraid. What can mere mortals do to me?"
—Hebrews 13:6 (NIV)

AUGUST 11

The Influencer

I have learned in whatever state I am, to be content.

—PHILIPPIANS 4:11 (NKJV)

CECILY IS AN influencer—you know, one of those photogenic, charismatic figures whose social media feeds inspire others to follow their advice about fashion and life. Sixteen thousand Instagram followers eagerly anticipate photos of Cecily modeling—and rocking—her latest fashion attire. More than thirty-two thousand people follow her Facebook page.

Cecily is also a cat, with blue eyes and a coat of white and gray, whose inspiring true story recently made the national news. She was born with Manx syndrome, a term that can cover a lot of inherited conditions. In Cecily's case, it affected her organs and resulted in poor spinal development. Because of this, her hind legs were removed, and she must wear a diaper.

But, as her Instagram bio tells us, "I'm not sad!"

Cecily is a permanent resident of The Cattery, a no-kill Texas animal shelter, having arrived there when she was just 2 months old. To cover her diaper, a friend of the shelter began making bespoke dresses and outfits for the fashionable feline. Once a week, Cecily poses in her special outfits, which are shared on her social media pages. The staff members at The Cattery call her their fashionista.

Her seeming disadvantages don't slow her down at all. By all appearances, Cecily loves to dress up in her special outfits, and her sunny disposition and positive outlook inspire people even as her social media presence helps raise awareness of feline disabilities. She is helping to spread a message of positivity.

We're all influencers, aren't we? Compared with Cecily, I am not always so upbeat, and I can sometimes find discontentment even among my blessings. When negative thoughts come to mind, when I open my mouth to say something critical or complaining, I will think of Cecily and her inspiring story, and ask God to help me encourage people, just as she does. —Jon Woodhams

Live simply, expect little, give much. Scatter sunshine, forget self, think of others. Try this for a week and you will be surprised.

—Norman Vincent Peale

AUGUST 12

Let Nothing Stand in the Way

I press on toward the goal to win the prize for which God has called me heavenward in Christ Jesus.

—PHILIPPIANS 3:14 (NIV)

WHILE ATTENDING A writers' conference in the Colorado Rocky Mountains, I drove into Rocky Mountain National Park to search for bighorn sheep. The ranger suggested a meadow below the mountain where I might see them feed. When I reached the area, I noticed a parking lot full of cars and pulled in.

Behind me, rams with horns curled around their face clambered down the cliff. They crossed the road, walked through the meadow in front of me, and joined a large herd of ewes with lambs. I crouched with my back against a boulder alongside the road. I turned off my shutter sound, faced the herd in the distance, and began to take photographs.

All was well until something alerted the sheep. It began slowly with one of the rams. He lifted his head and sniffed the air. The others noticed. The herd stood motionless at first. Then, as if on cue, they turned toward the mountain. Suddenly, the entire herd of bighorn sheep took off. Straight toward me and the boulder where I knelt beside the road.

There were more sheep than I could count. They ran so fast, I knew I couldn't get out of their way. All I could do was crouch low, press into the boulder, and pray I didn't get clipped by a hoof to the head. As I crouched, the sheep either ran around me or jumped over me. While I waited for the herd to pass, I marveled at their determination. Nothing was going to stop them from reaching the mountain. Certainly not me.

Those bighorn sheep taught me one thing. You either jump over or go around obstacles that stand between you and your goals. You don't let them stop you. Something I won't forget. —Sandy Kirby Quandt

Determination gives you the resolve to keep going in spite of the roadblocks that lay before you.

—Denis Waitley

AUGUST 13

The Power and the Glory

O Lord, what a variety of things you have made! In wisdom you have made them all. The earth is full of your creatures.

—Psalm 104:24 (NLT)

AFTER FLYING TO Pittsburgh some years ago to attend a wedding, my sister and I decided to visit the National Aviary while in the city. We are fascinated by birds and knew this would be a great opportunity to get up close and personal with feathered creatures we would never otherwise see firsthand.

The aviary was well worth the visit. We were delighted by the colorful variety of birds new to us, including a bearded barbet, fruit doves, and a golden pheasant. We made a point of stopping by the Andean condor display to admire these huge birds—one of the largest in the world, with a wingspan of up to 10 feet. But the Steller's sea eagle took my breath away. This rare and beautiful raptor was easily over 3 feet high as he sat on his perch coolly surveying his confined kingdom. After reading the posted information, I stared in awe at this massive eagle, marveling anew at God's majestic creativity.

Sandy and I talked about our visit to the aviary for weeks, grateful that God created so many birds in such rich variety. Like King David in many of his psalms, we couldn't stop praising God for His amazing handiwork. The apostles and early followers of Jesus surely stood speechless with amazement as they witnessed the Lord performing miracles, proving that He had absolute power over His creation. While I encourage you to visit the National Aviary if you're ever in Pittsburgh, you don't have to go to that zoo to be reminded of our God's power and glory. For that, you need to simply look out your window. —Shirley Raye Redmond

Nothing in the world is quite as adorably lovely as a robin when he shows off—and they are nearly always doing it.

—Frances Hodgson Burnett

AUGUST 14

Is That What I Think It Is?

Now faith is the substance of things hoped for, the evidence of things not seen.

—HEBREWS 11:1 (KJV)

I HAD JUST DROPPED my son off for his first-ever week of summer camp. The camp was operated by a fine Christian organization, but I knew my wife was a bit anxious about leaving him. "He'll be fine," I said as we pulled out of the driveway, professing more confidence than I felt.

A mile or so down the road, we pulled up to a country intersection. I noticed a large bird walking in the road just ahead. My wife saw it too. "What is *that*?" she asked. I had no idea.

We sat and stared for several moments as this stately black-and-white creature, a bit larger than a crow, paced a circle on the pavement. It stopped, turned its head from side to side, then spread its wings and took flight. That's when it hit me.

Searching my memory, I came up with a possibility. "Was it a magpie?" I asked.

"I think it was," my wife answered.

All I could think of was the old children's show *Heckle and Jeckle*, which featured a pair of mischievous smart alecks played by cartoon magpies. Honestly, I thought magpies were made up for television. If I hadn't seen the winged tuxedo wearer with my own eyes, I'd not have believed them to be real. But there he was, big as life.

Like that magpie, many of the things I believe are seldom, if ever, seen in this life. Though many have seen miracles of healing, I have not. Angels are real, I know that. But I've not seen one. Heaven, where so many of my loved ones have taken up residence, is an actual place. I've not seen it though and don't expect to until I join them there.

This is the life of faith, of accepting that many real things remain invisible or are seen only in fleeting glimpses. Yet they are real.

From that day to this, I've not seen another magpie. That one was enough for me. —Lawrence W. Wilson

Lord Jesus, give me the gift of faith, so I may keep moving toward that city I have not yet seen.

AUGUST 15

Inseparable

First we were loved, now we love. He loved us first.

—1 JOHN 4:19 (MSG)

WHEN MY FRIEND'S son Tim was a young boy he had a pet gerbil named Lisa. He loved her with all his heart and couldn't bear to be away from her. Tim often wore a blue windbreaker, both inside the house and outside. One day at lunch his mom wondered why he still had his jacket on. It wasn't long before she spotted bright, beady eyes peeking at her from one of the coat sleeves. Though Tim wasn't allowed to bring pets to the table, he'd smuggled Lisa into the dining room, hoping no one would notice.

During the summer months the two were inseparable. Lisa used Tim for a jungle gym, scampering up and down his arms, across his shoulders, even up onto his head. He foraged for food that he could sneak to her when his mom wasn't looking. Lisa was particularly fond of fruit and veggies, which should have been a definite mark in her favor where Tim's mom was concerned.

When summer break from school came to an end, Tim was disheartened at the thought of so many hours away from Lisa. So, even though it was against the rules, Tim brought Lisa to school, just like Mary did with her little lamb. Lisa's agile antics delighted Tim's friends while they awaited the start of classes. Unfortunately, an ever-vigilant teacher caught sight of a tail disappearing into Tim's blue windbreaker sleeve, and the gig was up. Lisa had to stay home from then on.

I yearn for time with Jesus, just as Tim and Lisa wanted to spend every moment together. I want to be so in love with the Lord that I can't bear to be away from Him. I know that's how He feels about me too. Of course, that desire of my heart came from Him in the first place. —Liz Kimmel

Thank You, Father, Son, and Spirit, for Your example of what it means to be in close community. Thank You for sharing every joy and sorrow, each challenge and victory, my gains and my losses. Your presence in my life is what enables me to live life to the fullest.

AUGUST 16

Feeling Squirrely

In his hand is the life of every creature and the breath of all mankind.

—JOB 12:10 (NIV)

GROWING UP IN a military family, we didn't live near most of our kin. My folks took trips across the US every summer to visit central Oregon, the stomping grounds of their youth. One of my favorite visits was with Cal and Wilma, who owned a cabin on the Deschutes River. They were my pseudo aunt and uncle, and I grew up enjoying their cozy cabin nearly every summer. The highlight? The appearance of a fluffy-tailed squirrel who came when called and took his position on a big stump, where he entertained us all, eating nuts from Cal's fingertips. Then Cal would extend his arm and outstretch his hand to where the squirrel sat. The little guy would climb up Cal's arm, straight to his shoulder. Sitting there victorious, he'd ride all over the yard. To a kid, this was akin to a sideshow in the circus. We were stunned at such animal friendliness and obedience out there in the wild. Cal was his friend, and a deep trust existed between the two.

After the show, I wanted more. But Cal had given us the squirrel's limit and protected him from too much human interaction. Looking around, I wasn't sure where the critter had gone. And we, the guests, were soon distracted with a delightful lunch served outside amid the sounds of the river rushing past.

Later, I realized Cal probably spent lots of time with the squirrel. How could the little guy perform those funny tricks without plenty of practice? I relaxed, keeping my eyes open. But my squirrely visit had ended. He was gone.

Though my childish self wanted many hours of the squirrel show, we all accepted when Cal closed it down. He knew the little beast personally and understood his ways. Though Cal's affection was evident, his respect for God's sovereignty was greater still. —Cathy Elliott

All things bright and beautiful,
all creatures great and small,
all things wise and wonderful,
the Lord God made them all.
—Cecil Frances Alexander

AUGUST 17

Wakeup Coo

Satisfy us in the morning with your unfailing love, that we may sing for joy and be glad all our days.

—PSALM 90:14 (NIV)

I DON'T NEED AN alarm clock or a cell phone alarm on summer mornings. My wakeup call is the repeated, gentle *coo-ah, coo, coo, coo* of light gray-brown mourning doves that have nested for many years in one of the silvertip fir trees in our backyard.

This year, I heard their arrival early and one day watched as the male led the female to the various options for nesting. Quickly, though, she settled into a spot close to where doves always nest—just a little bit higher each year in the fir tree's new growth. Over the next days, I watched as the male gathered the materials for the nest and the female wove them together.

Dove couples typically stay together during a breeding season, spending almost all their time together. And dove babies, called squabs, come and go several times during the warmer six months here in the largest alpine valley in North America, the Sierra Valley. While I don't know if the pair in my backyard is the same pair every year, their morning—not mourning—music soothes my soul and reminds me of God's daily loving presence.

While many of us may not be morning people, we all nonetheless can give thanks when we get another day of life with its rhythm of sweet morning sounds. A cooing dove. Children's voices. The drip-drip of a coffee maker. A spoon clicking against the side of a cereal bowl. The clip-clip-clip of a dog walking on a tile floor and the rattle of its dish.

While I do use an alarm most days, it's always lovelier when God uses the sweet coos of our mourning doves, which remind me of His love for me and the many simple joys He provides each day. —Janet Holm McHenry

In the morning when I rise, in the morning when I rise,
in the morning when I rise, give me Jesus.
—African American spiritual

AUGUST 18

What a Sight!

I will give you hidden treasures, riches stored in secret places, so that you may know that I am the Lord, the God of Israel, who summons you by name.

—Isaiah 45:3 (NIV)

I LOVE STROLLING THROUGH the Sunken Garden at the historical West Baden Springs Hotel. Long ago master gardeners designed the perfect patterned pathways and selected flora that thrived in the southern Indiana climate. The tiger swallowtail butterflies, variegated fritillary butterflies, and honeybees flit around the colorful blooms bordering the manicured lawn. On every visit, I am on the lookout for the orange-and-black monarch, my late mother's favorite. However, I never catch a glimpse of the elusive butterfly among the well-maintained garden plots.

One summer day, after my garden visit I pulled into the parking lot of a nearby fast-food restaurant. Next to the paved area was an overgrown patch of ground. What a sight! I walked around bits of trash littering the edge, with weeds towering 4 feet high.

For just a moment, I paused. The entire area vibrated with sounds, smells, and activity. Something colorful caught my eye. It was a bright orange butterfly milkweed, the perfect host plant for monarch eggs. I stood still and waited (and I think I held my breath). A pair of monarchs circled the plants, once, twice, and then landed. What an unexpected sight!

I reflected on those two gardens. One was monitored daily by paid staff and bloomed with a variety of exotic flowers. The other was tended by Jesus, the Master Gardener, and bloomed with a variety of weeds. That got me wondering. On many occasions, I have rushed past this disorderly place and many like it, disregarding the riches to be discovered. Unfortunately, I am also guilty of overlooking a person because I was too busy and therefore missed the treasure. Under God's trained eye, all are unique and special.

From now on, I am going to take my garden walks to the next level. I am "stopping to smell the roses" and noticing the secret garden in all of God's creations. What a sight awaits me, indeed! —Glenda Ferguson

Weeds are flowers too, once you get to know them.
—A. A. Milne

Don't Take Yourself Too Seriously

But he's already made it plain how to live, what to do, what GOD is looking for in men and women. It's quite simple: Do what is fair and just to your neighbor, be compassionate and loyal in your love, And don't take yourself too seriously—take God seriously.

—MICAH 6:8 (MSG)

A PLAQUE AT THE nature center read, "Otters are characterized by a play ethic."

"What's a play ethic?" I asked my new husband. He grinned. Steve was characterized by a play ethic too. It served him—and me—well through 30 years of ministry together and raising our family. When things got tough, Steve could be counted on to find some fun, to lighten the weight of shared burdens, to help us take ourselves less seriously even when we faced challenges.

But when Steve died of cancer, challenges seemed to mount to horrific proportion. I needed a break. So when a friend invited me to join her family on an Alaskan cruise, I hesitated for only a second. To float away from problems at home for a week with people I love? Yes, please!

As we sail into Glacier Bay National Park and Preserve on a sparkling blue day, an unfathomable ice wall fronting an ice river 21 miles long looms before us. Though breathtakingly beautiful, its sheer magnitude is an eerie reminder of challenges I have left on shore. I'm unsure whether my deep sigh reflects awe and wonder or resignation.

Then just below the ship appears what seems to be a floating log, then another and another. I look more intently. A dozen—no, four or five dozen—otters, not logs, cavort before our ship. They seem to be playing as they swim, dive, and crack shells against their chests. Smiling, I think of my husband. For the first 14 years of our marriage, we lived beside an otter habitat, but I haven't seen these animals in years. I had forgotten how much I enjoy them—how their antics refresh and inspire me. Otters seem not to take themselves too seriously. To honor Steve and survive his absence, I commit myself to play. —Susie Colby

The true object of all human life is play.
—G. K. Chesterton

AUGUST 20

For Their Own Good

And now, Israel, what does the Lord your God ask of you but to fear the Lord your God, to walk in obedience to him, to love him, to serve the Lord your God with all your heart and with all your soul, and to observe the Lord's commands and decrees that I am giving you today for your own good?

—Deuteronomy 10:12–13 (NIV)

GLANCING OUT THE window, I noticed a tangle of twigs and dried grasses atop the light fixture on our front porch. I soon saw the mated pair of birds appear, each with another twig in its beak, keeping a careful eye out for predators while seeming to sneak up under the porch roof. They were small and brown with speckled wings, and I identified them as house wrens using a birding reference from our bookshelf.

I was fascinated by their cooperative and persistent effort but soon realized their choice of nesting place was not ideal. My husband and I regularly used the porch door, and mail and packages were delivered to the mailbox there. Our dogs barked at any disturbance outside the front window. These birds would be constantly stressed by the activity and might eventually abandon their eggs or young. I decided to evict them before they got very far along in their project and it was too late to find a better location.

My husband and I tried several humane deterrents, finally settling for pulling a length of aluminum foil from the roll, cutting the bottom into fringe, and taping it above the porch light, where it fluttered in the breeze, noisy and shiny. The wrens attempted to return several more times, but finally left permanently. We had frightened them away for their own good.

That got me thinking about the things God asks of me that I find unpleasant but that are good for me in the end. Forgiving others is hard, but it cleanses my soul and ensures that God will forgive me as well. Not coveting keeps me from focusing on earthly desires. Like the flapping foil for the wrens, God's requests move me to a better place despite myself. Those commands are not arbitrary but designed for my own good. —Kim Sheard

Walk of Faith: *Think of a command or task God gives that you find difficult. Consider how it is good for you once accomplished.*

AUGUST 21

The Poop Deck

"Praise be to…the God of all comfort, who comforts us in all our troubles, so that we can comfort those in any trouble with the comfort we ourselves receive from God."

—2 CORINTHIANS 1:3–4 (NIV)

"OH NO, THEY came back," my husband said. We had arrived at our little getaway cottage and both noticed dark blobs on our deck. The prior weekend we'd spent most of that Saturday cleaning our deck of turkey excrement. We tried all the suggestions noted on wildlife websites to deter them from gathering on the deck again, but it was obvious the turkeys hadn't read those suggestions. In the intervening week, they apparently had their own fall gathering. By the volume of their droppings on our table, chairs, deck, and railing, it appeared that it was a large gathering and a good time was had by all.

"Did you know that the turkeys love acorns?" I asked my husband as we scrubbed and swabbed the deck.

"Well, no wonder they love it here. There are plenty of oak trees, and this year there's a bumper crop."

"I also found out that turkeys have a voracious appetite for ticks. I guess if that is the case, we can allow them a party every once in a while."

As I filled my bucket with soapy water, I thought of the people I came across in our church's caregiving ministry—the "messy" ones who left a wake of disaster behind them for others to clean up. I would grumble and complain when they came across my path, yet in retrospect, I realized that I had learned so much from encountering them—humility, caring, empathy, discernment. We all make "messes," and through God's grace we can help one another.

I was willing to clean up our "poop deck" knowing that the turkeys were beneficial to our yard. I need to be willing to extend the same grace to those who need help cleaning up their situations, knowing that being part of their story is beneficial to my growth. —Virginia Ruth

Thank You Lord for the "messy" people and situations You place in our lives. May we extend grace and see the benefits that You bestow through them. Amen.

AUGUST 22

Tiny Angel Bird

The whole earth is full of His glory!

—ISAIAH 6:3 (NKJV)

I HAVE HUNG HUMMINGBIRD feeders from a stand on our porch or in the yard many times. On occasion, I would see the colorful birds drink the sweet nectar I had prepared. Thinking they would return, I was disappointed when weeks went by and I didn't see any of these splendid little birds.

Last summer, I gave up on preparing my bright red feeder and told myself I just couldn't seem to attract hummingbirds like other people, no matter how hard I tried. I started watching for other birds, with my Audubon book on hand. But I still longed to see the hummers.

One early midsummer evening at our new home in the high desert, my husband, Tom, and I sat on our patio chairs with our feet propped up. A cool breeze bid us to stay, and we enjoyed relaxing there. Suddenly, out of nowhere, a hummingbird danced around the wildflowers not too far from our feet.

Zooming like a tiny supersonic plane, a rufous hummingbird had visited us, flying up and down and down and up. It hovered over the pink, red, and purple wildflowers, drinking the nectar. We watched the unusual phenomenon—including its ability to fly backward. Since hummers can't hop or walk, they put their energy into flying at an unbelievable speed, beating their wings up to seventy times per second.

Like the fast-fluttering Tinkerbell in the fairy tale, the teeny hummer, and sometimes two or three, danced in front of us through the remaining summer evenings in our backyard. Joining them in their natural habitat was key for me. I realized then that sometimes I try too hard to make things happen. The answer is in living, in enjoying the present, and even becoming a part of it. The Creator, once again, gave me a gift in nature: little angel birds, tiny but magnificent! —Kathleen R. Ruckman

Dear God, thank You for Your glory that covers heaven and earth. Help me to live my life, without striving, and surprise me with glimpses of Your glory.

AUGUST 23

A Cat-astrophe

The Lord will rescue me from every evil attack and will bring me safely to his heavenly kingdom. To him be glory for ever and ever. Amen.

—2 TIMOTHY 4:18 (NIV)

ONE SCORCHING SUMMER day, I received a phone call from the neighbor who has a horse stable behind my house.

"I think your cat is stuck under the roof of our riding arena," he said.

I quickly took inventory of our three cats and assured him the cat wasn't mine, but I offered to see if there was anything I could do.

Sure enough, a beautiful long-haired orange-and-white cat perched high up on an overhead beam below the sizzling tin roof of the arena. He had obviously climbed there to escape something frightening and couldn't figure out how to get down. The cat was in heat distress, and we needed to act quickly, but neither of us had a long enough ladder. However, since my neighbor is the chief of police and has connections, he summoned the fire department. To my surprise, firemen still rescue trapped cats.

The firemen placed their extension ladder, then argued about who would retrieve the cat.

"I'll probably get scratched to ribbons," grumbled the unlucky volunteer.

Since I am a veterinarian, I offered to climb the ladder and fetch the cat. The two strong young men politely declined the offer from me, the little old lady.

We watched in amazement as the fireman reached the top of the ladder and the cat rushed into his arms as if grateful. Both fireman and cat descended the ladder unscathed.

I am reminded of the parable Jesus told of the lost sheep. The shepherd left the other ninety-nine sheep and looked high and low until he found the lost one. Then he put it on his shoulders and went home, rejoicing. Like the lost sheep and the trapped cat, I could not find my way to safety, to Jesus. He had to save me from the darkness of sin in which I was trapped. I am humbled and grateful that He loved me enough to search for and rescue me. —Ellen Fannon

Jesus, thank You for not giving up on me.

AUGUST 24

Mule Ambassadors

We are therefore Christ's ambassadors, as though God were making his appeal through us. We implore you on Christ's behalf: Be reconciled to God.

—2 CORINTHIANS 5:20 (NIV)

I LOVED WATCHING THE children interact with Jolly and Belle, two mules from the only stock team in the US Forest Service east of the Mississippi. An eager young boy, with his palm up, fed a ranger-approved treat to gentle Belle. Usually the four-mule team and rangers worked remotely in the Charles C. Deam Wilderness, so this day at a local Indiana park was a unique opportunity for the public to interact with these hardworking animals.

This was also a reunion of sorts for me. Two years ago I met the team in the Hoosier National Forest and affectionately named them the mule ambassadors because of their excellent representation of the Forest Service. Under the direction of several rangers, I witnessed how the mules maintain the trails where no machines are allowed. Belle pulls 100-pound steel plows, and Jolly hauls more than 200 pounds of gravel in canvas bags.

I asked Ranger Summer about the other two mules back at the corral. She informed the audience about their personalities. Sammy, the smaller mule, was shy around crowds. Lollie is a people mule but doesn't stand still. Summer said, "If Lollie were here, she would be kicking the trailer, insisting on a treat."

Someone asked about mules being stubborn. Ranger Rod explained, "Yes, mules have that reputation, but they are smart and will know what to do or not to do."

Afterward, I reflected on the mules' gentle character and reputation. I laughed, because what I heard and learned about the mules' personalities could be applied to me: I'm stubborn, impatient when waiting for answers to prayers, and shy around a crowd. I strive to be more cooperative with others, display self-control, and step out of my comfort zone. With God, though, I never have to be perfect and can still be one of His ambassadors. —Glenda Ferguson

A good name is more desirable than great riches; to be esteemed is better than silver or gold.
—Proverbs 22:1 (NIV)

AUGUST 25

Hearing from God

My sheep listen to my voice; I know them, and they follow me.

—JOHN 10:27 (NIV)

LAST YEAR, MY husband and I began using the free Merlin Bird ID app designed by the Cornell Lab of Ornithology. The app's sound identification feature makes it easy for users to identify birds in real time as they're singing. Incredibly, it can identify individual bird species even when many of them are "talking" all at once.

The app's value was proven right away. We found more success in hearing birdsong than we ever had before. When engaged, Merlin's intense listening mode was phenomenal. The app wasn't confused by the clamor of overlapping songs. Merlin didn't appear to miss a sound, no matter how faint or high-pitched.

I'd like to be as attuned to hearing God's voice as the Merlin app is to hearing birdsong. Imagine never missing the privilege and comfort of hearing the Lord speak to me, readily recognizing His voice when I hear it and extracting His words from the clamorous, overlapping voices bombarding me daily and demanding my attention.

Yet I want more than any app might offer. I want a relationship, cemented through the practice of listening for the voice that I have come to know. I strive for a posture that is always in the "on" mode to hear from Him. As Charles Stanley said, we are "children who need for Him to speak, who need to listen, who need guidance every day of our lives."

The Lord says through the psalmist, "My sheep listen to my voice." Let me go a step further. This sheep wants to listen *for* His voice. My goal is to remain in a listening stance at all times, filled with anticipation to hear what He has to say to me. Just like the joy I experience in hearing birdsong in greater number and clarity, I yearn for the joy of hearing more from God who is speaking directly to my listening ear. —Darlene Kerr

Walk of Faith: *Find a quiet place where you will not be interrupted for a time. With the full expectation of hearing from Him, quietly and silently wait upon the Lord. Afterward, write down what you heard and thank Him.*

AUGUST 26

Trying to Hide

If I say, "Surely the darkness will hide me and the light become night around me," even the darkness will not be dark to you; the night will shine like the day, for darkness is as light to you.

—PSALM 139:11–12 (NIV)

THE DOGS WERE going crazy. It was after dark, and they were having a fit, barking at something on the deck. I headed outside to see what all the commotion was about and was greeted by the cutest sight ever. A mama raccoon had brought her babies up onto the deck to sample from our bird feeders.

At the sight of me, the mama raccoon took off, but the babies could not quite figure out what to do. They sat on the railing looking caught. As I approached, instead of running away these little fellows attempted to hide by hanging off the railing. I laughed as they ducked their heads. I could imagine them thinking, *If we can just get small enough, she won't see us*. But of course, I could see their little paws and their heads as they tried to hide. They weren't really causing any harm, and the little guys were so cute that I decided to simply go back inside and leave them in peace.

My encounter with the raccoons made me think about how silly I must look when I try to hide from God. How often do I deny my sins or hope that God doesn't notice the hurtful thoughts in my heart? God sees all of me even when I think I'm hiding from Him, just as I saw the raccoons trying to hide that night. Luckily, just as I did with the raccoons, God responds to my mistakes with grace and love.

There is nothing we can do to hide from God. But God always loves us first and foremost. —Heather Jepsen

God, help me to bring the whole of who I am to You today. Even the darkest dark cannot hide me from Your sight. Amen.

A Liberation of Light

And God said, "Let there be light," and there was light. God saw that the light was good, and he separated the light from the darkness.

—Genesis 1:3–4 (NIV)

NIGHT HAD FALLEN, and we still had hours of driving ahead. We were at the tail end of a 10-day road trip across the Midwest with our four young children and puppy. My husband and I were weary but determined to make it home to Colorado that night. With the sun below the horizon, we hoped our children would fall asleep for the remainder of the drive. But then, a flicker of light disrupted any thoughts of sleep.

"Fireflies!" My husband made a sharp turn for the off-ramp. He found a safe place to park, and we all spilled out of the SUV. The field adjacent to the highway was aglow with flickering creatures.

My husband and I both grew up in the Midwest. Our childhoods were marked by evenings spent chasing flickering fireflies. After we moved our family to the Rocky Mountains, people asked me if there was anything I didn't like about living in the mountains. I'm hard-pressed to find an answer, but I always reply, "I miss fireflies."

Now, as my kids ran through the field, I watched them fill with the same wonder of my childhood. It didn't matter that we were on the side of a highway in the middle of nowhere—all we saw was light splitting open the dark night sky.

As a kid, I was enamored of the wonder of a firefly's light. Now, as a certified naturalist, I'm even more in awe of how that light is created. Fireflies create "living light" when an enzyme called luciferase oxidizes a molecule called luciferin. It is a liberation of light. We watched God's incredible design as the fireflies, using this process, actually released light into the night sky. As small as they are, these creatures illuminate the landscape and remind me that when darkness surrounds, God's living light shines brighter. —Eryn Lynum

The light shines in the darkness, and the darkness has not overcome it.

—John 1:5 (NIV)

AUGUST 28

Mosquitoes and Me

Before I formed you in the womb I knew you,
before you were born I set you apart.

—JEREMIAH 1:5 (NIV)

ONE, TWO, THREE...twenty-one, twenty-two! Nothing quite like counting up my mosquito bites after a short hike in the woods. My husband had three bites. I have to practically bathe in insect repellent to get that few.

"See," I told my husband, "this is proof that I'm a delicacy in the mosquito world. I'm utterly seductive with my tantalizing come-hither scent." Now I remember why I never ventured out for hikes in the summertime before I married a naturalist.

"Well, at least I have a purpose within God's creation," I quipped. "Mosquitoes would definitely feel the hurt if my blood supply was cut off." *Yeah, tough luck for mosquitoes,* I thought. What benefits do these pesky insects bring anyway? Malaria surely isn't one of them.

I googled mosquitoes. First and foremost, mosquitoes are a food source for birds, fish, amphibians, and reptiles. Surprisingly, they are also pollinators. I found it interesting that mosquito larvae's voracious eating produces a lot of insect poop, which makes plants very happy.

OK, I hereby acknowledge that mosquitoes serve a purpose in creation. They aren't the product of God's quirky sense of humor to annoy Darlene. Memo to self: Never doubt God's creation wisdom.

Ditto for never belittling God's purpose in creating me. There have been difficult days when being mosquito fodder pretty much sums up my sense of significance. Those times are often the result of comparing myself to others or feeling I will never measure up to God's expectations. It's easy to drown in the comparison game and very dangerous to absorb a lie about how God responds to me.

Thankfully, God's Word directs me to the truth. Ephesians 2:10 says that I'm created anew in Christ to do the good things He has planned for me long ago. Yes, that's it—for me to do—even if I'm scratching mosquito bites as I go. —Darlene Kerr

Of all the things Christ wants for us, loving Him and focusing
our attention on Him are the most important.
—Charles Stanley

In Search of Greener Grass

Keep your lives free from the love of money and be content with what you have, because God has said, "Never will I leave you; never will I forsake you."

—HEBREWS 13:5 (NIV)

IT WAS A strange sight in the field across the street as we drove into our subdivision. A herd of cows was lined up along the fence eating contentedly, except for one cow. She was in line with the others, and there was plenty of green grass in front of her, but she had stuck her head between two strands of barbed wire (ouch) and twisted her neck into a strange position so she could devour the grass on the outside of the fence. It was a perfect visual image of the adage, "The grass is always greener on the other side of the fence."

Apparently this desire to eat on the other side is not uncommon among cows. Our daughter Kimberly helps her boss feed his herd, and one day she accidentally left the gate ajar for 30 seconds. One heifer wandered through. Her boss was not fazed, as he remarked, "Don't worry. She'll be ready to return as soon as she samples the grass outside the fence."

If I'm being honest, I must admit that I sometimes have the same impulse. My neighbor's house looks better than mine, my neighbors' flowers are more beautiful than mine, and how I wish I could afford one of those fancy cars that some of the neighbors drive. But as the author Karen Salmansohn puts it, "The grass is always greener on the other side—until you get there and see it's Astroturf." When I lapse into one of those yearning moods, I hear the Lord telling me loud and clear to be content with what He has given me. —Harold Nichols

Dear Lord, please help me to be mindful of those straying cows and to be content with what I have. Help me remember that You are always with me, fulfilling all of my needs. Amen.

AUGUST 30

When Fear Flees

Such love has no fear, because perfect love expels all fear.

—1 JOHN 4:18 (NLT)

BUZZ! BUZZ! THE incessant noise of carpenter bees burrowing on our porch drove me inside. From my earliest memories, I've feared bees. Not just honeybees, but bumblebees too. And not just bees, but wasps, hornets, yellow jackets. If it buzzes, get it away from me. My phobia causes me to freeze if I hear the telltale buzz. I don't even need to see what's making it. Even a picture of a bee in a child's storybook makes me tremble.

Once while hiking with our daughter and two grandsons, I took our German shepherd mix, Kenai, along. He loved the trails and enjoyed romping with the boys. Kenai delighted at jumping about in a creek, running on the flat rocks, and retrieving pebbles I tossed in the water.

At lunchtime, we sat in a shaded area to eat. Kenai lay on one large rock, content, yet hoping we'd throw bread crusts his way. Bees buzzed about, causing me much concern. Suddenly, Kenai yipped and began chewing frantically at his paw. I found nothing on him that would cause the yips, but because he kept chewing at his paw, I turned it over and dug my finger between the pads. I pulled out a bee that had crawled into his foot! Without thinking, I stuck my fingers back in to check for more.

With meds and a few days' rest, Kenai stopped limping and licking his paw, but the aftermath of my fearless foray to protect my dog from the bees stuck with me. I love my dog so much that I went to bat against my biggest fear to save him from harm. Love really does expel fear. —Cathy Mayfield

Fear and love can never be experienced at the same time. It is always our choice as to which of these emotions we want.

—Gerald G. Jampolsky

Ageless and Unhurried

Take My yoke upon you and learn from Me, for I am gentle and lowly in heart, and you will find rest for your souls.

—MATTHEW 11:29 (NKJV)

ONE OF MY favorite parts of gardening is watering plants, because it gives my mind a break from the concerns of the day. Usually, wandering from flower bed to shrubs to bushes relaxes me and separates my workday from dinnertime and a restful evening. One late-spring evening, my mind continued to swirl even out in the garden. No matter how I tried, the troubles of the day continued to dominate my thoughts.

The hose followed obediently as I began watering the geraniums along the entrance walkway. Then I noticed a small crowd of neighborhood children gathered on the lawn next door. My neighbor, Georgia, appeared to be explaining something. My curiosity grew amid the sound of children's excited reactions to her comments.

"That's so cool," said the Schultz boy from across the street.

"Can I pet her/him," a young girl asked?

There in the middle of the children crawled a huge tortoise, over 2 feet in diameter. His muted yellow-and-green shell was almost as tall as it was wide. The healthy-looking beast munched grass and eyed the growing circle of strangers. Every so often, Georgia would turn the tortoise in the opposite direction to keep it from moving too far from her front stoop. Even with the gentle course correction, the tortoise seemed undeterred from eating dinner. He looked content to chew and rest quietly, even amid all the attention from the giggling young people.

As I listened to my neighbor describe the animal, its expected long life span, and how it came to live with her, my cares drifted away. The beauty of God's creation in action brought needed peace and rest for me too. —David L. Winters

God, thank You that Your loving care surrounds all those who call on Your name. Hold me tight and teach me to trust You every day—even during days full of life's troubles.

September

SEPTEMBER 1

Traveling Companions

Whoever is not against us is for us.

—MARK 9:40 (NIV)

FOR SEVERAL YEARS I was an avid cyclist. The county roads near my home had very little traffic, and I spent many a summer day pushing myself to ride just a bit farther or just a bit faster. Sunshine, cornfields, and a healthy bit of physical exertion restored both body and soul.

The one danger on my solitary rides came from none other than man's best friend, the dogs kept as pets by my rural neighbors. Car after car might pass by a country farmhouse, and the family dog would never leave the porch. But the sight of a bicycle would turn that same canine into a raging beast, teeth bared, snarling and barking, streaking to intercept its prey—me.

After a few dicey encounters, I began to note the location of the more aggressive beasts and plan my rides accordingly.

One day, pedaling along a quiet road, I noticed a large black Labrador in a yard ahead. Labs are generally peaceful, but I quickened my pace to be on the safe side. Sure enough, the old boy spotted me and dashed out to intercept me. "Here it comes," I thought, bracing for an attack.

But there was none. The amiable pup fell into formation and trotted along beside me. Every few seconds, he would glance up as if to see that I was still with him. After a moment, I realized what was happening. This lonely Lab saw me as a friend, not a threat. With no other dogs in the neighborhood, he was glad to find a rambling partner. We continued for a mile or so before parting ways. And that was not the last time we teamed up for a buddy run.

Many people are hostile to the person, message, and followers of Jesus Christ. There are times to be wary, no doubt. But not every stranger poses a threat. "I have other sheep that do not belong to this fold," Jesus said (John 10:16, NRSVUE). They are brothers and sisters in Christ we haven't met yet, partners who can join us on our ride in this life. —Lawrence W. Wilson

God is Unity, but always works in variety.
—Ralph Waldo Emerson

SEPTEMBER 2

Love Lifted Me

He lifted me out of the slimy pit...he set my feet on a rock.

—PSALM 40:2 (NIV)

DID YOU SEE that?" My husband quickly pulled our vehicle over to the side of the rural road. It had been raining for days, and the roadside ditches threatened to overflow. When he pointed, I saw what had attracted his attention: two small puppies appeared to have struggled out of the ditch onto the grassy bank. Bill scrambled out of the car. Suddenly, I had two squirming little creatures plopped in my lap. I removed my windbreaker, wrapping the drenched and trembling puppies inside, hugging them close to keep them warm until we got home.

"Someone must have tossed them out of a car or truck," Bill noted with disgust. I silently agreed. The poor little things were far too young and too small to have wandered this far out in the middle of nowhere.

At home, we dried the puppies off, then fed and cuddled them. I longed to keep the adorable, curly haired mutts, but knew it wasn't feasible, as Bill and I worked full time. Reluctantly, we took the two puppies to the animal shelter the next morning on our way to work and were relieved when the staff member assured us that she would have no trouble finding forever homes for these little cuties.

I've always been thankful that Bill spotted the puppies on the side of the road that day so we could rescue them. I am thankful, too, that God sent His only Son Jesus to rescue me. The Lord hasn't eliminated the water-filled ditches in my life, but He's always been there to lift me up, dry me off, and set me on my feet again. Those little puppies were worth saving. God thinks we're worth saving too. —Shirley Raye Redmond

He will lift you by His love out of the angry waves.
—James Rowe

We're All in This Together

For the creation was subjected to futility, not willingly, but because of Him who subjected it in hope; because the creation itself also will be delivered from the bondage of corruption into the glorious liberty of the children of God.

—ROMANS 8:20–21 (NKJV)

THE METEOROLOGIST ON my local evening news was about to say what weather to expect overnight. He showed a view of our area from a weather cam perched high on top of a skyscraper. But instead of the city skyline, clouds, and sunset, viewers were treated to the face of a black crow peering into the camera.

"I might need a little more time for this weather segment," the meteorologist said, "because we have a little visitor."

Sitting on my couch at home, I laughed as the curious crow's head and beak obscured everything. *Well, we're not alone on this planet.* It was a comforting thought.

Sometimes when I look around, life seems so chaotic. It feels as though it's just me against the world. Whether it's disturbing news on the television, family squabbles, health issues, natural disasters, even an unexpected crow interrupting the weather report, so many things are out of my control. These disheartening things can be very isolating. But that crow peering into the camera reminded me that I'm not alone in my struggles this side of heaven. The crow and I share the same planet, with all its potential and failings, and, according to Scripture, we are both waiting expectantly along with all of creation to be rescued.

That crow barging in on a weather report reminded me that the same loving God who watches over it takes care of me, too, and He has a plan for my salvation and deliverance "into the glorious liberty of the children of God." —Marianne Campbell

I feel a soaring in my heart that the God who could create all this—
and out of nothing—can still count the hairs of my head.
—Madeleine L'Engle

SEPTEMBER 4

Commonplace Treasures

The LORD your God in your midst, the Mighty One, will save;
He will rejoice over you with gladness, He will quiet you
with His love, He will rejoice over you with singing.

—ZEPHANIAH 3:17 (NKJV)

AS I TURNED into our driveway, I noticed a familiar oval-shaped object in our yard. Excited, I leapt from the car, fumbling with my keys to find the one to the house. Once inside, I grabbed my camera, then bypassed the dog's welcoming kisses to rush back out the door.

Of course, hurrying was unnecessary. The gray-brown wood turtle awaited me in the grass, not an inch from where I'd first seen it. I walked close, focused the camera to catch its nearly 11-inch-long shell, and excitedly snapped several photos to send to my uncle.

Most people in Pennsylvania would think a turtle is a commonplace critter, barely worth noticing. Some people help a slow, road-crossing turtle to the other side to help it avoid being crushed. But generally, turtles lead unnoticeable lives. So what prompted my excitement to send photos of said wood turtle to my uncle?

Because Uncle Alan loves turtles! To him, finding one in the yard delights him like a litter of fluffy pups does other people. At one time, he built a turtle pond on his property, complete with dirt and rocks for the reptiles to burrow under, pools to cool off in, and plants to dine on. Visitors enjoyed seeing his shelled menagerie.

To my uncle, turtles aren't commonplace, but treasures of creation. Sometimes I consider myself commonplace—a homemaker, no college degree, a devotional writer. But to God I'm not common at all because He loves me, His special treasure created in His image. As my uncle delights in turtles, so God delights in me. —Cathy Mayfield

And we, out of all creation, became his prized possession.
—James 1:18 (NLT)

SEPTEMBER 5

Like an Eagle

He guarded him…like an eagle that stirs up its nest and hovers over its young, that spreads its wings to catch them and carries them aloft.

—DEUTERONOMY 32:10–11 (NIV)

MOM, I SAW an eagle!" my son, Henry, exclaimed as he came running into the cabin. We were on a family trip, cabin camping at a state park. Henry had been fishing with his dad down by the river when the two of them saw an eagle in a tree. "Wow!" I replied and hurried out the door to look. I walked the 100 yards to the river and eagerly scanned the skies. Unfortunately, I couldn't see anything but turkey vultures. The eagle was gone.

Later that night after dinner, my husband started building a campfire. I strolled down to the river's edge to sit a spell and take in the sunset. Low and behold, an eagle arrived. And then another! It appeared they had a nest in the tree across the river. I was filled with awe as I sat quietly and watched them.

What a marvel bald eagles are, full of beauty and grandeur. They have a commanding presence yet are also such an embodiment of grace. No wonder they are a symbol of our great nation.

As I sat watching the eagles come and go, I thought of many of the places in the Bible that say God is like an eagle. He is majestic and strong, carrying us on His wings as He holds us up, guides us, and loves us. But He is also a protector and caretaker, spreading His wings to keep us safe and to catch us when we sin.

We have an amazing God! —Heather Jepsen

God, thank You for all the ways You guide and protect me.
I am happy to have shelter in Your wings. Amen.

SEPTEMBER 6

Playing Tag

But for you that honor my name, victory will shine like the sun with healing in its rays, and you will jump around like calves at play.

—MALACHI 4:2 (CEV)

MY FRIEND DIANA struggled with health challenges last year, but her love for rabbits and all of God's creatures—especially county fair types—kept her going. An avid rabbit breeder and showman, Diana also loves and appreciates her daughter's family's menagerie of rabbits, pigs, chickens, dogs, and chickens.

Their angus heifer, Molly, has quite the personality. She apparently thinks she is a dog, because she loves playing soccer with her snout with Diana's three grandsons. And she also noses her way through the fence to slap on a big, slurpy kiss, so you always have to watch out for that huge cow tongue coming for you!

Although Diana wasn't able to kick a soccer ball with Molly, they enjoyed a game of tag through the fence—what Diana said was a common activity for the two of them. With a tap of her hand, Diana would tag Molly, then the not-full-grown calf would prance around the corral, eventually circling back to my friend and tagging her back. Molly helped Diana chuckle and forget about her health struggles for a few minutes.

God's creatures can indeed help us forget the difficulties in our lives, providing a delightful distraction that lightens our hearts and countenance. They put into perspective that God means for us to enjoy the beauty and joy of the world around us rather than let it weigh us down. A butterfly flutters in front of us and makes us smile. A rainbow appears in the sky, reminding us that storms are only for a season. And even a silly animal such as a cow who thinks she's a dog invites us into moments of play that can lighten our hearts. When we pause to delight in play, I think God smiles too. —Janet Holm McHenry

Play is our brain's favorite way of learning.
—Diane Ackerman

SEPTEMBER 7

Lil' Owl Given Grace

I am like a desert owl, like an owl among the ruins.... You will arise and have compassion on Zion, for it is time to show favor to her; the appointed time has come.

—PSALM 102:6, 13 (NIV)

YOU GOTTA SEE the video Grace posted!"

My daughter held the iPhone as I continued snapping beans for supper. Within seconds, however, I wiped my hands on my pants, directing my full attention to the story on the screen.

After it ended, I said, "Wow! Play it again." I was intrigued, taken by my niece's compassion as she rescued a tiny screech owl.

Once more, we watched the short clip depicting the owl's release into the wild. "That's so sweet!" I exclaimed. "I'll need to talk to her, hear more of the story."

The next day, I called. Though the miles between her Ohio home and our North Carolina farm are too many for frequent visits, Grace and I share a special bond: a love of animals as well as the same September birthday.

"Grace, please tell me more about rescuing the screech owl."

My 17-year-old niece explained how she'd noticed something on the side of the road late one night and thought it a piece of trash. Still there the next morning, she stopped to investigate and discovered the small, injured bird.

"It's a miracle it hadn't been hit. I called 911, and they connected me with animal rescue. When the game warden arrived, he told me it appeared the owl's wing was broken, but he thought it could be rehabilitated."

Grace continued, sharing how, after several weeks, she received a call inviting her to participate in the owl's release. "It made me so happy knowing I'd played a part in its healing."

"Oh, it's no mistake, dear. You were right where God wanted you. He cares for all His creation and loves using us, His kids, to assist Him sometimes."

I'm proud of my birthday twin—for her compassion and kindness. Yes, her grace! And I'm reminded to thank our good Father for allowing me to be born at His appointed time, that I might serve with compassion, even the least of those in His created world. —Maureen Miller

Here [is] your good creature, O Lord, pondered and called to life by your own compassionate design...
—Douglas Kaine McKelvey

SEPTEMBER 8

On the Trail of God's Work

Therefore, my dear brothers and sisters, stand firm. Let nothing move you. Always give yourselves fully to the work of the Lord, because you know that your labor in the Lord is not in vain.

—1 CORINTHIANS 15:58 (NIV)

CHATTER FROM TWENTY-FIVE children broke through bird conversations from overhead branches as we walked the trail. When I guide children's nature hikes with groups this size, there is always a mixed bag of enthusiasm. While some kids run eagerly ahead, others lag behind, trying to adjust backpacks and attitudes.

My own mindset wasn't first-rate that morning. As a naturalist, I was guiding two group hikes that week on top of lesson planning and writing assignments. I love the work God has called me to do both in and outside my home. But on this particular morning, I was tired. And it was all I could do to excite the kids about nature. That is until the children up ahead stopped abruptly. My oldest son was leading the way when he pointed to tall grass beside the trail.

"There is something in there!" he exclaimed. Children trailing behind eagerly caught up to glimpse whatever was moving the grass. Suddenly, a large wild turkey popped her head out from the brush and hesitantly stepped onto the trail ahead of us. I've seen many wild turkeys, but I wondered if this was the first time for some of these children.

"A baby!" the kids exclaimed—and not just a single chick. One by one, chicks only a few inches tall scurried out onto the trail. We began counting in unison. "Two…three! Four! Five, six…seven! Eight, nine, ten…eleven!"

I watched the children's God-given curiosity rekindle as they observed the wild turkey family with awe. My own fatigue and struggling attitude melted into pure joy. Just like the mama turkey, I had the opportunity to lead these little ones through God's wonderful creation.

Whether I'm guiding nature hikes in our community or teaching my kids, I remember that mama turkey and I press on in the work God lays before me. —Eryn Lynum

For this I toil, struggling with all his energy that he powerfully works within me.
—Colossians 1:29 (ESV)

SEPTEMBER 9

Simple Joys

They…went home, joyful and glad in heart for all the good things the Lord had done.

—1 KINGS 8:66 (NIV)

I HAVE TAKEN A daily walk for years now. I am often accompanied by my own entourage, be it dogs, husband, or kids. For years this has been a wonderful family time for us.

When my kids were in preschool, the walks were a lot slower. They would spy something in the grass or by the side of the road, and we would all stop to look and enjoy. A favorite on our walks were the little moths flitting about in the grass. The kids would name each one, and in their minds we saw the same moths every time. There was Whitey, Blueberry, and Sunshine, each named after its color.

Now my kids are in school, so my walks are a solo adventure. But sometimes on the weekends, if their schedule isn't too full, they will join me for a stroll. Last Saturday as we were out on the trail, my daughter cried out with joy, "Look! It's Whitey!"

We all laughed as she pointed out a little white moth flying through the grass. It was a silly moment, but it reminded me of the simple pleasures of God's created world. When our kids are small, every moment, plant, animal, and insect is a miracle. As we get older, it's rare that we take pleasure in such simple things. And yet the wonder of God's good earth has not lost its splendor. A small white moth is still just as glorious now as it was when my children were small.

Noticing the wonders of creation, especially the things we are tempted to overlook, is a particular joy in my life. God has given us so much to rejoice in. —Heather Jepsen

Walk of Faith: *Today, try to notice something you may have looked past before. What part of God's good creation can you take joy in?*

SEPTEMBER 10

A Hidden Heron

And surely I am with you always, to the very end of the age.

—MATTHEW 28:20 (NIV)

IT'S FUNNY HOW you can be standing right next to something and not even know it's there. Last Saturday I was walking down an old towpath along a canal. Some of the birds that hang around the water are less familiar to me, so I got out my phone and consulted my Merlin Bird ID app, which has the wonderful ability to identify birds from a photo and by sound. When I tap the record button, the app identifies the birds it hears while they are actively singing. As I heard a raspy bark of a call, the words *Great Blue Heron* showed up on my app. I looked around, bewildered. How could such a large, beautiful bird be nearby, and I didn't know it?

It can be the same way with me and the Lord. So many times I go through my day without thinking that the Lord is with me, right beside me, even within me! I eat my meal without thanking Him; I do my work without asking for His direction. I worry about tomorrow without the awareness that He already has the details ironed out. There are also times when He feels very far away, as if He's left my side. But that is my fault. I need to keep my thoughts where they belong—on Him—and not try to handle life's challenges alone. I have a loving Father who is present and ready to help. I don't need an app to tell me that!

I'm missing a lot when I'm not conscious of God's presence beside me. Just like the birds around me, waiting to be discovered. I took a few steps along the path and peered across the canal. Maybe if I looked really hard, I'd spot that heron. —Peggy Frezon

Dear ever-present Father, I don't always see You, feel You,
or hear You, but Your Word assures me that You are always there.
Thank You for Your loving and constant presence in my life.

SEPTEMBER 11

If I Could Talk to the Animals

Therefore he had to be made like his brothers in every respect, so that he might become a merciful and faithful high priest in the service of God, to make propitiation for the sins of the people.

—HEBREWS 2:17 (ESV)

IN MY 40-PLUS years as a veterinarian, I sometimes envied my physician colleagues. In particular, I coveted their ability to communicate with their patients to figure out a problem. Being presented with an animal who "wasn't doing right" or "wasn't himself" made diagnosis challenging. Many times, I wished I could get inside my patient's head, even for a few minutes, and know what was going on. If I only had the ability to "talk to the animals" like Dr. Dolittle. Surely my maiden name of Little was close enough for me to be endowed with this skill. But no, I could only try to put myself in the animal's place and do the best I could.

Fortunately, we have a God who doesn't just sit back and wonder what it's like to be human. He loved us enough to put Himself in our place, leaving the splendor of heaven to step into our world in the form of a human and walk in our shoes. Jesus showed us how to live abundant, joyful lives by setting the perfect example. Although He experienced every trial, temptation, heartache, and physical and emotional suffering we do, Jesus never sinned. Finally, in a demonstration of supreme love, Jesus took our sin upon Himself by dying on the cross so we might have eternal life with Him.

As much as I would like to identify with my patients, I'm not sure I would want to live as one—at least not for long. I'm grateful for a God who humbled Himself to live as a human to *show* me the way. —Ellen Fannon

Who, being in very nature God, did not consider equality with God something to be used to his own advantage; rather, he made himself nothing by taking the very nature of a servant, being made in human likeness.

—Philippians 2:6–7 (NIV)

SEPTEMBER 12

A Cry for Help

He will rescue the poor when they cry to him; he will help the oppressed, who have no one to defend them...he will rescue them.

—PSALM 72:12–13 (NLT)

THE FIRE WAS blazing in our remote camping location along the river. As we talked, one friend alerted us to a chattering noise in the dark. Training flashing lights on a giant tree, we saw three masked faces pop up. Baby raccoons! Mama Raccoon was higher up the tree and glaring down. She had brought the babies, called kits, up the tree after we had eaten dinner alongside it and was now perhaps second-guessing that decision. The kits were curious about us but must have been worried about their mom. Two began a futile attempt to climb up the huge trunk.

After about 30 minutes, Mama Raccoon headed down the tree and into the woods, but the babies could not descend without help. The intensity level of their cries grew. We were worried that Mama would abandon them and we would be camping with a trapped nursery of young ones.

We eventually saw her shadow creeping back up. She grabbed one kit by the scruff and carried it down the tree to deliver it to safety. She repeated the process, then was gone for a long while. The last kit was now screaming, a panicked mess. His cries were painful to hear, especially knowing that with one misstep, he would tragically fall out of the tree.

Finally, it was silent. Our worries turned to celebration after a quick search revealed that the kit was out of the tree and must be safe with Mama. What a rescue!

The cries of that raccoon remind me of moments when I have been in deep grief. Raw pain is not pretty, and in it, I have felt so alone. Incredibly, God has rescued me many times through a timely and connected message from a friend or a physical sign that only I would recognize as having come from Him. When it feels like I am alone, He is never far. Just like Mama Raccoon. —Twila Bennett

Lord, thank You for hearing my cries, for knowing my wounded heart, and for the miraculous ways that You rescue me time and again. May I never forget.

SEPTEMBER 13

Alcatraz Bunny

In peace I will lie down and sleep, for you alone,
Lord, make me dwell in safety.

—Psalm 4:8 (NIV)

SEVEN YEARS AGO, when we rescued a stray bunny that hopped into our yard, my husband and I knew little to nothing about rabbit care. But we learned as much as we could, helping BunBun through several health crises and building bigger and better enclosures in our backyard.

My husband, a retired US Marine, insisted on a shipshape rabbit house, neatly organized with heat lamps, cooling fans, and green Astroturf for flooring. He trained BunBun to use a litter box and regularly tidied her area. For the most part, she was happy. But she always wanted out of her pen. And she loved to dig.

Every few days, BunBun dug under the flooring in her enclosure and tunneled as far as she could go. As soon as we found the holes, we'd fill them in or place rocks or bricks to discourage her from continuing to dig. But she wouldn't give up. BunBun was determined to break out of her personal Alcatraz, that famous San Francisco Bay prison.

I've explained to our dear bunny that her greenhouse-size enclosure is a mansion meant to keep her safe. Outside its borders, owls, raccoons, and other predators might attack her. She could graze on plants that make a rabbit sick. Whether or not she digs holes, she must stay in her pen.

I can relate to BunBun's yearning to run free. I often chafe at the parameters God sets for me, and I mistakenly think I should plan a prison break of my own. Yet when I remember why BunBun stays locked up, I see God's gentle hand protecting me rather than restraining me.

While she won't be able to escape, we'll also let her keep digging—even if we have to keep filling in her holes. Thanks to BunBun, I see how God gives us enough room to stretch while still enclosing us—and bunnies—in love. —Linda S. Clare

Walk of Faith: *Visit a shut-in or a nursing home and remind a resident that "some bunny loves them."*

SEPTEMBER 14

What's So Special about Grace?

From his abundance we have all received one gracious blessing after another.

—JOHN 1:16 (NLT)

WHILE TRAVELING WITH his family in Europe, my brother-in-law Ian sent me and my parents a gorgeous sunrise photo of a swan floating on the lake with one of her little cygnets. I had several images of swans on my phone already. One I took at St. James's Park in London during my first overseas trip. Another I'd spotted near a dock on Lake Geneva while at a writing seminar in Switzerland. I saved a short but glorious video that a friend captured in Ireland of a swan lifting her graceful wings just long enough to rise off the surface of the water.

Ian's picture was no less special because I'd seen and taken snapshots of other European swans. I have always been attracted to these graceful, winged creatures. With their long slender necks, lush feathers, and ability to glide across the lake like ballerinas, wild swans never fail to stop me in my tracks to marvel at and take a picture of if I have my camera handy.

I can't remember if Ian took that photo of the mother swan with her cygnet in Italy, Greece, or somewhere near Zurich, but its beauty was as unique as each experience I've had with God's grace. Each act of His goodness in my life is cause for thanksgiving. No matter how big or small, every gift that I know could only have come from Him is worth pausing to acknowledge, record in my journal, or even share with others: "Look what God just did."

Each instance deepens my trust in Him, confirms His sincere love for me, and provides memories for me to look back on when I'm tempted to lose hope.

I pray that, just as I'll never delete that swan picture, I will never lose my sense of wonder over the beauty of grace. —Jeanette Hanscome

Amazing grace! How sweet the sound.
—John Newton

SEPTEMBER 15

The Surety of Salmon

Know therefore that the L*ORD your God is God; he is the faithful God, keeping his covenant of love to a thousand generations of those who love him and keep his commandments.*

—DEUTERONOMY 7:9 (NIV)

I HEARD ABOUT THE return of Chinook salmon to nearby Sonoma Creek and grabbed my camera, eager to capture this special event. The spawning area is far up the watershed from the Pacific Ocean and, depending on rainfall during the year, it isn't always accessible to the salmon. But even after a couple of dry years when they couldn't make it this far, the way was swimmable and the salmon returned to spawn.

It was an amazing sight—about two dozen large gray fish swirling around in a small pool just off the hiking path. Signs nearby requested that we not disturb them, and every human being I saw was being respectful of the fishes' "home," observing them in quiet awe.

Instinct brought the Chinook back to their spawning pool, this place that is the source of life for them. It's remarkable that they remember precisely where they need to go and live. Year after year, generation after generation, the fish swim for hundreds of miles, braving predators and other obstacles, to come back to this exact spot and ensure the lives of future salmon.

Just like that specific pool of water is the source of life to these salmon, God's Word is my specific source of life. Within the pages of my Bible I find rich promises of love and mercy that I can get nowhere else. Each time I read it, I remember what God tells me about His love, my salvation, and eternal life. All around me are examples of His care and provision and protection, but if I ever doubt it, I remember the salmon. Just like they return home to ensure their continued life, I can return to God's Word and be reassured of my forever life. —Marianne Campbell

The L*ORD himself goes before you and will be with you; he will never leave you nor forsake you. Do not be afraid; do not be discouraged.*

—Deuteronomy 31:8 (NIV)

Surprised by a Snake

For the Lord your God moves about in your camp to protect you and to deliver your enemies to you. Your camp must be holy, so that he will not see among you anything indecent and turn away from you.

—DEUTERONOMY 23:14 (NIV)

A COUPLE WEEKS AGO, I opened the screen door to my patio to see my dog practically sitting on a young snake. Stunned, I snatched my dog out of the way, then watched as the small snake slowly slithered away. Once my heartbeat calmed, I briefly researched the snake to make sure it wasn't poisonous.

Turns out, the snake was harmless, which was a good thing, because it found its way back. Now, I watched it more closely. Grateful it hadn't tried to bite my dog, I began to feel sorry for the creature. The Florida heat that afternoon was extreme, and I am sure the snake was trying to find cooler shelter wherever it could. I prayed it would find what it needed—a nice distance away from my patio.

After my encounter with the snake, I began to think how challenging it must be for cold-blooded animals to regulate their body temperature. They are so dependent on outside factors that affect their well-being.

Though I often think of my spiritual walk as self-regulating, in reality, I'm a lot more like that snake than I realize. What I allow into my heart and mind have the power of life and death, both to myself and to those around me. My influences regulate my spiritual temperature, so to speak. I can choose to consume fear, strife, and negativity, or I can choose to meditate on temperate, good things. The choice is up to me—but the end result makes all the difference. —Ashley Clark

Father, help me find shelter in the promise of Your love—in the safe and bountiful spaces of Your provision—rather than seeking blessing through my own means. Thank You for Your goodness and faithfulness toward me. Guard my eyes and fix them on You.

Watch Out for the Guard Raven

But I will sing of your strength, in the morning I will sing of your love; for you are my fortress, my refuge in times of trouble.

—Psalm 59:16 (NIV)

WHILE WRITING AT my friend Susy's house, I was startled by the sound of her daughter, Teddy, yelling, "Hey!" and jumping up from her place at the kitchen table. She rushed outside.

From my desk in the upstairs bedroom, I heard squawks and frantic fluttering that told me Teddy's chickens and rooster were clearly in a crisis, most likely involving a predatory bird or animal. I sat frozen in front of my laptop and listened as Susy stopped typing and hurried outside to help her daughter. When the front door finally opened again, I ventured downstairs and found Susy in the kitchen.

"Is everything OK?"

Susy took a moment to regroup. "Teddy saw a coyote on the property." Her tone lightened. "When she went outside to scare it away, a raven was already chasing it off." She described the hilarious scene of a coyote running frantically with a raven, who'd declared himself the official protector of the chickens, at its tail. "Teddy and I just spent the last 20 minutes coaxing the chickens out of their hiding places. They're all fine."

Later that day, while feeding veggie scraps and leftover granola to the chickens, we spotted the hero raven and rewarded him with something from the bin.

Two months after that heart-stopping afternoon, Susy texted me to report that Teddy had just watched a raven—possibly the same one as before—chase a bobcat off their property, also to protect the chickens. I started seeing that raven as a reflection of God's protective presence. If He cared enough to use a raven to shield chickens from unwelcome guests, I can trust Him to stand between me and unforeseen danger. I can trust Him with those I love and celebrate each time I experience His faithful hand of safety. —Jeanette Hanscome

But the Lord is faithful, and he will strengthen you and protect you from the evil one.
—2 Thessalonians 3:3 (NIV)

SEPTEMBER 18

Screwed-Up Bee

So, big mountain, who do you think you are? Next to Zerubbabel you're nothing but a molehill.

—ZECHARIAH 4:7 (MSG)

I SHOULD'VE BEEN SAFE driving down a highway with my window open. When I'm on a country road, I close my car windows to avoid bees flying in. But none could get in with driving speeds of 65 miles per hour—or so I thought.

However, something black whacked the inside of the windshield, flew by my face, and landed on the seat between my legs. A glance down showed no sign of the insect, which meant it went deeper on the seat, almost under my bum! Fear grew to massive proportions as I imagined the pain the soon-to-be sting would produce.

I looked for a safe place to pull over, and seeing none, I prayed the bee had been stunned or killed from its collision with the window. I knew the exit I wanted wasn't far and had a parking lot near the off-ramp. Panting from fear, I navigated the last few miles while peering down every 50 yards, assuming the bee would come crawling out between my legs.

When I reached the lot, I zoomed into a parking space, opened the car door, and leapt out. Freed from the precarious situation, I looked at the small dark object on the driver's seat—a half-inch screw, one that had kept falling out of the frame of the sun visor!

How often does this scenario play out: me panicking unnecessarily over imagined "stingers" in my life, ones that end up as "screwed-up bees"? As with all the gifts God gives me, my imagination needs a little discipline thrown in now and then. And maybe some prayer. —Cathy Mayfield

Walk of Faith: *When your imagination goes wild, tame it with prayer.*

SEPTEMBER 19

Our Rescuer

To you they cried and were rescued; in you they trusted and were not put to shame.

—PSALM 22:5 (ESV)

I LOVE FEEDING MY rabbits. Each morning, they hop around, thumping and putting their paws on their food bowls, eager for the green pellets of yumminess. Chip was doing just that this particular morning. He was a wild guy who was never still for long, and when I fed him, he wolfed down his food. A moment later, his eyes widened and foam poured out of his mouth. My young daughter pointed at him and screamed, "Chip is choking."

Our cries of alarm alerted my husband who raced to the garage and pulled Chip out of the cage. I ran inside to search the internet: Heimlich for rabbits. Once I told him how, my husband laid Chip over his arm and made the downward swinging motion to push the air out of Chip's lungs and dislodge the food blocking his windpipe. It took a few attempts, but the food came out and Chip could breathe. Because of his rescue efforts, my husband is the only one Chip relaxes around. He's Chip's best friend.

Heroes are often celebrated, especially by those who have been rescued. It's an incredible thing to be saved from a scary situation. Because we are Christians, our Savior saves us not only from one scary event, but also from the ultimate death that comes from sin. That kind of saving should inspire us to get close to Him, just as Chip does with my husband. As a thank-You to Jesus our Savior who rescued us, we can snuggle close and celebrate Him as our ultimate Hero. —Kristen G. Johnson

God does not stop at rescuing us; the purpose of that rescue is to enjoy fellowship with us.

—A. W. Tozer

SEPTEMBER 20

What the Lizards Taught Me

A man's pride will bring him low, but the humble in spirit will retain honor.

—PROVERBS 29:23 (NKJV)

THE FIRST THING I noticed was a flash of bright red. I turned and saw the morning sun shining through a brown lizard's dewlap. Out and in that thin flap of skin moved. With each extension of the dewlap beneath its chin, the lizard bobbed up and down as if to say, "Look at me, everyone. Look at me."

I searched for the cause of the lizard's display. Another male was a few feet away. He, too, puffed his dewlap in and out and bobbed up and down. From what I've discovered observing lizards, these two were trying to make themselves appear bigger than they actually were. They were trying to figure out who was the strongest. By flashing their dewlaps in and out, they were establishing their territory.

As I watched their display, I realized something important. I'm not so different from those two lizards. I may not have a flashy red dewlap, but I have been guilty of puffing myself up with pride. I have bobbed up and down in an effort to make myself appear larger. I have expended energy trying to make my influence greater than need be. I've gotten into standoffs with others, not wanting to show weakness or back down.

At the time, I found the lizards' antics rather funny. Although the prideful behavior of these two creatures posturing to look impressive might look humorous, there is nothing humorous about it when I do the same thing. —Sandy Kirby Quandt

Pride is a person having too high an opinion of himself. Pride is the first sin that ever entered into the universe, and the last sin that is rooted out.

—Jonathan Edwards

Little Flock

Do not fear, little flock, for it is your Father's good pleasure to give you the kingdom…a treasure in the heavens that does not fail, where no thief approaches nor moth destroys.

—LUKE 12:32–33 (NKJV)

DRIVING TO THE Pacific Coast or along Interstate 5, I often see flocks of sheep in amazing numbers. When visitors come from out of state to see my family in Oregon, they comment on the beauty of the Willamette Valley, where green fields are dotted with white. Some mention the resemblance to the hillsides of England and the western coastline of Ireland.

Raising sheep in Oregon is prevalent along the grassy slopes of the rugged coastline and in the western valleys, where soil and climate conditions are ideal. Oregon is one of the top ten states for its number of sheep. To see these gentle creatures in such great numbers has blessed me. More and more, I am inspired by the parallels to my Christian life.

Our Good Shepherd, Jesus, calls His children "little flock." I have pondered this thought and how we need one another as Christians. We need to remain in the flock to stay connected as prayer partners and to encourage one another, and we are less likely to go astray if we are accountable to one another. We are safer in the parameters of the herd, rather than walking alone where the enemy of our souls may lurk. When members of the fold are kept home due to immobility or other health issues, we can still be together in spirit and in prayer—calling one another, writing a note, or making a visit to stay connected. God shepherds His flock, as they care for one another—just as Jesus said to Peter, after Peter declared his love for Jesus, "Tend My sheep" (John 21:16, NKJV).

The Lord is my Shepherd, and He leads me to an inheritance that lasts forever. In the pasture of life, I am part of His flock—as we walk each other home to heaven. —Kathleen R. Ruckman

Dear God, thank You for reminding me how important it is to stay in the sheepfold, rich with fellowship, where You count and cherish each one.

SEPTEMBER 22

Not Alone in Our Struggles

Both you and these people who are with you will surely wear yourselves out. For this thing is too much for you; you are not able to perform it by yourself.

—EXODUS 18:18 (NKJV)

MY YORKIE'S STITCHES lay exposed. I sat on the bathroom floor with bandages strung about. She needed my assistance yet refused to allow me to help her.

Minnie had surgery to remove a lump from her back left leg and had to wear an Elizabethan collar. She struggled to maneuver with the cone around her neck. I had to keep the wound covered for 10 days to allow the incision time to heal.

Keeping a dressing on Minnie's tiny leg was a challenge. At first the bandage was too tight, so the vet rewrapped it. The looser bandage lasted only a day or so before sliding off and requiring another visit.

After a week, I could re-dress her wound myself. At first Minnie let me replace the wrapping with ease. I even changed her bandage once in the middle of the night. But then her patience disappeared. She kicked and wiggled whenever I tried to replace the bandage. Wrapping the gauze around her tiny leg took more than 30 minutes.

On the day of her final vet appointment to remove the stitches, the bandage had slipped down, exposing them. I attempted to rewrap the wound before we headed out, but she put up too much of a fight. I gave up the challenge.

Minnie fidgeted the entire car ride. During the time of removal, one tech worked on the stitches. Another assisted by holding Minnie while I attempted to soothe her with soft words. Minnie continued to kick and wiggle, so they brought in another tech to hold her leg still. They traded positions to get out the last of the stitches.

Three to four people were needed to complete what I tried to do on my own, a good reminder that God provides others to come alongside us so we don't have to do everything all alone. —Crystal Storms

Bear one another's burdens, and so fulfill the law of Christ.
—Galatians 6:2 (NKJV)

SEPTEMBER 23

Never Tired of Seeing Me

He will not let your foot slip—he who watches over you will not slumber.

—PSALM 121:3 (NIV)

SEVENTEEN, EIGHTEEN! WAIT, there's another one! Nineteen!" Counting deer at my aunt and uncle's property delighted me. I raced like a child from the sliding door to their deck to the front bay window, numbering the deer that fed on their trees and shrubs, much to my aunt's consternation.

"You'd think they'd eat the corn and bread we feed them and leave my bushes alone." But she still fed them, watched them gallivant, coddled the one with the limp. Every day, every season (except during hunting season). On each visit to their home, I was right beside her, trying to hand-feed the timid doe, exclaiming over the antlers on the buck, swooning over the dotted fawns.

In Pennsylvania, white-tailed deer—our state animal—abound. I see them several days a week depending on the season. Other than the occasional trophy buck with wide spreads and numerous points that entice hunters, or possibly a piebald with splotches of white covering places on its hide, these deer are nondescript. Brown coats that change hues by season, brown eyes, white fur on the underside of their bellies and tails—nothing to say, "Look at me! I'm incredible!" And yet I never tire of watching them, loving them.

I'm sort of the same as those deer. A typical woman, graying hair, medium build, brown eyes. I see nothing special in the mirror, no one calling me for TV interviews or feature articles in the newspaper. Nothing to say, "Look at me! I'm incredible!" Yet, every day, God tells me, "Yes, you are!" He never gets tired of watching me, loving me. —Cathy Mayfield

Some days, Lord, I feel nondescript, nothing special. But
You lovingly say, "Look at you! You're incredible!
I'll always be watching you, loving you." Thank You.

SEPTEMBER 24

A Beautiful Life

Be kindly affectionate to one another with brotherly love, in honor giving preference to one another.

—ROMANS 12:10 (NKJV)

AS MY BABY daughter, Avery, crawled on the floor, she rounded the corner from the dining room to the kitchen. There, she was greeted with a sloppy wet kiss from my in-law's black-and-white spotted Boston terrier. Bella had a wonderful temperament and looked like a puppy even at full-grown. She suffered from allergies and had to be on a special diet, but her ailments didn't define her. *Bella* means "beautiful," and this pup lived that out to the fullest.

Toward the end of her life, Bella struggled with poor eyesight and body pain. Nearly a decade since their first greeting, my daughter knew she would have to say goodbye to her best friend. Avery's questions about Bella allowed us to talk about living for eternity with God, in heaven.

Before Bella died, our two oldest children wrote her letters. They read them to Bella as she sat on our mudroom floor one last time. Their words taught me about the importance of appreciating a life filled with beauty. They shared stories and the qualities they loved the most about Bella. I realized that she made their life better because of friendship. Finally, my husband and I took one last picture of our three kids next to Bella, to be hung up in their bedrooms later.

As I think about Bella's life, I reflect on my own. I want to be kind and considerate and to have the playful energy that she did. I want to walk up to friends and give them a big hug. I want to be gracious to others and experience God's abundant blessings in return. What a legacy she left us as we follow in her paw prints. —Stacey Thureen

Walk of Faith: *Think about the people in your life who have influenced you in a significant way. Reach out to them through a phone call or send them a handwritten note. Thank them for their love and friendship.*

SEPTEMBER 25

Termite Troubles

Cast all your anxieties on him because he cares for you.

—1 PETER 5:7 (NIV)

WHAT THE...?!" A large commotion was coming from the basement. My husband and I had just bought a 100-plus-year-old home and were having the basement remodeled. The contractor was demolishing the knotty paneling that had been installed some 50 years earlier. When I went downstairs, I saw the old paneling splintered on the floor with tiny white insects wriggling in the daylight.

"Termites!" the workers declared. I was flummoxed and had no idea what to do next. Fortunately, the contractor gave me the number of an exterminator. As the exterminator explained, the termites were discovered early in the renovation process and could be addressed before any damage and any new work was completed. She explained the nature of the bugs and how they invade. Once I understood that, I was not worried.

By allowing the experts to take care of the problem, I was not anxious. Much of my fear about the insects was based on horror stories I'd heard or read about termite infestation. But by speaking with the experts, I learned not to fear the termites and instead to appreciate how they break down debris and "clean up" the wood.

There have been so many times in my life when I worried about my children and their decisions. At times I've worked myself up with preconceived problems and what-ifs to the point of not knowing what to do next. It was only when I learned to turn those worries over to "the expert"—God—that I felt peace. The more I prayed to God and read His Word, the more I understood that He cares about all the things that I care about.

Once I accepted the "homeowner's worst nightmare," I was able to make decisions and move forward, realizing that having termites was not the worst thing. And once I accepted that my children's future was between them and God and that He cares for them even more than I do, I was able to worry less and find peace with their decisions. —Virginia Ruth

Thank You, Heavenly Father, for being the expert of my life. Thank You that I can cast my worries upon You and You relieve my fears. Amen.

SEPTEMBER 26

Guard Goose

I long to dwell in your tent forever and take refuge in the shelter of your wings.

—PSALM 61:4 (NIV)

MY 89-YEAR-OLD MOTHER lives alone in a senior facility. It's hard to watch her retreat from the world, but even harder to get her to turn off the blaring television. "It makes me feel safe," she declared.

One spring day, I asked her to turn off the TV. She scowled but obliged. Then I pointed to a scene beyond her apartment window. "Look," I said. "Goslings! The lawn is covered in goslings!" Sun glinted off the babies' downy coats as the adult Canada geese fed.

Mom's face lit up. "Aren't they adorable?" She stared out the window. Then she frowned. "Why are those two adults just standing around?"

I chuckled. "All the geese except those two are feeding or teaching the babies how to find food." I laid a hand on Mom's shoulder. "See how those two geese aren't looking at the ground? They're sentries. Guard geese. They make sure everyone stays safe while they feed. Soon, another pair will start guarding so these two can forage."

We watched the flock pull worms and other tasty snacks from the grass, with two adults always watching for danger. I patted Mom's hand. "Those two keeping watch are like God promising to protect us," I said. "Just like geese on duty, God never leaves us on our own."

Before I said goodbye that day, I made sure Mom had everything she needed. "Want me to put your TV back on?"

But Mom surprised me. "No, I think I'll sit here and watch the geese awhile." She set the remote aside. "Those goslings are cute as can be." She smiled. "Besides, I love that the geese are on duty. They make me feel safe." I thanked God for geese that take their duties seriously and prayed for Mom to feel secure under the shelter of His wings. —Linda S. Clare

I held my breath as we do sometimes to stop time when
something wonderful has touched us.
—Mary Oliver

SEPTEMBER 27

A Strange Stranger

Do not forget to entertain strangers, for by so doing some have unwittingly entertained angels.

—HEBREWS 13:2 (NKJV)

I WISH I HAD been a fly on the wall…or a mouse in the corner.

My daughter and husband were sharing a heart-to-heart conversation late one night in our basement. She sat on the stairs, while my husband had swiveled his office chair to face her. What they were discussing remains unknown to me, but it must have been a tender conversation. Suddenly they noticed they were not alone. A small rat sat between them, watching their conversation as if it were a tennis game, turning his head side to side as each spoke.

I became aware of the situation when after some audible commotion downstairs, my husband loaded a small cardboard box into the car and drove away. Later he recounted the story: He had taken the rat to the beach and released it. As he backed his car away from the log that marked his parking space, shadows of two small ears, like those of a famous mouse, appeared in the headlight beam. That was the last he saw of the rat.

Generally, we are anti-pest, anti-rodent sorts of folks. When we had a mouse invasion, I was quick to get a cat, and another cat sits on my desk as I write this very minute. I asked my husband why so much mercy was shown to this particular rat.

"He seemed friendly—like he wanted to help." I love that my husband's interpretation of the small intruder's appearance was beneficence and that the interpretation led him to an act of mercy too. Certainly, the impact of the Incident of the Big-Eared Rat, as it came to be called, was positive for our family, serving as a reminder to listen to one another with "big ears." —Susie Colby

Walk of Faith: *What opportunities for mercy might emerge today if I assume positive intent when I encounter people and if I listen with my big ears?*

SEPTEMBER 28

Daily Walk

Enoch walked faithfully with God; then he was no more, because God took him away.

—GENESIS 5:24 (NIV)

ROUTINES ARE GREAT for people and their pets. Raleigh, our golden retriever, looks forward to our morning walks. We head out through the back portion of our property onto the short trail I cleared that leads to a seldom used community park. When Raleigh hits the openness of the park, he takes off running in wide circles as fast as he can. He has a lot more energy than I do since in dog years, he's quite a bit younger.

Our daily walks build a tight bond of companionship between us. At certain spots along the way, I call him in close and give him a dog treat. Our routine is so well established that he will sometimes run ahead of me and wait at one of those proper spots. I am pretty sure he is glad I retired, because we get to share our daily walk together.

I admire the close relationship God had with Enoch. They had their own routine of daily walks. They committed to spending time together, which strengthened the bond they shared. Their friendship deepened to such a point that God did something unique with Enoch. He allowed him to forgo experiencing death. Here's how I think it could have happened.

One day they were walking together, engaged in conversation. Not realizing how far they had traveled, God might have said to Enoch, "You know something? We have walked together for so long that we are closer to My home than yours. Why don't you just come home with me today?" And Enoch agreed. What a unique experience.

Raleigh gets to walk home with me every day. I wonder if my four-legged friend senses our bond growing ever stronger. It makes me realize that my daily walk with God strengthens my relationship with Him. A relationship that isn't born out of obligation, but one that matures out of a desire to know Him more. As my relationship with Him grows deeper throughout my earthly life, my anticipation of my heavenly home with God becomes sweeter. —Ben Cooper

Lord, help me to walk with You daily, like Enoch did. Allow our bond to grow tighter each day as You lead me closer to Your heavenly home. Amen.

Family Reunion

There is neither Jew nor Greek, there is neither bond nor free, there is neither male nor female: for ye are all one in Christ Jesus.

—GALATIANS 3:28 (KJV)

PEOPLE FILLED THE stands in anticipation of the sea lion show as the graceful mammals glided through the water. When the program started, the trainer called one of her charges onto the deck for an introduction.

"This is Ely," she said. "He's a California sea lion. Unfortunately, many people think he's a seal."

Ely covered his face with his flipper, feigning disbelief. The trainer went on to point out the distinctions between sea lions and the harbor seals also swimming in the tank. In addition to external ear flaps, the sea lions had large winglike front flippers as opposed to the harbor seals' smaller front appendages. The sea lions' bigger flippers, along with their greater flexibility, allowed them to "walk," more easily on land. Harbor seals, on the other hand, used an undulating movement called galumphing. Though the two marine animals had many similarities, they also had many differences.

I, too, have many differences from my brothers and sisters in Christ, but as Paul told the Galatians, those differences don't matter. I have the same Savior, the same Father in heaven, and the same mission here on earth as my fellow believers. We are all "children of God by faith" (Galatians 3:26, KJV). Because of that, I can count on support from my extended family. I don't have to galumph along on my own. That's a relief to know in this increasingly wacky world in which we live.

And someday, I'll be united with other brothers and sisters I don't even know yet. What a reunion that will be! —Tracy Crump

Walk of Faith: *Look for a fellow believer you can draw into fellowship with your church or small group. Show that person the unconditional love of being "one in Christ Jesus."*

SEPTEMBER 30

Protection from the Storm

He who dwells in the shelter of the Most High will abide in the shadow of the Almighty. I will say to the LORD, "My refuge and my fortress, my God, in whom I trust."

—PSALM 91:1–2 (ESV)

THE STRAY TORTOISESHELL cat we fed and housed on our front porch delivered three kittens, two black and one cream-colored. We couldn't provide a forever home for any of them because of cat allergies, but we gave temporary protection, care, and love.

Mama Cat didn't like our front porch and moved her babies to an unprotected depression beside the house. A day later, with the onset of raindrops, I made my way to her hideout. The nursing mother cat glared. I ran inside to get a bowl of food as a bribe.

Drops turned into torrents, thunder crashed, and lightning flashed. Scared, Mama Cat leaped onto the porch but left her babies in the deluge. Three kittens with closed eyes mewed frantically as the depression filled with rain. Water from the gutter above pounded the tiny babies.

The storm was raging when I stepped off the porch a second time. I grabbed the three kittens, placed them into my already-soaked T-shirt, and ran. I dried all three, settled them into the cardboard box on the porch, and prayed they wouldn't get pneumonia. After coaxing Mama back into the box to warm them, I retreated inside for my own towel. "What a crazy cat," I mumbled to an empty house. "Why did you leave the shelter of the porch? We fixed up a cozy, warm place for you. How did you think your plan was better than ours?"

Suddenly, I laughed at my musing and wondered if God had similar questions about my behavior. Like the time I strayed from His protection to pursue my own plans instead of His. Or the time I abandoned my prayer time and Bible reading because "I was too busy." Fortunately, those storms sent me running back to the shelter of the Most High, right where I belong. —Julie Lavender

Dear God, help me dwell in Your shelter, especially when the storms of life assail. Amen.

October

OCTOBER 1

Buzzard's Gulch

O LORD, what a variety of things you have made! In wisdom you have made them all. The earth is full of your creatures. Here is the ocean, vast and wide, teeming with life of every kind, both large and small.

—PSALM 104:24–25 (NLT)

MY TWO 11-YEAR-OLD nephews and I made our way along a familiar trail in the woods. As the path zigged and zagged, we engaged in small talk and just enjoyed being on another adventure. The boys arrived first at the place where the path crossed County Line Road. Suddenly, they both fell silent as three giant turkey buzzards came into view. Almost as tall as the boys, the buzzards stood over a large animal carcass, picking at it and eating hungrily.

Although the name of the trail, Buzzard's Gulch, might hint at the presence of the big birds, neither young man had seen one before. They were astonished at the size of the black-and-white-feathered monstrosities. As the birds moved to reposition themselves, their huge wingspans seemed wide enough to completely encapsulate a boy. As I caught up to them, I heard their excited voices.

"That is the biggest bird I've ever seen," Justin exclaimed.

"What are they eating?" Peyton asked.

"Not sure, but the buzzards seem to be enjoying it."

Just as quickly as the birds appeared, they dispersed when a blue SUV came up the road. The majesty of the birds became even more apparent when they beat their wings wildly to fly away from the rapidly approaching Chevy.

As the boys recounted their story at the dinner table, I couldn't help but think of the infinite wonders of my Father's world. He created birds, forest animals, fish, and insects of so many colors, sizes, and shapes, each one a reminder of the creativity of our God. He knew as He created the world how and why each creature would enhance our lives, even predatory birds like the turkey buzzard. Oh Lord, what a variety of things You have made! —David L. Winters

Thank You, God, for all of Your creation. Each animal reminds us of the complexity and joy in this world. I praise You for all these gifts.

OCTOBER 2

My Oversize Bottle of Tears

You keep track of all my sorrows. You have collected all my tears in your bottle. You have recorded each one in your book.

—PSALM 56:8 (NLT)

WE KNEW WE couldn't keep the felines when we rescued the pregnant stray from the woods near our house. After providing a temporary place to stay for her and her three kittens, we knew it was time to find them new homes.

We soon found out that the wife of my husband's colleague rescued stray cats and placed them in forever homes. The day finally came, almost 9 weeks after we fell in love with the mother feline, to deliver all four to the rescue home. Fortunately, Mama Cat was easily coaxed into the pet carrier, and we slipped the kittens inside one at a time to join her. Their puzzled stance, questioning eyes, and forlorn mews tugged at my heart.

The tears began to flow as I watched my husband walk to his car with the carrier. I prayed my husband wouldn't have an allergy attack during the hourlong commute, and I prayed for an amazing, loving home for the cats. I cried off and on all day.

It comforted me to know that God caught each one of my tears, while consoling me with the warmth of His presence. I thought about other tears shed in recent years—grieving ones over the loss of my 47-year-old brother, empty-nest ones when my youngest child moved to another state, devastated ones for my friend who lost her husband to COVID, sad ones for a young friend who suffered a miscarriage, frustrated ones over a dishwasher fiasco that resulted in a flooded kitchen, and so many more.

My temporary furry friends who etched a permanent place on my heart remind me that God catches *all* my tears, those shed from big matters and seemingly small losses too. —Julie Lavender

Dear God, thank You for loving me so much that you don't delineate the importance of my tears; You hold me close and catch them all.

OCTOBER 3

Nature's Defensive Weapons

Call upon Me in the day of trouble; I will deliver you, and you shall glorify Me.

—PSALM 50:15 (NKJV)

AS WE WALKED around the beautiful Arizona-Sonora Desert Museum a placard caught my attention. In bold letters, it read, "Gross! Chew on this: Adaptations are nature's way of giving species the upper hand." Indeed the information listed was repulsive. The turkey vulture pukes. The Sonora mud turtle emits a foul-smelling stink. The regal horned lizard squirts blood. Hooded skunks, well, everyone knows what skunks do.

The placard gained new significance for me during early fall's stink bug jamboree at our house. These insects have become my nemesis as they relentlessly look for any crack to enter our home, bringing with them their obnoxious, defensive odor.

Defensive maneuvers. "Stay away, don't hurt me, don't eat me, don't take what's mine" weapon. It's a useful adaptation that works for insects and animals.

We humans also gravitate toward using personal defenses: sarcasm, avoidance, retreat, confrontation, altercations, and isolation to name a few. We've honed them through frequent practice. We are ever ready to fight our battles using our comfortable strategies instead of relying on the One who is our greatest defense.

Throughout the Psalms, King David sang of God's reliable defense. He refers to the Lord as his defender, his stronghold, and his sanctuary. He acknowledges his complete reliance on God, calls for God's deliverance, and speaks of unwavering expectations of the Lord's provision. I'm humbled by David's grasp of God as his defender.

David remembered and proclaimed. I likewise want to proclaim the many times the Lord's defense has been proven in my life. Remembering gives me the courage to believe I'm always safe under His loving wing. Unlike stink bugs, which must rely on their own defenses, I'm grateful that my best defense is always God's defense and He's always on the watch. —Darlene Kerr

Walk of Faith: *Today, recall one instance of God's protection that you've experienced. Declare His past faithfulness to help you build your trust in Him when you face a new challenge.*

OCTOBER 4

The Blue Jay Battle

Put on the full armor of God, so that you can take your stand against the devil's schemes.

—EPHESIANS 6:11 (NIV)

MY HUSBAND, TIM, and I strolled around the large cemetery located at a remote country church. We walked one lap on the paved pathway before the peacefulness was interrupted.

"Jeer! Jeer!" From behind us came the attack call of blue jays. Whatever was causing the chatter and aggression was shielded from our sight. We could only see the pair strafing some unknown vicious predator. Despite the birds' warnings, we crept a bit closer.

The intruder rushed out from behind a row of headstones. Striding straight toward us was…a little black kitten. He was mewing, but acted like he had nothing to fear.

Again the blue jays dive-bombed the fearless feline, attempting to peck him on top of his head. Tim acted quickly by scooping up the kitten and jogging toward our truck. He gently settled the kitten on the seat. As I hurried to follow him, I observed the blue jays heading toward their nesting area in the trees. *"Jeer! Jeer!"* The battle had been won.

We checked on the kitty. He had curled up in the middle of the seat and was fast asleep! His purring sounded like the truck's motor was running. Tim named the rescue kitten Stamper, after the church where we had been walking.

I want to be more like Stamper (and Tim), maintaining tranquility while a battle rages around me. Tim was fighting cancer but was at peace with the diagnosis and trusted fully in God. As for me, I was struggling with being strong among all the enemy's attacks on my faith and positive mindset. I am reminded of what Paul writes in Ephesians about the full arsenal of God's protection. Wearing the shoes with sure footing, I can stand firm. The shield of faith over my heart deflects doubts.

While fleeing the blue jays, we could have all benefited from "the full armor"! From now on, as I start my day, I will visualize the armor deflecting attacks on my peace of mind. —Glenda Ferguson

Walk of Faith: *Read Ephesians 6:10–17. Visualize donning the full armor as you begin your day.*

OCTOBER 5

The Golden Arrow

He will cover you with his feathers, and under his wings you will find refuge; his faithfulness will be your shield and rampart.

—PSALM 91:4 (NIV)

I'M AN ANXIOUS traveler, and a few days before I depart, I worry. I worry about all the details, and then I worry about all the details I might have forgotten. Sometimes I can get so knotted up, I snap at loved ones who innocently ask about my travel plans. I've tried all sorts of techniques to deal with it—breathing, praying, making lists, drinking tea—but nothing has helped me completely relax before a trip.

About a week before my most recent journey, I was sitting on a bench in the park looking up at the sky. It was a deep bright blue, filled with the thick light-rimmed clouds that the Gulf Coast sky so famously produces. Far above me, I saw a heron, not an uncommon sight in this area. But this heron did not take a horizontal flight path. It flew higher than herons normally do, approaching the heavens at such an angle that it looked like it was made of pure gold. With its wide wingspan and its legs extended behind it, it looked like an ancient arrow, shot from the bow of a hero, flying as if it would never stop and never descend.

Far below, I realized that all the worries on earth meant nothing to that heron. It was connected to God in pure flight. *I want to be free like that heron,* I thought. *I want to soar above anxiety and crabbiness and just take in the world around me.* I stood up and returned home, vowing to approach my coming departure as pure adventure, an opportunity to see the wonders wrought by God. —Lucy Chambers

Help me to journey beyond the familiar
and into the unknown.
Give me the faith to leave old ways
and break fresh ground with You.
Christ of the mysteries, I trust You
to be stronger than each storm within me.
I will trust in the darkness and know
that my times, even now, are in Your hand.
Tune my spirit to the music of heaven,
and somehow, make my obedience count for You.
—St. Brendan

OCTOBER 6

Squirrel Gluttons

When you sit to dine with a ruler, note well what is before you, and put a knife to your throat if you are given to gluttony. Do not crave his delicacies, for that food is deceptive.

—PROVERBS 23:1–3 (NIV)

ON A VISIT to see my family in Louisiana in the early fall, I noticed the immense size of the squirrels. I suppose squirrels everywhere try to beef up for the winter, but I swear these squirrels were the size of large house cats.

My sister explained that her squirrels enjoyed the cardinal food, the bluebird food, and fruit scraps thrown into the yard. "They gorge themselves! A nurse I met told me that one day she heard a thud outside and found that one of her fat squirrels had fallen out of a tree, probably because he was so heavy, he couldn't hang on to the branches!"

There are a lot of deceptive things in life that pull at our focus and tempt us with the promise of bigger, better, and more. Material things will never give us true satisfaction. They are distractions that just make us want more and more and *more*. Craving these things doesn't mean they are good for us either. In fact, they probably aren't.

It's easy to think of gluttony as a little sin, something we gloss over on the list of things we are not to do, because it doesn't sound as bad as some of the bigger sins. But is it? Ask that fat squirrel who fell out of the tree with a thud. Better yet, ask yourself how you can change your gluttonous ways so that your "falls" in life may be met with the cushion of Jesus's grace and forgiveness. —Devon O'Day

God, draw me to good things and teach me my limits.

OCTOBER 7

Waiting for the Food Bowl

How much more will your heavenly Father give good gifts to those who ask him.

—MATTHEW 7:11 (NLT)

WAIT." I HAD my hand up. Our little rescue dog was sitting, looking at me as I filled his dog bowl. We'd had a very active day, hiking at a nearby park. I knew Scuppers was hungry.

We were training Scuppers to sit while we filled his bowl and then "release" when we were ready. Sometimes we would make him repeat the waiting because he would eagerly start eating before we gave the command.

I was planning on filling the bowl with a little more food and needed for him to sit just a little bit longer while I dipped the scooper a second time into the food canister.

"Wait...way-ate," I singsonged to him. As I stepped away from his bowl, he raised up on his haunches and before I had a chance to dip the second scoop into the food container, he was eating from the food bowl.

"Oh Scuppers. You needed to wait." I was disappointed. If he'd just waited a little bit longer, he would've received more food.

I wonder how often God has me waiting. In my impatience, do I miss out on more? So many times I complain that God did not act quickly enough. But what if He was training me to wait so that He could bless me even more? Like Scuppers, I need to learn to wait and trust that God will give me what is needed at just the right time. —Virginia Ruth

Giver of all good gifts, thank You that You remind us of Your timing for all that we receive. Amen.

OCTOBER 8

Toward a Destination

I have fought the good fight, I have finished the race, and I have remained faithful. And now the prize awaits me—the crown of righteousness, which the Lord, the righteous Judge, will give me on the day of his return. And the prize is not just for me but for all who eagerly look forward to his appearing.

—2 TIMOTHY 4:7–8 (NLT)

IT WAS DUSK as I sat on my front porch steps. A movement caught my eye. I assumed it was a black cat crossing the street. Then I noticed the white stripe.

It meandered into our yard, making its way into our backyard. *Please don't decide to live under our deck,* I thought. I could imagine that animal's scent working its way through our open windows. Gingerly peeking around the corner of the house, I was too slow and cautious to see where it went.

It's not an everyday event to mistake skunks for cats in our suburban neighborhood. Despite my concern, I smiled at nature coming for a visit.

My thoughts turned to Daddy, now gone for 25 years. I remembered when he and I had watched cartoons together. His favorite was Pepé Le Pew, that over-amorous skunk who irrepressibly chased a black cat. Daddy would have enjoyed watching this skunk. We would have laughed together and named our visitor Pepé.

I can no longer remember my father's voice. This saddens me. But he left a legacy I'll never forget. I'll remember that he ran the race to the end, faithful to the Lord until his dying breath. I'm so thankful that it is his witness that I've remembered through the years. It spurs me toward a faithful walk. Each day, each step forward toward the goal of eternity with the Lord.

I think of my own spiritual trek as I recall that skunk off on its own trek to somewhere. Thank You, Lord, for the example of those who have lived and died faithful to you. I'm so grateful for the gift of one of them being my daddy. —Darlene Kerr

Walk of Faith: *Was there someone in your life who was a faithful witness until death? Stop and remember, then thank God for this person.*

OCTOBER 9

Habit of Forgiveness

Praise the Lord! Oh, give thanks to the Lord, for He is good! For His mercy endures forever.

—Psalm 106:1 (NKJV)

ONE OF THE great joys of my life bounded into my home when Snowy the golden retriever came to live with me. Just a pup at the time, she quickly grew to a 90-pound white bundle of personality. She is quite the clown and enjoys stealing socks, slippers, rolls of toilet paper, and even a remote control.

Occasionally, she will do something cute like interrupting a show by standing in front of the television. When I request that she move, Snowy dips her head a little, gets a shy smile on her face, and slowly walks away. It's as if she's saying, "Oh, you caught me trying to get your attention." She completes her antics by marching over to me and putting her head in my lap, hoping for some ear scratches.

When walking out in the neighborhood, Snowy enjoys taking it slow and sniffing all the smells along the way. Some days, I'm in a bit of hurry. She doesn't appreciate being rushed from her favorite spots like the fire hydrant on the corner or the tree several doors down from my house. Occasionally, she will just sit down and obstinately refuse to move. I forgive her, though, because she can't communicate clearly everything that might be bothering her.

One of her antics is harder for me to forgive. I like sleep, particularly at night, so when Snowy wakes me up for the third or fourth time hoping to play or get a treat, I put her in her crate for a while. By morning, I've forgiven her, and she extends the same grace to me.

Snowy's quickness to forgive reminds me of God's grace in many ways. He never holds a grudge or brings up previously forgiven sins. God wants a relationship with me, and He's willing to wipe my slate clean if only I ask Him. Surely, one of the best benefits of faith is the advocate we have: God's own Son, Jesus. He knows our hearts and still forgives us with just a word. How can I do less for my furry and human friends? —David L. Winters

Blessed is he whose transgression is forgiven, whose sin is covered.
—Psalm 32:1 (NKJV)

OCTOBER 10

Neighborly Chickens

And do not forget to do good and to share with others, for with such sacrifices God is pleased.

—HEBREWS 13:16 (NIV)

THOUGH I LIVE in town, I usually keep a backyard flock of chickens both for eggs and as pets. I'm currently between flocks, and, truth be told, I am enjoying my nice clean back patio where my messy but adorable free-ranging chickens would normally hang out. Still, I do miss my feathered companions! I miss the organic pest control, free fertilizer, and fresh eggs too. I've considered getting a new flock, but it takes some time and effort to turn chickens into good pets. With new grandchildren to watch over, I simply don't have the time to develop a new flock right now. Perhaps when the grands are a little older, we can do it together.

For now, I enjoy the chickens my young neighbor, Maria José, keeps. Inspired by the success of my backyard flock, she started keeping a few hens of her own. I can hear their clucking and chirping noises through our shared fence, and though these chickens aren't pets, I enjoy having them near.

The other day, there was a knock at my door. It was Maria José, stopping by to give me eggs from her chickens. She knew I had loved my chickens and missed them, and this thoughtful gesture really touched me. I couldn't thank her enough. Her smile told me she understood what her gift meant to me.

My neighbor's simple and kind gesture elevated my day and inspired me to look for opportunities to be kind to those around me. Those expressions don't have to be in the form of a big, expensive gift or a flashy surprise. Showing I care by sharing from my heart are God-pleasing things I can do. —Marianne Campbell

Where charity and love prevail,
there God is ever found;
Brought here together by Christ's love,
by love are we thus bound.
—Unknown (ninth-century hymn)

OCTOBER 11

God's Perfect Timing

He has made everything beautiful in its time.

—ECCLESIASTES 3:11 (NIV)

ON AN EVENING walk in October, my husband pointed out an imperial moth caterpillar. "On our busy street, it's going to get crushed if we don't move it," he said. My entomologist hubby recognized that the caterpillar was preparing to pupate.

David keeps an old glass cookie jar on the porch to use as a terrarium of sorts for rescued critters. We filled it with soft dirt, added some leaves, and watched in awe as the caterpillar immediately burrowed in. "It should emerge in the spring," David announced.

We kept the jar on the kitchen counter so we could watch the changes. Even into late summer, however, our terrarium looked the same. David flicked dirt away and held the pupa in the palm of his hand. "It's moving, so it's definitely still alive." He laid it back in the hole and replaced the dirt.

A dishwasher disaster and kitchen remodel fiasco later, I'd almost forgotten about the caterpillar. With most of my cabinets removed, part of my tile floor scraped away with bare subfloor showing beneath, and no sink, oven, or dishwasher to access, I'd just about had all I could take of insurance claims, contractor disappointments, and cabinetry appointments.

"My kitchen is so ugly right now," I complained through tears. "I have nowhere to cook; I have to wash dishes in this tiny island sink, and I have no idea when they'll finish all the repairs."

One day when I felt like throwing in the dish towel—literally—David and I saw the fluttering of pink and yellow wings in the terrarium. Our imperial moth had emerged an entire season after we thought it would. What a joy to release the beautiful insect into the world.

I couldn't help but be reminded that God makes all things beautiful in His perfect timing, and not just the moth. My kitchen may not be ready on my time schedule, but when it finally emerges again as a usable part of our home, it will be a joy to behold. —Julie Lavender

Never lose an opportunity of seeing anything beautiful.
Beauty is God's handwriting.
—Charles Kingsley

OCTOBER 12

From Misfit to Family Fit

You are God's chosen and special people.

—1 PETER 2:9 (CEV)

WE ADDED A young couple and their much-loved English bulldog to our family last fall. Because we have a detached guest house, visiting folks and those between homes occasionally stay with us for a season… and then become wrapped up in our crazy, fun, extended family circle.

We thought the brindle-and-white-colored Mollie would be with us here in the Sierra Valley for just a couple of months until her owners moved to the Philippines, but when she refused to walk in the San Francisco airport, my son-in-law Ozzie got a late-night plea over the phone. "Would you consider adopting Mollie?"

Despite the fact that my daughter Rebekah and her husband, Ozzie, thought Mollie was on the last legs of her 12-year-old life, she began to rebound in their actively robust life with six children, four other dogs, four horses, two kittens, a bird, and several beef cattle. Miraculously, Mollie started moving, lost weight, and transformed from an inactive misfit to a much-loved fit for their family. Eight months later, she even keeps the oldest child, Josiah, company when he feeds his show steer. And when we visit our nearby daughter and family, Mollie jogs to greet us, her former landlords.

Mollie's story reminds me that each of us belongs to the extended family of God. He has chosen us, so each of us is special. No matter what our position is in our own family or in our group of friends, we are all important, and God has purpose for us in those relational circles. And that kind of belonging can be transformational to a person—physically, mentally, and emotionally. Knowing we are a part of God's family helps us get up and go each day of our lives. —Janet Holm McHenry

Walk of Faith: *When you feel alone and useless, simply look around, find someone else who might feel the same way, and invite them into your family.*

OCTOBER 13

The Highway

For "you were like sheep going astray," but now you have returned to the Shepherd and Overseer of your souls.

—1 PETER 2:25 (NIV)

MY DAUGHTER'S BOSS, Dennis, had a herd of about fifty cows. His neighbor 2 miles down the road had some horses but only one cow, and he wanted to expand his herd. So Dennis sold him a single cow. One day our daughter Kimberly, who worked for Dennis, was driving down the highway and saw that the lone cow had gotten loose. As Alison Krauss says in her song, "Two highways lay before me, which one will I choose?/Down one lane I'd find happiness and down the other I would lose." The cow had chosen the road home and was slowly meandering back toward Dennis's house. Kimberly called Dennis, and the two neighbors quickly struck a deal for him to repurchase the cow and reunite her with her original herd.

My daily walk with God often goes like that. Many times I have to choose the highway I will travel; sometimes I stray from the path that I know the Lord wants me to take. When that happens, it's easy to become discouraged and feel frustrated, broken, weak, and alone. But I know that if I ask for His forgiveness and forgive myself, the Lord will take my hand and show me the way back to Him. —Harold Nichols

Precious Lord, take my hand,
Lead me on, let me stand
I'm tired, I'm weak, I'm worn.
Through the storm, through the night,
Lead me on to the light.
Take my hand, precious Lord, lead me home.
—Thomas A. Dorsey

OCTOBER 14

Penny's Promise

Even to your old age and gray hairs I am he, I am he who will sustain you. I have made you and I will carry you.

—ISAIAH 46:4 (NIV)

NO DOUBT ABOUT it. The woman needed help.

In one hand, she held a leash attached to a floppy-eared dog who couldn't wait to get to the beach. It sniffed the air like a teenager in a pizza joint and wiggled so hard its whole body gyrated.

Her other hand rested on the push bar of a pet stroller. Tucked under her leash-holding arm, she held an aging pup. Bony hip bones protruded through its coarse gray fur, and its legs dangled beneath its body.

I'd seen her the day before at the water's edge, but this day we met several hundred yards from the ocean. A long stretch of soft sand stood between her and the beach.

"May I push your stroller for you?" I asked.

"You don't know how glad I would be if you did that."

She backed away and shifted her pup so one arm supported its back end and the other cradled its chest. She tightened her grip on the other dog's leash, and we headed toward the beach.

"Penny's 17½" she said. "She can't see and can barely walk, but she loves the beach. I just couldn't leave her behind."

When we reached the shore, she settled Penny into her stroller. As the waves crashed in front of her, Penny lifted her nose to catch a whiff of the salty air. She closed her eyes and smiled—I swear she did—as the sunshine warmed her face.

As I watched Penny's owner care for her senior pup, the Holy Spirit reminded me of God's promise to His children through the prophet Isaiah 46:4 (NIV), "Even to your old age and gray hairs I am he, I am he who will sustain you. I have made you and I will carry you."

I'm grateful we don't need to fear that God will abandon us when we're no longer healthy, spry, or productive. He promises to meet our needs—physical, emotional, and spiritual—all the days of our lives. And then, He'll take us home to live with Him forever. —Lori Hatcher

Thank You, Father, for promising to care for me from my first breath until my last.

OCTOBER 15

My Dear Pursuer

Your beauty and love chase after me every day of my life.

—PSALM 23:6 (MSG)

I'VE BEEN A city girl all my life, but I am a Minnesota city girl. This means that while I enjoy the convenience of the metro area, I love any opportunity to venture out into the wilds of greater Minnesota. We have so many options, including prairies, farmlands, river valleys, and incredible forests.

My husband and I make the hourlong trip between St. Paul and Elk River at least once, and sometimes twice, a week. We've connected with an awesome church there, and the drive gives us time to interact with each other without distraction.

On one of these trips we witnessed something I had never seen before. It is quite common to view a lovely doe dashing across an outstate freeway. Sometimes she will be followed by one or two fawns. I wonder if she is giving them the equivalent of driver's ed training, teaching them to navigate the roads and avoid the metallic monsters that come and go at all hours of the day.

On this day we spotted a deer as we were about a mile from our church. And then another...and another...They kept coming until at least twelve deer had leaped past our car, right in front of us. Fortunately, we had slowed with the first sighting and came to a complete stop as we witnessed each successive creature running after the one who went before it.

Where were they all going? Why were they together in such great numbers? Were they family or just friends? Were they fleeing danger? I wish I had the answers. But one thing I know—God's goodness toward me will keep on coming and coming, just as these deer did. Bethel Music has a song whose chorus refers to God's goodness as "running after me." And what I love about God is that this is not an occasional occurrence. He does it every day. —Liz Kimmel

Thank You, Heavenly Father, for Your pursuit of me. As God, You go before me, You are with me, and You follow after me. You completely encircle me with Your love and Your care.

OCTOBER 16

Blown Away

But our citizenship is in heaven. And we eagerly await a Savior from there, the Lord Jesus Christ, who, by the power that enables him to bring everything under his control, will transform our lowly bodies so that they will be like his glorious body.

—PHILIPPIANS 3:20–21 (NIV)

I AM AN ANIMAL LOVER, so not much could top my safari in Kruger National Park in South Africa. We stumbled out of bed at 4:15 a.m. to gulp strong coffee at our hotel. Then we loaded into a van for the ride to the park. Once we entered the park and hopped into a safari jeep, we had a few minutes to grumble about the early wake-up on a vacation. All the grumbling stopped a few minutes into the drive, however, when we came upon our first animal sighting, a giraffe. I excitedly exclaimed to our tour guide, Elaine, "Giraffes are my favorite!" The words were hardly out of my mouth before a group of zebras came into view, to which I joyfully babbled, "Zebras are my new favorite!"

"And so, what's your next favorite?" Elaine dryly addressed me. "Seems like we'll probably see that next."

In all we saw what's referred to as the big five—leopards, lions, water buffalos, rhinos, and hippos—and much more including elephants, elands, and more giraffes and zebras. I hardly had time to take a breath the sights were so amazing. I knew this trip would be fun because I was with my sister, but I didn't know I'd be so blown away by the sheer numbers of exotic animals we would see. It was a once-in-a-lifetime chance to witness these amazing creatures in their natural habitat.

It made me wonder how I can ever take in the scope of heaven. Earth's sights are incredible enough. We've been told to buckle up and hold on because heaven will be a sight like no other. I can't wait. —Linda Bartlett

However, as it is written: "What no eye has seen, what no ear has heard, and what no human mind has conceived"—the things God has prepared for those who love him.

—1 Corinthians 2:9 (NIV)

OCTOBER 17

Come!

Come to me, all you who are weary and burdened, and I will give you rest.

—MATTHEW 11:28 (NIV)

A BLUR OF QUICK movement caught my attention. Slowing the car, I realized it was a medium-size brown dog galloping down the sidewalk toward the intersection with a major road, no owner in sight. And it was rush hour. Without thinking, I pulled ahead of his trajectory and to the side of the road, flashers on. Grabbing the leash and treats I keep in my car for my work as a pet sitter, I hurried to the sidewalk between him and the traffic on the busier street. The dog was still headed in my direction, dodging other pedestrians who didn't seem to notice him. Wide-eyed with ears pinned back, he managed to stay on the sidewalk instead of swerving into the road where cars continued to whoosh by. As he got closer, I squatted and opened my arms, calling, "Come, puppy!" The terrified dog ran right into my embrace.

Once I had secured him with the leash, I was able to read the tags on his collar, call his frantic owner, and take him home. She had no idea what might have spooked him and caused him to dart out her front door, but now he was safe because he had been willing to come to me.

I, too, have darted in fear from challenges in my life, not ready to take them on. Sometimes I run in the wrong direction, toward trouble instead of away from it. I may not think before I act, or I let my emotions overflow before taking a breath and asking for help. But like that lost dog, I have a rescuer who gladly reaches out, saying, "Come to me."

No matter my burdens or how frightened I feel, Jesus calls me, welcoming me to peace and safety in His arms. I need only to run to His embrace. —Kim Sheard

Lord Jesus, when I am frightened or worried or in danger,
help me remember to listen for Your call and run to the
safety of Your arms. Thank You for Your loving care. Amen.

OCTOBER 18

Boo?

And the Holy Ghost descended in a bodily shape like a dove upon him, and a voice came from heaven, which said, Thou art my beloved Son; in thee I am well pleased.

—LUKE 3:22 (KJV)

WHEN OUR SON Brian was 4, he ventured into our fenced-in backyard one afternoon to play by himself. A few minutes later, he rushed back inside. "There's a ghost out there!"

"What?" I said. "Baby, there's no such thing as a ghost."

"Yes, there is. It said, 'Boo, boo!'"

I walked out with him and listened. Then I heard it too. "Honey, that's not a ghost. It's a dove. He's not saying, 'Boo, boo.' He's saying, 'Coo, coo.'"

Mourning doves still inhabit our backyard, and I smile every time I hear one, remembering that day with Brian. But instead of picturing a scary ghost, I think of the Holy Ghost appearing as a dove. Instead of fear, I experience the peace only God's Spirit can bring.

Sometimes I wonder why the Holy Spirit chose to appear in the form of a dove, but then I watch the gentle nature of those around our house. Unlike blue jays or mockingbirds, the doves are quiet and soothing. In the same way, the Holy Spirit is my comforter, sent by Jesus Himself to walk with me on this earth, instilling hope and peace. Yet He has all the power of God—because He is God.

With whom else would I want to entrust my spiritual life rather than the all-powerful Being? Even when this world says boo, I will have nothing to fear with the Holy Spirit by my side. —Tracy Crump

May the God of hope fill you with all joy and peace as you trust in him, so that you may overflow with hope by the power of the Holy Spirit.

—Romans 15:13 (NIV)

OCTOBER 19

Keeping It Fresh

Because of the LORD's great love we are not consumed, for his compassions never fail. They are new every morning; great is your faithfulness.

—LAMENTATIONS 3:22–23 (NIV)

WE'VE HAD OUR bunnies, Lemon and Nimbus, for more than 3 years. I had gotten into a regular routine with them—feeding them, changing their water and litter, giving them greens and treats. I still thought they were adorable, but I wasn't as compelled to sit and watch them play as when they first arrived.

While cleaning my house one afternoon, I came across a stack of rabbit magazines I'd bought in the heyday of my excitement. Flipping through the pages reminded me of how smart bunnies are and how much they need stimulation to thrive. I had justified my lack of attention with the idea that there were two of them, and they were keeping each other company. Not enough, I told myself. I need to enrich their environment and spend more time with them.

I went online and ordered some new tunnels for them. I cut little doors in cardboard boxes and made an improvised warren. I ordered treats made of herbs and dried vegetables that would help their digestion, their coat, and their energy. I began sitting and playing with them again, offering the treats from my hand, setting up foraging puzzles, and hiding fresh arugula and rosemary around the hutch for them.

Now the bunnies are noticeably happier, and so am I. They're showing me different aspects of their personalities, and after spending quiet time in their presence, I feel more peaceful. Bun time had become an obligation, but it is sacred time again. This transformation in our hutch life made me realize that in order to keep my relationship with God fresh, I should change things up there too. I got a new prayer journal and some pretty pens so I can sit in the hutch and write. Thank You, Lord, for using Your creatures to teach me a great spiritual lesson. —Lucy Chambers

Just a closer walk with Thee,
Grant it, Jesus, is my plea,
Daily walking close to Thee,
Let it be, dear Lord, let it be.
—Unknown

OCTOBER 20

Kindness Makes All the Difference

And God is able to bless you abundantly, so that in all things at all times, having all that you need, you will abound in every good work.

—2 CORINTHIANS 9:8 (NIV)

MY FRIEND KATHY recently shared a praise at our weekly Bible study. She told us about her family's new German shepherd puppy and the beautiful progress she had made. The dog had come to them so malnourished that her backbone showed beneath her skin. They could count every rib. When she was first adopted, the poor thing would gorge on her food because she had been starving before being rescued.

Kathy told us that it took a while, but the change in the pup was incredible. She said she was thrilled to announce their new pet had come a long way, that she now feels secure and settled in. She has become very affectionate, happy, and well-adjusted, simply from the kindness of a loving family.

God is so good to us that I think sometimes we're surprised by it, like Kathy's puppy, who probably didn't understand the gift of being in her new home with a loving family because she was not used to such lavish care. I grew up in the church, but as I matured into my teens, I pursued a more personal relationship with God on my own. When I asked for God's forgiveness, I had a hard time accepting it. I felt unworthy. I even felt doubt about whether God could love me. Then I dug deeper into studying the Bible, trying to absorb everything I could about God's love, about Jesus's gift of grace. I was also blessed to have mentors who guided me through high school and helped me discover God's unconditional love.

Like Kathy's puppy, I had to learn that I was loved and would be cared for. I found I could rest secure in God's provision for my life. —Missy Tippens

Walk of Faith: *Show gratitude to those who mentor and teach you. And most of all, thank God for His loving-kindness.*

OCTOBER 21

Consider the Consequences

Trust in the Lord with all your heart, and lean not on your own understanding.

—PROVERBS 3:5 (NKJV)

WHILE TAKING A boat tour through the swamp at Jean Lafitte National Historical Park and Preserve in Louisiana, we saw furry creatures swimming through the water. They looked rather like beavers without the distinctive flat tail. "What is that?" I asked, pointing. The guide called it a nutria rat. He explained that the invasive species had been brought to the United States from South America in the late 1800s to boost the fur industry. When the business collapsed in the 1940s, the nutria—which have a high reproductive rate—became a serious problem. The US Department of Agriculture has declared the animals to be highly destructive to marshlands and wetlands. They erode levees, dams, and roadbeds. They also destroy rice, wheat, and corn crops as well as aquatic vegetation. "The decision to bring the nutria here has had dire consequences," the guide added with a sigh.

I thought how true that was of life in general—that many decisions have dire consequences. No wonder the Bible has so many verses warning us to seek God's wisdom, to harness our tongues, to pray for the Lord's guidance and not to lean on our own understanding. Consider the numerous incidents recorded in the Bible, such as Aaron reluctantly agreeing to construct the golden calf. His decision had deadly consequences for thousands of Hebrews.

We probably all know people who decide to take on more commitments than they can realistically handle. Such behavior often leads to burnout or more serious health problems. I'm trying to take more time to pray and consider thoughtfully before making decisions. What about you? —Shirley Raye Redmond

Good and evil both increase at compound interest. That is why the little decisions you and I make every day are of such infinite importance.

—C. S. Lewis

OCTOBER 22

Message from a Dog

Place me like a seal over your heart, like a seal on your arm; for love is as strong as death, its jealousy unyielding as the grave. It burns like blazing fire, like a mighty flame.

—SONG OF SONGS 8:6 (NIV)

OUR BELOVED DOG, Moose, died last summer. Many years before, we had found him on a late November day running scared on a country road. It was freezing rain, and tiny icicles hung from his face. He had no collar and was diagnosed with Lyme disease that same night.

We advertised on the radio and notified our local vet and humane society. But no one claimed him, which was a good thing. Because the goofy mutt, whose DNA showed him to be half golden retriever and a quarter each bloodhound and Jack Russell terrier, bonded with us immediately and we to him.

For the next 11 years, he stayed lovingly by our side. He was the friendliest, gentlest dog we've ever known. Our older son once witnessed a surprising encounter between Moose and a wild turkey. They came face-to-face on a wooded path. Instead of Moose chasing the turkey, as most humans would expect, both animals stopped, touched noses, and then went their separate ways—without a "cross word" between them.

So it was a sad day that fall when my husband, Neil, offered Moose's bag of leftover treats to our visiting younger son, who has a dog named Ellie. Neil said, "I'm putting these treats in your bag because I think Moose would want Ellie to have them." Feeling a bit overcome with emotion, our son sank into a kitchen chair, which is over the register. Immediately, the heat came on, surprising everyone when a puff of Moose's black hair blew into the air.

It felt to me like confirmation that Moose was listening and telling us that he did, indeed, wish for Ellie to have his leftover treats. The special link between us is still strong and always will be. —Aline Alexander Newman

There is a land of the living and a land of the dead and the bridge is love.
—Thornton Wilder

OCTOBER 23

A Gentle Giant

I have told you these things, so that in me you may have peace. In this world you will have trouble. But take heart! I have overcome the world.

—JOHN 16:33 (NIV)

SO THERE I was, sitting on a bench, eating my overpriced Bongo Burger and Monkey Fries, and staring up at a giraffe. Zoos are supposed to be happy places, but I was feeling flustered, beset with persistent problems for which I had no solutions. Relationships that had gone off the rails. Butting heads with coworkers. Financial anxieties. I pulled out my cell phone and looked at the daily news. Is it just me, or does it seem sometimes that the world has gone crazy?

The giraffe and I appeared to be having a staring contest, me looking up, him looking down, his large head peering over the retaining wall. The Almighty must have been in a whimsical mood when He made giraffes. Everything about this animal is exaggerated: an 18-inch prehensile tongue (or so the placard on the wall said), a heart that weighs 20 pounds, outrageous eyelashes, hooves the size of dinner plates, and of course the signature long neck. The giraffe was chewing. The placard said that giraffes appear always to be chewing because they are. They are ruminants, constantly working their cud.

Staring up at this gentle, silent animal had a calming effect. The giraffe had an expression that seemed to exude serenity. I felt relaxed, at peace. I reminded myself that I live out my life in the palm of God's hand, and that nothing is going to happen to me that I cannot handle with His help. My life may sometimes feel discombobulated, and the daily news may be a torrent of sin and sadness, but this world has not spun out of the Father's control. In the end all will be well. The giraffe continued chewing and seemed to nod. —Louis Lotz

Worrying does not take away tomorrow's troubles.
It takes away today's peace.
—Randy Armstrong

OCTOBER 24

Come Right In

You will receive a rich welcome into the eternal kingdom of our Lord and Savior Jesus Christ.

—2 PETER 1:11 (NIV)

JOJO THE CAT was a welcome gift after my son's family lost their two dogs in a short period of time. Justin and his wife, Megan, were on an evening bike ride along a canal in Bakersfield, California, when they decided to take a detour into an area where they usually didn't cycle. As they pedaled along, they noticed a gray tabby kitten, who immediately went to Megan. Because coyotes frequent that area, they took the kitten home, and their three children immediately welcomed him.

Jojo quickly embraced their busy lifestyle of backyard baseball, trampoline acrobatics, and motorized dirt bikes. Wherever the family was, Jojo wanted to be in the middle of the action. They found this to be laughingly true when the cat learned to let himself in the back door by jumping up to grab the lever door handle, then pushing himself off against the wall to open the door. Jojo has become so adept at opening lever doors that Justin had to change some of the handles and even lock his and Megan's bedroom door at night.

It's true that hospitality reigns in their home—all feel welcomed. And 13-year-old Dillan summed it up one day when he said, "You guys have given this cat such a good life." And that is true for Jojo, yes, but as we watch him perform his door-handle and other acrobatics, we all know that God has given the whole family a good life.

Extending hospitality to visitors of all kinds—two-footed or four-footed—is a natural when we have an understanding that God has embraced us into His family and that someday His people will all live together in His heavenly home. And we don't even have to jiggle a handle to get there. —Janet Holm McHenry

Father, thank You for my home and my family, and thank You for welcoming me into the family of God.

OCTOBER 25

Best Foot Forward

But let each one test his own work, and then his reason to boast will be in himself alone and not in his neighbor. For each will have to bear his own load.

—GALATIANS 6:4–5 (ESV)

I FOLLOWED MY DOG, Galen, into the house, dropping his leash so he could walk where he pleased while I closed the door and removed my jacket.

After a few moments, I noticed my giant Leonberger wasn't moving. He seemed frozen in one spot in the foyer.

"What's the matter, Galen?" I walked toward him to investigate the problem. My gaze fell to his leash, stuck under one of his huge paws.

He looked over his shoulder at me as if he thought I was holding him back. But, in fact, he was holding himself back by stepping on his leash.

I chuckled as I lifted his foot and freed the leash so he could move. *What a silly boy*, I thought.

But then I realized I'm just as silly. When my life isn't going the way I want, I have a tendency to look for causes only outside myself. I look for someone to blame. But if I admit the truth, I'm often the one holding myself back.

Perhaps because of fear or pride or sometimes sheer laziness, I'm not willing to put in the work required to succeed. Even when I'm doing work for the Lord, I shouldn't expect to stay in my comfort zone or get by with little effort. But it's so much easier to blame others than to take responsibility for my mistakes or failure to do what God desires of me.

Instead of looking over my shoulder to see who I can find to blame for my circumstances, I need to look inward and see where I'm at fault. And then I need to look up and ask the Lord to forgive me and strengthen me to walk on, bearing my load in faith and perseverance. —Jerusha Agen

Striving for excellence in our work, whatever it is, is not only our Christian duty, but a basic form of Christian witness.
—Ted Engstrom

OCTOBER 26

The Squirrel and the Acorn

Blessed is the one who perseveres under trial because, having stood the test, that person will receive the crown of life that the Lord has promised to those who love him.

—JAMES 1:12 (NIV)

THE FALL LEAVES were a glorious mixture of red and orange, and the crisp air gave notice that winter would be coming soon. When you live in Michigan, taking a drive in the fall is a definite treat after summer's heat and knowing that the hard winter season lies ahead.

My husband and I were in our SUV, enjoying the moment. As we rounded a sharp corner, I saw a large squirrel with an acorn in his hand sitting directly in our path. There was no time to swerve, but miraculously our tires flew by this steadfast creature with inches to spare. I looked back in the mirror and was shocked to see him still standing there, solid as a rock. The acorn had never left his hands.

We called him stubborn, brave, determined, and more—laughing at the way his stomach must have held out over his own safety and how his life must have flashed in front of his eyes. He may have been too shocked to move after those big wheels were in his face.

Standing firm when the unexpected is barreling down the road takes its own kind of strength, doesn't it? The shock and awe caused by the breeze of the "almost" takes my breath away some days. If I can find the strength to look that trial in the eye, God promises rewards. Being rooted in the Holy Spirit and in His Word, clinging tightly to His promises, is the only way that I will come out on the other side with my faith still intact. —Twila Bennett

Walk of Faith: *How will you stand firm when lightning strikes? Are you filling your spirit with God's Word? Are you committed to your prayer life? Begin today to hold on to what's important in order to face what comes with courage and God's power.*

OCTOBER 27

Sore Feet and Prayerful Poops

Be joyful in hope, patient in affliction, faithful in prayer.

—ROMANS 12:12 (NIV)

I RESCUED RITA ROSE from an online auction of last-chance horses headed for some pretty dire circumstances. She went from skin and bones to a beautiful burgundy with a spirit that was pure fire.

I like my horses to graze, and it was very hard for me to limit a formerly starved horse from enjoying a beautiful green pasture, especially with winter coming. And Rita Rose developed a tendency to overindulge in the grassy summer pasture. In my inability to set boundaries for her, she got ill, so I had to pull her off the pasture during the day and feed her hay instead of grain. Her excessive eating not only caused sore feet, known as founder, but also gave her a bellyache, a combination that can be fatal.

I called the vet to come out and provide treatment, but Rita was in a miserable place. When the vet left, I lay my hands on her and prayed…for poop. I knew if she could just overcome her destructive overindulgence, there would be hope that she would recover.

I believe God puts great stock in faith and hears all prayers, even those that might seem frivolous or insignificant to some. But God hears all prayers as significant. Rita had a healthy "answer to prayer" within minutes, and I took that to heart. It reminded me that you and I are invited to take every thought and need to Him, and He answers with love and compassion every time regardless of where we pray—in a church, by the bedside, or even in a horse pasture. —Devon O'Day

God, hear my prayers and know that my faith is in Your answers.

OCTOBER 28

My Furry Guardians

Cast all your anxiety on him because he cares for you.

—1 PETER 5:7 (NIV)

LAST YEAR, DUE to unexpected postmenopausal bleeding, I had major surgery—a complete hysterectomy. These days, even major surgeries are mostly outpatient, as was mine. The medical team got me in and out and on my way home in a matter of hours. I was happy about that, as I knew I'd feel more comfortable at home rather than being stuck in the hospital, despite the better use of pain control I may have had if I'd remained there overnight.

The most comforting aspect of recovering and resting at home was the company of my furry guardians, especially my schnauzer, Gabby, and my bonded brother black tuxedo cats, Hype and Dab. These three didn't leave my side during my entire recovery period, which lasted a couple of weeks. I sleep with an extra pillow above my head so Gabby or one of the boys has a place to lie, and during my recovery time, there was at least one animal there 24-7. Gabby would curl around my head, while Dab liked to press his paw on my temple to let me know he was there. They must have sensed when I was in pain, as they'd move a little closer. It almost appeared as if they were taking shifts. I was never alone.

I learned a lot from my pets during my recovery. As an introvert, I often find myself uncomfortable with people who are in pain, not really knowing what to say. Gabby, Hype, and Dab taught me that I don't need to fill the silence with words. Sometimes it's enough just to be there. —Deb Kastner

Just being there for someone can sometimes
bring hope when all seems hopeless.
—Dave G. Llewellyn

OCTOBER 29

The Bat Condo

The L*ORD* *is good to all; he has compassion on all he has made.*

—PSALM 145:9 (NIV)

MY FRIEND SUSY pointed to the sky as we rode home from shopping. "There's a bat." She continued driving as if seeing a bat flapping not too far away wasn't a big deal at all. Susy and her family live in the mountains, so spotting critters of all sorts is part of daily life. I, on the other hand, cringed inside at the idea of a bat getting so close to the vehicle. "I'm glad I didn't see it. I don't like bats."

She reminded me, "Bats get a bad rap, but they aren't dangerous. They are extremely helpful around here. They eat mosquitos and other pests." That was when I found out that, in addition to housing her daughter's injured squirrels, free-range chickens and a rooster, and a blind owl named Marbles (she's an educational animal), Susy and her husband had a small structure over the garage where bats were welcome to roost in exchange for their pest control services. Bats weren't Susy's favorite animal in the world either, but my friend valued their place in the big picture of life in the mountains. By providing them with a space to hang out, she had the peace of mind of facing fewer mosquitoes, moths, and crickets. Her approach changed my attitude toward bats.

The memory of Susy pointing out a bat in the same tone she would use for a bird or squirrel reminded me that God made each creature on the planet, as well as each human being, with a plan and place in mind. Her family saw the beauty in what many of us fear, in the same way our Creator sees purpose and value in those others ignore or cast aside. I want to follow the example of Susy building a bat condo in the way I think about others. —Jeanette Hanscome

Walk of Faith: *Think of a time when you felt purposeless or friendless and someone—even a group—made a place for you. What difference did it make? Who needs you to do the same for them?*

OCTOBER 30

The Importance of Wings

Look at the birds of the air; they do not sow or reap or store away in barns, and yet your heavenly Father feeds them. Are you not much more valuable than they?

—MATTHEW 6:26 (NIV)

I GOT MY WINGS!" No, I didn't become an angel—far from it. But I did become a flight attendant at the age of 53. It was a fantasy of mine to become a fly girl when I graduated high school in the 1960s. In order to become a flight attendant (then called a stewardess) at that time, you needed to have beauty, confidence, and poise. It felt out of reach for me and became just a dream. Instead, I started my career as a teacher and loved it for 30 years.

At the dawn of the millennium, the requirements for a flight attendant had changed drastically. What was needed then was a good work ethic. That I had, so I interviewed and spent the next 10 years living my dream. To prepare, though, I had to learn fly codes for the world, emergency procedures, and safety measures. I was tested every year to keep current.

The process it took for me to get my wings made me envious of birds whom God has supplied with ready-made wings. Birds don't have to work for their wings. God also gives them everything else they need for the life He planned for them. They toil not nor do they primp before a mirror. Birds must, however, learn to use their wings to fly, find food, and stay safe. Life is a challenge for all living things, but God always equips us for the journey, whether we have wings or not. —Linda Bartlett

Heavenly Father, whenever I begin to doubt Your care for me may I remember how You provide for all Your creation. Thank You, Father, for supplying me all my needs and many of my wants as well. Amen.

Prone to Wander

I will search for the lost and bring back the strays. I will bind up the injured and strengthen the weak, but the sleek and the strong I will destroy. I will shepherd the flock with justice.

—EZEKIEL 34:16 (NIV)

I CHECK THE BACKYARD. "Windsor!" I check every room. "Windsor!" Windsor was nowhere to be found.

It was a warm but wet Halloween night. My guests from Germany, where Halloween is not as popular, were eager to experience handing out candy to the trick-or-treaters that would soon start ringing the doorbell. My guests had been helping me with a project that meant a lot of coming and going out the door of the kitchen, to the garage, and out the garage door. Everyone assumed everyone else was keeping an eye on Windsor, my silver-gray schnoodle.

And then the realization slammed home. Windsor was gone. Everyone felt terrible that they'd let him slip away.

I grabbed my keys and ran through the pouring rain to my car and proceeded to search for my prodigal boy. Up one street...nothing. Down another street...nope. Finally I made it to the final street in the subdivision, driving slowly along, wipers struggling to keep up with the torrent, and peering out through the water streaming over my windows. Nope... nope...nope...*yes!* There he was. At the dead end of the street, sniffing around. I pulled up and ran around the car to open the door, and Windsor hopped up onto the seat (soaking wet, of course, though it didn't matter, because I was so happy to find him).

Left to his own devices, Windsor wandered, his curiosity spiriting him away, first a little and then a little farther yet.

I'm not so different. Left on my own, I can easily let my heart wander, my thoughts and actions drifting away from God and the home He provides me. But I know He will always come after me, searching for me, waiting for me, to bring me back home where I belong. —Jon Woodhams

Not all those who wander are lost.
—J. R. R. Tolkein

November

NOVEMBER 1

A Mockingbird Visitation

Like birds hovering overhead, the LORD Almighty will shield Jerusalem; he will shield it and deliver it, he will "pass over" it and will rescue it.

—ISAIAH 31:5 (NIV)

MY DADDY LOVED birds, but he was drawn especially to mockingbirds. He'd whistle and carry on a musical conversation with almost any mockingbird, and he'd get that glimmer in his eye whenever he told me to listen for its response.

Ever since his passing, I find myself drawn to mockingbirds. I try to get them to respond to my whistles, and even though I've not been as successful as my father at getting responses, the birds make my father seem near and intensify my memories of him.

On a particularly hard day, I got into my truck, the last vehicle my father ever drove, put the key in the ignition, and…nothing happened. I rolled down the window, laid my head on the steering wheel, and started to pray. Suddenly, I felt the presence of something near me. I lifted my head to find a mockingbird cocking its head and looking at me from its perch on my side-view mirror. It was close enough to touch. I talked to this bird as if it were my daddy. "What do I do? I have to get home. I'm exhausted. I can't get this truck to start!" That bird kept staring at me as I cried out in my frustration. All of a sudden, I remembered I had bought a membership in an auto-assistance company, and after I called them, they came to my rescue.

That bird may not have been my rescuer, but it calmed my spirit enough for me to figure out what to do. It stayed right beside me on that side-view mirror until help arrived and then flew off in a flash. God knows what we need to settle us when life becomes overwhelming or scary. —Devon O'Day

Lord, help me to pay attention to the little things in my path that calm me and help me make better decisions.

Mouse in the House

The LORD is my light and my salvation—whom shall I fear? The LORD is the stronghold of my life—of whom shall I be afraid?

—PSALM 27:1 (NIV)

I WAS QUIETLY READING a book in our living room when I heard my husband, Craig, stumble on the first steps of our staircase and then shriek loudly.

Even before I could utter a sound, I saw a small brown thing jump like lightning up and around the bend of the stairs into the darkness of our second floor.

"We've got a mouse!" Craig confirmed from the top of the stairs.

We have a field behind us and a field in front of us at the edge of our isolated, rural community in a mountain valley, and I am not a fan of rodents and other things creepy-crawly. I went for the weaponry: a broom.

But after an hour of opening closets and sweeping under furniture, the mouse did not turn up again. Convinced it was hiding in my closet, I said, "I think I'll sleep downstairs tonight."

But then reason took over: The poor thing was probably more afraid of me than I of it. And since the mouse never reappeared, we figured it found its way back to its field home.

Fear can raise its ugly head into the living spaces of our lives. We can often go to that worst-case-scenario thinking and hang out there, dreading what might jump out at us in the days ahead. It can have a strong hold on our minds and emotions, even affecting us physically with headaches, stomachaches, or anxiety-caused chest pain.

In those times, we can turn from the fearful what-ifs to what we know is true. God is our light and salvation. Not a bit of that situation has taken Him by surprise. And He can be our place of strength, as well as our guide so that we do not stumble. —Janet Holm McHenry

Lord, because You are with me, I know that I need not fear, as You will lead me and be my companion as I face the unknown.

NOVEMBER 3

When "Woof" Equals "I Do"

But do not forget to do good and to share, for with such sacrifices God is well pleased.

—HEBREWS 13:16 (NKJV)

BECKY LOOKED STUNNING in her wedding gown. The white lace, though stark against her ebony tresses, illumined her dark eyes, which held a wee bit of uncertainty, as I'm sure many brides before have shown. Of course, Becky…was a dog.

For years, my mom worked with therapy dogs at senior care centers. As these dogs and handlers walked the halls, the elderly folks reached out to touch the animals' fur or receive a slurpy kiss, which never failed to bring smiles. Mom enjoyed planning events for them, such as a dog wedding. Her Scottish terrier played the bride, while a dapper Great Dane stood up as the groom. Our daughter offered to be the couple's photographer, and a local pastor came to officiate.

As the dog duo walked down the aisle between wheelchairs, the seniors laughed, probably remembering their own weddings, sans wagging tails and an occasional yip from the accompanying canine wedding party. Watching from the sidelines, I listened to the pastor as he welcomed the wedding guests and went on to the vows. I assumed he would make a joke with them. But this servant of God had chosen to create special doggy vows, whose relevance to us as humans brought smiles. I was amazed at the pastor's sensitivity. He showed a true servant's heart, striving to turn what some may have thought a silly event into a time of blessing.

When working with seniors or children, people often make light of their unique needs. Jesus called little children to Him, and the book of Proverbs holds reverence for the aged. This pastor did likewise. —Cathy Mayfield

When occasions arise for me to do good,
I pray I will serve as Jesus would.
—C.M.

NOVEMBER 4

Her Master's Voice

The LORD is close to the brokenhearted and saves those who are crushed in spirit.

—PSALM 34:18 (NIV)

THE WAGON RIDE was the last thing I planned to do at the harvest festival that November day. As I stepped off the back of the hay wagon, the black draft horse tethered to the fence caught my attention. She was majestic and beautiful and looked exactly like the horse pulling the wagon I'd been on. I couldn't help but be drawn to her.

She seemed agitated, pawing the ground as the next group of visitors loaded onto the hay wagon. The horse lifted her head and strained at her halter. When she whinnied, it was obvious she was distressed. The man beside the horse tried to comfort her, but it did no good. She continued to whinny, snort, and paw the ground.

From across the yard, the driver of the hay wagon called to the horse. After he said her name several times, the horse calmed. She lowered her head. She ceased whinnying. She gave one last snort, then stopped pawing the ground.

As the wagon pulled away, the man beside the tethered horse looked at me. He nodded toward the wagon. "Her sister's pulling the wagon. She doesn't like being left behind." I could relate to that. In the midst of the horse's distress, she let her feelings be known. She cried out to her master. He was the only one she knew who could help. Her master heard. He called her name and calmed her.

As I watched this interaction between horse and master, God reminded me He is my Master. He is the One who hears me when I cry out. I am comforted when I remember that God is close to the brokenhearted. He cares for me, just as surely as the horse's master cares for her. —Sandy Kirby Quandt

Father, thank You for being my Master who hears my cries and comforts me, just as the draft horse's master heard and comforted her when she cried out. Amen.

NOVEMBER 5

Risking Like a Fox

Greater love has no one than this: to lay down one's life for one's friends.

—JOHN 15:13 (NIV)

LAST SPRING, A mated pair of foxes established their den in the brush just outside my backyard fence, and I had the pleasure of watching seven kits learn about the world. They tumbled over one another like acrobats and played hide-and-seek under my neighbor's shed. They stretched their necks to nurse from their mother where she stood, and later learned to eat meat that Mom or Dad dragged home. The fox parents gradually went from observing them closely to keeping an eye out more distantly, and I could eventually distinguish the bolder babies from the more skittish ones. By the time the family abandoned the den in the fall, the kits' coats had changed from grayish brown fuzz to sleek adult red.

In general, the foxes and my dogs coexisted peacefully, because of the fence. However, on occasion (especially at night), when I let the dogs into the backyard, the male fox would immediately cough up a screeching bark. I could follow the sound as he ran from the den around the inside perimeter of the fence to the opposite corner of our yard, attempting to draw the dogs away from his kits in the den. The fox risked his own safety to keep them secure. He took this action instinctively. Humans have more choice in the matter.

I'm not a police officer, a secret agent, or in the military, so I doubt I'll ever have to risk my life to save someone else's. At least I hope that's the case, because I don't think I have the right skills! But there are certainly risks and sacrifices I can make for others. I could leave my comfort zone to tell a desperate stranger about God's love. I might miss work to care for a child as their parent is taken away by ambulance. I could choose to use some of my retirement money to support a relative in need. When these opportunities present themselves, I pray I run inside the fence barking like that fox dad and make the godly choice. —Kim Sheard

Jesus, You sacrificed Your life for me. Help me choose to make smaller sacrifices for others, and please guide me when I do. Thank You, and amen.

NOVEMBER 6

To the Rescue

When I walk into the thick of trouble, keep me alive in the angry turmoil.... With one hand strike my foes, with your other hand save me.

—PSALM 138:7–8 (MSG)

MY FRIEND JANET lives on a ranch in Texas and has a heart big enough to care about animals from around the world. She regularly supports rescue organizations in Europe and Asia, as well as those that are closer to home. In her own words, "If it walks into my yard and is hungry, it has a home."

She was alarmed one day to step out of her barn and discover that a baby bird had fallen from a tree and was in grave danger from a chicken snake. Of course, the snake was only behaving as a snake knows how to behave. But Janet could not sit idly by and watch the baby suffer.

It wasn't a huge snake, but it was large enough to be a danger to the tiny bird. Janet called for her handyman, who quickly came to the rescue and disentangled the young one from the grasp of the limbless reptile. Once the bird was safe and the snake tossed a far enough distance away that it was no longer a threat, the man returned to the barn. To Janet's surprise, within moments he came back out into the yard and held up a handmade birdcage that would offer protection to their new feathered friend. She had no idea the cage had been there and was delighted at the unimagined provision.

It was fortunate that the bird was soon nestled safely inside, because it also had to be protected from the curiosity of the family dog.

I see God in this story in so many ways. Like Janet and the bird, God cares about me. He does not leave me defenseless. He is ever ready to come to my rescue. He offers a way of escape for whatever is threatening me. And He provides safe havens in a way I could never have imagined.
—Liz Kimmel

How could I cope in this life, Lord, without the knowledge that You are my strong support, my strong rescuer, my strong provider. Thank You for always knowing what I need and for watching out for me.

NOVEMBER 7

The Chosen Ones

You did not choose me, but I chose you and appointed you so that you might go and bear fruit.

—JOHN 15:16 (NIV)

I FOUND MYSELF DOGLESS for the first time in many years after my two dogs passed away within a few weeks of each other. So my friend and I headed to the animal rescue hoping to find two perfect dogs to take into my home and heart. I specifically asked for adult small-breed dogs, and after the attendant deliberately led me past run after run filled with large-breed puppies, she finally took me to a small fenced-in area housing a group of Chihuahuas that had been removed from a hoarding situation.

Ah, that was more like it. I have always been partial to Chihuahuas, having had one as a child. Now came the question of which ones should I choose? In the past, the obvious answer to this question was not which ones *I* chose, but which ones chose *me*. I entered the enclosure and sat on the ground, waiting. Within a few seconds, Frannie, a tiny, beautifully marked black-and-tan dog climbed onto my lap and started licking me. By selecting me, Frannie made the process of acquiring a new dog easy. She was also the sweetest and most attractive animal in the group. I waited for dog number two to choose me, while my friend pointed out nicely marked dogs among the several available. But dog number two turned out to be a plain, tan fellow named Fritz, who demanded my attention. I ultimately adopted Fritz not because of his beauty, but for his desire to make me his.

This experience reminds me that I did not choose Jesus—He chose me. Scripture tells us that on our own, we cannot come to Him unless the Father draws us (John 6:44). By myself, I could have done nothing worthy or righteous enough to deserve salvation. It humbles me to realize that in spite of that, the Creator of the universe chose me to be His child. —Ellen Fannon

For we know, brothers and sisters loved by God, that he has chosen you.
—1 Thessalonians 1:4 (NIV)

A Fierce Fisher

Watch and pray so that you will not fall into temptation.
The spirit is willing, but the flesh is weak.

—MATTHEW 26:41 (NIV)

MIKE, I THINK this is a fisher," I told my husband as we sat at the table, scanning images from our video doorbell. The previous day we'd seen a long, low, dark shape slinking across the yard. Because of its stealthy beauty, I was immediately attracted to the animal. A quick web search helped reveal its identity. "Fierce," I read online, and "one of the most vicious animals in the woods!"

Yikes! I learned that fishers are members of the weasel family and have been known to prey on domestic cats and small dogs. They may even climb trees and pounce on unsuspecting pets below, although they do prefer smaller rodents and squirrels, which make for a much easier meal.

I paused to remind myself that the fisher is one of God's creatures, just trying to survive. But I also made the connection that what can seem attractive could also be harmful. Just the other day I'd felt a pang of regret as I sat on the porch with a group of friends and the talk turned to a fifth friend, who wasn't there that day. It wasn't mean-spirited, I justified, but we were definitely gossiping. But then I thought of the ways it could be hurtful, possibly harmful, to that friend. I closed my mouth, but I was still listening.

Harmful habits like gossiping may slink around and be sneaky and pique my curiosity, then pounce on me when I am weak. Just like I protect my pets in the yard from the dangerous potential of the fisher, I have to protect myself from the dangerous potential of unhealthy habits. I thought back to the conversation on the porch and how I could have handled that better—I could have changed the subject, or if need be, walked away. I made a silent promise to work on making myself strong so I won't be an easy target for temptation and instead enjoy the bounty of beautiful friendships. —Peggy Frezon

May I always remember that when weaknesses strive to take me down, You, Lord, are the strength I can depend on.

NOVEMBER 9

For the Love of Red

We have different gifts, according to the grace given to each of us. If your gift is prophesying, then prophesy in accordance with your faith.

—ROMANS 12:6 (NIV)

FOR GENERATIONS MY family has sworn by big dogs. When I made the littlest peep about a cute Chihuahua or toy poodle, eyes widened as if to say "no small dogs." Just when I had had enough of this inexplicable canine censorship, my friend announced that her Cavalier King Charles spaniel was having puppies. Not the three she had anticipated, but seven. Would I like one?

I chose a tricolored boy with rakish eyebrows. Named Rocky for the boxer, he was a perfect dog. In my eyes. The rest of my family had difficulty with him because he bonded only, and fiercely, with me. Years passed, and finally I said my very tearful goodbyes to Rocky. After I felt we had mourned him appropriately, we started talking about new dogs.

We got Ruby, a darling black Labrador puppy. I welcomed her with open arms and the caveat that we would now have two dogs since we were going to get another Cavalier. Finally, we found Red.

Red is not Rocky. Where Rocky had been tricolored and jaunty, Red is a rich russet and distinguished. Red does not love me best; he loves my whole family. Even more, he loves Ruby. He curls up close to her and gives her kisses. He will occasionally play the part of lapdog, but he'd rather romp. When he does decide to cuddle, he doesn't play favorites. The nearest lap is the best lap.

My family is delighted with Red, and I have not heard the "no small dogs" mandate in quite some time. As for me, I will always miss Rocky, but I love how Red connects with everyone. Each little dog is perfect in his own way, and both remind me of God's great love—the unique love He has for me, and the way He created me to live in community, embracing the others He loves just as dearly. —Lucy Chambers

If God had wanted me otherwise, He would have created me otherwise.
—Johann von Goethe

NOVEMBER 10

Butterfly in Trouble

I am the good shepherd. The good shepherd lays down his life for the sheep.

—JOHN 10:11 (NIV)

I WANDERED WITH MY granddaughter through an enchanting butterfly exhibit. Nellie and her mom had spent many hours raising monarchs, so she was familiar with their care. Yet she was thrilled to see the variety of butterflies from all over the world now flitting around her. She fed them nectar, pointed out her favorites, and laughed when one landed on Granddaddy's nose to camp out a while.

Nellie paused at the glass-enclosed nursery where hundreds of chrysalides hung from the tops of cages. Suddenly, she grabbed my arm. "Grandma, that butterfly is in trouble!" She dragged me through the exhibit toward an employee and described the problem. The woman listened intently and assured Nellie she would take care of it. Only then could we relax and enjoy the rest of our visit.

I was so proud of Nellie. She cared about one of the smallest creatures in God's kingdom and wouldn't rest until she found help for it. In the same way, I'm grateful that my Father in heaven is concerned about me. No matter what burden or crisis presents itself that day, I can carry it to God, and He says, "Don't worry. I'll take care of it."

That doesn't mean His answer won't require action on my part, and it doesn't mean everything will turn out as I want it to. But knowing that God cares about my problems and He promises to shoulder my load eases my heart. Even though I often feel like one of the least in His Kingdom, He watches over me and lifts the weight of my anxiety, allowing me to escape its binding grasp and fly free. —Tracy Crump

When songs give place to sighing, when hope within me dies,
I draw the closer to Him, from care He sets me free.
—Civilla D. Martin

My Piece of God

Now this is our boast: Our conscience testifies that we have conducted ourselves in the world, and especially in our relations with you, with integrity and godly sincerity. We have done so, relying not on worldly wisdom but on God's grace.
—2 Corinthians 1:12 (NIV)

MY HUSBAND AND I often joke that our German shorthaired pointer, Scout, is a very good girl…until she isn't. Perhaps once a year, she takes offense at being left home alone and scours the kitchen for something yummy to eat or items that are fun to chew. She once met me at the door when I returned, tail wagging madly, proud to present the bag of nacho chips she clutched in her teeth. Once I'd finished laughing despite myself, I worked for hours to clean up orange crumbs and spice dust. We have since put everything she might find tempting behind closed doors or out of reach for her safety, since Scout must stay at home alone sometimes.

Multiple studies done in the past 25 years have documented what Scout taught us: Even dogs that have been trained not to eat accessible food when told no will almost always eat it anyway when the human leaves the room or when a human is present but not paying attention. In essence, a dog does not have a conscience to guide her actions the way a human does. This is one of the traits that allows dogs to happily live in the moment (nacho chips are yummy!) rather than agonizing over past wrongs.

The Bible gives many instructions on how to be good and avoid doing wrong. I do not have them all memorized. But in addition to the Word, God has given me the blessing of a conscience to guide my actions, as well as to prod me to ask for forgiveness when I err anyway. I think of conscience as a little piece of God in my soul, speaking to me as needed to keep me on the right path. All I have to do is listen. —Kim Sheard

Conscience is God present in man.
—Victor Hugo

NOVEMBER 12

Watson, the Game's Afoot

Finally, brothers and sisters, whatever is true, whatever is noble, whatever is right, whatever is pure, whatever is lovely, whatever is admirable—if anything is excellent or praiseworthy—think about such things.

—PHILIPPIANS 4:8 (NIV)

AFTER MANY YEARS of having a mixed-breed Chihuahua named Minnie, my brother, Dan, and family decided she was their last small dog. They were ready for a change. When they welcomed a gonna-be-a-giant-boy into the family, they were expectant. Black and shiny, he didn't stay small for long. A purebred Lab, Watson wagged with his whole body. But he acted like a lapdog. In spite of his increasing size, he felt comfortable resting on Dan's wife, Nancy, when she'd recline to watch her Netflix favorites.

In spite of his detective-inspired name, Watson has no clue about his size or mass. Good-natured and full of love, he assumes everyone was thrilled to see him. Dan shared that it's not always the case. In fact, they long for the pup to grow a little older and slower. While they wait, they wonder if there is a class for happiest Lab? If so, Watson had it covered.

In fact, it's as if Watson has the outlook of the message in Philippians 4:8. Every day, all the time. There is no bad mood. Only happy expectation. And of course, the pup's attitude makes everyone a fan. He might knock over a bucket, but he's pleased about it. That wasn't a mistake! Nooo. Instead, a happy accomplishment for his friends to enjoy. How lovely to move through each day with such intense self-appreciation.

I've often heard the old saying, "Attitude is everything." When I consider young Watson's accidental adventures, I agree. Maybe God gave him a quiet hint along the way to enjoy it all and shove shame to the side. As if God said, *If you're going to kick that bucket, do it well*. That's advice worth noting. Something I've not done often enough.

Thanks to Watson, I'm now trying to do my best to enjoy all I see before me, finding the good everywhere. —Cathy Elliott

If you look the right way, you can see the whole world is a garden.
—Frances Hodgson Burnett

Breakfast at the Beach

Man does not live on bread alone but on every word that comes from the mouth of the LORD.

—DEUTERONOMY 8:3 (NIV)

STANDING ANKLE-DEEP IN the sand, I watched the morning's air traffic along the windswept Florida beach. First a pelican caught my eye, cruising along through the sky with eyes trained on the depths below, then diving deep and repeatedly for whatever fish might become breakfast. Next I studied the sandpipers, flitting across the sand to my right in shifting cells made of a dozen birds all moving as one. Eventually they separated and started picking through voluminous clumps of beachside sargassum algae, hopping and hoping for insects to eat. Finally, I was startled by a gull in the sand so close that I could have stroked his white head. I half giggled, rolling my eyes, as he snatched an old Cheeto poking out of the sand.

God made special kinds of breakfast for each bird. For some, like the pelican, it is fish. For the sandpipers, tasty bugs. The birds who frequent my feeders love seeds and berries. Many different tastes for many different birds, though I find it hard to imagine that God had Cheetos in mind for all the great gulls of the world. Admittedly, plenty of birds might go after a Cheeto in a pinch, but it often seems to be gulls who go after the convenience of junk food or garbage.

In a similar way, I find I am often tempted by the convenience of whatever images and words are fast at hand on my smartphone, rather than taking time to pursue the richness and depth of God's Word. I fill my mind with stories I see as I scroll through my Facebook feed or get lured in by the ads posted alongside each web page. I stare mindlessly at the TV as I binge-watch a show. All of this, instead of intentionally seeking out the most nourishing Word that fills me through the simple act of reading Scripture. I want to fill myself with the bread that God intended for me, the only sustenance I need. —Katy W. Sundararajan

O God, may Your Word nourish every part of my life, to Your great glory. Amen.

NOVEMBER 14

Running Interference

We beseech you brethren...that ye study to be quiet, and to do your own business, and to work with your own hands, as we commanded you.

—1 THESSALONIANS 4:10–11 (KJV)

WHILE ON A walk one evening, I spotted a wren at the edge of the street. As my husband, Stan, and I neared, it just sat there. "It looks pretty young," I said. "Maybe it can't fly yet."

"Well, it's going to get run over sitting there," Stan replied. He tried to nudge the little bird into the grass, but it refused to budge. When Stan reached down to relocate it, the fledgling hopped unafraid onto his hand. Before we could find a good place to set it down in the yard, the bird surprised us by flying toward a tree in the opposite direction. Immediately, mockingbirds appeared and dived at the newcomer, squawking threats.

What had we done? By interfering, had we put the young bird in greater danger? Our intentions were good, but we know what road is paved with those. My favorite wildlife rehabber's words came to mind: "When it comes to fledglings, it's usually better to leave nature alone." Finally, we saw the recipient of our "aid" land in a large oak tree, where we hoped it would be safe.

The whole incident made me wonder how many times God was working in someone's life to teach or to discipline and I interfered. I tend to want to make things all better, but that's not always God's plan. Rather than jumping into action, the best tactic may be to step back and pray. Is helping someone avoid painful consequences what God desires? Or would I better serve by standing by to lend a listening ear and support God-honoring decisions?

Maybe next time I face that decision, I'll take a lesson from my little wren friend. —Tracy Crump

Lord, forgive me for trying to run interference without consulting You first. Help me remember that I don't see the whole picture as You do and need Your wisdom in every situation.

NOVEMBER 15

Not My Home

The L*ORD watches over the foreigner.*

—PSALM 146:9 (NIV)

SOMETHING'S WRONG IN the pasture."

Standing outside, our daughter scanned the acreage above our house. Sure enough, our horse and sheep were staring intently.

"Maybe you should check it out," I encouraged my husband. "Might be a bear or a coyote.

Bill nodded. "I'll go look."

Moments later, I watched as he maneuvered our farm four-wheeler up the steep terrain, then disappeared over the brink of a hill. Suddenly, the motor stopped. My daughter and I waited, wondering what he'd found.

The sound of a motor again, and Bill reappeared in the upper pasture, then followed the path back to the barn.

"So?"

"You'll never believe it."

"What, Dad? What was it?"

"An elk. Huge. Antlers that stretched..." My husband used both arms to show how large the bull's rack was. "Even bigger than that!"

It wasn't the first time one of these majestic creatures visited our farm. Elk were brought to North Carolina decades ago to encourage tourism, then relocated to an area known as the Cataloochee Valley.

Sometimes they wander, winding up on local farms, where, though not particularly dangerous to animals, they damage fences and trample crops. Indeed, these foreigners aren't meant for this part of the country. They're better suited someplace else.

Their presence reminds me that my true home is somewhere else also, a perfect place still being prepared. One day, I'll be there, and all will be as was first intended.

Until then, I'm thankful God watches over the foreigners, like me, others, and the elk. —Maureen Miller

Walk of Faith: *Heaven will one day be our home.*
Watch for someone with whom you might share this truth.

NOVEMBER 16

Special-Delivery Mouse

God made the wild animals according to their kinds, the livestock according to their kinds, and all the creatures that move along the ground according to their kinds.

—GENESIS 1:25 (NIV)

I LIKE MICE. STRANGE? Maybe, but my feelings date back to my childhood. That's when I opened an old desk drawer and discovered a dead mother mouse and three live babies. I tucked the babies into a bed of grass in my Easter basket and fed them milk through an eyedropper. My mother, bless her heart, handled a week's worth of nighttime feedings. Unfortunately, unknown to either of us then, cow's milk isn't good for baby mice. And none of my little orphans survived.

These sad memories came rushing back one late fall day, when my husband, Neil, opened our mailbox and a mouse jumped out. It hit him in the chest and ran away, so we thought it had returned to the field. But we thought wrong. Two days later our mail lady called us on the phone. "There's a mouse in your box," she said. "Can you get it out? I'm afraid it will jump in my car."

So we went out to the box, and when Neil opened it, the same little mouse came flying out again. I tried to catch it in a box, but it landed on the ground and took off. Then we discovered it had built a nest in the mailbox! The nest was empty, so Neil pulled it out. Still, this persistent little critter refused to leave. How she kept getting in, we don't know, but she returned again and again.

The obvious, easy solution was a mousetrap. Only I couldn't bring myself to trap and likely kill her. She was outside, after all, and just trying to prepare for the winter. So, we tried a variety of approaches. Finally, peppermint oil on a ball of cotton worked as a deterrent, providing a happy ending for us all. —Aline Alexander Newman

Please, God, help me to refrain from the easy fix and always try my hardest to do the kind thing.

NOVEMBER 17

Hawk Highway

You will show me the path of life; in Your presence is fullness of joy; at Your right hand are pleasures forevermore.

—PSALM 16:11 (NKJV)

WHILE WALKING ALONG my local creek trail, I watched a majestic red-tailed hawk sail noiselessly past me. Wings outstretched, feathers riffling, it glided just above the water's surface but below the overhanging trees along the clear path of the creek. No doubt it was hunting for the small rodents that live along the creek.

As I watched it sail by, I was struck by the ease with which it moved. It was so close that I could see its large alert eyes darting back and forth as it carefully scanned the way forward. Nothing obstructed its path. It was smooth sailing all the way. In just a few moments it had traveled upstream and vanished from my sight. Clearly the creek made a good highway for a hawk.

Wouldn't it be nice if all the places I had to go each day were just as smooth sailing as this hawk highway? I thought as I continued my walk. Whether I'm driving in my car or walking on a crowded sidewalk in town, other cars and people can get in my way and slow me down. But that's just life, right? And then I thought of my life's path, the one God has promised to show me. Am I seeing it? Is the path clear, or do I let worries and troubles block my way? Yes, I confess, sometimes I do. And am I so intent on getting where I need to go that I miss His presence all around me? Yes, sometimes I do that too.

The hawk knew well its chosen path and carefully followed the best route for food and safety. I, too, can see my way clear by reading God's Word and praying. As God shows me the path of life, I will prayerfully do my best to follow it and rejoice in the infinite pleasures found in Him.
—Marianne Campbell

Proceed with much prayer, and your way will be made plain.
—John Wesley

NOVEMBER 18

From Failure to Success

"For I know the plans I have for you," declares the LORD, "plans to prosper you and not to harm you, plans to give you hope and a future."

—JEREMIAH 29:11 (NIV)

THE BOBCAT CAME slinking around the corner of the house across the street from Mom's apartment. It was in pursuit of a rabbit that zipped into a hedge of juniper bushes. We stood watching the drama through Mom's large front window, surprised to see the wildcat, with its stub of a tail and distinctive ears, hunting during the day. Normally, these predators—common where we live in the foothills of the Rockies—hunt at night and snooze during the daytime. The bobcat lunged at the bushes, then stepped back. He pounced again. This went on for quite some time as the cat made several attempts to catch his prey. But in the end, he failed. With a shake and a snarl, he finally gave up. He turned back toward the canyon that borders our small neighborhood.

I waited until he was well out of sight before saying goodbye to Mom and venturing outside to return to my own house around the corner. As I strolled down the sidewalk, I thought about the bobcat's failure to secure his prize. I thought about my own failures too. With God's help, I've been able to overcome most of them. Frankly, I've often been amazed at how the Lord takes broken plans—and broken people—to accomplish something wonderful for our good and for His glory. Like the bobcat, I can give myself a little shake and try again tomorrow. I'm trusting the Lord to give me the strength to do so. —Shirley Raye Redmond

Walk of Faith: *Be transparent with someone today. Share how God turned one of your failures into a victory. Your testimony will be a source of encouragement.*

NOVEMBER 19

Lost, but Not Alone

God will command his angels to protect you wherever you go.

—PSALM 91:11 (CEV)

MY FRIEND COLLEEN had a Yorkshire terrier named Colby who was a tiny bundle of energy and was known to escape from time to time. Colleen knew his normal routes and was usually able to find him. One night during a rainstorm, he went roaming again, but this time Colleen couldn't see through the downpour to locate him. It was too dark and too wet. She called for him and prayed for help but soon realized that she had no choice but to leave him in God's care.

As she slept that night, she had a vivid dream. Just as in real life, Colby had run away. A man on a late-night walk happened to find him, and using the information attached to Colby's collar, he was able to call Colleen in the morning with the good news. When she arrived at the address supplied to her, the man was wearing a red plaid shirt. He welcomed her into his kitchen, where Colby was relaxing on a towel in front of the refrigerator. The man in the dream picked up her dog, and handing him over, said, "We gave him a bath."

Colleen woke to the sound of her phone ringing. The voice said, "I believe we found your dog, and I brought him to my home." Imagine her awe when the back door leading into the kitchen was answered by a man wearing a red plaid shirt. He pointed to the errant dog warming himself on a towel in front of the fridge. "He was pretty dirty, so we gave him a bath."

God knows that my heart is sometimes wayward. I may dash about without a care and without taking note of my surroundings. This often lands me in a situation that is unfamiliar, possibly even dangerous. Even though I have stepped outside of the security of God's presence, I am never outside of His protection. —Liz Kimmel

Lord, You are so good to watch over me every moment of every day. Thank You for sending angels to guard and protect me in spite of my moments of carelessness.

A Lion's Roar

Behold, these are but the outskirts of his ways, and how small a whisper do we hear of him! But the thunder of his power who can understand?

—JOB 26:14 (ESV)

ANTICIPATION STIRRED IN my belly as I watched Kitty, the African lion, open his mouth wide. He started slowly at first, as if in an abbreviated yawn. His sounds were short, like snarls. He tilted his head up and opened his mouth again, revving up for the big moment.

I'd heard Kitty's roar from a distance several times. When at a friend's house 4 miles away from our local zoo, I had heard Kitty roar. I couldn't believe one animal could make a sound so loud that it could carry so far. Now I was about to have a rare experience, to see the lion produce his magnificent roar, to hear how loud and powerful it would be up close.

The vocalizations lengthened, growing stronger from deep in Kitty's throat as he opened his mouth wider. I watched through the fence of the exhibit, bracing myself for the deafening sound I was sure would come. Then he finally roared.

But it didn't sting my ears. I didn't have to cover them as I'd expected. Instead, the roar seemed, well, quiet. The big, cacophonous sound that could be heard up to 4 miles away was comparatively small up close. I couldn't have been more surprised.

Yet maybe I shouldn't have been surprised. After all, isn't that how God often seems? The truth of the similarities struck me deeply. When I stay close to God, His grace and daily mercies seem so small I forget to notice them. I overlook that He is at work in mighty ways because He uses a still, small voice I take for granted. Other times, His voice booms as He wields storms, floods, health crises—His might on display as He calls me to come near again. Kitty helped me understand that behind God's whisper is power beyond imagination. —Jerusha Agen

The voice of the LORD is powerful; the voice of the LORD is full of majesty.
—Psalm 29:4 (ESV)

NOVEMBER 21

Bird Calls

But, brothers and sisters, when we were orphaned by being separated from you for a short time (in person, not in thought), out of our intense longing we made every effort to see you.

—1 THESSALONIANS 2:17 (NIV)

WHILE IT SOUNDS a little like the setup for a corny joke, it's true: scientists have taught parrots how to participate in videoconferences, and the results have been amazing.

Parrots, like humans, are not by nature solitary creatures. In the wild, the garrulous, gregarious birds live in flocks (so many that the group is sometimes called a pandemonium). But most parrots kept as pets are by themselves. Scientists wondered if video interaction might help alleviate the parrots' isolation.

The process of teaching the parrots this new skill was slow and methodical, culminating in the birds being able to voluntarily make their own video calls to other parrots. The owners also were carefully trained to watch for signs of aggression, distress, or fear and to end the call if they observed such behaviors. (Please note: scientists caution people against trying this with their own pets without the important training.)

Between them, owners recorded a thousand hours of the birds' calls. Researchers are convinced the birds knew that the parrot at the other end of the call was, in fact, another parrot and not just a recording. The variety of behaviors the birds exhibited convinced them. The birds would be playful, sing, and show the other caller their toys. Some birds even befriended their feathered friends' owners across the miles. Clearly, the parrots enjoyed and benefited from their virtual interactions, and researchers believe videoconferencing can improve the lives of lonely parrots for whom face-to-face interaction is not feasible.

We live in what has the potential to be the golden age of communication, thanks to social media, texting, emails, voice calls, and video calls. While all these methods can sometimes be overwhelming and frustrating, they offer us unprecedented ways to connect with loved ones near and far.

The parrots benefited from their virtual fellowship—and so can we. —Jon Woodhams

Dear God, technology can be a two-edged sword, but thank You for the opportunities it gives me to connect with others. Amen.

NOVEMBER 22

Waiting for the Good Stuff

Trust in the LORD with all your heart and lean not on your own understanding; in all your ways submit to him, and he will make your paths straight.

—PROVERBS 3:5–6 (NIV)

MY COLLEGE-AGE DAUGHTER, Julia, and I were walking on a popular trail in a nearby park. It was around dusk, and we'd met to talk and catch up. "All of my friends have a boyfriend," she said. "But I haven't met anyone I want to go out with. Am I being too picky?"

"I've been praying for your future spouse since you were a little girl," I said. "We need to trust God that He will guide your steps in this area."

Julia sighed. "I know. It's just hard."

I started to respond, but I was startled by a large raccoon sitting on top of a trash can, just watching the people walk by. Julia and I couldn't believe how unafraid he seemed.

"He's probably sitting on the trash can so he can go through it to find food," I said. "Raccoons have a not-so-nice nickname: trash pandas."

The man walking behind us piped up. "Not that raccoon. He knows to wait for the good stuff." The man explained that every day around this time, the food vendor walked by and dumped his leftover hot dogs and popcorn in that trash can. "When the raccoon figured that out, he started waiting for the man. He doesn't eat trash. He waits for the good stuff," the man said.

We stood there, watching that raccoon patiently waiting for the hot dog vendor. We could see that there were food wrappers in the trash can, but the raccoon knew that if he just waited a few minutes, he would have something better.

"If the raccoon can trust the food vendor to bring his dinner, I can trust God to bring me the right guy in His time," Julia said. "I just have to be patient."

"Just like the raccoon, you're waiting for the good stuff." I squeezed her hand. "Not just the good stuff. But God's best for you. It will be worth the wait." —Diane Stark

You can save a lot of time waiting on God.
—Adrian Rogers

NOVEMBER 23

Hidden Parts

For You formed my inward parts; You covered me in my mother's womb. I will praise You, for I am fearfully and wonderfully made; marvelous are Your works, and that my soul knows very well.

—PSALM 139:13–14 (NKJV)

MY MOM, HUSBAND, and I went to the Sunken Gardens in St. Petersburg, Florida. The shaded paths offered a tranquil escape from the outside world and protected us from the sun's rays. A couple of rescue parrots squawked as we passed their way.

Lush tropical foliage lined the trail. The sound of water falling added to the peaceful scene. I paused to watch the red-footed tortoises. One was napping under a rock cave and another munched on something green.

Farther ahead a small group gathered to watch the flamboyance of Chilean flamingos. Their salmon-pink feathers and scarlet-wing coverts contrasted with the green lily pads that floated in the pond surrounding them.

I stood on a small bridge that overlooked the birds. The flamingos went from dunking their heads underwater in search of food to pecking at their rivals to honking at all the people.

My close position allowed me to better observe the flamingos at the water's edge. Their feet were webbed like a duck's rather than traditional bird's feet. This surprised me. I pointed out their unexpected appendages to my mom and husband. I later discovered their webbed feet support them on soft mud and also learned that flamingos can even swim.

Just like the flamingos, I have some hidden qualities. My sensitivity and introverted nature can't be observed, but the fact that I'm sensitive attunes me to the needs around me. And my introversion makes it easier for me to sit in the quiet and write.

God gives us all different gifts. Although some of mine are hidden, He created me to be me—a good reminder from flamingos. —Crystal Storms

Walk of Faith: *What makes you unique? Find ways to use the gifts God has given you to better love those around you.*

NOVEMBER 24

Braggin' Rights

Let not the wise boast of their wisdom or the strong boast of their strength or the rich boast of their riches, but let the one who boasts boast about this: that they have the understanding to know me, that I am the Lord, who exercises kindness.

—Jeremiah 9:23–24 (NIV)

CHICKEN PEOPLE WILL tell you that you don't need two roosters. They will fight and be territorial and trouble, in general. However, when I took two rooster brothers into the rescue, raised by two little boys as pets, I figured they would be loving toward each other because behavior is based all on how they are raised, right? Wrong. These mixed-breed mongrels came of age with a hen house of potential mates and lived up to their instinct.

One day I came home to some rooster drama as these two were each sticking their heads in a box and strutting back and forth. Inside that box was a hen sitting on a nest of hatching eggs. The proud papas seemed to be saying, "That's my baby," bragging and crowing as if they were the only reason there were babies. Soon they were in a full-fledged fight, with neck feathers puffed out like bearded dragons.

I have certainly met people like that. I may even have been someone like that, collecting kudos for something I really had little to do with. Every amazing accomplishment comes from the amazing God who gives us the ability for the achievement. I can only imagine how God must smile at our puffed-up pride in the midst of His handiwork! —Devon O'Day

God, when I begin to believe that I am solely responsible for something amazing, remind me of who You are and what You have created me to do.

NOVEMBER 25

Sticking with Gratitude

O our God, we thank you and praise your glorious name!

—1 CHRONICLES 29:13 (NLT)

I'M SORRY, MA'AM, but we can't finish your kitchen by Thanksgiving. Maybe by Christmas."

The cabinet installer's words shattered my hopes for turkey, dressing, and all the fixings and left me vacillating between anger and heartbreaking sadness. I'd been without a kitchen for almost 7 months. Water mitigation technicians, cabinet demolition team members, installers, repair people, and delivery drivers visited my home as if we had a revolving front door.

I was so hopeful the kitchen would be finished by Thanksgiving, and when dinner with my family was yanked away, I grumbled then cried. I felt like I had nothing to be thankful for in the month of gratitude.

"Let's drive over to your brother's farm," my husband, David, suggested. He knew the outdoors always cheered me up, and the 30-minute drive to the next county would feel like a mini-getaway.

Walking near the pond's edge, we heard rustling noises and splashes. David grabbed my arm, shushed me with a finger to his lips, and pointed. Two beavers made their way effortlessly through the water, both carrying broken limbs in their mouths. We watched them approach a mound of sticks and mud—their lodge—and push new sticks into place.

We stood motionless and watched them swim, dive, retrieve new sticks, spread mud, and then vanish under the water again. "They build and repair their lodge constantly," David whispered. "They keep the same lodge year after year, raising pups inside. Water pushing against their home results in the need for frequent repairs."

"Wow—they're hard workers," I whispered back.

As I watched the busy beavers, I thought about the workers who'd been in and out of my house recently. "I'm grateful for hard-working repairmen and women," I told David. Which reminded me that I was thankful for good insurance. And a roof over my head. And my mom's dishwasher just 10 minutes away from my house. And fast-food workers. And the promise of turkey and the fixings at Christmas.

Thanks to those beavers, I realized I had a lot to be grateful for after all. —Julie Lavender

Grumbling and gratitude are, for the child of God, in conflict. Be grateful and you won't grumble. Grumble and you won't be grateful.

—Billy Graham

NOVEMBER 26

Dave the Squirrel

A merry heart does good, like medicine.

—PROVERBS 17:22 (NKJV)

A SILLY SQUIRREL MY son named Dave kept us busy, as we tried to keep it from eating the seeds in our bird feeder. It would hang from the feeder, swaying back and forth. My husband, Tom, and I tried everything we could think of, even hanging a squirrel-proof, tubular bird feeder in a tree. But Dave would dangle from a high branch, upside down, trying to get to the seeds. This persistent squirrel even did a somersault once, falling and landing on its feet. Because of our love for birds, we didn't want to take the feeder down.

The squirrel's escapades kept us annoyed and losing patience. I scattered some nuts, trying to satisfy its stomach so it would leave the bird feeder alone. But Dave only got fatter and continued his gymnastics, trying to reach the seed in the feeder. Sometimes, he would come up to the patio glass door with his two front legs in a begging position. I knew then I also had a spoiled squirrel who wanted more of the walnuts I kept in my pantry.

When my young grandchildren came to visit, I taught them not to chase or touch the squirrel because he was a wild creature. Instead, they pulled up a chair by my glass patio door and watched Dave. This acrobatic squirrel mesmerized them and brought smiles and giggles, as he also scampered back and forth across the top of the fence, as though he knew he had an audience. When I heard the sweet giggles of my little ones, I knew it was time for me to laugh too.

I was reminded, through the antics of a rascal squirrel, that I can laugh at and embrace what I cannot change as long as doing so doesn't hurt anyone. When we moved to a new home, I wondered what became of Dave the squirrel. But I imagine, as long as he lives, he will continue his silly stunts, wild and free. —Kathleen R. Ruckman

---

Trouble knocked at the door, but, hearing laughter, hurried away.
—Benjamin Franklin

NOVEMBER 27

Beware the Camel!

Because you are my help, I sing in the shadow of your wings.

—PSALM 63:7 (NIV)

I HAD SEEN CAMELS in zoos but never in the wild before my trip to Egypt. Seeing these "ships of the desert" up close and personal was mesmerizing. Our tour guide advised us, "Don't hop on any camel. I will find one for you." My traveling companion ignored the warning and mounted a camel as soon as one became available. She rode for free but paid a heavy price to dismount, which is why our guide told us to wait. It is a rooky tourist mistake, one the camel drivers appreciate.

My approach to life is a lot like that. I often run headlong into situations before thinking of the cost. Some people who know me well would agree that I am wearing out my guardian angel.

My next encounter with camels is a case in point. I was in the United Arab Emirates with another chance to ride a camel. This time there was no guide to help. I figured that since I had successfully ridden before, I knew what to do. The camel was down on its knees, so I climbed on board. The next thing I knew I was flung forward as the camel rose; I almost did a somersault off its back. I managed to hang on, then realized I was in for an unescorted ride with no help to dismount. Oh, how I wished I thought before acting.

So many situations in life look enticing that I eagerly jump into them while God watches and warns. Although He has literally saved my life at times, His most important saving was long ago when I knew I was defenseless by myself and needed His care.

Like the Bedouin who saved the day by helping me down from the camel, God always saves the day by taking care of me, no matter where I am or what I've done, in spite of myself. —Linda Bartlett

Heavenly Father, thank You for the many times
You have been my help and salvation. Amen.

NOVEMBER 28

A Special Connection

But Jesus came and touched them and said, "Arise, and do not be afraid."

—MATTHEW 17:7 (NKJV)

EVER SINCE CHILDHOOD, I've been enamored of horses. The first horse I met was at my grandparents' house. Grandpa had a beautiful palomino named Chance, and I fell in love at first sight. When I went back home to suburbia, I visited the local library and borrowed every book on horses I could find. It didn't matter if it was *The Black Stallion* or *How to Take Care of Your Horse.* I started collecting Breyer statues and naming each one. I just knew that the moment I became an adult, the first thing I would do was get a horse of my own.

To my dismay, adulting didn't exactly work out that way. I got married and had children. I was a (very young!) grandmother when my midlife crisis hit. No sports cars for me. I wanted to fulfill my lifelong dream of having a horse. And along came Moscato, a gorgeous bay Arabian gelding.

My head swims when I'm near him, breathing in his horsey scent, hearing his whickers and snorts, and running my hand down his neck. One of my favorite things to do with him is work in the round pen. I click my tongue and Moscato will walk, trot, and canter in a circle around me. It's magnificent to see. But the best part is our connection. I'll never forget the first time I stepped back a couple of paces and turned my back on him. He approached me and touched my shoulder with his muzzle. It's called a join-up, and it's a spectacular feeling. Horse and human in perfect harmony.

Just as I've had special moments in my relationship with Moscato, I've experienced many similar moments with the Lord. Sometimes in my walk with God, though, I feel as if He is just circling around me. But when I'm still and wait for Him, He approaches me and touches me in His special way, letting me know He's there. God and this human in harmony. —Deb Kastner

---

God, I am so grateful when You touch me in Your special way and let me know You're with me.

NOVEMBER 29

Buttercup Smiles

Be completely humble and gentle; be patient, bearing with one another in love. Make every effort to keep the unity of the Spirit through the bond of peace.

—EPHESIANS 4:2–3 (NIV)

BUTTERCUP IS A rescue dog I often see at church. She accompanies Hannah, the office assistant, to work. Buttercup doesn't like me. She scurries to hide near Hannah and growls whenever I come through the office. For many months, despite my best efforts to be nonthreatening and coaxing, there was a rumbling in Buttercup's throat. But the other day, she timidly approached me and gave me a single wag of her tail. I slowly stretched out my hand as I'd always done, and this time Buttercup let me scratch her behind the ears.

So, what changed? I admit, I don't know. But I do know that patience on my part paid off. I'm no longer greeted by a nervous, growling dog when I visit the church office. I was glad I had persevered in being kind and gentle and had not given up simply because a change of heart seemed unlikely. I wondered if this approach worked to sway a nervous, growling dog, would it also be a good practice when dealing with nervous, growling people? Do you know anyone like that? I do.

Forging successful relationships isn't entirely up to me. I believe the Holy Spirit is working behind the scenes to bring about His own perfect outcome, even though I don't always see it. My part is to be humble, acknowledging that God's will, not mine, is the goal. I need to be gentle and not try to force relationships the way I think they ought to go.

Just as I was patient with Buttercup, I need to be patient with God, waiting on His timing while "bearing with one another in love." —Marianne Campbell

It isn't what we say or think that defines us, but what we do.
—Jane Austen

NOVEMBER 30

Stray Love

My command is this: Love each other as I have loved you. Greater love has no one than this: to lay down one's life for one's friends.

—JOHN 15:12–13 (NIV)

OUR FAMILY VACATION in Mexico was packed with outdoor activities. Exhausted, we decided to take a break one day and relax in our hotel room. I settled down in the patio chair with a book, enjoying the ocean breeze and warm sunlight. A loud meow interrupted my deep reading. An orange tabby stood about 6 or 7 feet in front of me. I closed my book slowly, careful not to make any sudden movements. "Hey kitty, kitty!" I whispered. She meowed again and walked around my chair, surveying the area but not coming close.

Curious about the activity outside, my son turned off the TV in the room and joined me on the patio, his eyes fixed on the feline. She walked up to him and rubbed herself against his leg. Smiling ear to ear, Ryan stroked her head and back. While he bonded with the cat, I went inside our room to fetch our lunch leftovers. Our new friend gobbled up the food in a few minutes. I expected her to stay a little longer and enjoy our attention, but as soon as her hunger was satisfied, she walked away. We called, but she wouldn't come back to us.

That day, God taught me an important lesson about love. Sometimes, I want to love people my way and expect them to also receive love my way. I can be blind to their special circumstances, unaware of how they need to be loved. The cat came to us because she was hungry. She needed food more than cuddles. Just as God used me to provide for her, He can use me also to care for His people. I can show people love by putting aside my selfish expectations and focusing on meeting their wants and needs. —Mabel Ninan

Walk of Faith: *Prayerfully research and choose a local nonprofit organization that aligns with your values. Offer to volunteer your time and talents where they are most needed. Schedule volunteering in your annual calendar.*

December

DECEMBER 1

Old Dog, New Tricks

Wisdom is with the aged, and understanding in length of days.

—JOB 12:12 (ESV)

I THINK OLD DOGS are the best dogs. Yes, puppies are cute and cuddly and adorable. But old dogs bond with their humans in ways neither can imagine when they first meet—becoming sweeter companions day by day. The dogs are content simply to *be* with their people, to hang out, to be by our sides or at our feet (and sometimes *under*foot!).

My schnoodle Windsor is moving into his golden years. He is bonding with me more and more as he ages. With some anxiety and trepidation (certainly more than Windsor is demonstrating), I'm aging too. I watch Windsor as he slows down a bit and mellows out, and I hope I can follow his example. Each day, he is becoming better and better. My good boy is becoming a sweet old man.

Schnoodles are known to be stubborn, and Windsor is no exception. He has always seemed to enjoy pushing my buttons, particularly when it comes to food. I'd put a bowl of food down for him, and he'd give me a baleful look, as if maybe he thought I was trying to poison him, before walking away. That look, that haughtiness is just one of the ways.

Something has changed between us recently, though. Whereas sometimes I've felt the need to raise my voice in order to get Windsor to listen, I now find that a quiet word or even a whisper captures his attention. And they say you can't teach an old dog new tricks. But who's changed? Now that I think about it, maybe Windsor isn't the only one learning new things—maybe I am too.

The Bible tells us that wisdom comes with age, but it's not automatic. Just because we get older doesn't mean we get wiser. Wisdom is something we must seek out, pray about, and practice. As we get older, either we can become harder, more entrenched, and more cantankerous, or we can mellow out and become more tolerant and loving of others. I know which one I would rather be. —Jon Woodhams

But the wisdom that comes from heaven is first of all pure; then peace-loving, considerate, submissive, full of mercy and good fruit, impartial and sincere.

—James 3:17 (NIV)

DECEMBER 2

Inward Beauty

Do not let your adornment be merely outward—arranging the hair, wearing gold, or putting on fine apparel—rather let it be the hidden person of the heart, with the incorruptible beauty of a gentle and quiet spirit, which is very precious in the sight of God.

—1 PETER 3:3–4 (NKJV)

ALTHOUGH SMALL, THE aquarium my husband and I were visiting held several interesting specimens. One large semicircular tank drew my attention. Two unusual fish, each about a foot long, drifted in the water. They had distinctive maroon-and-white zebra-like stripes across their bodies and checkerboard tails. Numerous long spines fluttered gracefully from them like mythical mermaid hair. I called my husband over for a photo op with the gorgeous fish.

Then I read the information card beside the tank.

Those spines contained a potent venom that can pack quite a punch. Though beautiful, the lionfish were not something I'd want to cuddle up with. As my mother often said, "Beauty is only skin deep" and "It's what's on the inside that counts."

While I don't neglect my appearance, the beauty that comes from within is what I want to cultivate, a sweet spirit that springs from knowing Jesus. I admit that sometimes I default to a venomous reaction. Jesus is still working on me, but the older I get, the more I try to respond in love as Jesus would.

Lionfish may be dazzling, but I think I'll opt for the hidden beauty Peter spoke of, the one that is precious to God. When Jesus's light shines from within, I hope people will be drawn to Him.

Wouldn't that be beautiful? —Tracy Crump

For beautiful eyes, look for the good in others; for beautiful lips, speak only words of kindness; and for poise, walk with the knowledge that you are never alone.

—Audrey Hepburn

DECEMBER 3

The Hamster Ball

Jesus replied, "What is impossible with man is possible with God."

—LUKE 18:27 (NIV)

I AM NOT A fan of hamster balls. I often frowned when my grandson Wyatt placed his hamster, Mr. Winky, inside the clear plastic ball to watch the little critter roll hither and yon around the living room. It's cute, I suppose. It may even provide necessary exercise for cage-bound creatures. But sometimes when the ball slammed into a table leg or when Wyatt accidentally kicked the ball because he wasn't watching where he was going, Mr. Winky would spin topsy-turvy with such velocity, it was a wonder the hamster didn't get motion sickness.

Was it my imagination or did Mr. Winky appear stunned and disoriented after such an episode? That's how I feel when I get kicked around by life. The unpleasant surprise of a heart attack, the sudden death of a close friend, the distressing news of another divorce in the family, the unexpected loss of a job. These things have left me feeling as though I'd been tumbled about in a hamster ball. I've felt trapped inside a ball of worry unable to see a way out.

I read somewhere that the phrase *do not be afraid* appears more than 300 times in the Bible. Often these words are used by Jesus, and I try to take them to heart, for He knows how easily I worry and fret over things I can do absolutely nothing about. The only thing that has kept me from emotional and mental collapse is my trust in the Lord. I sit and pray, waiting patiently for Jesus to remove me from the hamster ball of worry.
—Shirley Raye Redmond

If you want to be happy, do not dwell in the past, do not worry about the future, focus on living fully in the present.
—Roy T. Bennett

DECEMBER 4

Winter Buddies

He will call on me, and I will answer him; I will be with him in trouble, I will deliver him and honor him.

—PSALM 91:15 (NIV)

THAT DECEMBER, FREEZING temperatures threatened a winter storm, and the wind howled outside a friend's door. *Good stay-at-home weather,* she thought. But when she looked outside, her jaw dropped. A large gray cat and a raccoon sat huddled together on her front porch.

My friend sprang into action, setting food, water, and a heated shelter on her porch. She assumed the raccoon would run off, but he and the cat stayed side by side for three weeks, eating together and sleeping next to each other in the shelter. They seemed to understand that on this porch they were safe. The curious arrangement lasted until the weather warmed up.

One day the raccoon disappeared, presumably back into the wild, most likely to do raccoon things. But the cat stayed on my friend's porch, becoming more and more tame as time went on. His new adoptive humans had him neutered and named him William Graeber, after a client my friend had known in a law practice. Not more than a year old, this gray kitty knew where to go to find deliverance from the cold.

When the winds of trouble threaten to blow me sideways, I want to be like these two critters that survived a harsh time by banding together. They remind me that I need not suffer alone. I can ask for help from both my community and my God.

William doesn't seem to miss his raccoon pal, and he is now living his best cat life. Each time I think of the cat and raccoon who bonded to get out of the weather, I think of God's promises to answer me when trouble knocks on my door. —Linda S. Clare

Walk of Faith: *Help unwanted animals by giving to a shelter, setting out food or water, or adopting a stray.*

DECEMBER 5

Rescued from Darkness

For he has rescued us from the dominion of darkness and brought us into the kingdom of the Son he loves, in whom we have redemption, the forgiveness of sins.

—COLOSSIANS 1:13–14 (NIV)

DURING MY COLLEGE years in India, I shared a rented house with four friends. One morning, we woke up to a plumbing emergency. Our landlord dispatched a plumber that afternoon to resolve the problem. The plumber first unsealed the underground water tank situated just outside our house, in the foyer, to assess our water levels. It was half full. In India, some homes use these tanks to store water. Relieved that the tank was not the issue, the plumber was about to shut it when I noticed something move and requested that he keep the tank open. I ran inside the house, returned with a flashlight, and lit up the tank. I gasped. *Was that really a turtle?* Seeing my horrified expression, the plumber explained that some landlords leave turtles in water tanks so the animal can purify the water by feeding on any insects or worms.

My heart sank. The tank had not been opened during the time I had been living there, which was more than a year. I could not imagine that this creature lived by itself without light in an enclosure underground. The plumber went inside the house to investigate the water problem while I dialed a local animal rescue organization. Two trained volunteers arrived within an hour and extracted the turtle from the tank. The organization treated the turtle for lung disease and eventually released it into the wild.

The memory of the rescued turtle remains etched in my mind because it helps me appreciate and value my salvation. Jesus sacrificed Himself on the cross so my sins can be forgiven. He rescued me from the bondage of sin so I can be free from guilt and condemnation and free to love and live for God. —Mabel Ninan

But you are a chosen people, a royal priesthood, a holy nation, God's special possession, that you may declare the praises of him who called you out of darkness into his wonderful light.
—1 Peter 2:9 (NIV)

DECEMBER 6

Standing Guard

Be alert and of sober mind. Your enemy the devil prowls around like a roaring lion looking for someone to devour.

—1 PETER 5:8 (NIV)

MOST CATS ARE serious types, but Twitch was the soberest cat I ever knew. He had the demeanor of a veteran patrol cop: alert, watchful, and purposeful. This was no cat to be trifled with.

Like any cat, Twitch believed he owned the entire house in which he lived, that is to say *my* house. And his lordship extended to the yard and property of some 4 acres. He watched over his charge with the vigilance of a warden. Mice in the basement? Not on Twitch's watch. Stray dogs wandering through the yard? Absolutely not.

By day, the gray tabby reigned over the grounds from the big yellow chair near the window—between naps, of course. At dusk, he slipped out the back door to patrol the perimeter and, presumably, the rest of the neighborhood too.

Yet with the onset of cold and snow, the threat level was reduced considerably. The mice had all found other places to live. Neighborhood dogs stayed close to home. It would have been easy for Twitch to curl up on the yellow chair and take a long winter nap. But he had no intention of allowing his formidable skills to degrade over the long winter.

To keep sharp, Twitch ran attack drills nearly every day—on me. When I entered the walk-in closet, he would pounce from an upper shelf, then dart away. As I napped through a football game, Twitch would swat at my head, then disappear behind the couch. Like Cato, faithful servant of the fictional Inspector Clouseau, Twitch was liable to attack from any place at any time. I had to admire his discipline.

During the occasional seasons when threats from our spiritual enemy have diminished, I've tended to relax my guard. That lack of attention has too often provided an opening for sin. I've learned that the enemy takes breaks but never retreats. Vigilance is the price of victory. —Lawrence W. Wilson

Sure I must fight if I would reign.
Increase my courage, Lord;
I'll bear the toil, endure the pain,
Supported by Thy Word.
—Isaac Watts

DECEMBER 7

A Posture of Confidence

But blessed is the one who trusts in the Lord, whose confidence is in him.

—Jeremiah 17:7 (NIV)

OUR TWO DOGS come from very different backgrounds. We adopted Honcho when he was 6 months old. He had been surrendered by a family that was moving to a living situation that didn't allow pets. We suspect he was treated well because he has always seemed confident and at ease. He came into our home and quickly acted as if he owned the place and deserved our attention.

A year later we adopted Simone. She was about 1½ years old, and the worker at the shelter said the owner mistreated Simone as they dropped her off, so we assumed she had not had a happy life. She lacked confidence, and if we moved toward her too quickly, she would cower fearfully. We learned to approach her slowly and have worked to make her feel loved and secure over the past year. Thankfully, she is developing trust and gaining confidence. My husband recently marveled that she will now lie on her back in a vulnerable position and allow him to pet her belly.

Simone still has a very different posture from Honcho, though. He walks with his head held high, with an almost regal bearing. It may sound silly, but whenever Simone plods across the floor with her head down, I tell her to lift her head like Honcho and be proud because she's a beloved part of our family.

God could say the same to me on occasion. Anytime I lack confidence or feel like I'm not good enough, God reminds me—through Scripture or through someone who cares about me—that I am loved. Like Simone, I need to lift my head and claim my status as a beloved child of God, worthy of my place in His family. —Missy Tippens

See what great love the Father has lavished on us, that we should be called children of God! And that is what we are!

—1 John 3:1 (NIV)

DECEMBER 8

The Backyard Nativity Scene

And he will be called Wonderful Counselor, Mighty God, Everlasting Father, Prince of Peace.

—ISAIAH 9:6 (NIV)

FIVE GOLDEN RETRIEVERS posed in front of our old backyard shed. Zeke, our son's gentle dog and faithful friend for 8 years, sat at one end. Our own female golden rescue came next, looking down at Jack, our son's new wiggly puppy, who was attempting to dive out of an open wooden crate. Next came our senior dog, followed by our slightly younger golden.

When I'd thought about our Christmas card photo for last year, the idea had immediately jumped to my mind—we had the perfect grouping for a nativity scene! A shepherd, a wise man, Mary, Joseph, and 10-week-old Jack to portray the babe. We simply draped a plain towel around each dog and attached a rustic star to the shed. While it was unique, I made sure the scene was reverent; we were doing it in complete respect and honor to commemorate the birth of the blessed babe. The dogs sat attentively for their picture. The scene was adorable and poignant.

A few weeks later I looked at the finished product and wiped away a tear. After we'd sent the card to be printed, we'd unexpectedly lost our precious granddog, Zeke, to cancer. The Nativity picture—our Christmas greeting—was now a source of sorrow. I debated even sending it out. Yet, along with the sadness, I also felt grateful that Zeke was present in that very special picture, that we could look back upon it and remember him well. It didn't take me long to realize that the photo served to reinforce the true meaning of Christmas. The holidays can be an emotional season, one of great joy yet also one of grief that someone special is no longer celebrating with us. But the season is, foremost, a time to give glory to the baby in the manger, the Son, who gives us comfort and hope for the future. Oh come, let us adore Him! —Peggy Frezon

Yea, Lord, we greet Thee, born this happy morning;
Jesus, to Thee be all glory given.
—John Francis Wade

DECEMBER 9

Painted Paw Prints

Love is patient, love is kind.... It keeps no record of wrongs.

—1 CORINTHIANS 13:4–5 (NIV)

AS NEWLYWEDS, OUR first gift to ourselves was a sweet puppy, Sebastian, a Pomeranian-Chihuahua mix. His fluffy golden coat and captivating smile melted our hearts. We filled our days setting up our new home and playing with our furry little ball of energy.

One afternoon, in a fit of budget-inspired creativity, I decided to tackle the bathroom's dated linoleum floor. I gave it a good sanding and then applied a thick coat of sticky white paint. It looked fantastic! After cleaning the brushes, I came back to find white paw prints up and down our pine staircase. I looked in the bathroom—little paws had stepped all over the wet paint. I found Sebastian curled up in the living room, trying to figure out what the white stuff on his feet was! I gathered him in my arms and brought him into the kitchen to carefully wash the paint off his paws. My husband and I laughed over the mess our curious puppy had made. He'd intended no harm—he just wanted to be part of the decorating fun! I scrubbed the paw prints off the stairs and grabbed a clean paintbrush.

As I touched up the bathroom floor, I thought of the many times I'd wandered into messes myself. Most times, I didn't intend to cause harm—they just seemed to happen. Caught up in my own agenda or desires, I'd suddenly find myself stepping all over someone else's needs, leaving a mess in my wake. And like Sebastian leaving paw prints on the stairs, I'd leave a trail of harm as I exited the scene. But God always showed up when I seemed to need Him the most, ready to cradle me in His arms and let me know that everything would be OK.

Just as I wiped away Sebastian's sticky paw prints, God always cleans up my mess, erasing every record of my wrongs. —Allison Lynn

Loving God, I try to be good, but there are times when I just get things wrong. Thank You for cleaning up the messes I make and forgiving my wrongs. Thank You for Your never-ending grace. Amen.

DECEMBER 10

Velvet at My Window

My beloved is like a gazelle or a young stag. Behold, he stands behind our wall; he is looking through the windows, gazing through the lattice.

—SONG OF SOLOMON 2:9 (NKJV)

LIVING ON THE high desert of central Oregon has brought many of God's creatures to our yard. But one summer morning, up close and personal, I saw velvet from my window.

After starting the coffee, I opened the blinds on my big kitchen window. Like a miracle, at that very moment in time, a buck with majestic antlers walked by. Not even 3 feet away, I could see its antlers covered with velvet. The male deer didn't run or even startle when I opened the blinds, but it paused before strolling by, as if to give me a glimpse of its crown.

I had never seen a deer walk so near my window. Usually, they come through the yard and the remote desert behind us. Part of me wished I could touch the velvet. Of course, I would never even dare, nor would the buck allow me. Instead, my window separated me from this wild but elegant animal, and I thanked God for an up-close glimpse.

The soft, fuzzy layer that covers the male deer's antlers during spring and summer provides nourishment and protection while the antlers underneath harden and turn to bone. The velvet is living tissue that includes all the nutrients needed to grow thick, strong antlers. Soon, around Labor Day, the velvet would shed and turn uncomely, but on that early summer morning, I saw its unique beauty. I am so thankful I didn't miss it.

That morning, I discovered something. I have a window of opportunity *every day* to experience God's blessings. I will see the miracles around me, even just glimpses that make a memory, if I only open the symbolic shutters of my heart to receive them. God's blessings come in many ways and in many forms—like when I looked out my window and saw velvet.
—Kathleen R. Ruckman

If you believe in God, He will open the windows of heaven
and pour blessings upon you.
—Mahalia Jackson

DECEMBER 11

The Elephant Whisperers

Be merciful to me, LORD, for I am in distress; my eyes grow weak with sorrow, my soul and body with grief.

—PSALM 31:9 (NIV)

ALL MY FRIENDS were talking about the award-winning documentary *The Elephant Whisperers*, so I decided to check it out for myself. At the time, I was going through an animal documentary phase, and I wanted to be able to participate in discussions about the one that was generating so much buzz. I was surprised by how deeply I connected with a story of a couple in South India who cared for abandoned elephants. The story focuses on the couple's bond with an orphaned baby elephant named Raghu. Helping Raghu recover from being left motherless required round-the-clock feeding and nurturing. The wife was especially close to the newest addition to their wildlife preserve. She shares that caring for Raghu helped her come out of depression after the death of her daughter. She doesn't say how her daughter died, only that she was lost in grief and pouring her affection and attention into helping a baby elephant survive, grow strong, and thrive became like medicine to her soul. She shared her love for Raghu with her granddaughter by allowing her to spend time helping her at the preserve.

I have never suffered the pain of losing a child, but I have experienced other losses that left me drowning in grief. God often showed me the way out through sending something or someone for me to invest my time and energy in. A friend who needed me. A new hobby that gave me joy. While those distractions didn't make the pain disappear, they did remind me that joy and sorrow could exist at the same time. That life would be good again. And most important, that God is with us in the sadness and knows exactly how to guide us back into the light. —Jeanette Hanscome

For I am the LORD your God who takes hold of your right hand and says to you, Do not fear; I will help you.
Isaiah 41:13 (NIV)

DECEMBER 12

Speckles' SOS

The Lord watches over you—the Lord is your shade at your right hand; the sun will not harm you by day, nor the moon by night.

—Psalm 121:5–6 (NIV)

SPECKLES' YOWLING WOKE up my husband and me in the middle of the night...again. We were losing sleep over our tortoiseshell cat's noisy insomnia. All three of us were seniors now, so we sympathized with her nighttime restlessness, as well as any aches and pains. Before bedtime, we left out tasty treats (and snacks for us), a new cat toy (for us, interesting books), and switched on a hallway night-light (for all of us). But something had to be done.

The next morning, despite ill-tempered glares from Speckles, I phoned the veterinarian. She asked me about any changes in her routine, attempts to hide from us, or decrease in appetite. After ruling out an emergency situation, she said, "Speckles may be sending out a yowl because she is experiencing some distress. Cats are very good at masking their pain." The vet recommended that before Speckles' next appointment, we read a few websites with information about interpreting our feline's body language, vocalizations, and facial expressions. I learned that cats have a natural instinct to hide their discomfort, since a cat's yowling signals it is weak and prone to a predator's attack.

One night I couldn't fall asleep, but not because of Speckles. This was of my own doing, regarding a relationship conflict at my job. I realized I was disguising my distress during the day by faking a smile and speaking like everything was fine. My natural instinct was self-protection, and I didn't want any coworkers detecting my vulnerability. During the night, my anger, along with the stress, was keeping me awake. Something had to be done.

The next morning my husband and I prayed over the relationship situation. I confided in our pastor, and he recommended reading Psalm 121 before bedtime. In those eight verses, there is hope and assurance from God. Speckles' SOS was just the signal we both needed. —Glenda Ferguson

The Lord will keep you from all harm—he will watch over your life.
—Psalm 121:7 (NIV)

DECEMBER 13

Stronger Than Silk

Then he said to me, "...Not by might, nor by power, but by my Spirit, says the LORD of hosts."

—ZECHARIAH 4:6 (ESV)

A FRIEND WHO VISITED Italy brought me a lovely silk scarf. One day I showed it to my mother, who fingered the fine material and asked, "Do you remember when you brought that silkworm home from school in a jar?" I paused, suddenly recalling my second-grade field trip to a silkworm farm.

We were living on the island of Okinawa at the time. I still recall the odd sound of thousands of silkworms munching mulberry leaves. As we walked among the large wooden tables inside a sprawling building much like a hothouse, our guide explained how the worms were carefully hatched. After reaching maturity at 6 weeks, they spew out a jellylike substance that hardens in the air. This is silk. It takes 3 days for the worms to enclose themselves tightly in cocoons that consist of approximately 1,000 feet of continuous silk thread.

The silkworms stay in the cocoons for just 8 days. If allowed to remain longer, they will change into moths that break out, destroying the silk thread. On the eighth day, the farmworkers place the cocoons in hot water to loosen the thread. The silk is wound into reels and given several twists to make the threads stronger.

As a child, I recall being amazed that such small worms could help produce everything from lovely ball gowns to parachutes. However, it wasn't until I donned my new scarf for the first time that I reflected upon the fact that the silkworms' productive strength—like my own—comes from the Lord. He will never expect me to do anything without giving me the strength and ability to do so. Jesus promises to be with me. He holds my hand. I can accomplish amazing things and get through the most difficult of days because He is with me. —Shirley Raye Redmond

She is clothed with strength and dignity; she can laugh at the days to come.

—Proverbs 31:25 (NIV)

DECEMBER 14

Stand Your Ground

Submit yourselves, then, to God. Resist the devil, and he will flee from you.

—JAMES 4:7 (NIV)

SNOWY HAD ONE of those late-night urges to relieve himself. I grumbled as I put down the book I was reading and dragged myself out of bed. When I opened the back door to let my furry friend out, he charged with loud barks toward the lawn. But his barking stopped abruptly. Curious, I turned on the light in the backyard just in time to catch sight of a standoff between my dog and a large raccoon. I was afraid Snowy would try to attack the animal and hurriedly put on my slippers, prepared to break up a fight. But the two animals simply stared at each other. I expected the raccoon to run away or back down, but he stood his ground. Much to my surprise, Snowy turned around and ran back inside the house.

I admired the raccoon's courage. It inspired me to stand my ground when the enemy plays havoc with my thoughts and makes me doubt who I am in Christ. During my teens, I wrestled with low self-esteem. Even now as an adult, sometimes I think I'm not pretty enough, not intelligent enough, not funny enough, not strong enough, not talented enough. The list can drag on. But I can remember that God has empowered me to fight the enemy's lies with His Word. I can hold on to biblical truths that assure me I'm a beloved, beautiful child of God, created by Him in His image to bring Him glory. The best part is knowing that the battle belongs to God. I must only show up and stare down the enemy, sword of God in hand. —Mabel Ninan

Dear God, help me to remember to put on the spiritual armor daily so I can take down the unholy and untrue lies of the enemy. Thank You for empowering me with Your Holy Spirit and equipping me with Your Word to overcome evil.

DECEMBER 15

God Knows Best

Every good gift and every perfect gift is from above, and comes down from the Father of lights, with whom there is no variation or shadow of turning.

—JAMES 1:17 (NKJV)

THE TOAST POPPED up from the toaster, and my parrot said his name. I spread almond butter on the warm bread as Lorito whistled. I turned my back to hide my breakfast snack and eat my buttered toast in secret.

My red-lored Amazon says his name or whistles to indicate he wants what I'm eating. For years I would hear his call and give him what he desired. Lorito made the cutest sound when he crunched down on warm toast. But people food came at a cost, and now Lorito needs special medicine and regular blood work.

I wish I could satisfy his desires and give my parrot what he wants, but I've learned to give Lorito only what is best for him—things like fruits, vegetables, tree nuts, and vet-recommended parrot food.

Lorito is not able to choose what's best for his health. He counts on me to say no to what would harm him. Lorito's requests give me a hint into how God might view my prayers. Some align with His desires. Others do not. As much as my good Father delights to give me good things, I can trust Him to deny some requests because He knows what's best.

Thankfully, Lorito's taste buds are changing, and he's learning to request the best—whistling and saying his name when he sees me open a banana or crunch a carrot. But when he does ask for food he shouldn't have, I remind myself that loving him means choosing what is best for him even when it's not what he wants—just like God does for me. —Crystal Storms

God sometimes answers our prayers by giving us what we would have asked for had we known what He knows.
—J. D. Greear

DECEMBER 16

Hiding Place

In the shelter of your presence you hide them from all human intrigues; you keep them safe.

—PSALM 31:20 (NIV)

IT WAS YET another snowy December day in the Sierra Valley—a day for hunkering down, not going out. Nonetheless, I had to plod through the heavy snow to our guest house to raid the freezer there for dinner. But just as I stepped out the door, I noticed some backyard guests: a mule deer doe and a large buck less than 20 feet away.

The doe was hiding from her companion underneath our trampoline, while the snow-covered buck kept trying to duck his eight-point antler rack underneath the fabric to join her or coax her out. My first instinct was to shoo him away so he wouldn't tear up the trampoline, but my husband, Craig, stopped me. "You don't want to get close to that big guy."

Before I could grab my phone to take a photo, the doe had moved out from under the trampoline and jumped back over the fence with the buck close behind.

Like that doe, we all need a safe place, a shelter from life's storms and the thunder of human unkindness. A tough diagnosis. A broken relationship. A job loss. Or even simply a sarcastic, hurtful comment from someone we thought cared about us.

God provides that shelter in many ways. Some have a cozy chair in a quiet room of their home. Others find shelter in the outdoors—a cross-country ski trail in the mountains or a walk on the beach. And yet still others have that one special friend who provides the graceful shelter of a warm hug and confidential conversation.

That sweet doe reminded me that day that even when safe shelter isn't found in anything earthly at all, God has His arms wide open to each of us, ready to protect us from any storm that blows into our lives.
—Janet Holm McHenry

Under His wings, under His wings,
Who from His love can sever?
Under His wings my soul shall abide,
Safely abide forever.
—William O. Cushing

Following Instructions

Where then does wisdom come from? Where does understanding dwell? ...God understands the way to it and he alone knows where it dwells.

—JOB 28:20, 23 (NIV)

I WAS RECENTLY AFFORDED the opportunity to visit an entire troop of friendly capuchin monkeys. Our guide pointed to a large set of cubbies and strongly suggested we set aside anything loose (or that could be set loose) on our persons, from watches to purses to baseball caps, although glasses were allowed if we needed them to properly see the monkeys. For me, I set aside my backpack and my very expensive hearing aids. I could only imagine what a cheeky monkey could get away with if he swiped those!

The capuchins were delightful, perching on my shoulders and the top of my head, and knocking my glasses askew, though thankfully not running off with them. One monkey even managed to take a particularly good selfie of the two of us. I sure appreciate that because I've never been particularly good at taking selfies. I guess capuchins have a lot of practice with cell phones.

What struck me was how many people in the group chose to ignore the guide's instructions. Several brought in their purses and backpacks and then were surprised when the naturally curious capuchins rifled through their things. One man wore his baseball cap, and the monkeys tossed it around in a game of keep-away. I'm not sure if the man ever got his cap back.

Like the guide's instructions about interacting with the capuchins, the Bible offers me the instructions I need to live my best life, starting with God's commandments. Jesus tells us how to live our best life when He's speaking to the Pharisees in Matthew 22:37 (NIV): "Love the Lord your God with all your heart and with all your soul and with all your mind." Instructions for life from the Guide of my life. —Deb Kastner

Lord, help me to listen to You and remember it's easier to follow Your Word than to chase after my own will.

DECEMBER 18

Love Can Find a Way

Do not judge, and you will not be judged. Do not condemn, and you will not be condemned. Forgive, and you will be forgiven.

—LUKE 6:37 (NIV)

I MISS MY DOG Cesar. For 3 years I took him walking when I volunteered at the dog shelter. One day I just walked him home with me. He didn't have many options. You do not make many friends when you growl at anyone willing to peek into your kennel at the adoption center. And that sure doesn't help you find your forever home. I had no choice; Cesar chose me as his only friend.

It is Christmas time, and Cesar loved opening gifts. He would rip into packages he thought were his based on how they smelled. He loved the paper almost as much as he loved the gifts. It was his most redeeming quality. I knew he had been abused and didn't trust people. That's why I could overlook his scary exterior to see into his heart. Once he felt safe enough, he expressed his love and devotion with his sappy doggy smile to me and other close family members. He seemed more grateful than the other pooches just to have a walk, a rub, and a treat. Although Cesar never became a lover of all people, he did love his family.

I know people like Cesar, people who have been abused by the world and have trouble trusting others. When I meet someone with a crusty manner like Cesar's, I need to dig deeper to find the beautiful soul that God sees. Even though we might growl at God—believe me, I have—for the hard things in life, He loves us anyway and wants to help us through them.

Like Cesar with his Christmas gifts, if I can do something to open up a person's real self, I just might discover their lovely and loving heart. After all, that's exactly what God does for me. —Linda Bartlett

Walk of Faith: *Is there someone in your life that seems distant and unapproachable? Take time to listen and learn. Then make a plan to overlook their outside in order to see their heart.*

Confidence Builders

This is the confidence we have in approaching God: that if we ask anything according to his will, he hears us.

—1 JOHN 5:14 (NIV)

WHILE DECIDING WHETHER to accept a new position in a writing organization, I took my friend Susy up on an offer to read through a leadership book together. One day, while discussing a chapter, we got on the subject of my struggle with confidence.

Susy told me, "I think I developed confidence early on because I grew up riding horses." She explained all that was required to stay safe while riding a large, strong herd animal. She had to constantly remember that her horse had the ability to size her up and figure out who was in charge. And "who is in charge" needed to be her. Her horse could sense fear, anxiety, even her mood. I'd seen Susy with her retired racehorse, Stetson, and marveled over her calm confidence in his presence. As we talked and I remembered the day when she introduced me to Stetson, it made perfect sense why my kindhearted, generous, encouraging friend could walk into a room with a confidence that told everyone, "She knows who she is and what she's talking about." She had been practicing for leadership while bonding with the horses she loved.

Her horse analogy opened my eyes to the things God had used to build a confidence in me that I didn't always recognize. In high school, I discovered my talents for drama, music, and public speaking. So I grew into an adult who doesn't fear being in front of an audience. I learned to act confident even when I'm terrified.

I didn't end up taking the leadership position that prompted me and Susy to read a book together and talk about confidence. But considering it allowed me to recognize God's work and to grow in my ability to trust Him to equip me for whatever He has in mind next. —Jeanette Hanscome

Walk of Faith: *How has God used a past hobby or passion to prepare you for what you are doing now?*

DECEMBER 20

Visit to a Family Farm

And God blessed them, and God said unto them, Be fruitful, and multiply, and replenish the earth, and subdue it: and have dominion over the fish of the sea, and over the fowl of the air, and over every living thing that moveth upon the earth.

—GENESIS 1:28 (KJV)

WE WERE SPENDING Christmas at my grandparents' family farm in northeast Iowa. It was bitterly cold, snow covered the ground, and the house did not have indoor plumbing, so we had to use bed pans and make trips to the outhouse and the water pump. But in my 10-year-old eyes, it was a great adventure. There were chickens and pigs and sheep to play with, and even the outhouse was a new adventure. I hardly noticed that once the presents were opened, my grandfather, dad, and uncle were nowhere to be seen as my brother, my cousin, and I played with our new toys. Where had they gone? They were outside tending to the livestock.

The difficult life of a family farmer was brought home to me vividly by a recent discussion with a friend, who had grown up on such a farm. He said there were no vacations and no days off, for even on holidays, the animals needed care and food. It's easy to forget that having "dominion" over animals means more than lording over them. It also means taking the responsibility to provide for them and to care for them.

I may not be a family farmer, but the lesson here still applies. I can care for my pets or the birds in my backyard. And when I cannot provide animal care directly, I can help and support animal shelters and rescue organizations. I can serve as a family farmer to God's animals in a multitude of ways. —Harold Nichols

The greatness of a nation and its moral progress can be judged by the way its animals are treated.
—Mahatma Gandhi

DECEMBER 21

Equine Empathy

Share each other's burdens, and in this way obey the law of Christ.

—GALATIANS 6:2 (NLT)

WE'VE ALL HEARD about therapy dogs and other small animals that help bring comfort and cheer to hospital patients. But you might be surprised to learn about Peyo, a very special horse in France, that, since 2016 has visited more than 1,000 patients in the palliative care unit of Calais Hospital.

News articles tell the story of Peyo and the patients—many terminally ill—he helps, just by being there. But there's more to Peyo's story.

Like many horses, the large chestnut stallion competed in dressage competitions, in which the horse and trainer perform a sequence of controlled movements before a panel of judges. He and Hassen Bouchakour, his owner and trainer, won many awards and accolades together. But Bouchakour began to notice something unique about his equine friend. When they greeted audience members at the dressage competitions, Peyo pulled Bouchakour to certain people in the audience and stayed near them. Over time, Hassen realized that Peyo was choosing people who were physically or mentally fragile—he sensed their need and sought to comfort them.

This observation eventually led Bouchakour and Peyo to Calais Hospital, where Peyo began to work with patients in end-of-life stages. The pair spend 2 hours before each visit washing and disinfecting to prepare Peyo for his days at the hospital. Peyo not only brings joy and peace with his daily patient visits and helps make hospital visits less scary and sad for the children of terminal patients, but he also stays with patients until their last breath. Hospital staff call him Doctor Peyo.

Peyo's gift is truly unique—from a test of 500 horses, only he demonstrated this ability. But we humans have the ability to learn how to be empathetic, to listen, to care about others, and share others' burdens. Peyo's example inspires me to be more in tune with the needs of others so I can perhaps lighten their burden a little too. —Jon Woodhams

Truly I tell you, whatever you did for one of the least of these brothers and sisters of mine, you did for me.
—Matthew 25:40 (NIV)

DECEMBER 22

Following Directions

If you pay attention to these laws and are careful to follow them, then the LORD your God...will love you and bless you.

—DEUTERONOMY 7:12–13 (NIV)

I HAVE A MALTIPOO named Fizz, and even though he is small, he has a big personality. Fizz loves to go on walks, but he is always pulling at the leash. Like a sled dog, Fizz is often tugging as hard as he can, trying to get to whatever spot he has in mind.

My big golden retriever, Candie, also used to pull on the leash until I got her a chest harness, which attaches to the chest of the dog instead of the neck. It worked like a charm! Whenever she pulled on the leash to go where she wanted, she instead was directed toward the way I was going.

I decided to get Fizz a chest harness like the one Candie has. Fizz was not happy. He squirmed and fought the whole way, but I was determined to train him to be a better-behaved leash-walking dog.

One day as we were approaching a busy traffic light, Fizz started to fight the chest harness. To my horror I saw him get one leg out of the straps and then the other. Hurriedly I reached down and picked him up before he could run out into the street.

After crossing the intersection, I strapped Fizz back into the harness. "That's it," I said. "We are going back to the earlier model." I would rather fight his pulling than risk him running into the street.

Struggling to work with Fizz reminds me of my own struggles in life. Like Fizz, I struggle when I don't feel free. How often am I running off in the wrong direction, despite the Lord trying to lead me another way? How many times have I headed into danger because I ignored the Word of God?

Following God's direction can be a challenge, but Scripture reminds me that if I follow the ways of the Lord, He will bless me. —Heather Jepsen

Gracious God, help me to trust You to be a guiding presence in my life. Amen.

In Search of Nests

There is a time for everything, and a season for every activity under the heavens…a time to tear down and a time to build…a time to keep and a time to throw away.

—ECCLESIASTES 3:1, 3, 6 (NIV)

MINNESOTA TREES OFFER something delightful in every season: brilliant green buds bursting from the branches in spring, lavish foliage filling out the treetops through the summer, golds and reds setting the fall trees on fire. And in the winter, bare, leafless branches prominently display their structure against the monotone landscape. I love when the leaves have fallen away and I can see the twists and turns of every trunk, branch, and twig. But what I noticed this past winter was that there weren't many nests.

A wide assortment of birds remain in Minnesota through the winter, hearty enough to withstand our weather from November to March. This includes sparrows, cardinals, woodpeckers, blue jays, finches, nuthatches, chickadees, and crows. I just assumed that they continued to sleep in their nests throughout the year. But I now know that most birds only use these temporary homes during the nesting season.

In spring, birds inherently know that it's time to prepare a place for their eggs, a place that will provide protection as their young develop, both pre- and post-hatching. Nests serve a purpose, but only for a limited time. As birds mature, and as the weather changes, they adapt, finding new places to settle in for the night. It's not unusual to find them in tree cavities, bird boxes, barns, holes in homes, thick vegetation, and clefts in rocks.

I want to be like the birds in this way. There is a time for everything—a time to rest in my nest, and a time to cocoon inside the sturdy crevice of a rock. God knows when and how my circumstances will change. I choose to say yes to Him when He moves me into a new environment. I can do all things when I am secure in Him. —Liz Kimmel

I'm so grateful, Lord, that You never abandon me. You have taught me to trust in You and in Your sovereign hand. You lead me and guide me every step of the way in this adventure called life.

"Grandma Needs That!"

Your Father knows what you need before you ask him.

—MATTHEW 6:8 (NIV)

GRANDMA NEEDS THAT!" Our then 2-year-old grandson made a beeline through the store to show his mama what he knew I would need for my Christmas tree—a 15-inch-tall, feathery owl Christmas tree topper. He insisted they buy it. When they presented this gift to me, the story of how our grandson claimed I needed it thrilled me. It sat on that year's Christmas tree, presiding over the smaller owls and other animals filling the branches.

The relationship between owls, our grandchildren, and me has a long history. I enjoy owls, and I love hearing their calls in our backyard and sharing stories and information about them with our grandkids. But owls didn't become a thing I "needed" until the youngest grands came along. Their excitement in relating anything with owls to me when I visit delights me. I especially love reading books such as *Owl Moon* to them over and over.

My whole family has a love of animals, and when our daughter's family moved near a zoo, we purchased a yearly membership for them to enjoy the animals whenever they wanted. On their first trip, their then 3-year-old daughter chose the one-eyed barred owl as her favorite. Every time we visited and went to the zoo, she needed to make sure we spent some time with that owl.

A few days before writing this, I heard they again visited the zoo. Upon seeing the snowy owl, our grandson exclaimed, "Grandma needs to see that!" And I shall next time I visit my grands who know exactly what "Grandma needs"!

Each time I look at the owls that inhabit our house—tree ornaments, books, and handmade pictures—or hear the great horned or barred owls outside, I thank God for knowing just what this child of His needs and how He delights in fulfilling my needs—whether owls, grandchildren, or the gift of His Son. —Cathy Mayfield

Thanks be to God for his indescribable gift!
—2 Corinthians 9:15 (NIV)

Our Good Golden Receiver

For those who find me find life and receive favor from the LORD.

—PROVERBS 8:35 (NIV)

LET'S NAME HER after one of Santa's reindeer, since she came at Christmas!" Our 8-year-old daughter danced around the living room, the pure white puppy prancing at her feet.

"Hey! How about Prancer?"

The name stuck. Our English cream golden retriever's full name, Prancer Dancer Miller, was even stamped on her registration papers.

Sadly, less than a year later, our pup contracted blastomycosis, a nasty lung fungus we knew little about. After several hospital stays and many months of medication, Prancer survived, though her keen eyesight did not.

"Just don't let her drive a car," our friendly veterinarian joked, trying to lighten the mood. "Dogs are resilient and adapt well. You'll see. Soon she'll be getting around with very little trouble."

And while that's true, our golden retriever—her breed instinctively prone to retrieve—possesses an interesting characteristic. While Prancer will fetch a tossed ball, for example, she's more a receiver than a retriever.

She loves to sit and *receive* a good belly rub.

She loves visits from our UPS driver—certain those golden letters stand for *Ummy Puppy Snacks*, which she always *receives* with a wag of her tail.

And she loves to harness up to *receive* exercise when we, her humans, take our walks, Prancer on her leash, leading the way.

But our pup's got a point. This dog who's overcome so much in only half a dozen years reminds me that life's not all about *retrieving*—going out to obtain that which I desire. Rather, more important, it's about *receiving*.

Receiving wisdom from God, to know His plans for me.

Receiving affirmation from the One whose opinion matters most.

Receiving life-giving truths from His Word which sustain me and offer me life.

Indeed, Prancer is teaching me a lot, the best reminder coming when we take our walks. After all, our nearly blind golden girl, the pup who loves to retrieve her fair share of balls, prances by faith, not by sight.

And this reminder of God's favor is something I receive, with both conviction and joy. —Maureen Miller

Lord, help me receive Your favor, then walk by faith,
even when I can't see ahead.

DECEMBER 26

Sleeping Sea Lion

You are my hiding place; you will protect me from trouble and surround me with songs of deliverance.

—PSALMS 32:7 (NIV)

WHAT A SURPRISE! One day on our trip to the Galapágos Islands, my husband, Neil, and I ate lunch in a restaurant on Santa Cruz, one of the Archipelago's very few inhabited islands. When we left, Neil forgot his cap, and when we went back for it, it was gone. So he went hat shopping while I walked out on a busy pier and sat on a bench. I probably rested there, engaged in people watching, for at least 30 minutes. When I saw Neil coming, I stood up to meet him. And that's when a local person pointed at my sitting spot.

"Did you know he was sleeping under there?" she asked, pointing to my former seat. Following her gaze, I spotted a Galapagos sea lion pup curled up underneath. Galapagos sea lions are the most abundant marine mammal in the islands and are often seen sleeping on beaches. But not snoozing silently on a wooden pier under a bench and almost touching my legs! That was unusual. "His mother hid him there to keep him safe while she's gone fishing," the stranger explained. "And he won't move until she comes back for him."

The smooth-bodied, light brown pup looked adorable, and I longed to pet him. But I knew better than to interfere. This pup, although able to swim and dive, would remain dependent on his mother for a full year. During that time, she would find him countless hiding places safe from orcas, sharks, and other dangers.

God, our heavenly Father, has promised to protect us in times of fear and trouble by granting us a hiding place in Him. And what hiding spot could be safer? So why do I struggle to feel as secure as that sea lion pup? Next time I fear some approaching storm, I will remember that relaxed little creature and try to muster up as much trust as he had. —Aline Alexander Newman

Rock of Ages, cleft for me,
Let me hide myself in Thee.
—Augustus Montague Toplady

DECEMBER 27

Sparrows in the Snow

The eyes of all look to you, and you give them their food at the proper time. You open your hand and satisfy the desires of every living thing.

—PSALM 145:15–16 (NIV)

WHEN WE LIVED in the Willamette Valley of Oregon, 400 feet above sea level, we rarely got snow. So when a freak snowstorm came at Christmastime, I felt especially blessed. But I worried about the sparrows in my yard, as I kept watch over them daily.

How did these sweet songbirds keep warm? What did they eat when 6 inches of snow lay on the ground? I found myself placing bowls of water on my patio so they could take a drink, but by morning the water was frozen solid. I scattered sunflower seeds and fine grains, and wondered if they would starve if I didn't help them.

My baby granddaughter enjoyed watching the sparrows hop across the yard. I pulled her highchair close to the patio window and said, "God made the birdies." But did I really believe their Creator gave them instincts to stay warm and find food in several inches of snow?

Then I discovered that in order to survive freezing temps, sparrows seek out shelter in dense foliage, like the shrubs in my yard. They huddle together to share warmth and tuck their heads and feet in, while fluffing up their feathers. Sometimes they puff up into tiny balls to minimize heat loss.

I also learned that sparrows find food in the snow, such as seeds or insects trapped in the ground or food dispersed by other animals. Many plants keep their mature seed heads throughout the winter, which may fall and remain under leaves and are easy for the birds to reach. As for drinks, the sparrows get their water from the snow.

My greatest Christmas gifts that year were the sparkling snow, sparrows thriving in a winter storm, and learning along with my grandchild that "God made the birdies and provides for them too—and much more for me and you." —Kathleen R. Ruckman

Walk of Faith: *Remember Jesus's words about sparrows when you worry about your needs: "And not one of them is forgotten before God.... Do not fear therefore; you are of more value than many sparrows."*
—Luke 12:6–7 (NKJV)

DECEMBER 28

Urban Beauties

He has made everything beautiful in its time. He has also set eternity in the human heart; yet no one can fathom what God has done from beginning to end.

—ECCLESIASTES 3:11 (NIV)

I LIVE IN THE city where I grew up, but except for the name, it's hard to recognize it as the same place. I can shut my eyes and see the field behind my house where dewberries grew, the cows that grazed across the street from my school, and the flocks of geese that crowded the skies with their V formations each fall. But looking around now, I am faced with townhouses, high-rises, mid-rises, shopping malls, and chain restaurants sprawling for miles. Sometimes I find all this change disheartening: How can I find God when I can't find His creatures in the landscape around me?

Stuck in traffic recently, I began lamenting about urbanization when I looked up and saw a big flock of pigeons in the overpass. Pigeons! Rats with wings! These city birds seemed to be another indication that there was no beauty in my city.

But with nowhere to go and nothing to see but the bumper ahead of me, I began studying them. The pigeons shimmered with iridescent blues, purples, and pinks, as colorful as peacocks. Their plump bodies, gently rounded heads, and small beaks looked just like those of doves, those marvelous messengers of God's presence. I remembered a story I had heard in school of two legendary pigeons, Cher Ami and G. I. Joe, and others like them that carried messages to save troops during World War I. I extended a silent apology to pigeons throughout time.

As the traffic began to move, I realized that God is more pervasive and persistent than even the most prolific urban developer. I simply need to remove the blinders of nostalgia and self-pity and look around to find evidence of the ongoing splendor of creation. —Lucy Chambers

Wherever there are birds, there is hope.
—Mehmet Murat Ildan

DECEMBER 29

Fear in Safe Places

When the disciples saw him walking on the lake, they were terrified. "It's a ghost," they said, and cried out in fear.

—MATTHEW 14:26 (NIV)

MY FOSTER DOG, Cookie, is a boxer mix with an underbite that is both adorable and intimidating at the same time. She has a grunting growl that is scary to some, but it really only comes out when she is afraid.

I seldom travel, but recently when I did have to leave town, I boarded Cookie at my veterinarian's office because the staff had seen her on several occasions and it was a familiar place. Everyone there loves her and always greets her with treats. The young girls who walk and play with the boarders spend so much extra time with them that I thought Cookie would feel happy and safe.

But when we walked into the lobby, Cookie hit the floor and refused to move. She was terrified of the bell on the door and the other dogs, and when the young lady reached for her leash to take her back to the kennel area, Cookie tried to bite. Cookie was trembling in fear, so I had to walk her back with the lady, who kept explaining how much she loves her and how Cookie really has nothing to worry about.

I knew Cookie was in the safest place she could be, but that didn't stop her from being scared.

Even for us, unexplainable fear can pop up in the most secure moments because we are marked by things that have hurt us or frightened us in the past. It is in the moment we allow ourselves to trust that love never leaves us in a bad place. Only then can we truly start living bravely. —Devon O'Day

God, help me to trust that You are always with me, even when I am unreasonably afraid of the unknown.

DECEMBER 30

Acting Like a Drip

A quarrelsome wife is like the dripping of a leaky roof in a rainstorm.

—PROVERBS 27:15 (NIV)

MY HUSBAND, ERIC, knelt on the floor in front of our dogs' water dish. When he stood up, he was frowning. "The water that drips onto the floor from Peyton's beard when she drinks is starting to damage the hardwood," he said. "We need to do something about it."

I felt irritation spark. "Peyton is a furry dog. It's not like I can train her to stop dripping."

Moments later, my son, Nathan, walked into the kitchen. He scowled and said, "I stepped in Peyton's drips and now my sock is wet."

"Can everyone stop blaming poor Peyton?" I snapped again. "She can't help dripping water onto the floor."

My bad mood got worse still when I realized we were out of milk. I griped under my breath about people not writing needed items on the grocery list.

"Are you crabby today, Mom?" Nathan asked.

It was the wrong thing to say, and I let him know it. After my tirade, I headed upstairs to clean out a closet and, more important, be alone for a bit. While cleaning, I came across an old bath mat I thought might help protect the floor from Peyton's drips. And then I thought about my behavior and realized that I needed something to protect my family from my bad attitude. Just like Peyton's drips could damage the floor, my unkind words could damage my relationships. *Help me to control my emotions instead of snapping at loved ones,* I prayed.

I laid the bath mat under the water dish. When Peyton came for a drink, I rubbed her fuzzy chin. "You can't help your drips, but with God's help, I'm going to learn to control mine," I said. I apologized to Eric and Nathan and showed them my solution for Peyton's drips. "And God and I will be working on my drippy behavior," I promised. —Diane Stark

Lord, help me to treat others well, even when I'm feeling cranky.

DECEMBER 31

His Beautiful Ninth Life

You should clothe yourselves instead with the beauty that comes from within, the unfading beauty of a gentle and quiet spirit, which is so precious to God.

—1 PETER 3:4 (NLT)

DON'T PET THAT ugly cat!"

Looking up, I watched a woman squeeze hand sanitizer onto her child's palms, her face wrinkled with disdain.

"Now, rub your hands together, and don't touch it again. It's a stray."

Her daughter obeyed, but her eyes were fixed on the feline at her feet.

Turning to my husband, I whispered, "Must not be from round here."

After all, anyone from our small town who frequents this restaurant knows Siobhan, the coffee shop cat. He showed up more than a dozen years ago, and no one knew where he'd come from or his age upon arrival.

Understanding he wasn't welcome, Siob turned and, with the flip of his tail, sauntered toward our table tucked in the shade of a large oak. Seconds later, soft fur brushed my leg, and I reached to scratch his head.

The cat's wet nose touched my finger before he rubbed his face along the length of my hand, and I laughed. "He may not be handsome, but he sure is sweet!"

I stroked him a few moments more, then apologized: "I'm sorry, Siob! Lunch is calling."

He blinked his one good eye, the other long gone, probably lost in some back-alley scuffle.

I watched as he strolled toward another table, pausing to wash his face. Turning to Bill, "I sure hope he knows he's beautiful."

Bill smiled. "Well, just look at him."

Again, I peered over my shoulder. Siob was already receiving a tummy rub from another patron, his lanky frame stretched out in sunshine.

My husband squeezed my hand. "Despite how he looks, I'm guessin' he knows."

And I heard God whisper, *What matters most is what's on the inside—within you. Within others.*

Indeed. Because what's most beautiful is a matter of the heart. —Maureen Miller

Your true character is most accurately measured by how you treat those who can do "Nothing" for you.

—Mother Teresa

About the Authors

As a teacher and student of God's Word, **JERUSHA AGEN** is awed by the letters of love the Father writes into every moment of our lives, including through the animals we encounter. Jerusha is the daughter of two veterinarians and has always shared her life with a menagerie of pets, which she now uses as models for the animals featured in her suspense novels. You'll often find Jerusha sharing adorable photos of her two big dogs and two little cats in her e-newsletter. Get a free suspense story from Jerusha and find more of her writing at jerushaagen.com.

JEAN ALFIERI is a writer, speaker, and dog fan. When her eyes locked with those of a smooshy-faced little dog who sat inside a kennel at the Humane Society, it was love at first sight. He captured her heart, and she went on to capture their many adventures in short stories starring Zuggy the rescue pug. She and her husband joke that although they pay the mortgage of their home in Colorado, it's really the dogs' house—they have three altogether. Jean gets much of her writing inspiration from her "vintage puppies" and her work at the Pikes Peak Humane Society.

LINDA BARTLETT considers it an honor to immortalize some of her favorite four-footed friends in the pages of *All God's Creatures*. She has written stories for Chicken Soup for the Soul books and articles for her local paper, but most of her writing is just for fun. *Christian, wife, mother, grandmother, great-grandmother, teacher, flight attendant, lover of the world and all its creatures* are words that spell out her journey. She belongs to a local writing group, which she has led for many years, as well as a local Bible study, which keeps her grounded.

A regular contributor to *All God's Creatures*, **TWILA BENNETT** is also a contributing writer to *The Cat on My Lap, The Dog at My Feet*, and *Guideposts One-Minute Daily Devotional*. Twila is the communications manager for Camp Roger and Camp Scottie. She is also the founder of Monarch Lane Consulting (monarchlaneconsulting.com), helping writers create proposals and providing branding consultation. For 20 years, Twila was a branding and marketing executive for Revell books. Twila loves camping, boating, and sunsets, and lives with her husband, Dan, in Rockford, Michigan. Connect with Twila on Facebook and Instagram.

Homemaker **MARIANNE CAMPBELL** lives in Sonoma County, California. She developed her love of animals during her childhood spent on her family's Gravenstein apple farm. Her spirit of adventure led her to visit Japan, Thailand, Nepal, Israel, and Egypt in the early 1980s. She served in the US Navy from 1984 to 1990, where she met her husband, Scott. They have two married daughters and two grandchildren. When not writing, Marianne enjoys watching her grandchildren, reading, studying history, baking, gardening, hiking local trails, and playing World of Warcraft.

LUCY CHAMBERS serves Christ Church Cathedral and the downtown Houston community as the manager of the historic Cathedral Bookstore. A firm believer in the power of sharing stories to deepen connection and improve lives, she has worked with books for more than 35 years as an editor, publisher, teacher, and writer. In addition to reading and writing, she makes miniature gardens and volunteers for the altar guild and literary and green organizations. She and her husband, Sam, have two grown daughters, two very soft rabbits, a big dog, and a small dog.

LINDA CLARE is the award-winning author of eight books, including *Thank God for Cats!* (BroadStreet Publishing Group, 2023), *Prayers for Parents of Prodigals* (Harvest House, 2020), and the novel *The Fence My Father Built* (Abingdon Press, 2009). A frequent contributor to Chicken Soup for the Soul and Guideposts, Linda is a writing coach and mentor.

No matter how chaotic life becomes, God and her fur babies carry her through it. She lives with her family in Oregon. Connect with her on Twitter (@lindasclare), Facebook, or her website, lindasclare.com.

ASHLEY CLARK (ashleyclarkbooks.com) writes devotions for Guideposts and Southern fiction for Bethany House. With a master's degree in creative writing, Ashley teaches literature and writing courses at the University of West Florida and also homeschools her son. She lives with her husband, her son, and a rescued cocker spaniel on Florida's Gulf Coast. When she's not writing, she's dreaming of Charleston and drinking all the English breakfast tea she can get her hands on.

SUSIE COLBY is a proud mom of three adult kids, Caleb, Phoebe, and Lily; she is the bereft widow of the funniest guy ever, Steve Colby; and she is a reluctant but devoted servant of an extremely extroverted cat, Tango. Susie has worked in student ministry for more than 30 years, and if that doesn't qualify her as an animal lover, nothing does! If she hadn't been hanging out with students all these years, she might have joined Team Otter at the aquarium.

BEN COOPER is a husband, father, author, speaker, educator, and beekeeper. He grew up on a family farm in western Pennsylvania and went on to get an agricultural science degree from Penn State University. Ben retired after working as an agricultural specialist for the State of Maryland. He teaches beekeeping courses at Allegany College of Maryland and mentors new beekeepers.

Ben and his wife live in southern Pennsylvania, where they homeschooled and raised their five children. He is the author of *All Nature Sings: A Devotional Guide to Animals in the Bible* and the children's picture book series that include *Created Critters with Wings* and *Created Critters with Fur.* Ben speaks at churches, youth groups, and camping ministries about God's wonderful creation and can be reached at cooperville@breezeline.net.

TRACY CRUMP dispenses hope in her multi-award-winning book, *Health, Healing, and Wholeness: Devotions of Hope in the Midst of Illness,* based on her experiences as an ICU nurse. Her articles and devotions have appeared in diverse publications, including *Focus on the Family, Mature Living, Ideals, The Upper Room, Woman's World,* and several Guideposts books. But she is best known for contributing twenty-two stories to Chicken Soup for the Soul books.

Tracy and her husband love observing wildlife near their country home and doting on five completely unspoiled grandchildren. Find encouragement from Tracy's blog for caregivers at tracycrump.com.

Shortly before publication of this book, **CATHY ELLIOTT** passed. Cathy was a full-time writer whose work included cozy mysteries, children's books, devotions for Guideposts' book *Every Day with Jesus*, and the Someone Cares greeting cards program. We will miss her meaningful, heartfelt contributions.

Award-winning author **ELLEN FANNON** is a retired veterinarian, former missionary, and church pianist and organist. She and her retired Air Force pilot-turned-pastor husband fostered more than forty children and are the adoptive parents of two sons. She has published five novels: *Other People's Children, Save the Date, Don't Bite the Doctor,* and *Honor Thy Father, Episodes 1 and 2.* Her articles and stories have appeared in *One Christian Voice,* Chicken Soup for the Soul books, *Divine Moments,* and *Guideposts.* In addition to being published in *All God's Creatures,* her devotions have appeared in *Open Windows* and *The Secret Place.* She also has had stories published in *You and Me, Sasee,* and *Go* magazine.

Follow Ellen's humor-at-everyday-life blog, ellenfannonauthor.com.

GLENDA FERGUSON has contributed to *All God's Creatures* since 2023. Her writings have appeared in *Angels on Earth, Guideposts, Mules & More, Sasee,* and Chicken Soup for the Soul books. The Indiana Arts Commission has included her poem "The Buffalo Trace Trail: Then and Now" in the INverse Poetry Archive. Her writing encouragement comes from the Writers Forum of Burton Kimble Farms Education Center and the ladies' prayer circle at Paoli Christian Church. Glenda and her husband, Tim, have an acre of land they share with Speckles the cat and a variety of wildlife visitors.

PEGGY FREZON is a contributing editor of *Guideposts* magazine, a contributing editor of *Angels on Earth,* and the author of many books about the human-animal bond. She especially enjoys writing about dogs and the people who love them. Peggy and her husband, Mike, rescue dogs at BrooksHaven, a forever retirement home for senior golden retrievers. They live with their goldens, Ernest, Petey, and Sophie, and two rescue guinea pigs, Petunia and Marigold. Find out more about her books at peggyfrezon.com and join her newsletter, *Dogs of BrooksHaven,* at tinyurl.com/brookshaven.

SONIA FRONTERA is an attorney, empowerment trainer, and author from New Jersey. Her writing invites readers to discover paths to spirituality in everyday situations and personal adversity.

An avid animal rescuer since age 3, Sonia believes that God's creatures are our greatest teachers. She is the proud mom of three street dogs turned princesses. Her dream is to run an animal shelter in her native Puerto Rico.

Though she doesn't have any creatures in her home, **JEANETTE HANSCOME** savors every opportunity to play with other people's pets and be inspired by critters she spots while traveling. She is the author of both fiction and nonfiction books, in addition to hundreds of articles and devotions. She is currently writing novels for Annie's Fiction and Guideposts' Whistle Stop Café Mystery Series. A proud mom of two grown sons, she now has more time on her hands for her many creative pursuits and practicing ukulele. Jeanette lives in the San Francisco Bay Area.

LORI HATCHER has loved animals since she received two tiny turtles at age 6. She and her husband, David, have cohabited with many fish, a pair of hermit crabs, four birds, and two amazing dogs in Lexington, South Carolina. They're currently petless due to a delightful influx of tiny humans, although they have recently acquired an amazing granddog, Halsey the Frenchie.

Lori is the author of *Refresh Your Faith, Refresh Your Prayers,* and *Refresh Your Hope.* She has also written for Guidepost's *Evenings with Jesus, Guideposts One-Minute Daily Devotional,* and *Pray a Word a Day.* She and David most recently coauthored *Moments with God for Couples* for Our Daily Bread Publishing. Connect with Lori on her blog, *Refresh,* at lorihatcher.com.

REV. HEATHER JEPSEN is the pastor at First Presbyterian Church in Warrensburg, Missouri. She has been serving small churches for more than 18 years. She and her husband, Lars, have two kids, Olivia and Henry, as well as a wide variety of pets. When she is not pastoring or writing, Heather likes to garden, quilt, and play the harp. In addition to writing for *All God's Creatures,* Heather also writes for Guideposts' *Strength and Grace* magazine. Read more at pastorheatherjepsen.com.

KRISTEN G. JOHNSON grew up as that kid who always had her nose in a book and a pen in her hand. She enjoys many different forms of writing, including devotionals, short stories, and articles. Kirsten is currently working on a series of middle-grade novels. She is married to a pastor, and they have two adopted girls, five rabbits, and one one-eyed cat. When she pops her head up from her computer, Kristen enjoys singing, acting, hiking small mountains in search of huckleberries, and serving in her church. She and her family live in Washington State.

As a *Publishers Weekly* award-winning author of more than fifty novels and with two million books in print, **DEB KASTNER** writes contemporary inspirational and sweet western stories set in small communities, often including animals as major secondary characters.

Deb lives in beautiful Colorado with her husband, her puppers Gabby and Sadie, and two mischievous bonded brothers, black tuxedo cats Hype and Dab. She recently went through what she terms a midlife crisis and adopted her very first real live horse, whose name is Moscato.

She is blessed with three adult daughters and two grandchildren, with a third on the way. Her favorite hobby is spoiling her grandchildren, but she also enjoys reading, watching movies, listening to music (The Texas Tenors and The High Kings are her faves), singing in the church choir, and exploring the Rocky Mountains on horseback.

DARLENE KERR lives in Ohio with her naturalist husband, Jeff, on a property increasingly overflowing with native plants, flowers, and vegetables—and all the creatures and insects that are attracted to them. She says, "Our goal is to have a living garden, where many hovering, crawling, buzzing, and burrowing critters are encouraged to thrive." Darlene is the garden tidier (with no calluses), whereas the true gardener (with calluses) is her husband. Much to her husband's chagrin, she has realized that calluses from writing are preferable, and she especially enjoys writing about God's creation, finding spiritual applications to encourage herself and others.

LIZ KIMMEL has self-published two books of Christian prose and poetry and a grammar workbook for middle-school students. She enjoys writing for Guideposts projects and for Grace Publishing's Short and Sweet series. Married to Cary for 44 years and living in St. Paul, Minnesota, she has two children and four grandchildren. Liz provides administrative support to four nonprofits,

Dare to Believe Ministries, Great Commission Media Ministries, Minnesota Christian Writers Guild, and Minnesota House of Prayer. Her new book is a photo-illustrated alliterative retelling of ten of Jesus's parables called *Putting Punch in the Parables.*

Having lived her whole life in the same house until she married, **JULIE LAVENDER** was excited to see more of God's beautiful world when her high school and college sweetheart, David, joined the navy. Reluctant to move at first, Julie ended up loving living in Florida, North Carolina, Virginia, California, and Washington before returning to Georgia.

A former elementary school teacher, Julie homeschooled their four children, while David served first as a navy medical entomologist and later as a wildlife biologist for an army installation. Julie is the author of *365 Ways to Love Your Child: Turning Little Moments into Lasting Memories* and other books and would love to connect with you at julielavenderwrites.com.

REV. LOUIS LOTZ is an ordained minister in the Reformed Church in America and has served as president of the Reformed Church General Synod. His writing for *The Church Herald* and *RCA Today* magazines has won multiple awards from the Evangelical Press Association. He is a frequent contributor to *Words of Hope* devotional magazine.

Lou and his wife, Mary Jean, live in rural Michigan. Caring for their land as stewards of God's creation is important to them. Lou enjoys gardening, beekeeping, long walks with his bride of 49 years, and tending his fruit trees—apple, peach, and cherry. He enjoys fishing but concedes there is a difference between fishing and catching. The Lotzes have two grown children and two grandchildren.

Singer, songwriter, and worship leader, **ALLISON LYNN** is drawn to the power of story to grow hearts and communities. She and her husband, Gerald Flemming, form the award-winning duo Infinitely More. Their ninth album, *The Sum of All Love,* explores the joys and challenges of living an authentic life of faith. Allison writes devotionals, songs, stories, and creative nonfiction to remind people how deeply they are loved by God. She has contributed to *Love STC* blog, The Upper Room, and Chicken Soup for the Soul books. You can reach Allison at infinitelymore.ca.

ERYN LYNUM is a certified master naturalist, an educator, a national speaker, and the author of *Rooted in Wonder: Nurturing Your Family's Faith Through God's Creation.* Eryn hosts the popular podcast for kids, *Nat Theo: Nature Lessons Rooted in the Bible.* She lives in northern Colorado with her husband, Grayson, and their four children, feisty cat, German shorthaired pointer, and pet axolotl, Spud. They spend their days hiking, camping, and adventuring through the Rocky Mountains. Eryn has been featured on broadcasts, including *Focus on the Family, FamilyLife Today, Christian Parenting,* and *Raising Christian Kids.* Every opportunity she gets, she is out exploring God's creation with her family and sharing the adventures at erynlynum.com.

CATHY MAYFIELD'S home exhibits her love of all animals. From the pictures on the walls to animal figurines in settings of driftwood and pine cones to the German shepherd mix who lounges on the couch, her home shows the huge part animals play in Cathy and her husband's lives. Cathy says, "I thank God often for the wildlife I see on our property and the joys of writing about them for *All God's Creatures.* Adding Scripture and devotional thoughts to our real-life stories allows me to see the reason God placed us in this home and gave me a love of animals and devotions."

JANET HOLM MCHENRY is the author of twenty-seven books. She often prayer walks her Sierra Valley, California, town, where she encounters all kinds of God's creatures. Janet and her husband, Craig, have raised four children and a variety of pets. A journalism graduate of UC Berkeley, Janet worked as a reporter and English teacher and is the creator of an online course called *Prayer School* and host of the Sierra Valley Writers Retreat. Through her business, Looking Up!, she encourages others to pursue a praying life. She loves traveling, kayaking, and spending time with their grandchildren. Connect with her at janetmchenry.com.

MAUREEN MILLER is an award-winning author and storyteller who writes for her local newspaper, a contributing author in numerous collaboratives, and a featured blogger for several online devotional websites. She loves life in all its forms, enjoying it with her husband and their three "born in their hearts" children and grandchildren on Selah Farm, their hobby homestead in western North Carolina. She blogs at penningpansies.com, sharing God's extraordinary character in the ordinary things of life, and she's finishing her first novel, *Gideon's Book*, for Redemption Press.

Last summer was a heartbreaker for **ALINE ALEXANDER NEWMAN** and her husband, Neil, of Turin, New York. After 11 years spent being their constant companion, their beloved rescue dog, Moose, suddenly died of cancer. "We hardly know what to do without him," Aline says. But visits from their four grandchildren, ages 2 to 29, distract them and help heal their grief. Their prayer now is that when they're ready, God will send them another rescue pup, one who needs them as much as they need him. Until then, Aline keeps busy writing animal books and magazine articles for kids.

HAROLD "NICK" NICHOLS is a retired university professor and administrator living in Lafayette, Louisiana, with his amazing wife of 30 years and best friend, Anna Marie. Nichols earned his PhD in theater history at Indiana University and taught at Kansas State University for 22 years before turning to administration. He served as a dean at the University of Nebraska at Kearney and at Georgia Southwestern State University before finishing his career as dean of the Mississippi State University Meridian Campus. Nick and Anna Marie have five children and thirteen grandchildren.

MABEL NINAN is an author, speaker, and host of the podcast, *Far from Home with Mabel Ninan*. In her award-winning book, *Far from Home: Discovering Your Identity as Foreigners on Earth*, Mabel draws from her personal experience as an immigrant and examines the lives of biblical heroes to shed light on how we can find purpose and joy as sojourners on earth. Her writings have appeared in *The Upper Room*, *CBN.com*, *Leading Hearts* magazine, *AriseDaily.com*, and *(in)courage.me*. She enjoys reading and traveling and lives in Northern California with her husband and son. Connect with Mabel at mabelninan.com or through social media @mabel_ninan.

DEVON O'DAY is an award-winning career radio broadcaster with songwriting credits for George Strait, Dolly Parton, Hank Williams Jr., and others. As an author, she has written several books for Thomas Nelson and United Methodist Publishing House, and has narrated more than one hundred audio books for HarperCollins, Thomas Nelson, and Zondervan. She has been a contributor to *All*

God's Creatures since the inception of the franchise, when devotions from her book, *Paws to Reflect,* were included.

Currently Devon works for Main Street Media of Tennessee, where she hosts three lifestyle streaming shows. She lives on a rescue sanctuary therapy farm outside Nashville called Angel Horse Farm, where senior equines and special-needs livestock offer an infinite well from which to draw stories about animals and their gifts and lessons connecting us to God. Look for Angel Horse Farm on Instagram to see pictures of the animal family that inspire her devotions.

SANDY KIRBY QUANDT is a former elementary school educator and full-time writer with a passion for God, history, and travel, which often weave their way into her stories and articles. She has written numerous articles, devotions, and stories for adult and children's publications, including *Today's Christian Woman, Power for Living, The Lookout, Mature Years, Standard,* and *Alive!* Her devotions appear in *So God Made a Dog, Let the Earth Rejoice,* and several Guideposts devotional books. She has won multiple awards for writing in the young adult, middle grade, and children's categories.

Are you looking for words of encouragement or gluten-free recipes? Check out Sandy's blog at sandykirbyquandt.com, where she posts twice a week. Sandy and her husband live in southeast Texas.

SHIRLEY RAYE REDMOND has written for many publications, including *Focus on the Family* magazine, *Home Life,* and *The Christian Standard.* Her devotions have appeared in multiple volumes of Guideposts' *All God's Creatures* and *Walking in Grace.* Her book *Courageous World Changers: 50 True Stories of Daring Women of God* (Harvest House) won the 2021 *Christianity Today* Book Award in the children's book category. Shirley Raye has been married for nearly 50 years to her college sweetheart. They live in Los Alamos, New Mexico, and are blessed with two adult children and five precious grandchildren.

KATHLEEN R. RUCKMAN enjoys several genres of writing. She is the published author of devotions, articles, short stories, poetry, and children's books and has taught women's Bible studies for several years. Kathleen is the mother of four adult children and nine young grandchildren, who are the loves of her life and her inspiration. Her desire as an author is to inspire readers to draw close to the heart of God and to His Word. Kathleen and her husband, Tom, and family live in Oregon, where the beauty of nature shines and all God's creatures are plentiful.

VIRGINIA RUTH has been a lifelong lover of animals and words. She sees God's creation and handiwork as examples of His love for us. Virginia has written for numerous Guideposts publications over the last 4 years and is currently working on a book about lessons learned during her recent move. Her website, wellofencouragement.com, provides encouraging words to fellow travelers on the road of life.

Virginia and her husband are the proud owners of a rescued "only his mother knows his background" mutt named Scuppers.

KIM SHEARD has owned a pet-sitting company in Northern Virginia since 2010, and as a result has lots of good animal stories to tell. Her devotions have appeared in Guideposts' *Pray a Word a Day Volume 2, The Upper Room, The Word in Season, The Secret Place,* and *Keys for Kids.* She participates in the music ministry of Vale United Methodist Church and enjoys writing liturgy for her congregation's special services. You can find her publications and flute choir arrangements listed at kimsheardauthor.com.

HEATHER SPIVA is a freelance writer from Sacramento, California. When she's not reading or writing, she can be found treasure-hunting for vintage clothing for her online vintage shop. When she's not doing that, she is hanging out with her two grown sons, her husband, and her fluffy 13-year-old goldendoodle. Learn more at heatherspiva.com.

DIANE STARK is a wife, mother, new grandma, and animal lover. She loves to write about the important things in life: her family and her faith. Connect with Diane at dianestark19@yahoo.com.

As an author, artist, and host of *The Heart Rest Podcast,* **CRYSTAL STORMS** equips you to release anxiety and experience peace in Jesus so you can live a peace-filled, purposeful life. She has been married to her dear husband, Tim, since 1995. They live in Florida with their sweet Yorkie, Minnie, and snuggly parrot, Lorito. When she's not creating, you can find Crystal exploring God's creation, cuddling with her husband, or working through her long list of books to read. She would love to connect with you at crystalstorms.me.

KATY W. SUNDARARAJAN is an ordained minister in the Reformed Church in America and has served as a youth pastor, college chaplain, missionary, and international student advisor. It has been her joy to learn and grow with God's people in these diverse settings, relishing the beauty and creativity of God and celebrating the vastness of God's love. Katy resides in west Michigan with her husband, two children, and an adoring goldendoodle named Honey.

Married since 2005, **STACEY THUREEN** is a mom of three children. Stacey enjoys writing about the Word of God and has contributed to many devotionals, including *3-Minute Daily Devotions for Moms*. She is thrilled to be sharing her stories in *All God's Creatures*. When Stacey is not putting words to paper, she can be found spending time with family. She also enjoys masters swimming and spends time at the local pool or rejoicing in God's creation by swimming in open water. Find out more at staceythureen.com.

MISSY TIPPENS is a pastor's wife, mother of three, and an author from the Atlanta, Georgia, area. She loves being involved in their church by singing in the choir and playing handbells. Missy has cared for many fur children through the years. Her family now has two rescue dogs, and she also enjoys pet sitting for the granddogs.

After more than 10 years spent pursuing her dream of being published, Missy sold her first novel to Love Inspired in 2007. She has been writing devotions for Guideposts since 2018. Visit Missy at missytippens.com.

LAWRENCE W. WILSON believes that God is love, life is good, and we can all be a bit better than we are now. He writes to remind people of simple truths so they will be inspired to live a better story. He got his start as a writer by penning and producing a play for his fourth-grade class. (It closed after half a performance.) Since then he has written five books and countless articles, lessons, scripts, sermons, podcasts, and news articles.

Larry lives in an Indiana small town, just like John Mellencamp—but not the same one.

DAVID L. WINTERS is an author and speaker living in Huber Heights, Ohio. David is a regular contributor to many Guideposts publications. His nonfiction books include *Exercise Your Faith, Taking God to Work,* and *The Accidental Missionary (A Gringo's Love Affair with Peru).* A 1981 graduate of The Ohio State University, David also earned an MBA from Regent University in 2003.

JON WOODHAMS enjoyed 10 great years as a Guideposts book editor, including serving as the editor of *All God's Creatures* for several years. While with Guideposts, he had the privilege of editing several Guideposts fiction series, including Miracles of Marble Cove, Mysteries of Silver Peak, and Tearoom Mysteries, and the nonfiction titles *Divine Interventions* and *Angels All around Us*. He now freelances as a writer and in editorial capacities for several publishers, including Guideposts.

In addition, Jon is an artist and photographer, shooting both film and digitally. You can see his work at jonwoodhams.com. Originally a Michigander, he currently lives and works in Memphis, Tennessee.

Author Index

Bible Acknowledgments

Every attempt has been made to credit the sources of copyrighted material used in this book. If any such acknowledgment has been inadvertently omitted or miscredited, receipt of such information would be appreciated.

Scripture quotations marked (CEV) are taken from *Holy Bible: Contemporary English Version*. Copyright © 1995 American Bible Society.

Scripture quotations marked (ESV) are taken from the *Holy Bible, English Standard Version*. Copyright © 2001 by Crossway Bibles, a division of Good News Publishers. Used by permission. All rights reserved.

Scripture quotations marked (GNT) are taken from the *Good News Translation® (Today's English Version, Second Edition)*. Copyright © 1992 American Bible Society. All rights reserved.

Scripture quotations marked (KJV) are taken from the *King James Version of the Bible*.

Scripture quotations marked (MSG) are taken from *The Message*. Copyright © 1993, 1994, 1995, 1996, 2000, 2001, 2002 by Eugene H. Peterson.

Scripture quotations marked (NASB) are taken from the *New American Standard Bible®*, Copyright © 1960, 1971, 1977, 1995, 2020 by The Lockman Foundation. All rights reserved.

Scripture quotations marked (NIV) are taken from *The Holy Bible, New International Version*. Copyright © 1973, 1978, 1984, 2011 by Biblica, Inc. Used by permission of Zondervan. All rights reserved worldwide. zondervan.com

Scripture quotations marked (NIRV) are taken from the *Holy Bible, New International Reader's Version*. Copyright © 1995, 1996, 1998, 2014 by Biblica, Inc. Used by permission. All rights reserved worldwide.

Scripture quotations marked (NKJV) are taken from *The Holy Bible, New King James Version*. Copyright © 1982 by Thomas Nelson.

Scripture quotations marked (NLT) are taken from the *Holy Bible, New Living Translation*. Copyright © 1996, 2004, 2007, 2015 by Tyndale House Foundation. Used by permission of Tyndale House Publishers Inc., Carol Stream, Illinois. All rights reserved.

Scripture quotations marked (NRSVUE) are taken from the *New Revised Standard Version, Updated Edition*. Copyright © 2021 by the National Council of Churches of Christ in the United States of America. Used by permission. All rights reserved worldwide.

A Note from the Editors

We hope you enjoyed *All God's Creatures 2025*, published by Guideposts. For over 75 years, Guideposts, a nonprofit organization, has been driven by a vision of a world filled with hope. We aspire to be the voice of a trusted friend, a friend who makes you feel more hopeful and connected.

By making a purchase from Guideposts, you join our community in touching millions of lives, inspiring them to believe that all things are possible through faith, hope, and prayer. Your continued support allows us to provide uplifting resources to those in need. Whether through our communities, websites, apps, or publications, we inspire our audiences, bring them together, and comfort, uplift, entertain, and guide them. Visit us at guideposts.org to learn more.

We would love to hear from you. Write us at Guideposts, P.O. Box 5815, Harlan, Iowa 51593 or call us at (800) 932-2145. Did you love *All God's Creatures 2025?* Leave a review for this product on guideposts.org/shop. Your feedback helps others in our community find relevant products.

Find inspiration, find faith, find Guideposts.

Shop our best sellers and favorites at

guideposts.org/shop

Or scan the QR code to go directly to our Shop